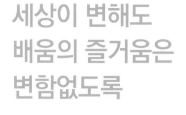

세상이 변해도
배움의 즐거움은
변함없도록

시대는 빠르게 변해도
배움의 즐거움은
변함없어야 하기에

어제의 비상은
남다른 교재부터
결이 다른 콘텐츠
전에 없던 교육 플랫폼까지

변함없는 혁신으로
교육 문화 환경의 새로운 전형을
실현해왔습니다.

비상은 오늘, 다시 한번
새로운 교육 문화 환경을 실현하기 위한
또 하나의 혁신을 시작합니다.

오늘의 내가 어제의 나를 초월하고
오늘의 교육이 어제의 교육을 초월하여
배움의 즐거움을 지속하는 혁신,

바로, 메타인지 기반 완전 학습을.

상상을 실현하는 교육 문화 기업 비상

메타인지 기반 완전 학습
초월을 뜻하는 meta와 생각을 뜻하는 인지가 결합한 메타인지는
자신이 알고 모르는 것을 스스로 구분하고 학습계획을 세우도록 하는
궁극의 학습 능력입니다. 비상의 메타인지 기반 완전 학습 시스템은
잠들어 있는 메타인지를 깨워 공부를 100% 내 것으로 만들도록 합니다.

GRAMMAR
TAPA

LEVEL 2

How to Study

구성과 특장

STEP 2 핵심 문법 Focus를 공부하고 이해도를 점검하세요.

핵심 문법 Focus

문법 Focus를 다양한 유형의 문제로 반복 학습하고, 〈교과서 문장 응용하기〉로 Writing 실력을 높이세요.

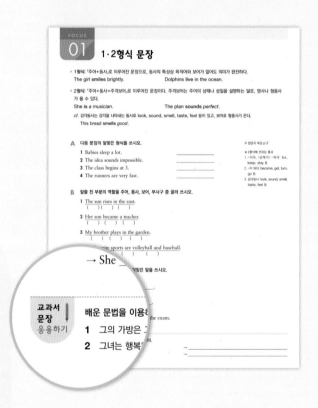

STEP 1 Chapter의 전체적인 내용을 파악하세요.

챕터 미리 보기

공부할 내용을 미리 파악하면서 〈용어 사전〉으로 어려운 문법 용어의 의미를 익히세요.

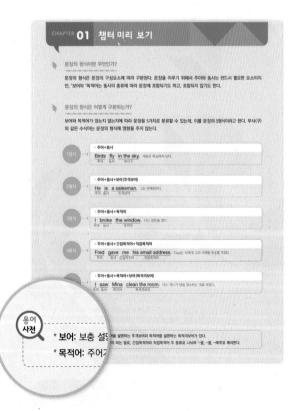

STEP 3
내신적중 실전문제로 문법을 학습하며 내신도 대비하세요.

〈내신적중 실전문제〉로 학교 시험 빈출 유형을 파악하고, 해당 Chapter의 문법을 이용한 〈서술형 평가〉의 Writing, Reading 문제를 통해 내신을 완벽하게 대비하세요.

STEP 4
Workbook으로 한 번 더 정리하세요.

공부한 내용은 〈요점정리 노트〉로 Chapter별 핵심 문법 사항을 다시 한 번 정리한 후, 문제를 통해 복습하여 완벽하게 이해하고 넘어가세요.

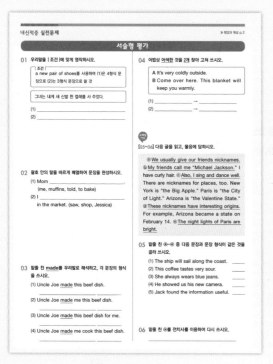

Contents

차례

CHAPTER

01

문장의 형식

🌿 **문장의 형식이란 무엇인가?**

문장의 형식은 문장의 구성요소에 따라 구분된다. 문장을 이루기 위해서 주어와 동사는 반드시 필요한 요소이지만, *보어와 *목적어는 동사의 종류에 따라 문장에 포함되기도 하고, 포함되지 않기도 한다.

🌿 **문장의 형식은 어떻게 구분하는가?**

보어와 목적어가 있는지 없는지에 따라 문장을 5가지로 분류할 수 있는데, 이를 문장의 5형식이라고 한다. 부사(구)와 같은 수식어는 문장의 형식에 영향을 주지 않는다.

1형식
- **주어+동사**

Birds fly in the sky. 새들은 하늘에서 난다.
주어   동사   부사구

2형식
- **주어+동사+보어 (주격보어)**

He is a salesman. 그는 판매원이다.
주어 동사   주격보어

3형식
- **주어+동사+목적어**

I broke the window. 나는 창문을 깼다.
주어 동사   목적어

4형식
- **주어+동사+간접목적어+직접목적어**

Fred gave me his email address. Fred는 나에게 그의 이메일 주소를 주었다.
주어   동사 간접목적어   직접목적어

5형식
- **주어+동사+목적어+보어 (목적격보어)**

I saw Mina clean the room. 나는 미나가 방을 청소하는 것을 보았다.
주어 동사 목적어   목적격보어

**용어
사전**

* **보어**: 보충 설명해 주는 말로, 주어를 설명하는 주격보어와 목적어를 설명하는 목적격보어가 있다.
* **목적어**: 주어가 행한 동작의 대상이 되는 말로, 간접목적어와 직접목적어 두 종류로 나뉘며 '~을, ~를, ~에게'로 해석한다.

01 1·2형식 문장

■ **1형식**: 「주어+동사」로 이루어진 문장으로, 동사의 특성상 목적어와 보어가 없어도 의미가 완전하다.

The girl **smiles** brightly.   Dolphins **live** in the ocean.

■ **2형식**: 「주어+동사+주격보어」로 이루어진 문장이다. 주격보어는 주어의 상태나 성질을 설명하는 말로, 명사나 형용사가 올 수 있다.

She **is** *a musician*.   The plan **sounds** *perfect*.

cf. 감각동사는 감각을 나타내는 동사로 look, sound, smell, taste, feel 등이 있고, 보어로 형용사가 온다.

This bread **smells** *good*.

A 다음 문장의 알맞은 형식을 쓰시오.

» 정답과 해설 p.2

1 Babies sleep a lot.   _____

2 The idea sounds impossible.   _____

3 The class begins at 3.   _____

4 The runners are very fast.   _____

◆ 2형식에 쓰이는 동사
1. ~이다, (상태가) ~하다: be, keep, stay 등
2. ~이 되다: become, get, turn, go 등
3. 감각동사: look, sound, smell, taste, feel 등

B 밑줄 친 부분의 역할을 주어, 동사, 보어, 부사구 중 골라 쓰시오.

1 <u>The sun</u> <u>rises</u> <u>in the east</u>.
  (   ) (   ) (   )

2 <u>Her son</u> <u>became</u> <u>a teacher</u>.
  (   ) (   ) (   )

3 <u>My brother</u> <u>plays</u> <u>in the garden</u>.
  (   ) (   ) (   )

4 <u>My favorite sports</u> <u>are</u> <u>volleyball and baseball</u>.
  (   )   (   )   (   )

C 우리말과 뜻이 같도록 빈칸에 알맞은 말을 쓰시오.

1 나의 어머니는 바빠 보인다.
  → My mother _____ _____.

2 이 음료는 단 맛이 난다.
  → This drink _____ _____.

3 그녀는 시험 후에 피곤하다고 느꼈다.
  → She _____ _____ after the exam.

교과서 문장 응용하기

배운 문법을 이용하여 영어 문장을 써 봅시다.

1 그의 가방은 그 의자 밑에 있다.   → _____

2 그녀는 행복해 보인다.   → _____

02 3·4형식 문장

- 3형식: 「주어+동사+목적어」로 이루어진 문장으로, 동사의 특성상 목적어가 있어야 의미가 완전하다.

My sister **likes** *chocolate cake.*

- 4형식: 「주어+동사+간접목적어+직접목적어」로 이루어진 문장으로, 간접목적어는 '~에게', 직접목적어는 '~을(를)'로 해석한다.

My aunt **bought** *me a bike.*

A 다음 문장의 알맞은 형식을 쓰시오.

» 정답과 해설 p.2

1 He has a car in his garage. _____

2 Dad bought me a birthday present. _____

3 You're going to meet my cousin. _____

4 Tony passed me the ball. _____

5 I play tennis on weekends. _____

◆ 목적어 자리에는 명사, 대명사, 동명사(구), 부정사(구), 명사절 등을 쓸 수 있다.
I started **keeping** a diary.
She wants **to visit** the zoo.
I think **that** she likes music.

B 밑줄 친 부분을 어법상 바르게 고쳐 쓰시오.

1 May I ask your a question? _____

2 Jenny often wrote he long emails. _____

3 My grandma showed our her old photos. _____

4 The designer made my a dress. _____

C 우리말과 뜻이 같도록 괄호 안의 말을 배열하여 문장을 완성하시오.

1 그의 팬들은 그에게 팬레터를 보냈다. (fan letters, him, sent)

→ His fans _____.

2 그 여자아이는 나에게 많은 질문을 했다. (me, asked, many questions)

→ The girl _____.

3 Nick은 그의 여동생에게 쿠키를 만들어 주었다. (his sister, cookies, made)

→ Nick _____.

4 그녀는 우리에게 그녀의 새 가방을 보여 주었다. (her new bag, showed, us)

→ She _____.

교과서 문장 응용하기 | 배운 문법을 이용하여 영어 문장을 써 봅시다.

1 우리는 사과나무 세 그루를 키운다. → _____

2 그는 그녀에게 다이아몬드 반지를 주었다. → _____

---

03 4형식 문장의 3형식 전환

■ 4형식 문장은 「주어+동사+직접목적어+전치사+간접목적어」의 3형식으로 바꿔 쓸 수 있다. 이때, 전치사는 동사에 따라 결정된다.

전치사 to를 쓰는 동사	give, send, tell, lend, show, teach, write 등	Andrew **gave** *her a rose.* → Andrew gave a rose **to** her.
전치사 for를 쓰는 동사	make, buy, get, cook 등	My mom **made** *me chicken soup.* → My mom made chicken soup **for** me.
전치사 of를 쓰는 동사	ask, require 등	May I **ask** *you a question*? → May I ask a question **of** you?

A 밑줄 친 부분을 어법상 바르게 고쳐 쓰시오.

» 정답과 해설 p.2

1 Please get some water <u>to</u> me.　　　　　　　_____

2 May I ask a favor <u>to</u> you?　　　　　　　_____

3 My uncle sent a Christmas present <u>for</u> me.　　　_____

B 다음 문장과 뜻이 같도록 빈칸에 알맞은 말을 쓰시오.

1 He teaches them music. → He teaches music _____ _____.

2 She made Mira a dress. → She made a dress _____ _____.

3 Fred asked me my address. → Fred asked my address _____ _____.

C 다음 4형식 문장을 3형식 문장으로 바꿔 쓰시오.

1 Josh's sister bought him a red hat.

→ _____

2 Kate lent me her earphones.

→ _____

3 Minsu made his brother a paper airplane.

→ _____

4 He sometimes asks his classmates funny questions.

→ _____

교과서
문장
응용하기

배운 문법을 이용하여 영어 문장을 써 봅시다.

1 Kevin은 나에게 그의 사진들을 보여 주었다. (to)　　→ _____

2 그녀는 우리에게 간식을 좀 사 주었다. (for)　　→ _____

04 5형식 문장 1_ 명사, 형용사, to부정사 목적격보어

5형식은 「주어+동사+목적어+목적격보어」로 이루어진 문장이다. 이때 목적격보어는 동사에 의해 결정된다.

- **명사 또는 형용사를 목적격보어로 취하는 동사**: call, make, keep, leave 등
  My mom **calls** me "*Sleepyhead.*" ⟨me = Sleepyhead⟩
  The news **made** her *happy*.
  Gloves **keep** your hands *warm*.

- **to부정사를 목적격보어로 취하는 동사**: want, ask, tell, expect, advise, get 등
  Jenna **wants** me *to come* to her party.

A 다음 문장에서 목적격보어를 찾아 밑줄을 그으시오.   » 정답과 해설 p.2

1 We call our cat "Kitty."
2 My mother told me to study harder.
3 Rainy days make me sad.

B 밑줄 친 부분을 어법상 바르게 고쳐 쓰시오.

1 She wants her son <u>win</u> the game.   _____
2 My little brother made me <u>angrily</u>.   _____
3 Peter asked Jane <u>singing</u> with him on the stage.   _____

C 우리말과 뜻이 같도록 괄호 안의 말을 이용하여 문장을 완성하시오.

1 우리는 그를 친절한 이웃으로 생각한다. (neighbor)
   → We think _____ _____ _____ _____.
2 그 영화는 우리를 신나게 했다. (make, excited)
   → The movie _____ _____ _____.
3 그녀는 그들에게 당장 시작하라고 말했다. (tell, start)
   → She _____ _____ _____ _____ at once.
4 너는 어떻게 나를 거짓말쟁이라고 부를 수가 있니? (call, liar)
   → How can you _____ _____ _____ _____?

교과서 문장 응용하기 │ 배운 문법을 이용하여 영어 문장을 써 봅시다.

1 그는 그의 몸을 건강하게 유지한다. (keep, healthy)   → _____
2 우리 선생님은 우리에게 조용히 하라고 말씀하셨다. (tell, quiet)   → _____

05 5형식 문장 2_ 동사원형 목적격보어

동사원형을 목적격보어로 취하는 동사의 종류에는 2가지가 있다.

- **사역동사:** make, let, have 등 '~가 …하도록 시키다, ~가 …하게 하다'의 뜻을 가진 동사
  My brother **made** us *laugh*.

  cf. help는 목적격보어로 to부정사와 동사원형을 모두 쓸 수 있다.
  He **helped** me *(to) find* my backpack.

- **지각동사:** see, hear, feel 등 '~가 …하는 것을 보다(듣다 / 느끼다)'의 뜻을 가진 동사
  I **saw** you *dance* on the stage.

A 괄호 안에서 알맞은 것을 고르시오.

1 Tony's mom made him (wash / to wash) his feet.
2 We saw a man (jump / to jump) into the river.
3 My dad had me (save / saving) water.
4 They helped him (solving / to solve) the puzzles.
5 I watched raindrops (falling / to fall) on my left hand.

» 정답과 해설 p.2

◆ 지각동사의 목적격보어로 현재분사가 쓰이는 경우: 진행의 의미를 강조할 때는 현재분사를 쓸 수 있다.
He **felt** the building *shaking*.
(그는 건물이 흔들리고 있는 것을 느꼈다.)

B 밑줄 친 부분을 어법상 바르게 고쳐 쓰시오.

1 I saw Emma and Susie <u>went</u> out. _____
2 She made us <u>to keep</u> our desks clean. _____
3 Jack felt somebody <u>touches</u> his shoulder. _____
4 Please let me <u>knowing</u> what to do. _____

C 괄호 안의 말을 바르게 배열하여 문장을 완성하시오.

1 Anna _____ for help. (someone, ask, heard)
2 Did you _____ a motorcycle? (ride, see, my brother)
3 Mom _____ the flowers. (water, us, makes)
4 He should _____ back home. (the child, let, go)
5 Let's _____ the boxes. (carry, the boy, help)

교과서 문장 응용하기

배운 문법을 이용하여 영어 문장을 써 봅시다.
1 나는 그에게 내 의자를 고치게 했다. (have, fix) → _____
2 그녀의 어머니는 그녀가 설거지하는 것을 보았다. (see, wash) → _____

→ 내신적중 실전문제를 풀기 전에 Workbook p.2에 있는 요점정리를 참고하세요.

내신적중 실전문제

[01~02] 빈칸에 알맞은 것을 고르시오.

01

> This soap smells _____.

① well　　　　② sweetly
③ nicely　　　④ strange
⑤ freshly

02

> Bob _____ an airplane fly in the sky.

① watched　　② gave
③ wanted　　　④ sent
⑤ expected

03 우리말과 뜻이 같도록 괄호 안의 말을 배열하여 문장을 완성하시오. 주관식

> 우리는 숙제를 우리의 선생님에게 이메일로 보낸다.
> (our teacher, to, the homework, send)

→ We _____ by email.

04 빈칸에 공통으로 알맞은 것은?

> • You shouldn't give chocolate _____ your dog.
> • Helen asked me _____ take care of her bird.

① of　　② with　　③ for
④ about　⑤ to

05 빈칸에 알맞은 말이 바르게 짝지어진 것은?

> • We didn't want him _____ here.
> • She had her husband _____ smoking.

① come — stop
② come — stopping
③ to come — stop
④ to come — to stop
⑤ to come — stopping

06 우리말을 바르게 영작한 것을 모두 고르면?

> 그는 내게 라면을 요리해 주었다.

① He cooked ramen me.
② He cooked me ramen.
③ He cooked me for ramen.
④ He cooked ramen for me.
⑤ He cooked ramen of me.

07 문장의 형식이 |보기|와 같은 것을 모두 고르면?

> |보기|
> Brian is my best friend.

① The sun shines brightly.
② The leaves turned red and yellow.
③ Jason and I watched fantastic scenery on the mountain.
④ We kept quiet in front of the beautiful sunset.
⑤ After hiking together, we became better friends.

[08~10] 빈칸에 알맞지 <u>않은</u> 것을 고르시오.

08

> He _____ me go to sleep earlier than usual.

① had ② saw
③ told ④ let
⑤ helped

09

> These beautiful songs will make him _____.

① happy ② to smile
③ cheer up ④ very famous
⑤ a popular singer

10

> Mark _____ his son to read a lot of books.

① got ② told
③ expected ④ watched
⑤ advised

11 밑줄 친 우리말과 뜻이 같도록 빈칸에 알맞은 말을 쓰시오. 주관식

> **A** How does the blanket feel?
> **B** <u>그건 부드러운 느낌이에요.</u> I'll take it.

→ It _____ _____.

12 밑줄 친 부분의 쓰임이 나머지 넷과 <u>다른</u> 것은?

① The customer made the clerk <u>angry</u>.
② Everyone thinks Mr. Kim <u>a great teacher</u>.
③ My brother lent me <u>some money</u>.
④ We found the sci-fi movie <u>interesting</u>.
⑤ The parents named their child <u>Emily</u>.

13 다음 문장과 뜻이 같도록 할 때 빈칸에 알맞은 것은?

> Brian got his brother some stickers.
> → Brian got some stickers _____ his brother.

① in ② of ③ to
④ for ⑤ with

14 문장의 형식이 같은 것끼리 짝지어진 것은?

① • I asked Kevin to help me.
   • I dropped my cell phone in the toilet.
② • We helped Dad fix the bike.
   • I saw Kevin and Eric playing card games.
③ • Please tell me the truth.
   • Mom gave it to my sister and me.
④ • He is a nice and friendly teacher.
   • The sun sets in the west.
⑤ • Bad words make me angry.
   • My friend made me a pretty bracelet.

[15~16] 괄호 안의 말을 이용하여 문장을 완성하시오. 주관식

15

> My mother advised me _____ well.
> (dress)

16

> I felt the poor dog _____ in my arms.
> (shake)

17 문장의 형식이 나머지 넷과 다른 것은?

① I heard her talk on the phone.
② I bought my grandmother a book.
③ He keeps his money safe in the bank.
④ My homeroom teacher asked us to clean the classroom.
⑤ We found many people excited at the festival.

18 밑줄 친 ①~⑤ 중 어법상 어색한 것은?

> **A** Junho looks ① sadly today. What's the matter ② with him?
> **B** He ③ got a bad score on the math test.
> **A** Oh, let's ④ go out with him and make him ⑤ feel better.

19 밑줄 친 부분의 쓰임이 |보기|와 같은 것은?

> 보기
> My parents want me to save money.

① My classmates call Kevin a genius.
② His face turned red.
③ You must keep your promise.
④ He will buy blue jeans for his son.
⑤ My teacher asked me a difficult question.

20 빈칸에 알맞은 것을 모두 고르면?

> I helped Ms. White _____ the Korean food.

① cook
② cooks
③ cooked
④ to cook
⑤ cooking

21 두 문장을 한 문장으로 쓸 때 빈칸에 알맞은 것은?

> My neighbor walked his dogs. I saw him.
> → I saw my neighbor _____.

① walk him
② walk his dogs
③ walked his dogs
④ to walk his dogs
⑤ to walking his dogs

22 문장의 형식이 | 보기 |와 같은 것은?

> | 보기 |
> One of my friends showed me the photos.

① I got an A on the final exam.

② Don't let the boy run around.

③ I brought my neighbors some rice cake.

④ Dave bought the laptop computer.

⑤ Insu sent K-pop songs to his foreign friends.

23 어법상 어색한 것은?

① Your idea sounds great.

② The sky became cloudy.

③ My teeth hurt so badly.

④ His words made her happily.

⑤ Jun always keeps his body healthy.

24 어법상 올바른 것은?

① Let me to show you something.

② The rain made the ground wet.

③ I found the quiz show interest.

④ The coach advised me jogging every day.

⑤ Henry got them wait for him for an hour.

25 어법상 <u>어색한</u> 부분을 찾아 고쳐 쓰시오. 주관식

> I heard someone to knock on the door in the middle of the night.

_____ → _____

26 동사 make의 쓰임이 나머지 넷과 <u>다른</u> 것은?

① She will make you a great dancer.

② He makes his children feed the pigs.

③ I made the little girl a pretty doll.

④ Her voice made me feel comfortable.

⑤ Their boss made them nervous.

27 4형식 문장을 3형식으로 바꾼 것이 <u>어색한</u> 것은?

① I made the blind boy a special book.

　→ I made a special book for the blind boy.

② A native speaker teaches us English.

　→ A native speaker teaches English to us.

③ Can you show me your family album?

　→ Can you show your family album to me?

④ I want to ask him a tricky question.

　→ I want to ask a tricky question of him.

⑤ Mom bought me a pizza for lunch.

　→ Mom bought a pizza to me for lunch.

서술형 평가

01 우리말을 | 조건 |에 맞게 영작하시오.

> 조건
> a new pair of shoes를 사용하여 (1)은 4형식 문장으로 (2)는 3형식 문장으로 쓸 것

> 그녀는 내게 새 신발 한 켤레를 사 주었다.

(1) _____

(2) _____

02 괄호 안의 말을 바르게 배열하여 문장을 완성하시오.

(1) Mom _____ .
   (me, muffins, told, to bake)

(2) I _____
   in the market. (saw, shop, Jessica)

03 밑줄 친 **made**를 우리말로 해석하고, 각 문장의 형식을 쓰시오.

(1) Uncle Joe <u>made</u> this beef dish.

   _____ _____

(2) Uncle Joe <u>made</u> me this beef dish.

   _____ _____

(3) Uncle Joe <u>made</u> this beef dish for me.

   _____ _____

(4) Uncle Joe <u>made</u> me cook this beef dish.

   _____ _____

04 어법상 <u>어색한</u> 것을 <u>2개</u> 찾아 고쳐 쓰시오.

> **A** It's very coldly outside.
> **B** Come over here. This blanket will keep you warmly.

(1) _____ → _____

(2) _____ → _____

[05~06] 다음 글을 읽고, 물음에 답하시오.

> ⓐ<u>We usually give our friends nicknames.</u> ⓑ<u>My friends call me "Michael Jackson."</u> I have curly hair. ⓒ<u>Also, I sing and dance well.</u> There are nicknames for places, too. New York is "the Big Apple." Paris is "the City of Light." Arizona is "the Valentine State." ⓓ<u>These nicknames have interesting origins.</u> For example, Arizona became a state on February 14. ⓔ<u>The night lights of Paris are bright.</u>

05 밑줄 친 ⓐ~ⓔ 중 다음 문장과 문장 형식이 같은 것을 골라 쓰시오.

(1) The ship will sail along the coast. _____

(2) This coffee tastes very sour. _____

(3) She always wears blue jeans. _____

(4) He showed us his new camera. _____

(5) Jack found the information useful. _____

06 밑줄 친 ⓐ를 전치사를 이용하여 다시 쓰시오.

_____

CHAPTER

02

to부정사

🍃 **to부정사는 무엇이며 문장에서 어떤 역할을 하는가?**

to부정사는 「to+동사원형」의 형태로 문장 속에서 명사, 형용사, 부사의 역할을 한다.

명사 역할
문장에서 주어, 보어, 목적어로 쓰인다.

- **주어 역할**: ~하는 것은, ~하기는

> **To do** the housework isn't easy.
> 집안일을 하는 것은 쉽지 않다.

- **보어 역할**: ~하는 것이다

> My plan is **to bake** cookies for him.
> 나의 계획은 그를 위해 쿠키를 굽는 것이다.

- **목적어 역할**: ~하는 것을, ~하기를

> I want **to go out** with my friends.
> 나는 내 친구들과 외출하기를 원한다.

- **의문사+to부정사**: 목적어 역할

> I don't know **where to carry** these desks.
> 이 책상들을 어디로 옮겨야 할지 모르겠다.

형용사 역할
(대)명사를 꾸민다.

- **(대)명사+to부정사(+전치사)**: ~하는, ~할

> We need some bread **to eat**.
> 우리는 먹을 빵이 좀 필요하다.

부사 역할
동사, 형용사, 다른 부사를 꾸미며 문장의 의미를 풍성하게 한다.

- **목적의 의미**: ~하려고, ~하기 위해

> Jenny went to a store **to buy** a hairpin.
> Jenny는 머리핀을 사기 위해 가게에 갔다. .

- **감정의 원인의 의미**: ~해서, ~하다니

> I'm really glad **to meet** you.
> 당신을 만나서 정말 반갑습니다.

- **결과의 의미**: ~해서 (결국) …하다

> He grew up **to be** the president.
> 그는 자라서 대통령이 되었다.

- **형용사(부사) 수식**: ~하기에, ~하기가

> The river is not good **to swim** in.
> 그 강은 수영하기에 좋지 않다.

🍃 **to부정사의 관용적 표현에는 어떤 것이 있는가?**

too ~ to부정사	• 너무 ~해서 …할 수 없다
	He was **too** young **to** see the movie.
enough to부정사	• …할 만큼 충분히 ~하다
	She is smart **enough to** find the answer.

06 to부정사의 명사적 용법 1_ 주어, 보어

- **주어 역할:** '~하는 것은, ~하기는'의 뜻으로, 주어 자리에 가주어 it을 쓰고 to부정사(구)를 뒤로 보낼 수 있다.

  To get enough sleep is important.

  → **It** is important **to get** enough sleep.

- **보어 역할:** '~하는 것이다'의 뜻으로, 보통 be동사 뒤에 온다.

  My dream is **to travel** around the world.

A 다음 문장과 뜻이 같도록 빈칸에 알맞은 말을 쓰시오. 　　　　　　　　　　　　　》 정답과 해설 p.4

1 To read fantasy novels is fun.

→ _____ is fun _____ _____ fantasy novels.

2 To write Japanese character is difficult.

→ _____ is difficult _____ _____ Japanese character.

3 To play the drums is my favorite hobby.

→ _____ is my favorite hobby _____ _____ the drums.

4 To eat vegetables is good for your health.

→ _____ is good for your health _____ _____ vegetables.

B 우리말과 뜻이 같도록 괄호 안의 말과 to부정사를 이용하여 문장을 완성하시오.

1 내 소망은 그 배우를 직접 보는 것이다. (see)

→ My hope _____ _____ _____ the actor in person.

2 민지의 목표는 유명한 바이올린 연주자가 되는 것이다. (become)

→ Minji's goal _____ _____ _____ a famous violinist.

3 그의 꿈은 로봇을 발명하는 것이다. (invent)

→ _____ _____ _____ _____ _____ a robot.

C 다음 문장에서 밑줄 친 It이 가리키는 것을 찾아 밑줄을 그으시오.

1 <u>It</u> is a hard work to wash tennis shoes.

2 <u>It</u> is impossible to finish the puzzle in an hour.

3 <u>It</u> is a good idea to have a check-up with the dentist.

교과서 문장 응용하기 배운 문법을 이용하여 영어 문장을 써 봅시다.

1 자전거를 타는 것은 좋은 운동이다. (it) 　　　→ _____

2 나의 소원은 시험에 합격하는 것이다. (wish, pass) 　→ _____

07 to부정사의 명사적 용법 2_ 목적어, 의문사+to부정사

- **목적어 역할**: '~하는 것을, ~하기를'의 뜻으로, to부정사를 목적어로 취하는 동사에는 want, hope, need, plan, like, begin, decide, agree, learn, start 등이 있다.
  Brian *wants* **to have** a pet at home.
  We *need* **to talk** about your plans.

- **의문사+to부정사**: 문장에서 명사처럼 쓰이며, '~을 …할지'의 뜻으로, 「의문사+주어+should+동사원형」으로 바꿔 쓸 수 있다.
  I don't know **what to wear** to the party.
  → I don't know **what I should** wear to the party.

A 빈칸에 알맞은 말을 |보기|에서 골라 올바른 형태로 쓰시오.

》 정답과 해설 p.4

> 보기
>
> go   play   take   marry

1 He wants _____ mobile games now.
2 You need _____ a shower right now.
3 I like _____ to the movies on weekend.
4 She decided _____ him when she got a ring from him.

◆ 「의문사+to부정사」의 의미
  · what+to부정사: 무엇을 ~할지
  · when+to부정사: 언제 ~할지
  · where+to부정사: 어디로 ~할지
  · how+to부정사: 어떻게 ~할지
  · who(m)+to부정사: 누가(누구를) ~할지

B 괄호 안의 말을 바르게 배열하여 문장을 완성하시오.

1 I'm not sure _____ today. (cook, what, to)
2 She asked me _____ the word. (to, read, how)
3 Chris didn't know _____ you. (when, call, to)
4 We need to talk about _____ for vacation. (visit, where, to)

◆ **to부정사의 부정**: to부정사 앞에 not이나 never를 쓴다.
  We decided **not to stay** home.

C 다음 문장과 뜻이 같도록 빈칸에 알맞은 말을 쓰시오.

1 Tell me when to start.
  → Tell me _____ I _____ _____.
2 Serim showed me how she should make *gimbap*.
  → Serim showed me _____ _____ _____ *gimbap*.
3 She decided where she should go on a boat trip.
  → She decided _____ _____ _____ on a boat trip.

교과서
문장
응용하기

배운 문법을 이용하여 영어 문장을 써 봅시다.

1 Mary는 그를 다시 만나기를 희망한다. (hope)   → _____
2 나는 무엇을 구입할지 모르겠다. (to)   → _____

08 to부정사의 형용사적 용법

- '~하는, ~할'의 뜻으로, 앞에 오는 (대)명사를 꾸며 준다.

  It's time **to have** some fun.

  I have something **to tell** you.

- to부정사가 꾸며 주는 명사가 전치사의 목적어일 경우에는 to부정사 뒤에 반드시 전치사를 쓴다.

  The boy needs someone **to talk** *to*. (← talk to someone)

  My sister has many toys **to play** *with*. (← play with toys)

A 밑줄 친 부분을 어법상 바르게 고쳐 쓰시오.

1 I had no chance <u>talk</u> to Mr. Jones. _____

2 I have something interesting <u>show</u> you. _____

3 They're looking for a chair <u>to sit</u>. _____

4 Julie wanted a fork <u>to eat</u>. _____

» 정답과 해설 p.4

◆ 특정 대명사를 형용사와 to부정사가 동시에 수식하는 경우의 어순: -thing, -one, -body로 끝나는 대명사를 형용사와 to부정사가 동시에 꾸며 줄 때는 「대명사+형용사+to부정사」의 순서로 쓴다.

I want *something cold* to drink.

B 괄호 안의 말을 바르게 배열하여 문장을 완성하시오.

1 I need _____. (help me, to, someone)

2 Korea has _____. (visit, to, many places)

3 Give me _____. (wear, warm, something, to)

4 There are _____. (the problem, to, many ways, solve)

C 우리말과 뜻이 같도록 빈칸에 알맞은 말을 쓰시오.

1 Sarah는 Daniel에게 읽을 책 한 권을 주었다.

→ Sarah gave Daniel a _____ _____ _____.

2 너는 그 문을 열 열쇠를 가지고 있니?

→ Do you have a _____ _____ _____ the door?

3 나는 의지할 친구가 필요하다.

→ I need a _____ _____ _____ _____.

4 나는 그녀와 함께 쇼핑하러 갈 시간이 없다.

→ I don't have _____ _____ _____ _____ with her.

교과서
문장
응용하기

배운 문법을 이용하여 영어 문장을 써 봅시다.

1 우리는 거기에 갈 시간이 없다. → _____

2 Michael은 앉을 의자가 하나 필요했다. → _____

to부정사의 부사적 용법 1_ 목적, 감정의 원인

- **목적:** '~하려고, ~하기 위해'라는 뜻으로, 「in order to+동사원형」 또는 「so as to+동사원형」으로 바꿔 쓸 수 있다.

  Jennifer went out **to walk** her dog.

  → Jennifer went out **in order to(so as to)** walk her dog.

- **감정의 원인:** '~해서, ~하다니'라는 뜻으로, 형용사(sad, happy, surprised 등)와 함께 쓰인다.

  He was sad **to leave** his hometown.

  I was very happy **to see** them again.

A 빈칸에 알맞은 말을 | 보기 |에서 골라 올바른 형태로 쓰시오.   » 정답과 해설 p.4

> 보기
>
> see   save   get   ask

1 I am sorry _____ you this again.

2 Anna studied hard _____ a good score.

3 People sometimes take a taxi _____ time.

4 Chris was pleased _____ the movie star there.

B 우리말과 뜻이 같도록 빈칸에 알맞은 말을 쓰시오.

1 나는 점심을 먹기 위해 식당에 갔다.

→ I went to the restaurant _____ _____ _____.

2 우리는 그 소식을 듣고 놀랐다.

→ We were surprised _____ _____ _____ _____.

3 나의 오빠는 그 공을 놓쳐서 당황했다.

→ My brother was embarrassed _____ _____ _____ _____.

C 다음 문장과 뜻이 같도록 빈칸에 알맞은 말을 쓰시오.

1 He is going to Mexico to study Spanish.

→ He is going to Mexico in _____ _____ _____ Spanish.

2 I saved money to buy a new bike.

→ I saved money _____ _____ _____ _____ a new bike.

교과서
문장
응용하기

배운 문법을 이용하여 영어 문장을 써 봅시다.

1 그들은 쉬기 위해 그 소파에 앉았다. (take a rest)   → _____

2 나는 그 공원에서 Paul을 보아서 반가웠다. (glad)   → _____

to부정사의 부사적 용법 2_ 결과, 형용사 수식

- **결과:** '…해서 (결국) ~하다'의 뜻으로, 문장 앞에서부터 해석하는 것이 자연스럽다.

The boy grew up **to be** a great pianist.

- **형용사 수식:** '~하기(에)'라는 뜻으로, to부정사가 앞에 오는 형용사를 꾸며 준다.

This smartphone is easy **to use**.

The water in this bottle is safe **to drink**.

cf. 부사적 용법의 to부정사는 '~하다니, ~하는 것을 보니'로 해석되어 판단의 근거를 나타내기도 한다.

You must be foolish **to believe** such a thing.

A 빈칸에 알맞은 말을 | 보기 |에서 골라 올바른 형태로 쓰시오.

» 정답과 해설 p.4

| 보기 |
| be   find   move   learn |

◆ 「~, only+to부정사」: '…했으나, 결국 ~해 버렸다'는 뜻으로, 결과를 강조한다.
I tried again and again, **only to fail**. (나는 계속해서 노력했지만, 결국 실패했다.)

1 Folk dance is not hard _____.

2 He grew up _____ a brave soldier.

3 This box is not heavy _____.

4 They woke up _____ the house on fire.

B 밑줄 친 부분을 어법상 바르게 고쳐 쓰시오.

1 Justin woke up <u>be</u> a star. _____

2 This suitcase is <u>to carry easy</u>. _____

3 Chopsticks are difficult <u>using</u>. _____

C 다음 문장을 밑줄 친 부분에 유의하여 바르게 해석하시오.

1 My grandmother lived <u>to be</u> 80 years old.

→ _____

2 He must be smart <u>to answer</u> the question.

→ _____

3 Fred bought a new phone, <u>only to lose</u> it again.

→ _____

교과서 문장 응용하기 | 배운 문법을 이용하여 영어 문장을 써 봅시다.

1 그 시인은 87세까지 살았다. (poet) → _____

2 선글라스는 여름에 쓰기에 적절하다. (proper) → _____

too ~ to부정사 / enough to부정사

- **too+형용사(부사)+to부정사**: '너무 ~해서 …할 수 없다'의 뜻으로, 「so+형용사(부사)+that+주어+can't(couldn't) …」로 바꿔 쓸 수 있다.

  Sam is **too** busy **to make** time for his family.

  → Sam is **so** busy **that** he **can't** make time for his family.

- **형용사(부사)+enough+to부정사**: '…할 만큼 충분히 ~하다'의 뜻으로, 「so+형용사(부사)+that+주어+can(could) …」으로 바꿔 쓸 수 있다.

  She is strong **enough to** lift the box.

  → She is **so** strong **that** she **can** lift the box.

A 괄호 안에서 알맞은 것을 고르시오.   » 정답과 해설 p.4

1 I am (too / enough) tired to climb up the mountain.
2 Julia is tall (too / enough) to be a fashion model.
3 Do you know him well (too / enough) to ask for help?
4 The young girl is (too / enough) shy to say anything.

B 우리말과 뜻이 같도록 괄호 안의 말을 배열하여 문장을 완성하시오.

1 Harry는 너무 어려서 결혼을 할 수 없다. (get, too, to, young)
  → Harry is _____ married.
2 이 밧줄은 거기까지 닿을 만큼 충분히 길다. (long, reach, enough, to)
  → This rope is _____ there.
3 나의 할머니는 나이가 많이 드셔서 더 빠르게 걸으실 수 없다. (old, to, too, walk)
  → My grandmother is _____ faster.

C 다음 문장과 뜻이 같도록 빈칸에 알맞은 말을 쓰시오.

1 He is too upset to think clearly.
  → He is _____ upset _____ he _____ _____ clearly.
2 This bed is warm enough to sleep in.
  → This bed is _____ warm _____ I _____ _____ in it.

교과서 문장 응용하기	배운 문법을 이용하여 영어 문장을 써 봅시다.

1 그녀는 너무 어려서 그 책을 이해할 수 없다. (too)   → _____
2 그는 내 가방을 들어 줄 정도로 충분히 친절했다. (enough)   → _____

12 to부정사의 의미상 주어

to부정사의 행위의 주체를 to부정사의 의미상 주어라고 하며, to부정사의 행위의 주체가 문장의 주어와 다를 경우에
to부정사 앞에 「for(of)+목적격」의 형태로 쓴다.

- 「**for+목적격**」: 일반적인 형용사 뒤에 쓴다.

  This song is *difficult* **for me** to sing.

  It is not *easy* **for Kate** *to work out* every day.

- 「**of+목적격**」: 사람의 성격이나 태도를 나타내는 형용사 뒤에 쓴다.

  It is *nice* **of you** to help the boy.

A 빈칸에 알맞은 말을 쓰시오.

1 This smartphone is hard _____ my grandmother _____ use.

2 It was nice _____ you _____ take her to the airport.

3 It is important _____ students _____ do their homework.

4 It was silly _____ him _____ believe such a rumor.

» 정답과 해설 p.4

◆ 사람의 성격이나 태도를 나타내는 형용사: kind, nice, wise, careful, rude, foolish 등

◆ 의미상 주어의 생략: 의미상 주어가 일반인(people, we 등)인 경우 보통 생략된다.

B 괄호 안의 말을 바르게 배열하여 문장을 완성하시오.

1 It was _____ angry. (for, natural, to, get, Penny)

2 It was _____ the door. (careless, him, of, open, to)

3 It is not _____ "I'm sorry." (difficult, say, for, to, her)

4 It was _____ the chance. (you, miss, foolish, to, of)

C 우리말과 뜻이 같도록 빈칸에 알맞은 말을 쓰시오.

1 그 시험은 내가 통과하기에는 어려웠다.

→ The exam was difficult _____ _____ _____ pass.

2 그가 그 돈을 저축하다니 현명했다.

→ It was wise _____ _____ _____ _____ the money.

3 그들이 내 강아지를 돌봐 주다니 친절하다.

→ It is kind _____ _____ _____ _____ care of my puppy.

4 우리가 그의 설명을 이해하기는 쉽지 않았다.

→ It wasn't easy _____ _____ _____ _____ his explanation.

교과서 문장 응용하기

배운 문법을 이용하여 영어 문장을 써 봅시다.

1 그가 규칙적으로 운동하는 것은 중요하다. (it, regularly) → _____

2 네가 나에게 네 펜을 빌려주다니 친절하다. (it, lend) → _____

내신적중 실전문제

빈출유형 ★

[01~02] 빈칸에 알맞은 것을 고르시오.

01

> We decided _____ the child a card.

① send   ② sent

③ sending   ④ to send

⑤ to sending

02

> _____ is good for your health to work out regularly.

① It   ② This   ③ That

④ What   ⑤ Who

03 밑줄 친 부분의 쓰임이 |보기|와 다른 것은?

> 보기
> I came here early to get a good seat.

① She grew up to be a great artist.

② People go to the gym to work out.

③ I went to the airport to see off my aunt.

④ Nick went to the supermarket to get some snacks.

⑤ Sarah saved a lot of money to buy a new laptop computer.

04 빈칸에 알맞은 말이 바르게 짝지어진 것은?

> • I have no friends to play _____.
> • Homeless people want to have houses to live _____.

① on — to   ② on — with

③ with — to   ④ to — in

⑤ with — in

05 우리말과 뜻이 같도록 빈칸에 알맞은 말을 쓰시오. 주관식

> 나는 너 같은 친구를 가질 만큼 충분히 운이 좋다.
> → I am lucky _____ _____ _____
>   a friend like you.

06 빈칸에 알맞은 말이 나머지 넷과 다른 것은?

① It's strange _____ him to leave so early.

② It wasn't easy _____ me to solve this riddle.

③ Isn't it useful _____ you to learn how to cook?

④ It was nice _____ her to take care of my children.

⑤ It's important _____ teenagers to get along with friends.

07 밑줄 친 부분의 쓰임이 | 보기 |와 같은 것은?

> | 보기 |
> It is important <u>to help</u> people in need.

① My goal is <u>to win</u> a gold medal.
② <u>To remember</u> all their names is impossible.
③ We hoped <u>to leave</u> the small island.
④ I'm sorry <u>to keep</u> you waiting so long.
⑤ The way <u>to get</u> to the subway station is easy.

08 빈칸에 공통으로 알맞은 것은?

> • He is not old _____ to go to school.
> • The gate isn't wide _____ to get the car through.

① too
② enough
③ so as
④ that
⑤ in order

09 짝지어진 문장의 의미가 <u>다른</u> 것은?

① • I ran fast, only to miss the school bus.
　 • I ran fast, but I missed the school bus.
② • He was happy to win the race.
　 • He was happy because he won the race.
③ • Tom is wise enough to keep the secret.
　 • Tom is wise, so he keeps the secret.
④ • She tried harder not to fail.
　 • She didn't want to fail, so she tried harder.
⑤ • He is too old to go overseas.
　 • He is very old, so he can go overseas.

10 밑줄 친 <u>It</u>의 쓰임이 나머지 넷과 <u>다른</u> 것은?

① <u>It</u> is rather warm today.
② <u>It</u>'s kind of you to help me.
③ <u>It</u>'s easy to find the post office.
④ <u>It</u> is important to choose good friends.
⑤ <u>It</u> is impossible to master English in a month or two.

[11~12] 어법상 <u>어색한</u> 부분을 찾아 고쳐 쓰시오. 주관식

11
> We need a spoon and chopsticks to eat.

_____ → _____

12
> The doctor told me what to take medicine. So I took it in the evening.

_____ → _____

13 밑줄 친 부분을 어법상 바르게 고친 것은?

① It's time <u>to leaving</u>. → leaving
② I was too shocked <u>say</u> a word. → said
③ He woke up <u>find</u> his house burning. → found
④ The weather is <u>enough good</u> to go on a picnic. → too good
⑤ We are discussing <u>when</u> to buy for Sena's birthday. → what

14 우리말을 바르게 영작한 것은?

> 나는 너에게 할 놀라운 말이 있다.

① I have something surprising to tell you.
② I have something to tell you surprising.
③ I have something to tell surprising you.
④ I have surprising something to tell you.
⑤ I have surprising to tell something to you.

15 우리말과 뜻이 같도록 할 때 빈칸에 알맞은 것은?

> 네가 그 경기에서 이기는 것은 불가능하지 않다.
> → It is not impossible _____ the game.

① for you to win
② you to win for
③ for to you win
④ to you win of
⑤ of you to win

[16~18] 밑줄 친 부분의 쓰임이 나머지 넷과 <u>다른</u> 것을 고르시오.

16 ① She started <u>to climb</u> up the wall.
② The important thing is <u>to do</u> our best.
③ It is difficult <u>to lose</u> weight easily.
④ It's time <u>to do</u> your homework.
⑤ My hobby is <u>to take</u> pictures of wild flowers.

17 ① They were standing outside <u>to meet</u> him.
② My plan is <u>to play</u> with my cousins.
③ John saved money <u>to study</u> abroad.
④ Sue took the yoga class <u>to keep</u> in shape.
⑤ Joe went to the drugstore <u>to get</u> some aspirin.

18 ① Let's decide where <u>to go</u>.
② The stone is heavy <u>to lift</u>.
③ It's not good <u>to be</u> lazy.
④ What I want is <u>to show</u> you this.
⑤ My dream is <u>to travel</u> around the world.

[19~20] 다음 문장과 뜻이 같도록 빈칸에 알맞은 말을 쓰시오. 주관식

19
> I turned on the TV to watch the reality show.
> → I turned on the TV _____ _____ _____ watch the reality show.

20
> The lake was so deep that we couldn't swim in it.
> → The lake was _____ deep for us _____ _____ in.

21 우리말을 바르게 영작한 것을 <u>모두</u> 고르면?

> 그 선반은 너무 약해서 이 모든 책을 받칠 수 없다.

① The shelf is too weak to hold all these books.
② The shelf is weak enough to hold all these books.
③ The shelf is very weak, so it can hold all these books.
④ The shelf is so strong that it can hold all these books.
⑤ The shelf is so weak that it can't hold all these books.

22 빈칸에 알맞지 <u>않은</u> 것은?

It is _____ of him to do such a thing.

① nice   ② kind
③ stupid   ④ careful
⑤ necessary

23 다음 문장과 뜻이 같은 것은?

I'm not sure when to leave here.

① I'm not sure when I left here.
② I'm not sure where I should leave.
③ I'm not sure what I should leave here.
④ I'm not sure when I should leave here.
⑤ I'm not sure when I want to leave here.

24 빈칸에 enough가 들어갈 수 <u>없는</u> 것은?
① He is old _____ to go there alone.
② This book is _____ difficult to read.
③ Ian is tall _____ to reach the top shelf.
④ Bob is kind _____ to take care of my dog.
⑤ Two days are not long _____ to see everything here.

25 밑줄 친 부분의 쓰임이 같은 것끼리 바르게 짝지어진 것은?

ⓐ Cathy forgot <u>to bring</u> her report.
ⓑ This world is a good place <u>to live</u> in.
ⓒ My grandfather's wish is <u>to visit</u> Baekdusan.
ⓓ <u>To try</u> local foods is a fun part of any trip.
ⓔ Learning a foreign language is a way <u>to experience</u> a new culture.

① ⓐ, ⓑ   ② ⓐ, ⓓ
③ ⓑ, ⓒ   ④ ⓑ, ⓔ
⑤ ⓓ, ⓔ

26 어법상 <u>어색한</u> 것은?
① Let me know how to cook *bulgogi*.
② Can you tell me when to turn right?
③ Did you decide why to eat for lunch?
④ We didn't know whom to believe at that time.
⑤ Do you know where to get off to go to the City Hall?

27 어법상 올바른 것은?
① That is impossible for me to get an A.
② I need someone kind to depend on.
③ Can I have a piece of paper to write?
④ It was brave for you to say "no" to her.
⑤ It is difficult of me to speak in Chinese.

서술형 평가

01 밑줄 친 **to부정사**의 쓰임이 같은 것끼리 묶으시오.

> ⓐ I hope to take pictures of the players.
> ⓑ Yuri woke up to find a bag in her bed.
> ⓒ It is careless of her to forget his name.
> ⓓ The lady has two cats to take care of.
> ⓔ The frog was very happy to hear that.
> ⓕ He took the swimming class to stay healthy.

(1) 명사적 용법: _____
(2) 형용사적 용법: _____
(3) 부사적 용법: _____

02 빈칸에 알맞은 말을 괄호 안의 지시대로 쓰시오.

> **A** How can I get to the art museum?
> **B** Sorry, I don't know _____ to the art museum.

(1) _____ (to부정사 이용)
(2) _____ (should 이용)

03 다음 문장과 뜻이 같도록 빈칸에 알맞은 말을 쓰시오.

> They wanted to take pictures of wild animals, so they went to Kenya.

→ They went to Kenya _____
_____ wild animals.

04 두 문장을 괄호 안의 지시대로 한 문장으로 쓰시오.

> Miso got up very early. She could have breakfast.

(1) Miso got up _____
breakfast. (so ~ that 이용)
(2) Miso got up _____
breakfast. (enough 이용)

[05~06] 다음 글을 읽고, 물음에 답하시오.

> ⓐ <u>영어로 충고를 하는 방법이 몇 가지 있다.</u> Some ways are very strong. Other ways are not as strong. ⓑ <u>That's important of you to know when giving strong advice and when to making a suggestion.</u> In the United States and Canada, for example, you can give strong advice to a close friend or a family member. You should not give strong advice to your boss or your friend. Instead, you should make a suggestion.

05 밑줄 친 ⓐ의 우리말과 뜻이 같도록 괄호 안의 말을 이용하여 문장을 완성하시오.

There are _____
in English. (give advice, several ways)

06 밑줄 친 ⓑ에서 어법상 <u>어색한</u> 것을 <u>4개</u> 찾아 바르게 고쳐 문장을 다시 쓰시오.

_____
_____

CHAPTER

03

동명사

동명사란 무엇인가?

동명사는 동사의 의미와 성질을 가지면서 문장에서 명사의 역할을 하는 것을 말하며, 동사를 명사처럼 사용하기 위해 「동사원형+-ing」의 형태로 쓰인다.

Learning English takes a lot of time. 영어를 배우는 것은 많은 시간이 걸린다.

동명사는 문장에서 어떤 역할을 하는가?

동명사는 문장에서 명사 역할을 하여 주어, 보어, 목적어로 쓰인다.

동명사

- 주어 역할: ~하기는, ~하는 것은

Climbing rocks is dangerous.
암벽 등반을 하는 것은 위험하다.

- 보어 역할: ~하는 것이다

My hobby is **surfing** the Internet.
나의 취미는 인터넷 서핑을 하는 것이다.

- 목적어 역할: ~하는 것을, ~하기를

Jamie enjoys **collecting** stamps.
Jamie는 우표 모으는 것을 즐긴다.
Sarah is good at **solving** problems.
Sarah는 문제를 해결하는 데 능숙하다.

동명사와 to부정사를 목적어로 쓰는 동사에는 어떤 것들이 있는가?

동명사가 명사의 성격을 가졌다고 해서 모든 동사가 동명사를 목적어로 쓰는 것은 아니다. enjoy처럼 동명사만을 목적어로 쓰는 동사와 want처럼 to부정사만을 목적어로 쓰는 동사가 있다.

목적어의 형태	대표적인 동사
동명사만을 목적어로 쓰는 동사	enjoy, finish, stop, mind, give up, imagine 등
to부정사만을 목적어로 쓰는 동사	want, hope, expect, decide, plan, need 등
동명사와 to부정사를 모두 목적어로 쓰는 동사	like, love, hate, begin, start 등 〈의미 차이가 없는 경우〉
	remember, forget, try 등 〈의미 차이가 있는 경우〉

13 동명사의 쓰임 1_ 주어, 보어

동명사는 「동사원형+-ing」의 형태로 쓰며, 주어, 보어로 쓰인 동명사는 to부정사로 바꿔 쓸 수 있다.

- **주어 역할**: '~하기는, ~하는 것은'이라는 뜻을 나타낸다.

  Learning about other cultures is interesting.

  → **It** is interesting **to learn** about other cultures.

- **보어 역할**: '~하는 것이다'라는 뜻을 나타낸다.

  My goal is **getting** high scores on the test.

  → My goal is **to get** high scores on the test.

A 빈칸에 알맞은 말을 | 보기 |에서 골라 동명사 형태로 쓰시오. » 정답과 해설 p.6

> | 보기 |
> | fly   get   take   have |

1 _____ up early is easy for me.

2 The most important thing is _____ a dream.

3 My plan is _____ a dance class.

4 Is _____ in an airplane exciting?

B 우리말과 뜻이 같도록 괄호 안의 말을 배열하여 문장을 완성하시오.

1 오토바이를 타는 것은 어렵니? (hard, is, a motorcycle, riding)

  → _____

2 나의 숙제는 영어로 이메일을 쓰는 거야. (is, writing, my homework, in English, an email)

  → _____

3 밤에 외출하는 것은 위험하다. (dangerous, going out, is, at night)

  → _____

C 다음 문장과 뜻이 같도록 빈칸에 알맞은 말을 쓰시오.

1 Cheating during a test is wrong.

  → _____ is wrong _____ _____ during a test.

2 My dream is meeting the President of the USA.

  → My dream is _____ _____ the President of the USA.

교과서
문장
응용하기

배운 문법을 이용하여 영어 문장을 써 봅시다.

1 테니스를 치는 것은 재미있다. (fun)   → _____

2 그의 직업은 사진을 찍는 것이다. (picture)   → _____

14 동명사의 쓰임 2_ 목적어

- '~하는 것을, ~하기를'이라는 뜻으로, 동사나 전치사의 목적어로 쓰인다.

Yuna *enjoys* **running** along the river. 〈동사의 목적어〉

She *finished* **making** a model airplane. 〈동사의 목적어〉

Thank you *for* **inviting** me. 〈전치사의 목적어〉

I'm interested *in* **writing** a horror story. 〈전치사의 목적어〉

A 괄호 안의 말을 빈칸에 알맞은 형태로 쓰시오.

1 The kids started _____ in the snow. (play)

2 I stopped _____ birds in the tree. (watch)

3 She is proud of _____ the speech contest. (win)

4 The workers finished _____ the fence. (paint)

5 The villagers became interested in _____ one another. (help)

» 정답과 해설 p.6

◆ 동명사의 부정: 동명사 앞에 not (never)를 쓴다.
He felt bad about **not telling** the truth.

B 괄호 안의 말을 바르게 배열하여 문장을 완성하시오. (동사는 알맞은 형태로 바꿀 것)

1 Andy left _____. (finish, without, his lunch)

2 _____ me. (thank you, for, not, forget)

3 My friends _____. (enjoy, talk about, sports)

4 Many children _____. (mind, the medicine, take)

5 Ann's husband _____. (up, smoke, gave)

C 우리말과 뜻이 같도록 괄호 안의 말을 이용하여 문장을 완성하시오.

1 나는 양파를 먹는 것을 꺼려하지 않아. (mind, eat)

→ I don't _____ _____ onions.

2 Peter는 파티에서 그녀에게 이야기하는 것을 피했다. (avoid, talk)

→ Peter _____ _____ to her at the party.

3 Susan은 오늘밤 설거지할 것을 걱정한다. (worry, wash, about)

→ Susan is _____ _____ _____ the dishes tonight.

4 James는 강에서 수영하는 것을 두려워한다. (afraid of, swim)

→ James is _____ _____ _____ in the river.

교과서
문장
응용하기

배운 문법을 이용하여 영어 문장을 써 봅시다.

1 너는 너의 방을 청소하는 것을 끝냈니? (clean) → _____

2 우리는 그 계획을 바꾸는 것에 대해 이야기했다. (change) → _____

동명사나 to부정사만 목적어로 쓰는 동사

동명사만을 목적어로 쓰는 동사	enjoy, finish, stop, mind, give up, practice, imagine, avoid 등
to부정사만을 목적어로 쓰는 동사	want, hope, wish, expect, decide, plan, need, agree, promise 등

Jack and I *enjoyed* **flying** kites after school.
Let's *imagine* **climbing** Mt. Everest.
I *hope* **to hear** from you soon.
My father *decided* **to sell** his car.

A 괄호 안에서 알맞은 것을 고르시오.

» 정답과 해설 p.6

1 Would you mind (shutting / to shut) the door?
2 I practiced (drawing / to draw) dogs at first.
3 My family planned (going / to go) to Canada.
4 My brother enjoys (cooking / to cook) for my family.
5 Do you want (having / to have) lunch on the bench?

B 밑줄 친 부분을 어법상 바르게 고쳐 쓰시오.

1 Anna finished <u>to set</u> the table for dinner.   _____
2 Would you mind <u>to passing</u> me the bottle?   _____
3 Joanne promised <u>bring</u> her book tomorrow.   _____
4 Emma decided <u>buying</u> a new camera.   _____

C 우리말과 뜻이 같도록 괄호 안의 말을 이용하여 문장을 완성하시오.

1 Jennifer는 그녀의 컴퓨터를 고치는 것을 포기했다. (fix)
  → Jennifer _____ her computer.
2 나는 여름이 오기 전에 몸매를 가꾸기를 원한다. (get)
  → I _____ into shape before summer comes.
3 독후감 쓰는 것을 내일까지 끝낼 수 있니? (write)
  → Can you _____ the book report by tomorrow?

교과서
문장
응용하기

배운 문법을 이용하여 영어 문장을 써 봅시다.

1 Anne은 그녀의 여가 시간에 TV 보는 것을 즐긴다. (enjoy) → _____
2 나는 곧 너를 만나기를 희망한다. (hope)   → _____

16 동명사와 to부정사 모두 목적어로 쓰는 동사

- 동명사와 to부정사를 모두 목적어로 쓰는 동사: like, love, hate, begin, start, continue 등
  My stomach *began* **hurting(to hurt)** suddenly.

- 동명사와 to부정사를 모두 목적어로 쓰며, 의미가 다른 동사

remember + 동명사	(과거에) ~했던 것을 기억하다	remember + to부정사	(미래에) ~할 것을 기억하다
forget + 동명사	(과거에) ~했던 것을 잊다	forget + to부정사	(미래에) ~할 것을 잊다
try + 동명사	시험 삼아 ~해 보다	try + to부정사	~하려고 노력하다

I *remember* **telling** you the story.　　　　I *forgot* **to tell** you the story.

I'll *try* **reading** the book.　　　　The kids *try* **to read** the book.

A 빈칸에 알맞은 말을 |보기|에서 골라 올바른 형태로 쓰시오.

>> 정답과 해설 p.7

보기			
tell	work	hand	breathe

1 I love _____ the cool mountain air.

2 My father hates _____ on the weekend.

3 Don't forget _____ in your report by Friday.

4 She tried _____ him the truth, but she couldn't.

◆ stop + 동명사/to부정사
1. stop + 동명사: ~하는 것을 그만 두다
   He *stopped* chewing gum.
2. stop + to부정사: ~하기 위해서 (… 을) 멈추다
   He *stopped* to answer the phone.

B 괄호 안의 말을 빈칸에 알맞은 형태로 쓰시오.

1 I remember _____ Niagara Falls. It was wonderful. (see)

2 Remember _____ your swimsuit. We'll go to the pool. (pack)

3 If your wife is angry at you, try _____ her flowers. (give)

C 다음 문장을 밑줄 친 부분에 유의하여 바르게 해석하시오.

1 I <u>forgot reading</u> the book last year.　　_____

2 He <u>tried to remember</u> my name.　　_____

교과서
문장
응용하기

배운 문법을 이용하여 영어 문장을 써 봅시다.

1 나는 그녀를 전에 본 것을 기억한다. (before)　　→ _____

2 유리는 그 쿠폰들을 가지고 가는 것을 잊어버렸다. (coupon) → _____

17 동명사의 관용 표현

go -ing	~하러 가다	be busy -ing	~하느라 바쁘다
spend (on) -ing	(시간·돈을) ~하는 데 쓰다	How about -ing?	~하는 게 어때?
feel like -ing	~하고 싶다	look forward to -ing	~하기를 기대하다
on(upon) -ing	~하자마자	cannot help -ing	~하지 않을 수 없다
be used to -ing	~하는 데 익숙하다	It's no use -ing	~해도 소용없다

I **feel like going** out for a walk.
I **spent** the weekend **watching** movies.
I'll **look forward to seeing** you soon.

A 괄호 안에서 알맞은 것을 고르시오.

» 정답과 해설 p.7

1 I'm used to (live / living) in the city.

2 On (see / seeing) Daniel, I ran away.

3 He spent all the money (buys / buying) Christmas gifts.

4 Her family cannot help (to worry / worrying) about her wound.

B 어법상 어색한 부분을 찾아 고쳐 쓰시오.

1 Do you want to go ski? _____

2 How about read this article? _____

3 My father is very busy to run our store all day. _____

4 They're looking forward to join the band. _____

C 우리말과 뜻이 같도록 괄호 안의 말을 이용하여 문장을 완성하시오.

1 지금 후회해도 소용없다. (regret)

→ It is _____ _____ _____ now.

2 나는 그것에 대해 그에게 묻지 않을 수가 없다. (ask)

→ I _____ _____ _____ him about that.

3 그 소식을 듣자마자 그는 울기 시작했다. (hear)

→ _____ _____ the news, he began to cry.

4 그녀는 낮 동안 자는 것에 익숙하다. (sleep)

→ She _____ _____ _____ _____ during the day.

교과서
문장
응용하기

배운 문법을 이용하여 영어 문장을 써 봅시다.

1 나는 지금 집에 가고 싶다. (feel) → _____

2 나는 당신과 함께 일하기를 기대한다. (look) → _____

➡ 내신적중 실전문제를 풀기 전에 Workbook p.9에 있는 요점정리를 참고하세요.

내신적중 실전문제

[01~04] 빈칸에 알맞은 것을 고르시오.

01

_____ loudly is good for your health.

① Laugh
② Laughs
③ Laughed
④ Laughing
⑤ To laughing

02

He left Korea without _____ goodbye.

① say
② says
③ said
④ saying
⑤ to say

03

He won't agree _____ the rule.

① keep
② keeping
③ kept
④ to keep
⑤ being kept

04

I practice _____ ropes every day for the test.

① jump
② jumping
③ jumped
④ to jump
⑤ to jumping

05 우리말과 뜻이 같도록 빈칸에 알맞은 말을 쓰시오. 주관식

Brian은 서울에 도착하자마자 강남으로 갔다.
→ _____ _____ in Seoul, Brian went to Gangnam.

[06~07] 빈칸에 공통으로 알맞은 것을 고르시오.

06

- Don't forget _____ by the laundry shop later.
- People need _____ using cars so much.

① stop
② stops
③ stopped
④ stopping
⑤ to stop

07

A Rina, thank you for _____ me your bike. It was really useful.
B Oh! I completely forgot _____ it to you.

① lend
② lends
③ lent
④ to lend
⑤ lending

[08~09] 빈칸에 알맞지 <u>않은</u> 것을 고르시오.

08

> I _____ playing computer games.

① enjoy　　　　② hope

③ gave up　　　④ stopped

⑤ don't mind

[11~12] 괄호 안의 말을 이용하여 문장을 완성하시오. 주관식

11

> After the long journey, he tried _____,
> but he could not fall asleep. (sleep)

12

> The president finished _____ a
> speech in front of people. (make)

09

> _____ exercising in the morning.

① Todd is busy　　② I'm used to

③ They mind　　　④ We'll try

⑤ George planned

13 어법상 어색한 것은?

① He is busy doing his business.

② It's no use telling him the secret.

③ I'm looking forward to join the band.

④ Jack cannot help falling in love with her.

⑤ She wasn't used to carrying heavy bags.

10 밑줄 친 부분의 쓰임이 |보기|와 <u>다른</u> 것은?

> | 보기 |
> Our favorite activity is <u>playing</u> soccer.

① The dolphins are <u>swimming</u> in group.

② Her dream is <u>becoming</u> a member of an
   idol group.

③ Tom's wish is <u>meeting</u> the basketball
   player.

④ The Japanese girl's hobby is <u>watching</u>
   Korean dramas.

⑤ Their final goal was <u>taking</u> part in the
   Olympics.

14 우리말과 뜻이 같도록 할 때 빈칸에 알맞은 것은?

> 그들은 나에게서 편지를 받은 것을 기억하지 못했다.
> → They didn't remember _____ letters
>   from me.

① get　　　　　② got

③ getting　　　④ to get

⑤ to be got

15 어법상 올바른 것은?

① He's good at solve difficult puzzles.

② Imagine to be on the Broadway stage.

③ I spent a lot of money collect character dolls.

④ She remembered inviting some friends to her wedding next week.

⑤ They gave up traveling to the country because of the terror.

16 빈칸에 알맞은 말이 바르게 짝지어진 것은?

· She stopped _____ and closed the book.

· Jack hopes _____ from college next June.

① reading — to graduate

② to read — to graduate

③ reading — graduate

④ reads — graduating

⑤ to read — graduating

17 밑줄 친 부분이 어법상 어색한 것은?

① I go <u>swimming</u> every weekend.

② Thomas enjoys <u>reading</u> science fiction.

③ Paul is used to <u>getting</u> up early.

④ We're looking forward <u>working</u> with you.

⑤ Sora and her sister like <u>jogging</u>.

18 두 문장을 한 문장으로 쓸 때 빈칸에 알맞은 말을 쓰시오. 주관식

I learned to cook Italian food. I really enjoyed it.

→ I really enjoyed _____ Italian food.

19 우리말과 뜻이 같도록 할 때 빈칸에 알맞은 것끼리 바르게 짝지어진 것은?

· 다른 도구를 사용해 봐.

→ Try _____ a different tool.

· 그는 그 도구를 사용하려고 애썼다.

→ He tried _____ the tool.

① use — use

② using — to use

③ to use — used

④ used — to use

⑤ to using — used

20 어법상 어색한 것을 모두 고르면?

① My father is busy to clean the house.

② Sarah could not help to love the baby.

③ I don't feel like going to the concert.

④ The man spent his time walking his pet.

⑤ Kevin felt sorry for losing your comic book.

[21~22] 밑줄 친 ①~⑤ 중 어법상 어색한 것을 고르시오.

21

> Mandy promised ① taking care of ② our dog ③ while we ④ are ⑤ on vacation.

22

> A What made you decide ① being a zookeeper?
>
> B I like ② playing with animals. So I felt like ③ having the job.
>
> A What do you do ④ to be a zookeeper?
>
> B I ⑤ work part-time at the zoo.

23 밑줄 친 부분을 동명사로 바꿔 쓸 수 없는 것은?

① I want to return this book.

② It began to snow this morning.

③ They started to push the big gate.

④ Jina likes to play chess with her brother.

⑤ Richard hates to watch romantic movies.

24 우리말을 바르게 영작한 것은?

> 그에게 공부하라고 충고해도 소용없다.

① It is use advising him studying.

② He is use advising me to study.

③ He is no use to advise him to study.

④ It is no use advising him to study.

⑤ It is not use advising him studying.

25 짝지어진 두 문장의 의미가 같은 것은?

① • He tries to keep his promise.

  • He tries keeping his promise.

② • I forgot to visit the Grand Park.

  • I forgot visiting the Grand Park.

③ • She loved to ride a horse in the field.

  • She loved riding a horse in the field.

④ • We stopped to eat late at night.

  • We stopped eating late at night.

⑤ • They remembered to stay at that guest house in Jejudo.

  • They remembered staying at that guest house in Jejudo.

26 어법상 어색한 것을 찾아 고쳐 쓰시오. 주관식

> Your phone is ringing. How about answer the phone first?

_____ → _____

27 밑줄 친 부분이 어법상 올바른 것은?

① I didn't expect seeing you here.

② Don't you enjoy to play with them?

③ Debby plans studying abroad next year.

④ Do you mind to work another hour?

⑤ I forgot coming here when I was a kid.

서술형 평가

01 |보기|에서 알맞은 말을 골라 문장을 완성하시오. (동사의 형태를 바꿀 것)

> ┌ 보기 ┐
> learn a foreign language
> swim in deep water

(1) _____ dangerous.
(2) _____ helpful.

02 우리말과 뜻이 같도록 문장을 완성하시오.

(1)
> 나는 소라에게 이메일을 보냈던 것을 기억한다.

→ I _____ an email to Sora.

(2)
> 나는 소라에게 이메일을 보낼 것을 기억한다.

→ I _____ an email to Sora.

03 어법상 어색한 것을 2개 찾아 고쳐 쓰시오.

> **A** Serena, did you finish doing your science homework?
> **B** Not yet. It's really difficult.
> **A** Well, how about to do it together?
> **B** Sounds good. I need to doing it with someone.

(1) _____ → _____
(2) _____ → _____

04 밑줄 친 부분을 우리말로 바르게 해석하시오.

(1) You <u>cannot help crying</u> at this news.

_____

(2) I <u>feel like going shopping</u> today.

_____

(3) My dad <u>is busy preparing</u> dinner in the kitchen.

_____

[05~06] 다음 글을 읽고, 물음에 답하시오.

> Hi Alan,
> I got your email about ⓐ <u>go</u> hiking this weekend, and yes, I want ⓑ <u>go</u>. I'm really looking forward to ⓒ <u>leave</u> the city for a few days. ⓓ <u>Spend</u> time in the countryside will make me happy. What time are we going to take off on Saturday morning? Oh, by the way, ⓔ <u>I forgot to give back some books to you.</u> I'll drop by your house tomorrow morning.
>
> 　　　　　　　　　　　　　　Jessy

05 밑줄 친 ⓐ~ⓓ의 알맞은 형태를 쓰시오.

ⓐ _____　　ⓑ _____
ⓒ _____　　ⓓ _____

06 밑줄 친 ⓔ를 우리말로 바르게 해석하시오.

_____

CHAPTER

04

시제

시제란 무엇인가?

시제란 동작이나 사건을 시간적 흐름으로 표시하는 것으로, 시제에 따라 동사의 형태가 달라진다. 시제의 종류로는 단순시제(현재, 과거, 미래), 진행시제, 완료시제가 있다.

현재완료시제란 무엇인가?

현재완료시제는 과거에 시작된 동작이나 상태가 현재까지 영향을 미칠 때 쓰며, 「have(has)+*과거분사」로 나타낸다.

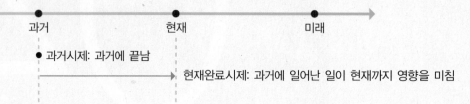

〈과거시제〉 I **was** a cheerleader two years ago. – 과거에 치어리더였고, 현재는 모름 (관련성 없음)
　　　　　나는 2년 전에 치어리더였다.
〈현재완료시제〉 I **have been** a cheerleader for two years. – 과거부터 현재까지 계속 치어리더임
　　　　　나는 2년 동안 치어리더이다.

현재완료시제는 어떻게 해석하는가?

현재완료의 의미

- 완료: (벌써, 지금 막) ~했다
  Alan **has** already **read** the magazine.
  Alan은 이미 그 잡지를 읽었다.

- 결과: ~해 버렸다
  Jisu **has lost** a new backpack.
  지수는 새 배낭을 잃어버렸다.

- 경험: ~한 적이 있다
  We'**ve** never **seen** the spaceship.
  우리는 우주선을 결코 본 적이 없다.

- 계속: ~해 오고 있다
  Yujin **has used** this computer for three years.
  유진이는 3년 동안 이 컴퓨터를 사용해오고 있다.

현재완료시제의 부정문과 의문문은 어떻게 만드는가?

부정문	주어+have(has) not+과거분사 ~.	I **have not(haven't)** been to the baseball field. 나는 야구장에 가본 적이 없다.
의문문	Have(Has)+주어+과거분사 ~?	**Have** you **worked** at the bank? 너는 그 은행에서 일한 적이 있니?

용어 사전

* **과거분사:** 「동사원형+-ed」의 형태 또는 불규칙 형태로, 문장에서 명사를 수식하거나 보어로 사용되며, 완료형 및 수동형을 만든다.

현재완료의 쓰임과 형태

- 현재완료는 「have(has)+과거분사」로 나타내며, 과거에 일어난 일이 현재까지 영향을 미칠 때 쓴다. 특정한 과거 시점을 나타내는 부사(구)나 when이 이끄는 부사절과는 같이 쓸 수 없다.

	현재완료	과거
형태	have(has)+과거분사	불규칙, 규칙 동사의 과거형(-ed)
의미	완료, 결과, 경험, 계속	과거에 있었던 사건이나 행동을 서술
같이 쓰는 부사	already, just, ever, before, once 등	yesterday, last year, ago 등

I **have been** to London before. 〈현재완료〉 I **went** to London last year. 〈과거〉

A 괄호 안에서 알맞은 것을 고르시오.   » 정답과 해설 p.8

1 They (went / have gone) to Jejudo yesterday.

2 I (was / have been) to New York for three weeks.

3 Jenny (see / has seen) the animation film before.

4 We first (got / have got) to know him ten years ago.

5 My brother (started / has started) to learn how to read last week.

B 괄호 안의 말을 빈칸에 현재완료 형태로 쓰시오.

1 She _____ _____ a diary in English. (keep)

2 They _____ _____ each other for ten years. (know)

3 There _____ _____ many earthquakes in California. (be)

4 I think you _____ _____ him once before. (meet)

5 Man _____ already _____ on the moon. (walk)

C 밑줄 친 부분을 어법상 바르게 고쳐 쓰시오.

1 I <u>have be</u> to Japan three times.   _____

2 My sister <u>has lost</u> her umbrella last week.   _____

3 Sally <u>have learn</u> Chinese since 2017.   _____

4 He <u>has been</u> out when I called him.   _____

교과서
문장
응용하기

배운 문법을 이용하여 영어 문장을 써 봅시다.

1 나는 전에 Matt를 만난 적이 있다. (before)   → _____

2 Jim은 이미 점심을 먹었다. (already)   → _____

현재완료의 부정문과 의문문

- 부정문: 「주어+have(has) not+과거분사 ~.」로 나타낸다.
  They **have not(haven't) seen** a rainbow.
  She **has not(hasn't) played** soccer before.

- 의문문: 「Have(Has)+주어+과거분사 ~?」로 나타낸다.
  Have you **finished** your homework?
  – Yes, I have. / No, I haven't.

A 밑줄 친 부분을 어법상 바르게 고쳐 쓰시오.   » 정답과 해설 p.8

1 <u>Do</u> you ever flown in a helicopter?   _____

2 The students <u>don't</u> had dinner yet.   _____

3 Have you <u>find</u> your library card?   _____

4 He has not <u>hear</u> from Amy since yesterday.   _____

B 괄호 안의 지시대로 문장을 바꿔 쓰시오.

1 I have traveled in Thailand. (부정문으로)

→ _____

2 They have sold all the tickets. (의문문으로)

→ _____

3 My sister has spoken to Andrew. (부정문으로)

→ _____

4 Yuri has bought him a present. (의문문으로)

→ _____

C 우리말과 뜻이 같도록 괄호 안의 말을 배열하여 문장을 완성하시오.

1 네 사촌은 멕시코로 돌아갔니? (to Mexico, your cousin, has, returned)

→ _____

2 우리는 그 새 방을 아직 보지 못했다. (yet, the new room, seen, not, we, have)

→ _____

3 그 만화책을 읽어 본 적이 있니? (you, have, the comic book, read)

→ _____

교과서 문장 응용하기 배운 문법을 이용하여 영어 문장을 써 봅시다.

1 초롱이는 아직 그의 편지를 읽지 않았다.   → Chorong _____.

2 너는 뉴욕에 가 본 적이 있니?   → Have _____?

20 현재완료의 의미 1_ 완료

■ 현재완료의 완료는 '(벌써, 지금 막) ~했다'는 뜻으로, 주로 already(이미, 벌써), yet(아직), just(지금 막) 등의 부사와 쓰여 과거에 일어난 일이 현재에 막 완료된 경우를 나타낸다.

Today's guest **has** *just* **arrived**.
We **have** *already* **had** dinner.
The students **haven't finished** reading the book *yet*.

A 우리말과 뜻이 같도록 빈칸에 알맞은 말을 쓰시오. 》 정답과 해설 p.8

1 수호는 이미 그녀에게 전화를 했다.
→ Suho _____ _____ _____ her.

2 Paul은 지금 막 모형 비행기를 만들었다.
→ Paul _____ _____ _____ a model airplane.

3 내 남동생은 벌써 그의 숙제를 다 했다.
→ My brother _____ _____ _____ his homework.

4 나는 막 엽서 쓰는 것을 끝마쳤다.
→ I _____ _____ _____ writing the postcard.

B 괄호 안의 우리말을 참고하여 대화를 완성하시오.

1 A Oh, I forgot to send the letter.
B Don't worry. I _____ _____ _____ it. (내가 그것을 이미 보냈어.)

2 A Are you hungry?
B No. I _____ _____ _____ lunch. (나는 지금 막 점심을 먹었어.)

3 A We should study chapter 3 today, right?
B Right. We haven't _____ it _____. (우리는 그것을 아직 공부하지 않았어.)

C 다음 문장을 밑줄 친 부분에 유의하여 바르게 해석하시오.

1 She has already left. _____

2 I have just finished doing the dishes. _____

3 He hasn't arrived at the airport yet. _____

교과서
문장
응용하기

배운 문법을 이용하여 영어 문장을 써 봅시다.
1 Kenny는 막 서울에 도착했다. (just) → _____
2 나는 이미 그 책을 샀다. (already) → _____

현재완료의 의미 2_ 결과

- 현재완료의 결과는 '~해 버렸다(그래서 현재 …하다)'는 뜻으로, 과거에 일어났던 일이 현재의 결과에 대한 원인일 때 쓴다.

I've **broken** my arm. I cannot play basketball now.
He **has lost** his smartphone. 〈현재완료 – 찾지 못했음〉
He **lost** his smartphone yesterday. 〈과거 – 찾았는지는 알 수 없음〉

A 우리말과 뜻이 같도록 빈칸에 알맞은 말을 쓰시오.

》 정답과 해설 p.9

1 나는 내 시계를 망가뜨려서 나는 그것을 고쳐야 한다.
→ I _____ _____ my watch, so I have to fix it.
2 그들은 그 차를 팔았고, 새 차를 샀다.
→ They _____ _____ the car, and they bought a new one.
3 Sarah가 내 우산을 가져가서 나는 우산이 없다.
→ Sarah _____ _____ _____ _____, so I don't have one.
4 그가 그것에 대해 나에게 모두 말을 해서 나는 지금 그것에 대해 잘 안다.
→ He _____ _____ _____ all about it, so I know about it well now.

B 두 문장이 한 문장이 되도록 괄호 안의 말을 이용하여 문장을 완성하시오.

1 Lindy went to Sydney. Lindy is still in Sydney.
→ Lindy _____ _____ _____ Sydney. (go)
2 Ann left her wallet at home. She doesn't have it now.
→ Ann _____ _____ _____ _____ at home. (leave)
3 I washed the shirt. It is clean now.
→ I _____ _____ _____ _____. (wash)

C 다음 문장을 밑줄 친 부분에 유의하여 바르게 해석하시오.

1 The players have left the stadium.
→ _____

2 My sister has eaten the cake.
→ _____

교과서
문장
응용하기 배운 문법을 이용하여 영어 문장을 써 봅시다.
1 나는 내 모자를 잃어버렸다. (lose) → _____
2 그 여자는 외출해 버렸다. (go out) → _____

22 현재완료의 의미 3_ 경험

- 현재완료의 경험은 '~한 적이 있다'는 뜻으로, 주로 ever, never, once, twice, ~ times, before 등의 부사와 쓰여 과거부터 현재까지의 경험을 나타낸다.

I **have been** to France three times. 〈경험〉

cf. She **has gone** to France. 〈결과〉

They **have eaten** pasta *many times before*.

A 빈칸에 알맞은 말을 | 보기 |에서 골라 올바른 형태로 쓰시오. » 정답과 해설 p.9

보기			
eat	climb	play	meet

1 I _____ his cousin many times.

2 Taehee _____ the mountain twice.

3 The woman _____ Vietnamese food three times.

4 Woobin _____ the piano in front of his classmates once.

B 우리말과 뜻이 같도록 괄호 안의 말을 배열하여 문장을 완성하시오.

1 아무도 화성에 가 본 적이 없다. (been, Mars, has, ever, to)

→ Nobody _____.

2 Mary는 피자를 여러 번 만들어 본 적이 있다. (a pizza, many times, made, has)

→ Mary _____.

3 나는 전에 연을 날려 본 적이 있다. (have, flown, before, a kite)

→ I _____.

C 다음 문장을 밑줄 친 부분에 유의하여 바르게 해석하시오.

1 We have seen his concert once.

→ _____

2 They have never been to a water park.

→ _____

3 Bob has ridden a horse before.

→ _____

교과서
문장
응용하기

배운 문법을 이용하여 영어 문장을 써 봅시다.

1 나는 중국에 두 번 가 본 적이 있다. (be) → _____

2 Peter는 전에 그 소식을 들은 적이 있다. (hear) → _____

23 현재완료의 의미 4_ 계속

- 현재완료의 계속은 '~해 오고 있다'는 뜻으로, 주로 for(~ 동안), since(~ 이후로) 등의 말과 쓰여 과거에 시작된 동작이 현재까지 계속되는 경우를 나타낸다.

She **has lived** in this town for ten years.
We **have learned** English *for* seven years. 〈for+시간의 길이〉
I **have learned** Japanese *since* last year. 〈since+시작한 시점〉

A 괄호 안에서 알맞은 것을 고르시오.

» 정답과 해설 p.9

1 My sister (works / has worked) here for six months.
2 She (was / has been) sick since last Wednesday.
3 This building has been here (for / since) 1967.
4 He has slept (for / since) ten hours.

B 밑줄 친 부분을 어법상 바르게 고쳐 쓰시오.

1 It has rained <u>for</u> this morning.   _____
2 They have been married <u>since</u> twenty years.   _____
3 Dr. Cook <u>is</u> a doctor for thirteen years.   _____

C 두 문장이 한 문장이 되도록 괄호 안의 말을 이용하여 빈칸에 알맞은 말을 쓰시오.

1 They moved here last year. They still live here.
→ They _____. (live, since)
2 Mina caught a cold two days ago. She has a cold now.
→ Mina _____. (have, for)
3 Eric started to enjoy baseball three years ago. He still enjoys it.
→ Eric _____. (enjoy, for)
4 This printer broke down last Monday. It still doesn't work.
→ This printer _____.
(break down, since)
5 She began to wear glasses when she was six. She still wears them.
→ She _____. (wear, since)

**교과서
문장
응용하기** 배운 문법을 이용하여 영어 문장을 써 봅시다.

1 지난 토요일부터 계속 비가 오고 있다.   → _____
2 나는 3년 동안 그 컴퓨터를 계속 써 오고 있다. → _____

→ 내신적중 실전문제를 풀기 전에 Workbook p.12에 있는 요점정리를 참고하세요.

내신적중 실전문제

[01~03] 빈칸에 알맞은 것을 고르시오.

01

> He _____ to England, so he is not in Seoul.

① goes
② is going
③ has gone
④ has been
⑤ has to go

02

> I _____ about his family before, so I don't know about his parents.

① don't hear
② haven't heard
③ am not hearing
④ don't have heard
⑤ haven't to hear

03

> I have met her in the library _____.

① now
② before
③ yesterday
④ two days ago
⑤ last weekend

04 어법상 어색한 부분을 찾아 고쳐 쓰시오. 주관식

> Have you watch the new movie before?

_____ → _____

05 빈칸에 알맞은 말을 쓰시오. 주관식

> A I went to Egypt last year. Have you ever been to Egypt?
> B _____, _____ _____ _____. B u t someday I hope to go there.

06 밑줄 친 우리말과 뜻이 같도록 빈칸에 알맞은 말을 쓰시오. 주관식

> A 너는 그녀가 바이올린 연주하는 것을 들어 본 적이 있니?
> B Yes, I have. It was wonderful.

→ _____ _____ _____ her play the violin?

07 우리말을 바르게 영작한 것은?

> 나는 3년 동안 태권도를 배워왔다.

① I learn *taekwondo* for three years.
② I learned *taekwondo* since three years.
③ I learned *taekwondo* for three years.
④ I have learned *taekwondo* for three years.
⑤ I have learned *taekwondo* since three years.

08 밑줄 친 부분의 쓰임이 같은 것끼리 바르게 짝지어진 것은?

> ⓐ He <u>has been</u> absent since last week.
> ⓑ Yujin <u>has gone</u> to India.
> ⓒ <u>Have</u> you ever <u>read</u> the novel?
> ⓓ Hojin <u>has just finished</u> taking a bath.
> ⓔ I've <u>posted</u> that on SNS several times.

① ⓐ, ⓒ   ② ⓐ, ⓔ
③ ⓑ, ⓒ   ④ ⓒ, ⓔ
⑤ ⓓ, ⓔ

09 우리말과 뜻이 같도록 할 때 빈칸에 알맞은 것은?

> Eric은 한 시간째 그의 가방을 찾고 있다.
> → Eric _____ his bag for an hour.

① looks for   ② looked for
③ have looked for   ④ has looked for
⑤ was looking for

10 두 문장을 한 문장으로 쓸 때 빈칸에 알맞은 것은?

> He started to paint the door blue three hours ago. Now the door is blue.
> → He _____ the door blue.

① paints   ② has painted
③ has painting   ④ has to paint
⑤ having painted

[11~13] 빈칸에 알맞은 말이 바르게 짝지어진 것을 고르시오.

11
> • I've learned Chinese hard _____ a few years.
> • It has snowed heavily in the area _____ last week.

① for — for   ② when — since
③ for — since   ④ for — when
⑤ since — since

12
> • Rita _____ here when she was a kid.
> • Ian _____ medical science for 4 years.
> • Kate _____ badminton a week ago.

① came — studied — played
② came — has studied — played
③ came — has studied — has played
④ has come — studied — played
⑤ has come — studied — has played

13
> **A** Have you _____ Ann's mother?
> **B** Yes. I _____ her an hour ago.

① see — saw   ② saw — saw
③ seen — saw   ④ saw — seen
⑤ seen — seen

[14~16] 밑줄 친 부분의 쓰임이 |보기|와 같은 것을 고르시오.

14

> 보기
> I have worked here for ten years.

① Sally has seen the movie once.
② Kate has already left for London.
③ I have never heard about his vacation.
④ Peter has gone to America.
⑤ Yuri has been in Paris since last year.

15

> 보기
> Have you ever talked to a movie star?

① Bob has been to China before.
② It has rained since last Friday.
③ Yuna has just arrived at the airport.
④ They have already finished their work.
⑤ I have kept a diary in English for five years.

16

> 보기
> The musical has just started.

① It has been stormy since last night.
② I have been to Australia twice.
③ He hasn't done his homework yet.
④ She has broken her left arm.
⑤ We have known each other for a long time.

17 밑줄 친 부분이 어법상 어색한 것은?

① Sora has stayed at the hotel last spring.
② I haven't been late for school this year.
③ Dad has just washed the dishes.
④ Woobin has never made a model airplane.
⑤ Singing has been my hobby since I was young.

[18~19] 두 문장을 한 문장으로 쓸 때 빈칸에 알맞은 말을 쓰시오. (주관식)

18

> They started to live in Korea three years ago. They still live there.

→ They _____ _____ in Korea for three years.

19

> Mike lost his cellphone battery. He has to buy a new one.

→ Mike _____ _____ his cellphone battery.

20 빈칸에 have(Have)가 들어갈 수 없는 것은?

① I _____ lost my bag on the subway.
② We _____ been friends for 5 years.
③ _____ Tom and John already gone out?
④ They _____ been to Canada three times.
⑤ The twins _____ met her two months ago.

서술형 평가

01 다음 문장을 괄호 안의 지시대로 바꿔 쓰시오.

> Jack has touched a spider before.

(1) _____

_____ (부정문으로)

(2) _____

_____ (의문문으로)

02 밑줄 친 부분의 의미가 같은 것끼리 묶으시오.

> ⓐ Has Dad come home yet?
> ⓑ Tom has spent all the money.
> ⓒ Some people have never seen snow.
> ⓓ I have already finished washing the dishes.
> ⓔ Ann has stayed a night at a friend's house before.
> ⓕ They have sold their house and moved to this city.

_____ / _____ / _____

03 두 문장을 한 문장으로 쓸 때 빈칸에 알맞은 말을 각각 쓰시오.

> Nicole started making the cheesecake at three o'clock. It's five o'clock and she is still making it.

(1) Nicole _____ _____ the cheesecake _____ three o'clock.

(2) Nicole _____ _____ the cheesecake _____ two hours.

04 다음 표를 보고, 대화의 빈칸을 완성하시오.

	Yes	No
Nick	play the drums	play the harp
Dave	eat Spanish food	eat Mexican food

(1) **A** Nick, have you ever played the drums?

    B _____, _____ _____. But _____ _____ _____ the harp.

(2) **A** Has Dave ever eaten Mexican food?

    B _____, _____ _____. But he _____ _____ Spanish food.

[05~06] 다음 글을 읽고, 물음에 답하시오.

> I'm studying really hard at school. I only started at this school last September, because we moved to this town a year ago. ⓐ Our Chinese teacher has left the school in December. ⓑ We had a new teacher, Mr. Cheng, last March. ⓒ We still have the teacher. He's really nice, and he doesn't give us tests very often. In fact, we haven't ⓓ had a Chinese test since three months. But we're going to have one tomorrow, so I have to do some more work.

05 밑줄 친 ⓐ, ⓓ에서 어법상 어색한 것을 찾아 고쳐 쓰시오.

ⓐ _____ → _____

ⓓ _____ → _____

06 밑줄 친 ⓑ와 ⓒ의 두 문장을 한 문장으로 쓰시오.

_____

CHAPTER

05

조동사

조동사란 무엇이며 어떤 형태인가?

조동사는 be동사나 일반동사의 앞에서 특정한 의미를 더해 주는 보조 동사이다. 조동사는 혼자서는 쓰이지 못하므로, 조동사의 뒤에는 반드시 동사원형이 온다. 주어의 수와 인칭에 상관없이 항상 같은 형태이며, 조동사가 있는 의문문은 조동사를 문장의 맨 앞에 쓰고, 부정문은 조동사 뒤에 not을 쓴다.

Can you come with me? 〈의문문〉 나와 같이 갈 수 있니?

I **cannot** play the guitar. 〈부정문〉 나는 기타를 칠 수 없다.

조동사는 어떤 의미를 나타내는가?

능력
- ~할 수 있다: can

  I **can** write in English. 나는 영어로 쓸 수 있다.

허락
- ~해도 좋다: can, may

  You **may** eat out tonight. 오늘밤은 외식을 해도 좋다.

요청
- ~해 주시겠어요?: can, could, will

  Can you give me a glass of water? 제게 물 한 컵 주시겠어요?

예정, 의지
- ~할 것이다, ~할 예정이다: will

  I **will** paint my bedroom tomorrow. 나는 내일 나의 침실을 페인트칠 할 것이다.

추측
- ~일지도 모른다: may, might
- ~임에 틀림없다: must

  They **may** not swim well. 그들은 수영을 잘하지 못할지도 모른다.
  He **must** be the son of Mike. 그가 Mike의 아들임이 틀림없다.

의무, 충고
- ~해야 한다: must, have(has) to, should, ought to
- ~하는 게 좋겠다: had better

  You must **follow** the school rules. 너는 학교 규칙을 따라야 한다.
  You **had better** study tonight. 너는 오늘밤에 공부하는 편이 좋겠다.

과거의 습관
- ~하곤 했다: used to, would

  I **would** get up early when I was a child. 나는 아이였을 때 일찍 일어나곤 했다.

24 can, could

- **can:** 능력, 허락, 요청 등의 의미를 나타내며, 능력은 be able to로, 허락은 may로 바꿔 쓸 수 있다. 부정형은 「cannot(can't)+동사원형」으로 쓴다.

  Anna **can(is able to)** solve the problem. 〈능력: ~할 수 있다〉

  I **cannot(can't)** come to the party on Friday.

  You **can(may)** watch TV after finishing your homework. 〈허락: ~해도 좋다〉

  Can you hand me the pencil case? 〈요청: ~해 주겠니?〉

- **could:** could가 의문문에 쓰이면 정중한 요청을 나타낸다.

  Could you give me a hand? 〈요청: ~해 주시겠어요?〉

A 밑줄 친 조동사의 의미를 괄호 안에서 고르시오.

» 정답과 해설 p.10

1 My brother <u>can</u> jump really high. (능력 / 허락)

2 You <u>can</u> feed animals at this zoo. (허락 / 요청)

3 <u>Can</u> you show me the map? (허락 / 요청)

4 Ted <u>can</u> fix the screen. (능력 / 요청)

5 <u>Could</u> you lend me your camera? (능력 / 요청)

B 다음 문장과 뜻이 같도록 빈칸에 알맞은 말을 쓰시오.

1 You may play online games for one hour.

→ You _____ play online games for one hour.

2 Jenny can make dolls with cloth.

→ Jenny _____ _____ _____ make dolls with cloth.

3 I couldn't play the violin last year, but I can now.

→ I _____ _____ _____ play the violin last year, but I can now.

C 우리말과 뜻이 같도록 괄호 안의 말을 배열하여 문장을 완성하시오.

1 너는 제주도에서 휴가를 보낼 수 있다. (spend, can, you)

→ _____ your vacation in Jejudo.

2 나는 어젯밤에 피곤했지만 잠을 잘 수가 없었다. (sleep, I, couldn't)

→ I was tired last night, but _____.

3 라디오 좀 꺼 주시겠습니까? (you, turn off, could)

→ _____ the radio?

교과서 문장 응용하기

배운 문법을 이용하여 영어 문장을 써 봅시다.

1 민호는 중국어를 말할 수 있다. (speak) → _____

2 네 공책을 내게 빌려줄 수 있니? (lend) → _____

will

- will은 미래에 대한 예정, 의지 또는 요청의 의미를 나타낸다. 부정형은 「will not(won't)+동사원형」으로 쓴다.

My sister **will** be ten years old next year. 〈예정: ~할 것이다〉

I **will** try my best. 〈의지: ~할 것이다〉

Will you open the door? 〈요청: ~해 주시겠어요?〉

They **will not(won't)** see the magic show this weekend.

A 밑줄 친 부분을 어법상 바르게 고쳐 쓰시오.

1 She will <u>goes</u> shopping this Saturday. _____

2 I <u>will don't</u> visit the museum this time. _____

3 <u>Did</u> it rain tomorrow? _____

4 Will you <u>invited</u> your classmates? _____

》 정답과 해설 p.10

◆ **will의 축약형:** will이 대명사와 쓰이면 I'll, you'll, he'll, she'll, it'll, we'll, they'll로 줄여 쓸 수 있다.

◆ **정중한 요청을 나타내는 would:** would는 will보다 좀 더 정중한 요청을 나타낸다.
Would you pass me the salt, please?

B will을 이용하여 미래를 나타내는 문장으로 바꿀 때 빈칸에 알맞은 말을 쓰시오.

1 I ate lunch with Andy today.
→ I _____ lunch with him tomorrow, too.

2 The students took a test yesterday.
→ They _____ another test today.

3 Jiho didn't wear a clean shirt today.
→ He _____ a clean one tomorrow, either.

C 우리말과 뜻이 같도록 괄호 안의 말을 배열하여 문장을 완성하시오.

1 내가 너에게 샌드위치를 좀 만들어 줄게. (some sandwiches, make, I'll, you)
→ _____

2 나는 다시는 거짓말을 하지 않을 것이다. (again, I, a lie, won't, tell)
→ _____

3 그는 너의 숙제를 대신 해 주지 않을 거야. (for you, he, not, will, your homework, do)
→ _____

4 우리에게 그녀의 앨범을 보여 주겠니? (us, her album, you, will, show)
→ _____

**교과서
문장
응용하기** 배운 문법을 이용하여 영어 문장을 써 봅시다.

1 Sue가 나중에 너에게 그 선물을 줄 거야. (gift) → _____

2 나는 나의 아버지와 낚시하러 갈 거야. (go fishing) → _____

26 may, might

- **may:** 허락 또는 불확실한 추측의 의미를 나타낸다. 부정형은 「may not＋동사원형」으로 쓴다.
  You **may** take my umbrella with you. 〈허락: ~해도 좋다〉
  Mike **may** know how to play this game. 〈불확실한 추측: ~일지도 모른다〉
  Lisa **may not** come to our meeting.

- **might:** 주로 불확실한 추측을 나타낸다.
  He **might** be in the classroom.

A 다음 문장을 서로 관계있는 것끼리 연결하시오.

1 I'm not feeling well. •
2 Tom wears a swimsuit. •
3 Don't you have a pen? •

• (a) You may use mine.
• (b) May I go home?
• (c) He might go swimming.

» 정답과 해설 p.11

◆ 허락을 나타내는 **may**와 **can**: 둘 다 허락의 의미를 갖지만 may는 격식을 갖춘 상황에서, can은 일상적인 상황에서 주로 쓰인다.

B 우리말과 뜻이 같도록 괄호 안의 말을 배열하여 문장을 완성하시오.

1 그는 학교에 결석했을지도 모른다. (be, absent, may, from school)
   → He _____.

2 나중에 비가 올지도 모른다. (might, later, rain)
   → It _____.

3 제가 창문을 열어도 될까요? (I, open, may)
   → _____ the window?

4 그 뉴스는 사실이 아닐지도 모른다. (not, be, may, true)
   → The news _____.

C 다음 문장을 밑줄 친 부분에 유의하여 바르게 해석하시오.

1 You <u>may eat</u> those cookies.   _____

2 <u>May I watch</u> TV now?   _____

3 Andy <u>might be</u> at the park now.   _____

4 Sena <u>may not like</u> soccer.   _____

교과서
문장
응용하기

배운 문법을 이용하여 영어 문장을 써 봅시다.

1 제가 안에 들어가도 될까요? (come in)   → _____

2 네가 틀렸을지도 모른다. (wrong)   → _____

27 must, have to

- **must**: 강한 추측 또는 의무를 나타내며, 부정형인 「must not+동사원형」은 금지의 의미를 나타낸다.

  He is tall with red hair. He **must** be Jerry. 〈강한 추측: ~임에 틀림없다〉

  I **must** take this book back to the library. 〈의무: ~해야 한다〉

  You **must not** lie to your friends. 〈금지: ~해서는 안 된다〉

- **have to**: 의무를 나타내는 must와 바꿔 쓸 수 있으며, 부정형인 「don't have to+동사원형」은 불필요의 의미를 나타낸다.

  You **have to**(must) finish your report today. 〈의무: ~해야 한다〉

  We **don't have to** go to school on Saturday. 〈불필요: ~할 필요가 없다〉

A 괄호 안에서 알맞은 것을 고르시오. » 정답과 해설 p.11

1 You (must / must not) waste time.

2 We (has to / have to) go home before dark.

3 We'll eat out today. You (don't have to / don't have) cook.

4 I have a test tomorrow. I (have / have to) study tonight.

B 우리말과 뜻이 같도록 괄호 안의 말을 배열하여 문장을 완성하시오.

1 Sam은 화가 난 것이 틀림없다. (angry, be, Sam, must)

→ _____

2 너는 내가 일할 때 내게 전화하면 안 된다. (call, not, me, you, at work, must)

→ _____

3 Tom은 설거지를 할 필요가 없다. (doesn't, Tom, wash the dishes, have to)

→ _____

4 그들은 승자를 결정해야만 한다. (have to, decide, they, the winner)

→ _____

C 다음 문장을 밑줄 친 부분에 유의하여 바르게 해석하시오.

1 We <u>must find</u> the hotel. _____

2 You <u>must not feed</u> the animals. _____

3 She <u>doesn't have to apologize</u> to Tony. _____

교과서 문장 응용하기

배운 문법을 이용하여 영어 문장을 써 봅시다.

1 우리는 지금 떠나야 한다. (leave) → _____

2 John은 아픈 것임에 틀림없다. (sick) → _____

28 should, had better

- **should**: 도덕적 의무 또는 충고를 나타내며, 의무를 나타낼 때는 ought to와 바꿔 쓸 수 있다. 부정형인 「should not(shouldn't)+동사원형」은 금지의 의미를 나타낸다.

  You **should(ought to)** be quiet in the library. 〈도덕적 의무: ~해야 한다〉

  You **should(ought to)** take some rest. 〈충고: ~하는 게 좋겠다〉

  You **should not(shouldn't)** take pictures in this museum. 〈금지: ~해서는 안 된다〉

- **had better**: 충고의 의미를 나타낸다. 부정형은 「had better not+동사원형」으로 쓴다.

  It's already six o'clock. You **had better** hurry up. 〈충고: ~하는 게 좋겠다〉

  You **had better not** waste your money.

A 괄호 안에서 알맞은 것을 고르시오.

» 정답과 해설 p.11

1 You should always (keep / keeps) your promise.
2 Children (should not go / should don't go) to bed late.
3 Jim (has better / had better) drink a lot of water.
4 We (had better not / had not better) waste our time.

◆ **had better**의 축약형: had better가 대명사와 쓰이면 you'd better, she'd better 와 같이 줄여 쓸 수 있다.

B 다음 문장과 뜻이 같도록 빈칸에 알맞은 말을 쓰시오.

1 You should follow the traffic rules.

   → You _____ follow the traffic rules.

2 You ought not to copy the report.

   → You _____ copy the report.

C 우리말과 뜻이 같도록 괄호 안의 말을 이용하여 문장을 완성하시오.

1 너는 식사 전에 손을 씻어야 한다. (should, hands)

   → You _____ _____ _____ before meals.

2 너는 그녀에게 진실을 말하는 게 좋겠다. (had better, tell)

   → You _____ _____ _____ her the truth.

3 우리는 박물관에서 시끄럽게 이야기하면 안 된다. (should, loud)

   → We _____ _____ _____ _____ in the museum.

4 너는 네 가방을 그곳에 놓지 않는 게 좋겠다. (had better, leave)

   → You _____ _____ _____ _____ your bag there.

교과서 문장 응용하기

배운 문법을 이용하여 영어 문장을 써 봅시다.

1 너는 네 비밀번호를 잊어버리면 안 된다. (password)   → _____

2 너는 커피를 마시지 않는 것이 좋겠다. (drink)   → _____

used to, would

- **used to**: 현재에는 하지 않는 과거의 습관이나 상태를 나타낸다.

  I **used to** go swimming on weekends. 〈과거의 습관: (과거에) ~하곤 했다〉

  The actor **used to** be very shy when he was a kid. 〈과거의 상태: (과거에) ~였다〉

- **would**: 과거에 반복되었던 행동을 나타낼 때 쓰며, 과거의 상태를 나타낼 때는 쓸 수 없다.

  I **would** visit my grandparents every Christmas. 〈과거의 습관: (과거에) ~하곤 했다〉

A 괄호 안에서 알맞은 것을 고르시오.

» 정답과 해설 p.11

1 Jennifer (would / would to) play tennis on Sundays.

2 I used (eat / to eat) sweets too much.

3 There (used to / would) be a tall tree here.

4 My grandpa (will / would) go fishing when he was young.

◆ **be used to+-ing**: '~하는 데 익숙하다'라는 의미이다.
My brother is used to staying up all night.
(우리 형은 밤새우는 것에 익숙하다.)

B 다음 문장을 밑줄 친 부분에 유의하여 바르게 해석하시오.

1 We <u>used to live</u> in a small town.

→ _____

2 He <u>used to have</u> long hair.

→ _____

3 Andy <u>would go</u> out of the room when he was angry.

→ _____

C 우리말과 뜻이 같도록 괄호 안의 말을 배열하여 문장을 완성하시오.

1 나는 작년에는 늦게 일어났었는데, 요즘은 일찍 일어난다. (used, get up, I, to, late)

→ _____ last year, but I get up early these days.

2 그 집은 기차가 지나갈 때 흔들리곤 했었다. (would, shake, the house)

→ When a train went by, _____ .

3 10년 전에 이곳에 깊은 우물이 있었다. (be, to, used, here)

→ A deep well _____ 10 years ago.

4 Brad는 기분이 좋을 때, 노래를 부르곤 했다. (would, sing, he, a song)

→ When Brad was happy, _____ .

교과서 문장 응용하기 배운 문법을 이용하여 영어 문장을 써 봅시다.

1 나는 저녁 식사 후에 산책을 하곤 했다. (take a walk) → _____

2 Nicole은 갈색 머리였다. (have) → _____

→ 내신적중 실전문제를 풀기 전에 Workbook p.16에 있는 요점정리를 참고하세요.

내신적중 실전문제

» 정답과 해설 p.11

[01~03] 빈칸에 알맞은 것을 고르시오.

01

> I had two dogs. They _____ jump into my lap when I sat on the sofa.

① used
② would
③ have to
④ should
⑤ had better

02

> **A** _____ I use your smartphone?
> **B** Of course. Go ahead.

① Will
② May
③ Must
④ Should
⑤ Do

03

> **A** Can you give me some advice to be healthy?
> **B** You _____.

① used to get up early
② may not eat breakfast
③ had better not exercise
④ should not eat fast food
⑤ should watch TV so much

[04~06] 밑줄 친 부분과 바꿔 쓸 수 있는 것을 고르시오.

04

> Monica is able to ride a horse.

① can
② had better
③ used to
④ would like to
⑤ has to

05

> **A** What time is it?
> **B** It's five. The movie starts soon. You should hurry up.

① might
② could
③ would
④ used to
⑤ had better

06 우리말과 뜻이 같도록 괄호 안의 말을 이용하여 문장을 완성하시오. 주관식

> 우리는 그 문제를 풀지 못할 것이다. (solve, the problem)
>
> → We _____.

07 빈칸에 알맞은 말을 쓰시오. 주관식

> **A** Do I have to wear a dress to your party?
> **B** No, you _____ _____ _____.

[08~09] 빈칸에 알맞은 말이 바르게 짝지어진 것을 고르시오.

08

> **A** _____ you speak Chinese now?
> **B** I _____ speak Chinese when I was young, but I can now.

① Can — couldn't ② May — shouldn't
③ Can — can't   ④ May — couldn't
⑤ Do — must not

09

> · It'll rain today. You _____ take an umbrella with you.
> · The elevator stopped suddenly. We _____ wait for the manager for ten minutes.

① will — have to
② will — had better
③ had better — must
④ had better — had to
⑤ had better — have to

10 다음 문장과 뜻이 같도록 빈칸에 알맞은 말을 쓰시오. 주관식

> There was an old palace, but not anymore.
> → There _____ _____ be an old palace.

[11~12] 밑줄 친 부분의 쓰임이 ㅣ보기ㅣ와 같은 것을 고르시오.

11

> ㅣ보기ㅣ
> Jake won the first prize. He <u>must</u> be happy.

① She <u>must</u> finish the work by 7.
② He <u>must</u> get to the airport in time.
③ Tim <u>must</u> not throw away cans.
④ You <u>must</u> not smoke in this restaurant.
⑤ He didn't eat anything. He <u>must</u> be hungry.

12

> ㅣ보기ㅣ
> You <u>can</u> use my smartphone.

① I <u>cannot</u> remember his face.
② My dog <u>can</u> jump through a ring.
③ <u>Can</u> I ask you something?
④ My little brother <u>can</u> ride a bike.
⑤ She <u>can</u> speak three languages.

13 어법상 어색한 부분을 찾아 고쳐 쓰시오. 주관식

> You had not better waste your money.

_____ → _____

[14~15] 짝지어진 문장의 의미가 <u>다른</u> 것을 고르시오.

14 ① · Could you open the window?
　　· Would you open the window?
② · You should be quiet in class.
　　· You ought to be quiet in class.
③ · You must not drive so fast.
　　· You don't have to drive so fast.
④ · I can remember her phone number.
　　· I'm able to remember her phone number.
⑤ · After lunch, he would take a nap.
　　· After lunch, he used to take a nap.

15 ① · He should bring her to a doctor.
　　· He ought to bring her to a doctor.
② · There used to be a tree here.
　　· There was a tree here, but not now.
③ · Jake must change his bad habits.
　　· Jake has to change his bad habits.
④ · We should not forget them all.
　　· We must forget them all.
⑤ · You need not tell him the news.
　　· You don't need to tell him the news.

16 밑줄 친 부분의 쓰임이 나머지 넷과 <u>다른</u> 것은?
① The rumor <u>may</u> be true.
② <u>May</u> I turn on the TV?
③ You <u>may</u> not go out at night.
④ <u>May</u> I use your computer?
⑤ You <u>may</u> close the door.

[17~18] 빈칸에 알맞지 <u>않은</u> 것을 고르시오.

17
```
_____ you tell us more about your cat?
```
① Will　　　　② Can
③ May　　　　④ Would
⑤ Could

18
```
Tim _____ exercise for his health from now.
```
① will　　　　② may
③ used to　　　④ should
⑤ had better

[19~20] 다음 글에 이어질 말로 알맞지 <u>않은</u> 것을 고르시오.

19
```
Yumi has got a bad grade again. She wants to improve her English.
```
① Yumi may study English harder.
② Yumi will study English every day.
③ Yumi must practice English harder.
④ Yumi doesn't have to study English now.
⑤ Yumi should practice English every day.

20
```
There are a lot of children around here. If you drive fast, it's very dangerous.
```
① You should drive carefully.
② You must not drive so fast.
③ You had better drive slowly.
④ You may drive fast around here.
⑤ You ought to drive slowly around here.

서술형 평가

01 밑줄 친 부분을 우리말로 바르게 해석하시오.

(1) Jessica has a high fever. <u>She had better take some rest.</u>

→ _____

(2) <u>Ron used to be my best friend.</u> Now my best friend is Brad.

→ _____

02 밑줄 친 부분을 같은 의미의 다른 말로 바꿔 쓰시오.

(1) <u>May</u> I reuse your old clothes?

→ _____

(2) Kate <u>must</u> go to yoga class every Friday.

→ _____

(3) People <u>should</u> learn public etiquette.

→ _____

03 밑줄 친 ⓐ~ⓔ 중 어법상 어색한 것을 <u>3개</u> 찾아 고쳐 쓰시오.

Classroom Rules
· You must ⓐ <u>comes</u> to class on time.
· You ⓑ <u>has</u> to take notes during class.
· You ⓒ <u>must</u> listen carefully to your teacher.
· You must ⓓ <u>not sleep</u> in class.
· You ⓔ <u>don't must</u> talk with your friends in class.

(1) _____ → _____
(2) _____ → _____
(3) _____ → _____

04 괄호 안의 말을 이용하여 충고하는 말을 완성하시오.

(1) **A** I can't sleep well at night.

B You _____

_____ .

(drink warm milk, before bedtime)

(2) **A** I have a test tomorrow.

B You _____

_____ . (watch TV for too long)

독해형
어법

[05~06] 다음 글을 읽고, 물음에 답하시오.

Body language will help you everywhere — in Japan, the United States, Greece, Mexico, or any another place. You may not understand a person's words, but <u>사람의 몸짓 언어는 이해할 수 있다</u>. Let's say you want to know how to go to a museum. Just ask a person on the street. He will usually turn and then point. Go in that direction, and you have to find the museum.

05 내용상 <u>어색한</u> 문장을 찾아 바르게 고쳐 다시 쓰시오.

→ _____

_____

06 밑줄 친 우리말과 뜻이 같도록 빈칸에 알맞은 말을 쓰시오.

(1) you _____ _____ the person's body language

(2) you _____ _____ _____ _____ the person's body language

CHAPTER

06
수동태

수동태란 무엇이며 어떤 형태인가?

문장의 주어와 동사의 관계에서 주어가 동작을 직접 행하면 능동태라고 하고, 주어가 행동에 영향을 받거나 행동을 당하면 수동태라고 하며, 수동태는 「be동사+과거분사+by+목적격(행위자)」으로 나타낸다.

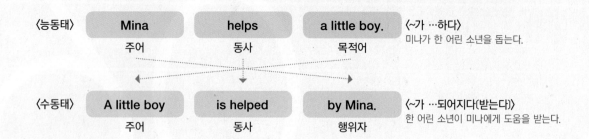

〈능동태〉 **Mina** / **helps** / **a little boy.**
주어 / 동사 / 목적어
〈~가 …하다〉
미나가 한 어린 소년을 돕는다.

〈수동태〉 **A little boy** / **is helped** / **by Mina.**
주어 / 동사 / 행위자
〈~가 …되어지다(받는다)〉
한 어린 소년이 미나에게 도움을 받는다.

수동태의 시제는 어떻게 나타내는가?

수동태의 시제

- 현재시제: am / are / is + 과거분사
  This comic book **is read** by many children. 이 만화책은 많은 아이들에게 읽힌다.

- 과거시제: was / were + 과거분사
  The paper flowers **were made** by Ann. 그 종이꽃들은 Ann에 의해 만들어졌다.

- 미래시제: will be + 과거분사
  The room **will be cleaned** by me. 그 방은 나에 의해 청소될 것이다.

수동태의 부정문과 의문문은 어떻게 나타내는가?

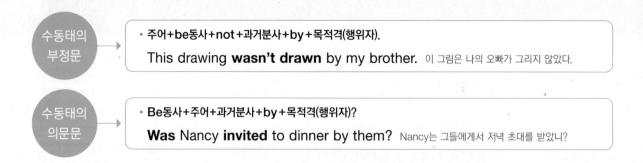

수동태의 부정문

- 주어+be동사+not+과거분사+by+목적격(행위자).
  This drawing **wasn't drawn** by my brother. 이 그림은 나의 오빠가 그리지 않았다.

수동태의 의문문

- Be동사+주어+과거분사+by+목적격(행위자)?
  Was Nancy **invited** to dinner by them? Nancy는 그들에게서 저녁 초대를 받았니?

용어 사전
*태: 주어가 동작을 행하는지 받는지를 말하는 것으로, 능동태와 수동태 두 가지가 있다.

30 수동태의 쓰임과 형태

- 수동태는 주어가 어떤 일을 당하는 것을 나타내며, 주로 동작을 받는 주체를 강조할 때 쓴다. 「주어+be동사+과거분사+by+목적격(행위자)」의 형태로 쓰며, '~가 …되어지다(받는다)'로 해석한다.

Everyone loves her.

She **is loved** by everyone.

cf. 수동태에서 행위자가 일반인이거나, 행위자를 알 수 없거나 밝힐 필요가 없을 때 「by+목적격(행위자)」은 생략한다.

English **is learned** all over the world (**by people**).

A 괄호 안에서 알맞은 것을 고르시오.　　　　　　　　　　　　　　　》 정답과 해설 p.12

1 The photo was taken by (he / him).

2 Gestures are sometimes (misunderstand / misunderstood).

3 The car (parked / was parked) on the street by Mr. Smith.

B 우리말과 뜻이 같도록 괄호 안의 말을 이용하여 문장을 완성하시오.

1 그 오래된 오토바이는 Jack의 아버지가 운전하신다. (drive)

→ The old motorcycle _____ _____ _____ Jack's father.

2 이 꽃들은 아이들에 의해 길러진다. (grow)

→ These flowers _____ _____ _____ children.

3 그 코치는 그의 선수들에게 존경받는다. (respect)

→ The coach _____ _____ _____ his players.

C 다음 문장을 수동태로 바꿔 쓰시오.

1 My daughter uses this room.

→ _____

2 A cat runs after a mouse.

→ _____

3 The director made this movie in 2017.

→ _____

4 They sell stamps in the post office.

→ _____

교과서 문장 응용하기

배운 문법을 이용하여 영어 문장을 써 봅시다.

1 그 나무들은 Mary에 의해 심어졌다. (plant)　→ The trees _____.

2 Montreal에서는 프랑스어가 말해진다. (speak)　→ French _____.

수동태의 부정문과 의문문

부정문	주어+be동사+not+과거분사+by+목적격(행위자).	The bridge **was not(wasn't)** built in 1895.
의문사가 없는 의문문	Be동사+주어+과거분사+by+목적격(행위자)?	A **Was** this chair **made** by your father? B Yes, it was. / No, it wasn't.
의문사가 있는 의문문	의문사+be동사+주어+과거분사+by+목적격(행위자)?	A When **was** the wine glass **broken**? B It was broken last week.

A 괄호 안의 말을 바르게 배열하여 문장을 완성하시오.   » 정답과 해설 p.12

1 Coffee _____ in cold countries. (grown, not, is)
2 The Statue of Liberty _____ by Americans. (not, built, was)
3 The store _____ by Thomas. (run, not, is)
4 This smartphone _____ in Korea. (not, is, made)
5 The dishes _____ by my sister. (were, washed, not)

B 대화의 빈칸에 알맞은 말을 쓰시오.

1 **A** _____ paper _____ in China?
  B Yes, it _____ invented in China many years ago.
2 **A** _____ this picture _____ by Gogh?
  B No, it _____. It _____ painted by Picasso.
3 **A** _____ _____ Diet Coke _____?
  B It was introduced in the early 1980s.

C 다음 문장을 부정문과 의문문으로 각각 바꿔 쓰시오.

1 This sad poem was written by Mike.
  → 부정문: _____
  → 의문문: _____
2 This art gallery is closed at 5 o'clock by them.
  → 부정문: _____
  → 의문문: _____

교과서
문장
응용하기

배운 문법을 이용하여 영어 문장을 써 봅시다.

1 이 신발은 그에 의해 만들어지지 않았다. (shoes)   → _____
2 언제 그 이메일이 보내졌니? (email)   → _____

수동태의 시제 / 조동사가 있는 수동태

■ 수동태의 시제

수동태과거	was(were)+과거분사	Chinese food **was cooked** by Cheng.
수동태미래	will be+과거분사	The fence **will be painted** by Tom.

■ 조동사를 포함하는 문장의 수동태

조동사+수동태	조동사+be+과거분사	Animals **should be protected** (by people).

A 밑줄 친 부분을 어법상 바르게 고쳐 쓰시오.   » 정답과 해설 p.13

1 The building is built in 2005 by the workers.   _____

2 The car will wash by Fred this weekend.   _____

3 The ball should thrown into the basket.   _____

4 The project can be doing in two days.   _____

B 우리말과 뜻이 같도록 괄호 안의 말을 이용하여 문장을 완성하시오.

1 그 자전거는 어제 Mike에 의해 수리되었다. (repair)

→ The bike _____ _____ by Mike yesterday.

2 많은 양의 올리브유가 사용될 것이다. (use)

→ A lot of olive oil _____ _____ _____.

3 먼지가 세계의 많은 지역으로 퍼질지도 모른다. (may, carry)

→ Dust _____ _____ _____ to many parts of the world.

C 다음 문장을 수동태로 바꿔 쓰시오.

1 Brian cleaned the bathroom yesterday.

→ _____

2 The secretary will copy the pictures.

→ _____

3 Sam must solve the problem.

→ _____

교과서
문장
응용하기

배운 문법을 이용하여 영어 문장을 써 봅시다.

1 음악이 한 밴드에 의해 연주되었다. (play)   → Music _____.

2 그 집은 곧 팔릴지도 모른다. (may, soon)   → The house _____.

33

4형식 문장의 수동태

- 4형식 문장은 두 가지의 수동태를 만들 수 있다.

Mom gave <u>me</u> <u>some apple juice</u>.
　　　　 간접목적어　　 직접목적어

→ I **was given** some apple juice by Mom. 〈간접목적어가 주어〉: 「간접목적어+be동사+과거분사+직접목적어」

→ Some apple juice **was given to** me by Mom. 〈직접목적어가 주어〉: 「직접목적어+be동사+과거분사+전치사+간접목적어」

- 직접목적어를 주어로 수동태를 만들 때 간접목적어 앞에 쓰는 전치사는 동사에 따라 to, for, of로 결정된다.

to	give, teach, tell, send 등	The camera **was given** *to* her by me.
for	make, buy, get, cook 등	A bicycle **was bought** *for* me by my father.
of	ask, inquire 등	A question **was asked** *of* her by them.

A 빈칸에 알맞은 전치사를 쓰시오.

>> 정답과 해설 p.13

1 A new job was given _____ Daniel by his boss.
2 The ring was bought _____ her by Todd.
3 Math was taught _____ us by Ms. Ryan.

◆ 직접목적어로만 수동태를 만들 수 있는 동사: make, write, buy, sell, cook 등과 같은 동사는 직접목적어만을 주어로 수동태를 만든다.
Judy made us pizza.
→ Pizza **was made for** us by Judy. (O)
→ We **were made** pizza by Judy. (×)

B 다음 문장을 수동태로 바꿔 쓰시오.

1 Dad made us some sandwiches.

→ _____

2 Mom got me a new computer.

→ _____

C 다음 문장을 두 가지 형태의 수동태로 바꿔 쓰시오.

1 Andy told them a scary story.
→ They _____.
→ A scary story _____.
2 Mr. Tullock asked me a hard question.
→ I _____.
→ A hard question _____.

교과서
문장
응용하기

배운 문법을 이용하여 영어 문장을 써 봅시다.

1 우리는 Ming에게서 중국어를 배운다. (teach) → We _____.
2 나의 형이 나에게 김밥을 만들어 주었다. (make) → *Gimbap* _____.

5형식 문장의 수동태 1_ 명사, 형용사, to부정사 목적격보어

■ 목적격보어가 명사, 형용사 또는 to부정사인 경우에는 목적어인 (대)명사를 주어로 수동태를 만든다. 이때 목적격보어는 원래의 형태 그대로 주격보어가 된다.

We called her Aunt Jenny. 〈목적격보어 – 명사〉
　　　　목적어　목적격보어

→ She **was called** Aunt Jenny by us.
　　주어　　　　　　주격보어

They asked you to explain this. 〈목적격보어 – to부정사〉
　　　　　목적어　목적격보어

→ You **were asked** to explain this by them.
　　주어　　　　　　주격보어

A 다음 문장을 수동태로 바꿔 쓰시오.　　　　　　　　　　　　　》 정답과 해설 p.13

1 He made me happy easily.

→ _____

2 We told Bob to exercise.

→ _____

3 They call a petrol station a gas station in America.

→ _____

4 Emma asked us to bring some food to the party.

→ _____

5 I named the rabbit Sally.

→ _____

B 괄호 안의 말을 바르게 배열하여 문장을 완성하시오.

1 (the Internet, to stop surfing, was told)
　→ I _____ by him.

2 (was kept, by his dog, warm)
　→ He _____.

3 (easy, was found, to use, by many people)
　→ The system _____.

4 (for their health, to drink, are advised, lots of water)
　→ People _____.

교과서
문장
응용하기

배운 문법을 이용하여 영어 문장을 써 봅시다.

1 그녀는 그 테니스 동아리의 리더로 선출되었다. (elect)　→ She _____.

2 그는 의사에게서 운동을 하라는 충고를 들었다. (advise)　→ He _____.

5형식 문장의 수동태 2_ 동사원형 목적격보어

- 목적격보어가 동사원형인 경우에는 수동태를 만들 때 목적격보어인 동사원형을 to부정사로 바꿔 쓴다.

능동태: 「동사+목적어+동사원형」 → 수동태: 「be동사+과거분사+to부정사」	We saw her *cross* the street. 〈지각동사〉 → She **was seen to cross** the street by us. My father made me *clean* my room. 〈사역동사〉 → I **was made to clean** my room by my father.

cf. 지각동사의 목적격보어가 현재분사인 경우, 수동태는 「be동사+과거분사+현재분사」로 쓴다.

A lot of people heard Justin *crying*. → Justin **was heard crying** by a lot of people.

A 다음 문장을 수동태로 바꿔 쓸 때 빈칸에 알맞은 말을 쓰시오.　　　　　　》 정답과 해설 p.13

1 I saw Noah jog in the park.

→ Noah _____ in the park by me.

2 Ann watched the dog run across the street.

→ The dog _____ the street by Ann.

3 Computers help us do a lot of things easily.

→ We _____ a lot of things easily by computers.

B 어법상 어색한 부분을 찾아 고쳐 쓰시오.

1 She was heard talk behind someone's back.　　　　　　_____

2 I was made look after my little brother by Mom.　　　　　_____

3 Something was felt touch me on the shoulder.　　　　　　_____

C 우리말과 뜻이 같도록 괄호 안의 말을 이용하여 문장을 완성하시오.

1 그녀가 노래를 부르는 것이 나에게 들렸다. (hear, sing)

→ She _____ _____ _____ _____ a song by me.

2 신선한 공기는 우리를 긴장이 풀리는 기분이 들게 해 주었다. (make, feel)

→ We _____ _____ _____ _____ relaxed by the fresh air.

3 동물들이 먹는 모습이 우리에게 목격되었다. (see, eat)

→ Animals _____ _____ _____ _____ by us.

교과서
문장
응용하기

배운 문법을 이용하여 영어 문장을 써 봅시다.

1 그 아이가 도로를 건너는 것을 우리가 보았다. (cross)　　→ The child _____

2 내가 지도를 가져오도록 Bob이 시켰다. (make, bring)　→ I _____

36

by 이외의 전치사를 쓰는 수동태

■ 수동태에서 행위자를 나타낼 때 by 이외의 전치사를 쓰는 경우도 있다.

be interested in	~에 관심이 있다	be made of(from)	~로 만들어지다
be worried about	~에 대해 걱정하다	be known to	~에게 알려져 있다
be surprised at	~에 놀라다	be known for	~로 유명하다
be satisfied with	~에 대해 만족하다	be filled with	~로 가득하다
be disappointed at	~에 대해 실망하다	be covered with	~로 덮여 있다
be pleased with	~에 기뻐하다	be crowded with	~로 붐비다

Jennifer **is interested in** K-pop music.

The movie **is known to** a lot of people in the world.

The street **is covered with** fallen leaves.

A 빈칸에 알맞은 전치사를 쓰시오. » 정답과 해설 p.13

1 This story is known _____ every student.

2 My brother is interested _____ wild flowers.

3 Ms. Winslet was very pleased _____ the result.

4 The mall was crowded _____ a lot of people.

B 어법상 어색한 부분을 찾아 고쳐 쓰시오.

1 I'm satisfied to my grade. _____

2 The store was filled of toys for the holiday sale. _____

3 They were disappointed of his response. _____

C 우리말과 뜻이 같도록 괄호 안의 말을 이용하여 문장을 완성하시오.

1 나는 그의 건강에 대해 걱정이 된다. (worry)

→ I _____ _____ _____ his health.

2 그녀는 그 소식에 놀랐다. (surprise)

→ She _____ _____ _____ the news.

3 이 장난감은 나무로 만들어졌다. (make)

→ This toy _____ _____ _____ wood.

교과서 문장 응용하기

배운 문법을 이용하여 영어 문장을 써 봅시다.

1 그 산은 눈으로 덮여 있다. (mountain) → _____

2 그녀는 그녀의 미모로 유명하다. (known, beauty) → _____

내신적중 실전문제

[01~02] 괄호 안에 주어진 말의 알맞은 형태를 고르시오.

01

> The gate (lock) during the winter period.

① locked
② is locking
③ to locking
④ is locked
⑤ to be locked

02

> The shoes (wash) by my mom yesterday.

① washed
② was washed
③ were washed
④ were washing
⑤ was washing

[03~04] 빈칸에 알맞은 것을 고르시오.

03

> A lot of things _____ online nowadays.

① can buy
② can bought
③ can be bought
④ can is bought
⑤ can are bought

04

> Judy's birthday party _____ next Friday.

① is held
② was held
③ will hold
④ will be holding
⑤ will be held

05 우리말과 뜻이 같도록 빈칸에 알맞은 말이 바르게 짝지어진 것은?

> 그 아이돌 가수는 십 대들로부터 사랑을 받았었니?
> → _____ the idol singer _____ by teens?

① Is — love
② Are — loved
③ Do — love
④ Was — loved
⑤ Were — loved

06 다음 문장을 수동태로 바르게 바꾼 것은?

> My father bought me a hat.

① I was bought a hat by my father.
② I was bought a hat for me by my father.
③ A hat was bought for me by my father.
④ A hat was bought to me by my father.
⑤ A hat has been bought for me by my father.

07 우리말과 뜻이 같도록 빈칸에 알맞은 말을 쓰시오. 주관식

> 이 상자는 꽃으로 가득하다.
> → This box is filled _____ flowers.

빈출
유형
★

[08~09] 어법상 어색한 것을 고르시오.

08 ① Your pen was found by my sister.
② The truck was driven by her.
③ This robot is made in Korea by they.
④ The singer is loved by teenagers.
⑤ Ted was introduced to us by Sejin.

09 ① Dad was pleased with my success.
② This model airplane was made of wood.
③ I was very disappointed at his behavior.
④ It is known for its wonderful sight.
⑤ What kind of music are you interested at?

10 수동태로 바꿀 수 <u>없는</u> 문장은?

① He plays the drum in his band.
② Michael became a great chef.
③ The artist showed us his paintings.
④ My teacher allowed me to go home early.
⑤ I watched the mother and her child play badminton.

11 빈칸에 알맞은 말이 나머지 넷과 <u>다른</u> 것은?

① My broken car was repaired _____ the engineer.
② The class president was elected _____ the students.
③ His house was burned down _____ a big fire.
④ The movie was directed _____ a 21-year-old university student.
⑤ They were satisfied _____ the result of the game.

[12~13] 괄호 안의 말을 이용하여 빈칸에 알맞은 말을 쓰시오.

12 The fan should not _____ _____ by babies. (touch)

13 When was the first train _____? (make)

[14~15] 다음 문장과 뜻이 같도록 빈칸에 알맞은 것을 고르시오.

14 I heard a bird sing by the window.
→ A bird was heard _____ by the window by me.

① sing   ② sings
③ to sing   ④ sang
⑤ to singing

15 They asked me to attend the meeting.
→ _____ to attend the meeting by them.

① I asked   ② I am ask
③ I was asked   ④ They are ask
⑤ They were asked

16 빈칸에 공통으로 알맞은 것은?

> - This place is known _____ many people all over the world.
> - Korean history is taught _____ us by Mr. Yoo.

① of   ② in
③ to   ④ for
⑤ with

17 밑줄 친 부분이 어법상 어색한 것은?

① Why <u>was</u> the field trip <u>canceled</u>?
② The book <u>was not lost</u> by Jake.
③ The same mistake <u>may be made</u> by him.
④ The dog <u>was named Choco</u> by its owner.
⑤ I <u>was made say</u> sorry to my sister by my mom.

18 밑줄 친 부분을 바르게 고친 것은?

> **A** Who painted *the Mona Lisa*?
> **B** It <u>paint</u> by Leonardo Da Vinci.

① painted   ② is painted
③ is painting   ④ was painting
⑤ was painted

19 다음 문장을 수동태로 바꾼 것이 <u>어색한</u> 것은?

① Sally uses the washing machine.
  → The washing machine is used by Sally.
② My mom made me learn Chinese.
  → I was made to learn Chinese by my mom.
③ Did he find his glasses in his room?
  → Were his glasses be found in his room by him?
④ She didn't invite me to her school festival.
  → I wasn't invited to her school festival by her.
⑤ You should hand in your report by tomorrow.
  → Your report should be handed in by tomorrow.

[20~21] 어법상 <u>어색한</u> 부분을 찾아 고쳐 쓰시오. 주관식

20

> The principal was seen come out of his office.

_____ → _____

21

> Beautiful flowers were sent for his girlfriend by Mark.

_____ → _____

22 빈칸에 들어갈 말이 바르게 짝지어진 것은?

> • The shopping mall was crowded _____ people.
> • She's pleased _____ the classical music.

① with — in   ② with — at
③ of — at   ④ with — with
⑤ about — with

23 밑줄 친 ①~⑤ 중 어법상 어색한 것은?

> **A** Did Jennifer ① break the window yesterday?
> **B** No, she ② didn't. The window ③ didn't break ④ by Jennifer. Bill ⑤ broke it.

24 다음 문장을 능동태로 바르게 바꾼 것은?

> I was made to learn *taekwondo* by my teacher.

① My teacher made learn *taekwondo*.
② My teacher made I learn *taekwondo*.
③ My teacher made me learn *taekwondo*.
④ My teacher made to learn *taekwondo*.
⑤ My teacher made me to learn *taekwondo*.

[25~26] 우리말을 바르게 영작한 것을 고르시오.

25

> 그는 의사에게 단 음식을 피하라는 말을 들었다.

① He told avoid sweet foods by the doctor.
② He told to avoid sweet foods by the doctor.
③ He was told avoid sweet foods by the doctor.
④ He was told to avoid sweet foods by the doctor.
⑤ He was told avoiding sweet foods by the doctor.

26

> 그 소포는 일주일 후에 배달될 것이다.

① The package delivers a week later.
② The package will deliver a week later.
③ The package will be deliver a week later.
④ The package will be delivered a week later.
⑤ The package will be to deliver a week later.

27 다음 문장과 뜻이 같은 것은?

> Why did you buy it at the market?

① Why was bought you it at the market?
② Why was it bought by you at the market?
③ Why did it bought you at the market?
④ Why did bought it by you at the market?
⑤ Why was by it you bought at the market?

서술형 평가

01 다음 문장을 괄호 안의 지시대로 바꿔 쓸 때 빈칸에 알맞은 말을 쓰시오.

> Yuri wraps the Christmas presents.

(1) The Christmas presents _____
_____ _____ Yuri. (수동태 긍정문으로)

(2) The Christmas presents _____ _____
_____ _____ Yuri. (수동태 부정문으로)

(3) _____ the Christmas presents
_____ _____ Yuri? (수동태 의문문으로)

02 빈칸에 알맞은 말을 쓰시오.

> **A** Was the telephone invented by Thomas Edison?
> **B** No, it _____. It _____ _____
> _____ Alexander Graham Bell.

03 우리말과 뜻이 같도록 괄호 안의 말을 이용하여 문장을 완성하시오.

(1)
> 그의 손은 페인트로 덮여 있다.
> → His hands _____
> paint. (cover)

(2)
> Josh는 그 사실에 놀랐다.
> → Josh _____ the
> fact. (surprise)

04 괄호 안의 말을 바르게 배열하여 문장을 완성하시오.

(1) The red button _____.
(be, not, must, pushed)

(2) _____ by people.
(is, called, a puppy, a baby dog)

(3) _____ by the host.
(us, to, was, given, a good dinner)

(독해형 어법)

[05~06] 다음 글을 읽고, 물음에 답하시오.

In a shop, ⓐ I heard two women talk in the next corner. "Jimmy and I have been together for 10 years now and ⓑ he makes me very happy," one said, "so ⓒ 그가 가장 좋아하는 음식을 내가 사 줄 것이다 even if it is very expensive." "Well, with my Benny I have no choice," her friend replied. I turned to corner. Both women were buying expensive cat food.

05 밑줄 친 ⓐ, ⓑ를 수동태로 각각 바꿔 쓰시오.

ⓐ _____
ⓑ _____

06 밑줄 친 ⓒ의 우리말과 뜻이 같도록 괄호 안의 말을 이용하여 문장을 완성하시오.

his favorite food _____
(will buy)

CHAPTER

07

분사

🍃 **분사란 무엇인가?**

분사는 동사를 형용사로 사용하기 위해 동사원형에 -ing(현재분사)를 붙이거나 -ed(과거분사)를 붙인 형태를 말한다. 명사를 수식하는 *형용사, 주어나 목적어의 의미를 보충하는 보어로 쓰인다.

🍃 **분사는 문장에서 어떤 역할을 하는가?**

분사는 현재분사인지 과거분사인지에 따라 그 형태와 의미가 다르다.

현재분사

형태와 의미
- **동사원형+-ing**: 능동·진행

  Dad is **reading** a newspaper. 아빠는 신문을 읽고 계신다.

역할
- **형용사 역할**

  This is an **interesting** storybook. 이것은 재미있는 이야기책이다.

- **보어 역할**

  I saw him **walking** into the office. 나는 그가 사무실 안으로 걸어 들어가는 것을 보았다.

과거분사

형태와 의미
- **동사원형+-ed**: 수동·완료

  The bread was **baked** by Susie. 그 빵은 Susie에 의해 구워졌다.

역할
- **형용사 역할**

  There were **broken** glasses on the floor. 바닥에 깨진 유리잔들이 있었다.

- **보어 역할**

  He looked **satisfied**. 그는 만족스러워 보였다.

🍃 **현재분사는 동명사와 무엇이 다른가?**

현재분사와 동명사는 「동사원형+-ing」로 형태가 같지만, 뜻과 용법에는 차이가 있다.

현재분사	형용사 역할	동작이나 상태를 나타냄 (~하고 있는)
		Look at the **sleeping** cat. 잠자고 있는 고양이를 보아라.
동명사	명사 역할	용도나 목적을 나타냄 (~하기 위한)
		I think you'd better buy a **sleeping** bag. 내 생각에 너는 침낭을 사는 게 낫겠다.

용어사전

* **형용사**: 명사의 모양, 색깔, 성질, 크기, 개수 등을 자세하게 설명하거나 꾸며 주는 말로 보통 '~하는(한)'으로 해석한다.

37 현재분사의 쓰임과 형태

현재분사는 「동사원형+-ing」의 형태로 '~하는, ~하고 있는'이라는 능동과 진행의 의미를 나타낸다.

- **형용사 역할:** 명사의 앞이나 뒤에서 명사를 꾸며 준다.

  The woman **running** over there is my music teacher.

- **보어 역할:** 주어나 목적어의 상태를 설명한다.

  I saw you **dancing** on the stage.

A 괄호 안의 말을 빈칸에 알맞은 형태로 쓰시오. (단, 원형은 쓸 수 없음)

» 정답과 해설 p.15

◆ 동사처럼 기능하는 현재분사: be 동사와 같이 쓰여 진행형을 만든다.
Tom *is* writing the letter to his parents.

1 I saw him _____ a walk in the park. (take)

2 Her daughter was _____ a novel last night. (read)

3 Sumi should take care of the _____ baby. (sleep)

4 Look at the sun _____ above the horizon. (rise)

5 Helen is _____ hot chocolate with her friends. (drink)

B 우리말과 뜻이 같도록 괄호 안의 말을 배열하여 문장을 완성하시오.

1 짖고 있는 이 개들을 무서워하지 마라. (barking, these, dogs)

→ Don't be afraid of _____.

2 피아노를 치고 있는 그 남자는 누구니? (playing, the piano, man)

→ Who is the _____?

3 나는 매우 피곤해서 다리가 후들거린다. (are, my legs, shaking)

→ I am very tired and _____.

4 나의 아버지는 물에 빠져 죽어가는 소년을 구하셨다. (saved, the, boy, drowning)

→ My father _____.

C 어법상 어색한 부분을 찾아 고쳐 쓰시오.

1 Who is the swim girl? _____

2 Everyone is waited for Christmas to come. _____

3 I like the girl stood in front of the gate. _____

4 The boys wear blue jakets are my classmates. _____

교과서
문장
응용하기

배운 문법을 이용하여 영어 문장을 써 봅시다.

1 나는 TV 쇼를 보는 중이다. (watch) → _____

2 웃고 있는 그 소년은 내 남자친구이다. (smile) → _____

38 과거분사의 쓰임과 형태

과거분사는 「동사원형+-ed」 또는 불규칙 변화의 형태로 '~되는, ~된'이라는 수동과 완료의 의미를 나타낸다.

- **형용사 역할**: 명사의 앞이나 뒤에서 명사를 꾸며 준다.
  Don't touch that **broken** window.

- **보어 역할**: 주어나 목적어의 상태를 설명한다.
  The police found the bag **thrown** in the woods.

A 빈칸에 알맞은 말을 | 보기 |에서 골라 올바른 형태로 쓰시오.

» 정답과 해설 p.15

◆ 동사처럼 기능하는 과거분사:
be동사와 같이 쓰여 수동태를, have와 같이 쓰여 완료형을 만든다.
The printer *was* repaired by Sam.
The lawyer *has* arrived here.

| 보기 |
learn   write   cover   call

1 Ben heard his name _____.
2 The mountains are _____ with snow.
3 My brother has _____ to play the violin for 3 years.
4 Do you have some books _____ by Charles Dickens?

B 괄호 안의 말을 빈칸에 알맞은 형태로 쓰시오.

1 The photo on the wall was _____ by Mike. (take)
2 That _____ car was found by a young man. (steal)
3 She didn't open the present _____ by Eric. (send)
4 Was your ball _____ on the ground? (leave)

C 우리말과 뜻이 같도록 괄호 안의 말을 배열하여 문장을 완성하시오.

1 이것은 내 여동생이 그린 그림이다. (painted, a picture, is)
  → This _____ by my little sister.
2 이것은 중고 의자이지만 새것처럼 보인다. (used, a, is, chair)
  → This _____, but it seems brand-new.
3 나는 한국에서 만들어진 이어폰을 가지고 있다. (have, an earphone, made)
  → I _____ in Korea.

교과서
문장
응용하기

배운 문법을 이용하여 영어 문장을 써 봅시다.

1 교실은 Jane에 의해 청소되었다. (clean)   → _____
2 나는 구운 감자를 좋아한다. (bake)   → _____

39 감정을 나타내는 분사

■ 현재분사는 주로 감정을 유발하는 능동의 의미를 갖고 있고, 과거분사는 감정을 느끼는 수동의 의미를 갖고 있다.

현재분사	~한 기분이 들게 하는	surprising, boring, tiring, exciting, disappointing, satisfying, confusing, shocking 등
과거분사	~한 기분이 드는	surprised, bored, tired, excited, disappointed, satisfied, confused, shocked 등

The news was very **surprising**.　　　　People were very **surprised** at the news.

cf. 감정을 나타내는 분사는 사물을 꾸며 주거나 사물이 주어일 때는 현재분사로, 사람을 꾸며 주거나 사람이 주어일 때는 과거분사로 쓰는 것이 보통이다.

A 괄호 안에서 알맞은 것을 고르시오.　　　　　　　　　　　　　　　　　　　》 정답과 해설 p.15

1 Last weekend was (tiring / tired).

2 At first I thought the movie was (boring / bored), but then it wasn't.

3 I was (interesting / interested) in the people in this book.

4 I don't think I will be (confusing / confused) by the changes.

5 The stories were (shocking / shocked).

B 우리말과 뜻이 같도록 괄호 안의 말을 배열하여 문장을 완성하시오. (동사는 알맞은 형태로 쓸 것)

1 Jack은 자신의 성적에 만족해했다. (was, with his grade, satisfy)

　→ Jack _____.

2 그는 너의 연설에 실망한 것처럼 보였다. (looked, with your address, disappoint)

　→ He _____.

C 두 문장을 비교하여 괄호 안의 말을 빈칸에 알맞은 형태로 쓰시오.

1 (a) Listening to pop music is _____. (interest)

　(b) I'm _____ in listening to pop music. (interest)

2 (a) The football game was _____. (excite)

　(b) Jake was _____ at the football game. (excite)

교과서
문장
응용하기

배운 문법을 이용하여 영어 문장을 써 봅시다.

1 그 서비스는 만족스러웠다. (satisfy)　　→ _____

2 우리는 그 서비스에 만족했다. (satisfy)　　→ _____

40 현재분사와 동명사

현재분사와 동명사는 둘 다 「동사원형+-ing」의 형태이지만, 그 의미와 쓰임은 각각 다르다.

- **현재분사**: '~하고 있는'의 의미로, 명사의 동작이나 상태를 설명하는 형용사 역할을 한다.

  My father is **folding** paper. 〈동작〉　　　　Look at the **moving** truck. 〈상태〉

- **동명사**: '~하기 위한'의 의미로 용도나 목적을 나타내며 문장에서 명사 역할의 주어, 목적어, 보어로 쓰인다.

  The tunnel has **moving** walkways. 〈용도〉　　My hobby is **folding** paper frogs. 〈보어 역할〉

  cf. **running** girls 〈현재분사〉　　**running** shoes 〈동명사〉

A 밑줄 친 부분의 역할로 알맞은 것을 고르시오.　　　　　　　　　　　　» 정답과 해설 p.15

1 Look at the <u>crying</u> boy.　　　　　　　　　　　　　(현재분사 / 동명사)

2 Don't forget to buy some <u>baking</u> powder.　　　　　(현재분사 / 동명사)

3 I felt something <u>moving</u> on my back.　　　　　　　(현재분사 / 동명사)

4 Knowing something is different from <u>doing</u> something.　(현재분사 / 동명사)

B 우리말과 뜻이 같도록 괄호 안의 말을 배열하여 문장을 완성하시오.

1 저 침낭은 내 남동생 것이다. (bag, sleeping, that)

  → _____ is my brother's.

2 소방관들은 불타고 있는 건물로 돌진했다. (the, building, burning)

  → The firefighters rushed into _____.

C 다음 문장을 밑줄 친 부분에 유의하여 바르게 해석하시오.

1 (a) They are in the <u>waiting</u> room.

  → _____

  (b) There were many people <u>waiting</u> in line.

  → _____

2 (a) My dream is having my own <u>swimming</u> pool.

  → _____

  (b) Look at <u>swimming</u> dolphins.

  → _____

교과서 문장 응용하기

배운 문법을 이용하여 영어 문장을 써 봅시다.

1 그 흥미진진한 게임은 우리를 행복하게 만들었다. (excite)　→ _____

2 그들의 목표는 그 경주에서 이기는 것이다. (race)　→ _____

41 분사구문

분사구문은 분사를 이용하여 부사절을 부사구로 나타낸 구문이다. 이유, 때, 양보, 조건, 동시동작 등의 다양한 의미를 나타낸다.

- **분사구문을 만드는 순서**

  ① 부사절의 접속사를 생략하고 ② 주절과 일치할 경우 부사절의 주어를 생략하고 ③ 부사절의 동사를 「동사원형+-ing」로 바꾼다.

  ~~As~~ ┼ felt so tired, I went to bed early. 〈이유〉
  ① ② ③
  Feeling so tired, I went to bed early.

  When he arrived at the station, he met his old friend. 〈때〉
  → **Arriving** at the station, he met his old friend.

A 밑줄 친 부분을 분사구문으로 바꿔 쓰시오.

1 <u>As she was busy</u>, Ann didn't go bike riding.
  → _____, Ann didn't go bike riding.

2 <u>If you turn left</u>, you'll find the museum.
  → _____, you'll find the museum.

3 <u>Though I live next door to him</u>, I don't know his name.
  → _____, I don't know his name.

》 정답과 해설 p.15

◆ **부정의 분사구문:** 부정의 분사구문을 나타낼 때는 부정어(not, never)를 분사 앞에 쓴다.
Not knowing what to do, Sam kept silent.

B 다음 문장과 뜻이 같도록 괄호 안의 접속사를 이용하여 빈칸에 알맞은 말을 쓰시오.

1 Coming back home, Ms. Robert found her house empty. (when)
  → _____, Ms. Robert found her house empty.

2 Having a headache, the man went back home. (because)
  → _____, the man went back home.

3 Reading a novel, I fell asleep. (while)
  → _____, I fell asleep.

4 Turning right, you will see the bank. (if)
  → _____, you will see the bank.

교과서 문장 응용하기

배운 문법을 이용하여 영어 문장을 써 봅시다.

1 피곤하다고 느껴서 나는 그녀의 파티에 가지 않았다. (feel)
  → _____

2 저녁을 먹는 동안에 소미는 전화를 한 통 받았다. (have)
  → _____

➡ 내신적중 실전문제를 풀기 전에 Workbook p.24에 있는 요점정리를 참고하세요.

내신적중 실전문제

빈출유형 ★

[01~03] 빈칸에 알맞은 것을 고르시오.

01

> It is an apartment _____ 50 years ago.

① build
② built
③ building
④ to build
⑤ being build

02

> The girl _____ a red hairpin is Minho's sister.

① wears
② to wear
③ wearing
④ is wearing
⑤ to be wear

03

> Kevin felt _____ during the musical.

① bore
② boring
③ bored
④ to boring
⑤ to be bored

04 두 문장을 한 문장으로 쓸 때 빈칸에 알맞은 말을 쓰시오. 주관식

> I saw Teddy at the park. He was flying his drone there.
> → I saw Teddy _____ his drone at the park.

[05~06] 우리말과 뜻이 같도록 빈칸에 알맞은 것을 고르시오.

05

> 저 깨진 창문들을 조심하도록 해!
> → Be careful with those _____ windows!

① break
② broke
③ breaking
④ broken
⑤ to break

06

> 그 남자는 노래를 부르면서 소파에 앉아 있었다.
> → The man sat on the sofa _____.

① sing
② singing
③ sings
④ to sing
⑤ being sung

07 우리말을 바르게 영작한 것은?

> 인터넷을 이용하면, 너는 그것에 관해 많은 자료를 얻을 수 있다.

① Use the Internet, you can get a lot of data about that.
② Used the Internet, you can get a lot of data about that.
③ Being used the Internet, you can get a lot of data about that.
④ Using the Internet, you can get a lot of data about that.
⑤ If use the Internet, you can get a lot of data about that.

08 밑줄 친 부분의 쓰임이 |보기|와 <u>다른</u> 것은?

> |보기|
> I felt my legs <u>shaking</u> a little.

① Jimmy was sitting in the <u>waiting</u> room.
② This lake is full of <u>swimming</u> fish.
③ Her <u>smiling</u> face makes me happy.
④ Bob is <u>talking</u> about his girlfriend.
⑤ Amy is a <u>walking</u> dictionary.

09 빈칸에 알맞은 말이 바르게 짝지어진 것은?

> **A** Sam, why were you _____ at the party?
> **B** I heard some news from Anna. It was _____.

① surprised — surprising
② surprised — surprised
③ surprising — surprised
④ surprising — surprising
⑤ to surprise — surprising

10 다음 문장과 뜻이 같도록 할 때 빈칸에 알맞지 <u>않은</u> 것은?

> Having no time, she doesn't put on makeup.
> → _____ she has no time, she doesn't put on makeup.

① As   ② When
③ Since   ④ Though
⑤ Because

[11~12] 밑줄 친 부분과 바꿔 쓸 수 있는 것은?

11

> <u>Wearing a thick coat</u>, she still felt cold.

① Though she wore a thick coat
② If she wore a thick coat
③ Since she wore a thick coat
④ After she wore a thick coat
⑤ Because she wore a thick coat

12

> <u>Having a lot of work to do</u>, I can't go to see a movie.

① Because I have a lot of work to do
② Though I have a lot of work to do
③ While I have a lot of work to do
④ Before I have a lot of work to do
⑤ After I have a lot of work to do

13 두 문장을 한 문장으로 쓸 때 빈칸에 알맞은 것은?

> This is a book. It was written by my mother.
> → This is a book _____ by my mother.

① write   ② to write
③ writing   ④ written
⑤ to be

14 어법상 <u>어색한</u> 부분을 찾아 고쳐 쓰시오. 주관식

> Be only six years old, she went to elementary school.

_____ → _____

15 다음 문장을 분사구문으로 바꾼 것이 <u>어색한</u> 것은?

① Because he is busy, he cannot help you.
→ Being busy, he cannot help you.

② When he saw the movie, he was moved.
→ Seeing the movie, he was moved.

③ If you read the letter, you'll be happy.
→ Reading the letter, you'll be happy.

④ Though the jeans are cheap, they're nice.
→ Cheaping, the jeans are nice.

⑤ While I took a walk, I met my friend.
→ Taking a walk, I met my friend.

[16~17] 밑줄 친 부분의 쓰임이 나머지 넷과 <u>다른</u> 것을 고르시오.

16 ① The <u>barking</u> dog never bites.
② Look at the <u>sleeping</u> kid.
③ She told me a <u>surprising</u> fact.
④ Be careful with the <u>boiling</u> water.
⑤ I enjoyed <u>playing</u> computer games.

17 ① <u>Being</u> rich, he can travel in space.
② <u>Being</u> late, we couldn't enter the theater.
③ <u>Being</u> shocked by the news about the accident, she didn't know what to do.
④ <u>Being</u> injured during the game, the player was carried to the hospital.
⑤ <u>Being</u> a good student is my New Year's resolution.

18 어법상 <u>어색한</u> 것은?

① Suji was bored of doing the dishes.
② We were exciting at the final match.
③ I went to the recycled art show.
④ Tom was interested in the board game.
⑤ The falling leaves make me sad.

[19~20] 빈칸에 알맞은 말이 바르게 짝지어진 것을 고르시오.

19
• Do you see the dog _____ toward us?
• This is the music _____ from the website.

① run — download
② run — downloading
③ running — download
④ running — downloading
⑤ running — downloaded

20
• He looked _____ because he didn't get the job.
• Our field trip to the old palace was _____.

① disappoint — satisfying
② disappointing — satisfied
③ disappointed — satisfied
④ disappointed — satisfying
⑤ disappointing — satisfy

21 밑줄 친 부분을 분사구문으로 바꿔 쓰시오. 주관식

> As I lifted a heavy flower pot, I hurt my back.

→ _____,

I hurt my back.

22 밑줄 친 ⓐ~ⓔ 중 어법상 어색한 것을 찾아 고쳐 쓰시오. 주관식

> I like ⓐ to see the top of the mountain ⓑ covering with snow. It is ⓒ disappointing ⓓ that we can't see ⓔ much snow this winter.

_____ → _____

[23~24] 밑줄 친 부분이 어법상 어색한 것을 고르시오.

23 ① The concert is amazing.
② He's excited to watch the baseball game.
③ The children were frightened of the dog.
④ I was shocking to hear about the accident.
⑤ They were disappointed at the score.

24 ① They finally found some hiding truth.
② He painted a mother looking at her child.
③ I couldn't read anything written on it.
④ You can see the stars shining in the sky at night.
⑤ This is the castle built five hundred years ago.

[25~26] 우리말과 뜻이 같도록 괄호 안의 말을 빈칸에 알맞은 형태로 쓰시오. 주관식

25

> 버스를 타면, 너는 그곳에 제시간에 도착할 수 없다.
> → _____ the bus, you won't be able to get there on time. (take)

26

> 그 요리사에 의해 요리된 음식은 매우 고급스럽다.
> → The food _____ by the chef is very luxurious. (cook)

27 분사구문의 쓰임이 나머지 넷과 다른 것은?
① Arriving at the office, I found no one was there.
② Turning his head, he saw a car running toward him.
③ Having no money, I couldn't buy anything at the flea market.
④ Playing a game on my smartphone, I heard Mom call me.
⑤ Traveling in Africa, I met many wild animals.

서술형 평가

01 우리말과 뜻이 같도록 괄호 안의 말을 이용하여 문장을 완성하시오.

> Nicole은 과일로 장식된 케이크를 샀다.

Nicole bought _____.
(the cake, decorate with fruit)

02 어법상 어색한 것을 <u>2개</u> 찾아 고쳐 쓰시오.

> **A** Peter, this movie is very interested, isn't it?
> **B** No, it isn't. I'm very boring.

(1) _____ → _____
(2) _____ → _____

03 밑줄 친 부분의 쓰임이 같은 것끼리 묶으시오.

> ⓐ Nari was <u>baking</u> chocolate cookies.
> ⓑ Sally started <u>reading</u> the comic book.
> ⓒ The parrot <u>sleeping</u> in the cage is very cute.
> ⓓ His hobby is <u>making</u> things with matches.
> ⓔ <u>Drinking</u> enough water is good for your health.
> ⓕ Look at the airplane <u>flying</u> in the sky.

_____ / _____

04 |보기|에서 알맞은 말을 골라 분사구문을 완성하시오.

> ┌ 보기 ┐
> sleep in class　　　　turn right
> clean the house

(1) _____,
you'll find the building.
(2) _____,
he didn't listen to the teacher.
(3) _____,
he found some old photos.

[05~06] 다음 글을 읽고, 물음에 답하시오.

> ⓐ<u>Be</u> a teen-aged boy, I took a long bus trip to visit our relatives with my mother. At that time, my mother was 40 years old, but she looked younger. On the return journey, a handsome driver stood outside the bus to help us in boarding. "Help your sister with her bag," he suggested. ⓑ<u>As I turned to correct him</u>, my mother touched me with her elbow. She looked ⓒ<u>excite</u> and said to me, "Never mind, brother. You heard what the man said."

05 밑줄 친 ⓐ, ⓒ의 알맞은 형태를 쓰시오.

ⓐ _____　　ⓒ _____

06 밑줄 친 ⓑ를 분사구문으로 바꿀 때 빈칸에 알맞은 말을 쓰시오.

_____, my mother touched me with her elbow.

CHAPTER

08

대명사

🍃 **대명사란 무엇인가?**

대명사는 명사를 대신해서 쓰이는 말이다. 대명사의 종류에는 인칭대명사(I, my, me 등), 지시대명사(this, that 등), 부정대명사(one, some 등), *재귀대명사(myself, yourself 등)가 있다.

🍃 **부정대명사란 무엇이며, 어떤 것들이 있는가?**

부정대명사는 정해져 있지 않은 불특정한 사람이나 사물을 가리킨다. 일부는 형용사로 쓰인다.

부정 대명사

- **one ~ the other ...:** (둘 중에서) 하나는 ~, 다른 하나는 …

  There are two books on the desk. **One** is mine, and **the other** is yours.
  책상에 두 권의 책이 있다. 한 권은 나의 것이고, 다른 한 권은 너의 것이다.

- **one ~ another ... the other –:** (셋 중에서) 하나는 ~, 다른 하나는 …, 나머지 하나는 –

  I have three sisters. **One** is 8, **another** is 10, and **the other** is 15.
  나는 자매가 세 명 있다. 한 명은 8살, 다른 한 명은 10살, 나머지 한 명은 15살이다.

- **some ~ others ...:** 어떤 것(사람)들은 ~하고, 또 어떤 것(사람)들은 …하다

  Some like red, and **others** like blue.   어떤 사람들은 빨간색을 좋아하고,
  또 어떤 사람들은 파란색을 좋아한다.

- **some ~ the others ...:** 어떤 것(사람)들은 ~하고, 나머지 전부는 …하다

  Some are shy, and **the others** are active.   어떤 사람들은 수줍어하고, 나머지는 전부 활발하다.

- **all:** 모든 사람, 모든 것 / **each:** 각각, 각자 / **both:** 양쪽, 둘 다

  All(**Each** / **Both**) of us went to the park.   우리 모두(각자 / 둘 다) 공원에 갔다.

🍃 **재귀대명사란 무엇이며, 어떤 역할을 하는가?**

재귀대명사는 문장의 주어와 목적어가 같을 때 목적어 자리에서 목적격을 대신하거나 대상을 강조할 때 쓴다.

재귀 대명사

- **재귀 용법:** 목적어 역할

  I saw **myself** in the mirror.
  나는 거울 속에서 나 자신을 보았다.

- **강조 용법:** 주어나 목적어 강조

  Jake **himself** solved the problem.
  Jake가 직접 그 문제를 풀었다.

용어 사전

* **재귀대명사:** 재귀(再歸)의 한자어를 풀면 '다시 돌아옴'이란 뜻으로, 주어의 동작이 다시 주어 자신에게 돌아온다는 의미가 된다.

FOCUS
42 one, another, the other

- **one ~ the other ... :** '(둘 중에서) 하나는 ~, 다른 하나는 …'이라는 뜻이다.

  Two boys are at the park. **One** is jogging and **the other** is feeding the birds.

- **one ~ another ... the other − :** '(셋 중에서) 하나는 ~, 다른 하나는 …, 나머지 하나는 −'이라는 뜻이다.

  I have three foreign friends. **One** is from Japan, **another** is from France, and **the other** is from Peru.

  cf. 정해진 수의 사물이나 사람 중에서 나머지 전부를 가리킬 때는 the others를 쓴다.

  I have five cats. **One** is big and **the others** are small.

  There are six caps. **One** is red, **another** is blue, and **the others** are black.

A 빈칸에 알맞은 말을 |보기|에서 골라 쓰시오. (중복할 수 있음)   » 정답과 해설 p.17

> | 보기 |
> |
> one   another   the other   the others

1 _____ of his eyes is blue and _____ is brown.

2 There are four flowers. _____ is a tulip, _____ is a carnation, and _____ are roses.

3 There are three bikes. _____ is mine, _____ is my mother's, and _____ is my father's.

4 I don't like this T-shirt. Can you show me _____, please?

B 우리말과 뜻이 같도록 빈칸에 알맞은 말을 쓰시오.

1 Mary는 두 벌의 치마를 샀다. 하나는 흰색이고 다른 하나는 빨간색이다.
  → Mary bought two skirts. _____ is white and _____ _____ is red.

2 네 명의 소녀가 벤치에 앉아 있다. 한 명은 책을 읽고 있고, 나머지는 음악을 듣고 있다.
  → Four girls are sitting on the bench. _____ is reading a book and _____ _____ are listening to music.

교과서
문장
응용하기 배운 문법을 이용하여 영어 문장을 써 봅시다.

1 Mike는 책을 두 권 빌렸다. 하나는 만화책이고, 나머지 하나는 요리책이다.
  → Mike borrowed two books. _____

2 그녀는 세 명의 삼촌이 있다. 한 분은 파리에 사시고, 다른 한 분은 뉴욕에 사시며, 나머지 한 분은 런던에 사신다.
  → She has three uncles. _____

43 some ~ others ... / some ~ the others ...

- **some ~ others ...:** '어떤 것(사람)들은 ~하고, 또 어떤 것(사람)들은 …하다'는 뜻으로, 이때 others는 나머지 중 일부를 가리킨다.

  Some like winter, but **others** like summer.

- **some ~ the others ...:** '어떤 것(사람)들은 ~하고, 나머지 전부는 …하다'는 뜻으로, 이때 the others는 나머지 전부를 가리킨다.

  There are ten members. **Some** agreed to the plan, but **the others** didn't.

A 빈칸에 알맞은 말을 |보기|에서 골라 쓰시오.   » 정답과 해설 p.17

보기
some   others   the others

1 _____ like the sea and others like the mountains.
2 Some people like classical music and _____ like dance music.
3 Here are nine pens. Some are mine and _____ are hers.
4 There are ten classrooms. Some are very clean, but _____ are dirty.

B 어법상 <u>어색한</u> 부분을 찾아 고쳐 쓰시오.

1 Some like to eat beef, but the others like to eat fish.   _____
2 I have five pets. Two are dogs and the other are cats.   _____
3 Some people hate math, but the other don't.   _____

C 우리말과 뜻이 같도록 빈칸에 알맞은 말을 쓰시오.

1 어떤 사람들은 사과를 좋아하고 또 어떤 사람들은 바나나를 좋아한다.
  → _____ like apples and _____ like bananas.
2 이 방에 있는 어떤 사람들은 아시아 출신이고 또 어떤 사람들은 아프리카 출신이다.
  → _____ in this room are from Asia and _____ are from Africa.
3 여기 15명의 학생들이 있다. 그들 중 일부는 공부하고 있지만, 나머지 전부는 자고 있다.
  → Fifteen students are here. _____ of them are studying, but _____
    _____ are sleeping.

교과서 문장 응용하기

배운 문법을 이용하여 영어 문장을 써 봅시다.

1 어떤 사람들은 부유하지만, 어떤 사람들은 가난하다.   → _____
2 책상에 열 권의 책이 있다. 그것들 중 일부는 Jane의 것이고, 나머지 전부는 Tom의 것이다.
  → There are ten books on the desk. _____

44 each, every

- **each:** '각각(의), 각자(의)'라는 뜻으로 문장에서 형용사, 대명사 역할을 하며, 단수 명사와 함께 쓰여 단수로 취급한다.
  Each player uses his own locker. 〈형용사〉
  I have three dogs. **Each** is lovely. 〈대명사〉

- **every:** '모든'이라는 뜻으로 문장에서 형용사 역할을 하며, 단수 명사와 함께 쓰여 단수로 취급한다.
  Every student wants to get good grades. 〈형용사〉

  cf. 「each of+복수 명사」는 '~ 중 각자, 각기'라는 뜻으로, each of 뒤의 명사가 복수이지만 단수로 취급한다.
  Each of us has a different answer. 〈대명사〉

A 다음 괄호 안에서 알맞은 것을 고르시오.

» 정답과 해설 p.17

1 I have three brothers. (Each / Every) has his own bad habit.
2 Alice has been to every (water park / water parks) in Korea.
3 Every room in the hotel (has / have) a private pool.
4 (Each / Every) of them is from a different city.
5 He shook hands and had a few minutes' talk with (each / every) of us.

B 밑줄 친 부분을 어법상 바르게 고쳐 쓰시오.

1 Every <u>members</u> of the club was at the party. _____
2 Jacob plays baseball <u>each</u> Sunday. _____
3 Each of the boys <u>have</u> his own desk. _____

C 우리말과 뜻이 같도록 빈칸에 알맞은 말을 쓰시오.

1 Dally 부인은 각각의 아이에게 피자 한 조각씩을 주었다.
  → Ms. Dally gave a slice of pizza to _____ _____.
2 모든 국가는 국기를 가지고 있다.
  → _____ _____ has a national flag.
3 그 반의 모든 학생들이 시험에 합격했다.
  → _____ _____ in the class passed the exam.
4 선생님은 그 학생들 각자에게 무엇을 해야 할 지 말해 주었다.
  → The teacher told _____ _____ the students what to do.

교과서
문장
응용하기 | **배운 문법을 이용하여 영어 문장을 써 봅시다.**
1 각각의 그룹은 다른 케이크를 만든다. (each) → _____
2 모든 방문객들이 이 쇼를 보고 싶어 한다. (every) → _____

45 all, both

- **all**: '모든 (것(사람))'이라는 뜻으로, 문장 내에서 대명사와 형용사 역할을 한다. 복수 명사와 함께 쓰이면 복수 취급하고, 단수 명사와 함께 쓰이면 단수 취급한다.

  All had a great time at the party. 〈대명사〉　　　**All** cheese is made from milk. 〈형용사〉

- **both**: '둘 다'라는 뜻으로, 문장 내에서 대명사와 형용사 역할을 한다. 복수 명사와 함께 쓰여 복수 취급한다.

  Betty has two sons. **Both** are soccer players. 〈대명사〉　　**Both** shirts look good on you. 〈형용사〉

  cf. 「all of+명사」는 뒤에 오는 명사에 맞춰 복수나 단수를 결정한다. all of 뒤에 the나 소유격이 오면 of를 생략할 수 있다.

  All (of) my friends will come to my birthday party.

  cf. 「both of+복수 명사」는 '~ 둘 다'라는 의미로, 복수 취급한다.

  Both of my parents are tall.

A 괄호 안에서 알맞은 것을 고르시오.　　　　　　　　　　　　　　　　》 정답과 해설 p.17

1 All of us (is / are) learning to drive a car.

2 All of the furniture (is / are) from England.

3 All of the boys (want / wants) to run in the marathon.

4 The weather wasn't good. It rained on both (day / days).

5 All the women on the beach (was / were) wearing sunglasses.

B 다음 문장을 밑줄 친 부분에 유의하여 바르게 해석하시오.

1 (a) <u>All</u> are present.　　　　　　　　_____

　(b) <u>All</u> is ready for the party.　　　_____

2 (a) <u>Both</u> sisters are diligent.　　　_____

　(b) I've read <u>both</u> of these books.　_____

C 우리말과 뜻이 같도록 빈칸에 알맞은 말을 쓰시오.

1 Sally는 하루 종일 바이올린을 연습했다.

　→ Sally practiced the violin _____ _____.

2 그들은 Jacob과 Sue이다. 그들 둘 다 15살이다.

　→ They are Jacob and Sue. _____ _____ _____ are fifteen.

教科書
文章
응용하기　**배운 문법을 이용하여 영어 문장을 써 봅시다.**

　1 우리 모두 공부를 열심히 해야 한다. (of, have to)　→ _____

　2 나는 그 그림 둘 다 좋아한다. (those)　→ _____

46 재귀대명사의 용법

재귀대명사는 주어 자신을 가리키는 말로, 인칭대명사에 -self(복수형은 -selves)를 붙여서 만든다.

- **재귀 용법**: 주어의 행위가 주어 자신에게 돌아오는 경우에 목적어로 쓰이며, 이때 재귀대명사는 생략할 수 없다.

  Don't burn **yourself**! The oven is very hot.

- **강조 용법**: 주어나 목적어를 강조하고자 할 때 쓰이며, 이때 재귀대명사는 생략할 수 있다.

  You don't need to help the kids. They can do it (**themselves**).

A 괄호 안의 말을 빈칸에 알맞은 형태로 쓰시오.

» 정답과 해설 p.17

1 Robert made this model airplane _____. (he)
2 I'm not a baby anymore. I can dress _____. (I)
3 Let's be careful not to hurt _____. (we)
4 Does the radio turn off _____ automatically? (it)
5 It was not your fault. Don't blame _____. (you)

◆ 다양한 재귀대명사
- myself: 나 자신
- yourself: 너(희) 자신
- himself: 그 자신
- herself: 그녀 자신
- itself: 그것 스스로
- ourselves: 우리 자신
- themselves: 그들 자신

B 밑줄 친 부분을 생략할 수 있으면 Y, 생략할 수 없으면 N을 쓰시오.

1 Alex <u>himself</u> closed the door. _____
2 I said to <u>myself</u>, "I can do it." _____
3 The students decided to go there <u>themselves</u>. _____
4 Be confident. You need to believe in <u>yourselves</u>. _____

C 우리말과 뜻이 같도록 빈칸에 알맞은 말을 쓰시오.

1 나는 나의 새 이웃에게 나를 소개했다.
  → I introduced _____ to my new neighbor.
2 그 어린 소녀는 스스로 자전거를 탈 수 있다.
  → The little girl can ride the bike _____.
3 Max는 저녁을 준비하는 동안 칼에 베었다.
  → Max cut _____ with a knife while he was preparing supper.
4 Peggy와 Jane은 이 맛있는 스파게티를 직접 만들었다.
  → Peggy and Jane made this delicious spaghetti _____.

교과서
문장
응용하기

배운 문법을 이용하여 영어 문장을 써 봅시다.

1 Sally는 가끔 거울 속의 자신에게 이야기한다. (talk) → _____
2 나의 아버지가 직접 이 의자를 만드셨다. (make) → _____

재귀대명사의 관용 표현

by oneself (= alone)	혼자서, 홀로	in itself	본래, 그 자체로
for oneself (= without others' help)	혼자 힘으로, 스스로	of itself (= automatically)	저절로
enjoy oneself	즐겁게 보내다	help oneself (to)	마음껏 먹다
between ourselves	우리끼리 이야기지만	talk(say) to oneself	혼잣말을 하다

Mr. Smith had his students think **for themselves**.　　　　**Help yourself (to)** the cookies.

A 우리말과 뜻이 같도록 빈칸에 알맞은 말을 쓰시오.　　　　≫ 정답과 해설 p.17

1 그들은 놀이공원에서 즐거운 시간을 보냈다.
　→ They _____ _____ at the amusement park.

2 아무도 없었다. 그녀는 온전히 혼자였다.
　→ There was nobody. She was all _____ _____.

3 Tim과 Gerry야, 우유를 더 마시고 싶으면 마음껏 마셔.
　→ Tim and Gerry, if you want more milk, _____ _____.

B 다음 문장을 밑줄 친 부분에 유의하여 바르게 해석하시오.

1 I can do the work <u>by myself</u>.　　　_____

2 Bob made the soup <u>for himself</u>.　　　_____

3 This stone is rare enough <u>in itself</u>.　　　_____

C 다음 문장과 뜻이 같도록 빈칸에 알맞은 말을 쓰시오.

1 The machine works automatically.
　→ The machine works _____ _____.

2 Sally tried to do the homework without others' help.
　→ Sally tried to do the homework _____ _____.

3 My grandparents are getting too old to live alone.
　→ My grandparents are getting too old to live _____ _____.

교과서
문장
응용하기　배운 문법을 이용하여 영어 문장을 써 봅시다.
　1 내 친구들은 콘서트에서 즐겁게 보냈다. (themselves)　→ _____
　2 그 노인은 저 집에서 혼자 산다. (himself)　→ _____

　→ 내신적중 실전문제를 풀기 전에 Workbook p.27에 있는 요점정리를 참고하세요.

내신적중 실전문제

» 정답과 해설 p.18

[01~03] 빈칸에 알맞은 것을 고르시오.

01

> Some people enjoy resting in their free time and _____ enjoy traveling.

① one   ② another
③ other   ④ others
⑤ the other

02

> Between _____, he likes a girl who has a boyfriend.

① myself   ② himself
③ herself   ④ itself
⑤ ourselves

03

> A My two sisters got first prize at the singing contest.
> B Wow! They must be so proud of _____.

① myself   ② her
③ herself   ④ them
⑤ themselves

04 밑줄 친 부분과 의미가 같은 것은?

> Sarah is thinking of going on vacation <u>alone</u> this year.

① of her   ② by her
③ of herself   ④ by herself
⑤ for herself

[05~06] 우리말과 뜻이 같도록 빈칸에 알맞은 말을 쓰시오.

05

> 어떤 사람들은 S사의 스마트폰을 좋아하고, 또 어떤 사람들은 I사의 스마트폰을 좋아한다.
> → _____ like S brand's smartphone, and _____ like I brand's smartphone.

06

> 나는 지갑이 두 개 있다. 하나는 Cathy가 준 것이고, 다른 하나는 Lisa가 준 것이다.
> → I have two purses. _____ is from Cathy, and _____ _____ is from Lisa.

07 우리말을 바르게 영작한 것은?

> 모든 사람들이 Jacob의 제안에 동의한다.

① Both agree to Jacob's suggestion.
② All agree to Jacob's suggestion.
③ All agrees to Jacob's suggestion.
④ Every agrees to Jacob's suggestion.
⑤ Each agree to Jacob's suggestion.

[08~09] 빈칸에 알맞은 말이 바르게 짝지어진 것을 고르시오.

08

> • All of us _____ friends.
> • Every student _____ friends.

① have — need ② has — need
③ have — needs ④ has — needs
⑤ having — needing

09

> There are three famous rivers in America:
> _____ is the Mississippi River,
> _____ is the Trinity River, and
> _____ is the Missouri River.

① one — the other — others
② one — another — the other
③ one — another — the others
④ some — the other — another
⑤ some — another — others

10 밑줄 친 부분의 쓰임이 나머지 넷과 <u>다른</u> 것은?

① I'm angry with <u>myself</u>.
② She fell down and hurt <u>herself</u>.
③ Andy only thinks of <u>himself</u>. He's so selfish.
④ We started to introduce <u>ourselves</u> to the people.
⑤ Fred, you'll have to do your homework <u>yourself</u>.

11 빈칸에 another가 들어갈 수 <u>없는</u> 것은?

① Please give me _____ glass of milk.
② There are ten more children in _____ room.
③ I don't like this one. Show me _____.
④ I haven't got a car. I'll need _____.
⑤ Yujin has three hairpins. One is red, _____ is yellow, and the other is blue.

12 어법상 <u>어색한</u> 부분을 찾아 고쳐 쓰시오. 주관식

> Each boys in the class expresses his opinion.

_____ → _____

13 밑줄 친 부분 중 생략할 수 <u>없는</u> 것은?

① Suji did the math homework <u>herself</u>.
② Grandpa designed this house <u>himself</u>.
③ We have no idea how to get out <u>ourselves</u>.
④ Guys, help <u>yourselves</u> to some tea, please.
⑤ To study biology is to learn about life <u>itself</u>.

14 밑줄 친 부분이 어법상 어색한 것은?

① You'd better do the work yourself.

② The brain in itself feels no pain.

③ The 10-year-old girl made this cake herself.

④ My cat was surprised to look at itself in the mirror.

⑤ The swimmer was disappointed at itself after the game.

15 밑줄 친 부분의 쓰임이 |보기|와 다른 것은?

> | 보기 |
> My dad painted our house himself.

① I made the ship myself.

② Did you see the actress herself?

③ He himself called me this morning.

④ Picasso drew himself many times.

⑤ The girl had to support her family herself.

[16~17] 빈칸에 공통으로 알맞은 말을 쓰시오. 주관식

16
> • Help _____ to anything on the party table. We have enough food.
> • Do not try to repair the broken phone _____.

17
> • If you don't like this one, I'll show you _____.
> • There are three shapes on the board. One is circle, _____ is star, and the other is square.

[18~19] 어법상 어색한 것을 고르시오.

18 ① Both cups is very dirty.

② All his money was gone.

③ Every actor wants to be slim.

④ Each team has five players.

⑤ One of my classmates is American.

19 ① Some like fishing, and others hate it.

② Some of the audiences liked the play, but the others didn't.

③ Two boys were fighting. One of them was taller than the other.

④ I have four hats. One is red, another is green, and others are blue.

⑤ Yuna has five pen pals. Some of them are in Canada. The others are in America.

20 밑줄 친 부분의 우리말 해석이 바르지 못한 것은?

① The door opened of itself. (저절로)

② I want to build a doghouse for myself. (나를 위해)

③ They enjoyed themselves at the festival. (즐겁게 보냈다)

④ Peter sometimes goes to the movies by himself. (혼자서)

⑤ Between ourselves, the movie was boring. (우리끼리 이야기지만)

서술형 평가

01 그림을 보고, 빈칸에 알맞은 말을 쓰시오.

There are three pairs of sneakers in the window. _____ is red, _____ _____ are blue.

02 빈칸에 알맞은 말을 쓰시오.

> **A** Where is Dave in this picture?
> **B** He is the one with his three dogs.
> **A** What are the dogs doing?
> **B** _____ is sleeping under the bench, _____ is playing with a ball, and _____ is eating some snacks.

03 어법상 어색한 것을 3개 찾아 고쳐 쓰시오.

> When Eddy saw him in the mirror, he was very shocked. Some of his eyes was blue and the others was red.

(1) _____ → _____
(2) _____ → _____
(3) _____ → _____

04 밑줄 친 부분의 쓰임이 같은 것끼리 묶으시오.

> ⓐ My mother often talks to herself.
> ⓑ Grandpa made this desk himself.
> ⓒ Hannah and I made these cookies ourselves.
> ⓓ I introduced myself to the new classmates.
> ⓔ Don't compare yourself with those around you.

_____ / _____

독해형
어법

[05~06] 다음 글을 읽고, 물음에 답하시오.

> Feeling down? Got the blues? You're not alone. ⓐEveryone get sad. ____ⓑ____ people have sad feelings just once in a while. ____ⓒ____ have sad feelings often. More than a half of teenagers go through a sad period at least once a month. When you're in a sad mood, it may feel like it will last forever. But usually feelings of sadness don't last very long — a few hours, or maybe a day or two.

05 밑줄 친 ⓐ에서 어법상 어색한 부분을 찾아 고쳐 쓰시오.

_____ → _____

06 빈칸 ⓑ, ⓒ에 알맞은 말을 각각 쓰시오.

ⓑ _____
ⓒ _____

CHAPTER

09

형용사와 부사

형용사는 문장에서 어떤 역할을 하는가?

형용사는 (대)명사의 앞이나 뒤에서 사람·사물을 수식하거나, 보어로 쓰여 주어나 목적어를 보충 설명해 준다.

형용사
- 명사 수식 — I bought a **nice** watch. 나는 멋진 시계 하나를 샀다.
- 보어 역할 — These cars are very **old**. 이 차들은 매우 낡았다.
- -thing+형용사 — I'd like to drink **something hot**. 나는 뜨거운 무언가를 마시고 싶다.
- the+형용사 — **The rich** are not always happy. 부자들이 항상 행복한 것은 아니다.

명사의 수와 양을 나타내는 형용사를 수량형용사라고 한다.

수량 형용사
- 셀 수 있는 명사 수식 — **many**: 많은 / **a few**: 약간의 / **few**: 거의 없는
There are **many** people in the store.
그 상점에는 많은 사람들이 있다.
- 셀 수 없는 명사 수식 — **much**: 많은 / **a little**: 약간의 / **little**: 거의 없는
How **much** money do you have?
너는 얼마나 많은 돈을 가지고 있니?
- 모두 수식 — **a lot of**: 많은 / **some**: 약간의 / **any**: 어떤 ~도
There are **a lot of** flowers in the garden.
정원에 많은 꽃이 있다.

부사는 문장에서 어떤 역할을 하는가?

부사는 문장 내에서 동사, 형용사, 부사 또는 문장 전체를 수식한다. 부사가 타동사와 함께 쓰여 「타동사+부사」의 형태로 하나의 동사처럼 쓰이는 경우에는 이것을 이어동사라고 한다.

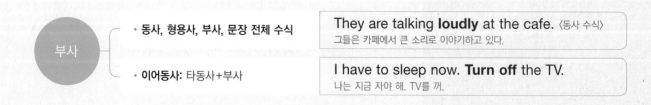

부사
- 동사, 형용사, 부사, 문장 전체 수식 — They are talking **loudly** at the cafe. 〈동사 수식〉
그들은 카페에서 큰 소리로 이야기하고 있다.
- 이어동사: 타동사+부사 — I have to sleep now. **Turn off** the TV.
나는 지금 자야 해. TV를 꺼.

48 -thing+형용사 / the+형용사

- **-thing, -body, -one으로 끝나는 대명사**: 형용사가 대명사를 뒤에서 수식한다.
  I feel cold. Give me **something hot**.
  Our company needs **someone diligent**.

- **「the+형용사」**: '~한 사람들'이라는 의미이며, 복수 취급한다. 「형용사+복수 보통명사(~ people)」로 바꿔 쓸 수 있다.
  The young have to respect **the old**.
  → **Young people** have to respect **old people**.

A 밑줄 친 부분을 어법상 바르게 고쳐 쓰시오. 　　　　　　　　　　　》 정답과 해설 p.19

1 David has <u>important nothing</u> to do now. 　　　＿＿＿＿＿＿＿＿＿＿

2 Mother Teresa helped <u>a poor</u> a lot. 　　　＿＿＿＿＿＿＿＿＿＿

3 I'll let you know <u>interesting something</u>. 　　　＿＿＿＿＿＿＿＿＿＿

4 We should always take care of <u>a handicapped</u>. 　　　＿＿＿＿＿＿＿＿＿＿

B 우리말과 뜻이 같도록 괄호 안의 말을 배열하여 문장을 완성하시오.

1 나는 똑똑한 누군가를 안다. (I, smart, somebody, know)
→ ＿＿＿＿＿＿＿＿＿＿＿＿＿＿＿＿＿＿＿＿＿＿＿＿＿＿＿

2 문에 낯선 누군가가 있다. (at the door, strange, someone, there is)
→ ＿＿＿＿＿＿＿＿＿＿＿＿＿＿＿＿＿＿＿＿＿＿＿＿＿＿＿

3 너는 뭐 특별히 생각해 둔 것이 있니? (do, have, you, anything, special, in mind)
→ ＿＿＿＿＿＿＿＿＿＿＿＿＿＿＿＿＿＿＿＿＿＿＿＿＿＿＿

4 나는 무언가 흥미로운 것을 찾고 있다. (looking for, interesting, I'm, something)
→ ＿＿＿＿＿＿＿＿＿＿＿＿＿＿＿＿＿＿＿＿＿＿＿＿＿＿＿

C 다음 문장을 밑줄 친 부분에 유의하여 바르게 해석하시오.

1 We build special houses for <u>the elderly</u>.
→ ＿＿＿＿＿＿＿＿＿＿＿＿＿＿＿＿＿＿＿＿＿＿＿＿＿＿＿

2 <u>The young</u> have the future in their hands.
→ ＿＿＿＿＿＿＿＿＿＿＿＿＿＿＿＿＿＿＿＿＿＿＿＿＿＿＿

3 He set up tents for <u>the homeless</u>.
→ ＿＿＿＿＿＿＿＿＿＿＿＿＿＿＿＿＿＿＿＿＿＿＿＿＿＿＿

교과서 문장 응용하기 | 배운 문법을 이용하여 영어 문장을 써 봅시다.

1 Bob은 나에게 웃기는 어떤 것을 말해 주었다. (funny) → ＿＿＿＿＿＿＿＿＿＿＿＿＿＿＿＿

2 우리는 가난한 사람들을 도와야 한다. (the poor) → ＿＿＿＿＿＿＿＿＿＿＿＿＿＿＿＿

수량형용사

• 수량형용사는 (대)명사 앞에 쓰여 명사의 수와 양을 나타낸다.

	몇 개의 / 약간의 (긍정)	거의 없는 (부정)	많은	
셀 수 있는 명사 앞	a few	few	many	a lot of / lots of
셀 수 없는 명사 앞	a little	little	much	

I have **a few** problems with my legs.　　　There is **little** sugar in the bowl.

He's getting too **much** stress.　　　　　There are **a lot of(lots of)** shops here.

cf. 셀 수 있는 명사 – tree, flower, egg, city, people, team 등

　　셀 수 없는 명사 – butter, water, love, stress, time, Seoul 등

A 괄호 안에서 알맞은 것을 <u>모두</u> 고르시오.　　　　　　　　　　》 정답과 해설 p.19

1 How (many / much) water did he drink?

2 There are (few / little) trees in the desert.

3 I have made (many / much / a few) mistakes in my life.

4 (Many / A little / A lot of) photos are collected in my scrapbook.

5 I've got (few / little / a little) money. Let's have some coffee and doughnuts.

B 어법상 <u>어색한</u> 부분을 찾아 고쳐 쓰시오.

1 Kevin wants a few sugar for his drink.　　　　　　_____

2 How much tomatoes do you need?　　　　　　　_____

3 There is few milk in the fridge.　　　　　　　　_____

4 There are little people on the road.　　　　　　　_____

5 Let's buy few toys for him.　　　　　　　　　　_____

6 We don't need many cheese to make the sandwiches.　_____

C 다음 문장을 밑줄 친 부분에 유의하여 바르게 해석하시오.

1 (a) I have <u>a few</u> questions.　　　　　_____

　　(b) I have <u>few</u> questions.　　　　　　_____

2 (a) Sue has <u>a little</u> time for reading.　_____

　　(b) Sue has <u>little</u> time for reading.　_____

교과서
문장
응용하기 | 배운 문법을 이용하여 영어 문장을 써 봅시다.

1 바구니 안에 당근이 거의 없다. (there)　　→ _____

2 매일 그 장미꽃들에 약간의 물을 주어라. (give)　→ _____

50 some, any

- some과 any는 셀 수 있는 명사와 셀 수 없는 명사 앞에 모두 쓸 수 있다.

some	긍정문, 권유문에 주로 쓰임	어떤 ~, 몇몇의
any	부정문, 의문문에 주로 쓰임	어떤 ~도, 아무 ~도

Some boy asked me how to get to the library. 〈긍정문〉

Will you have **some** more cookies? 〈권유문〉

You can't bring **any** food into the gym. 〈부정문〉

Are there **any** forks on the table? 〈의문문〉

cf. 조건을 나타내는 문장에서는 '약간의, 조금의'의 뜻일 때 any를 쓴다.

If you have **any** problems, call me.

A 괄호 안에서 알맞은 것을 고르시오.

» 정답과 해설 p.19

1 I'd like to see (some / any) koalas in the zoo.

2 Did you put (some / any) carrots in this soup?

3 We don't sell (some / any) posters in this gallery.

4 Would you have (some / any) more cake?

B 어법상 어색한 부분을 찾아 고쳐 쓰시오.

1 Peter didn't give his mother some help. _____

2 I don't have some books about stars. _____

3 I won't give some snacks to that monkey in the cage. _____

4 Let's decorate the room with any flowers. _____

C 우리말과 뜻이 같도록 빈칸에 알맞은 말을 쓰시오.

1 내게 물 좀 줄래?

→ Could you give me _____ _____?

2 방학에 어떤 특별한 계획들이라도 있니?

→ Do you have _____ _____ _____ for the vacation?

3 나의 가족은 함께 운동할 어떤 시간도 없다.

→ My family doesn't have _____ _____ to exercise together.

4 Peter는 학교 신문에 낼 사진을 몇 장 찍었다.

→ Peter took _____ _____ for the school newspaper.

교과서 문장 응용하기 | 배운 문법을 이용하여 영어 문장을 써 봅시다.

1 우리는 점심으로 샌드위치를 약간 먹었다. (sandwich) → _____

2 어떤 질문이라도 있나요? (question) → _____

이어동사

이어동사는 「타동사+부사」로 이루어진 동사이며, 목적어의 성격에 따라 어순이 달라진다.

- **목적어가 명사인 경우:** 「동사+명사+부사」 또는 「동사+부사+명사」의 2가지 순서로 쓴다.

  It's time to **turn off** the radio. = It's time to **turn** the radio **off**.

- **목적어가 대명사인 경우:** 「동사+대명사+부사」의 순서로만 쓴다.

  My aunt **tried** them **on** at the clothing shop.

cf.
- put on: 입다(↔ take off: 벗다)
- take out: 가지고[데리고] 나가다
- hand out: 나눠 주다
- put out: (불을) 끄다
- turn on: 켜다(↔ turn off: 끄다)
- turn down: (볼륨을) 낮추다(↔ turn up: (볼륨을) 높이다)
- give up: 포기하다
- put down: 내려놓다

A 괄호 안의 말을 바르게 배열하여 문장을 완성하시오.

1 _____ in the room. (off, your hat, take)

2 _____ to level 3. (down, turn, the volume)

3 _____ before you go out. (up, me, wake)

4 I'm going to _____ to the shop. (back, take, it)

》 정답과 해설 p.19

◆ **자동사+전치사:** 「자동사+전치사」의 경우 이어동사가 아니므로 목적어의 위치를 옮길 수 없다.
Look at the horse. (o)
Look the horse **at**. (x)

B 밑줄 친 부분을 대명사로 바꿔 문장을 다시 쓰시오.

1 Turn on the gas to boil the rice.

→ _____

2 He put out the fire with his clothes.

→ _____

3 Mom took out some tomatoes from the fridge.

→ _____

4 Mr. Cook handed out the test papers to the students.

→ _____

C 다음 문장을 밑줄 친 부분에 유의하여 바르게 해석하시오.

1 Put on this coat, it's very cold today.

→ _____

2 Jina stopped reading the newspaper and put it down.

→ _____

교과서 문장 응용하기 배운 문법을 이용하여 영어 문장을 써 봅시다.

1 선풍기를 틀어라. (fan) → _____

2 너는 그것을 포기하는 게 좋겠어. (should, give up) → _____

➜ 내신적중 실전문제를 풀기 전에 Workbook p.31에 있는 요점정리를 참고하세요.

내신적중 실전문제

[01~02] 빈칸에 알맞은 것을 고르시오.

01

> Your English grammar is correct. You make _____ mistakes.

① few
② a few
③ some
④ little
⑤ a little

02

> I'm not busy today. I don't have _____ work to do.

① many
② a few
③ little
④ much
⑤ some

03 다음 문장과 뜻이 같도록 빈칸에 알맞은 말을 쓰시오. (주관식)

> Mr. Na was a role model for young people.
> → Mr. Na was a role model for _____ _____.

(빈출유형) ★

[04~05] 빈칸에 들어갈 말이 바르게 짝지어진 것을 고르시오.

04

> I went out to buy _____ milk, but they didn't have _____ in the shop.

① any — some
② some — any
③ many — any
④ much — many
⑤ many — some

05

> • Will you give me _____ information?
> • I have only read _____ of his books.

① any — little
② any — a little
③ some — little
④ any — a few
⑤ some — a few

[06~07] 빈칸에 알맞지 않은 것을 고르시오.

06

> Ms. Smith always takes _____ sugar with her coffee.

① many
② some
③ much
④ a little
⑤ a lot of

07

> Sometime in the middle of the night, Lisa _____.

① woke her up
② woke up him
③ woke Tom up
④ woke her son up
⑤ woke him up

[08~09] 우리말과 뜻이 같도록 괄호 안의 말을 배열할 때 네 번째로 오는 것을 고르시오.

08

> 그 학생들은 식물들이 무언가 잘못되어 있는 것을 보았다.
> (the, with, students, wrong, plants, something, the, saw)

① saw   ② something
③ wrong   ④ students
⑤ plants

09

> 너는 그것을 내일 아침까지 제출해야 한다.
> (should, hand, you, in, it, by, tomorrow morning)

① it   ② in
③ you   ④ hand
⑤ tomorrow

10 어법상 올바른 것을 모두 고르면?

① Children like sweet something.
② Is there anything exciting around here?
③ I can't find anything wrong in this report.
④ Can you find interesting something in his article?
⑤ Our company needs professional someone for this job.

11 우리말과 뜻이 같도록 어법상 어색한 부분을 찾아 고쳐 쓰시오. 주관식

> 이 상점에는 내가 살 것들이 많이 있다.
> → There are much things for me to buy in this store.

_____ → _____

고난도

12 어법상 올바른 것은?

① I want cold something to drink.
② He saw strange someone in the town.
③ Did you find exciting anything?
④ The young is interested in fashion.
⑤ We helped a lot of the poor.

13 빈칸에 알맞은 것을 모두 고르면?

> We asked the waiter to bring _____ water.

① little   ② many
③ some   ④ any
⑤ a little

14 우리말과 뜻이 같도록 빈칸에 알맞은 말을 쓰시오. (주관식)

> 그 팬케이크 위에 시럽을 약간 더 얹어라.
> → Put _____ _____ more syrup on the pancake.

15 밑줄 친 부분이 어법상 어색한 것은?

① Would you like to have <u>some</u> kiwis?
② How <u>many</u> pairs of socks do you have?
③ Look up <u>a little</u> examples in the dictionary.
④ Don't you have <u>any</u> books about flowers?
⑤ There are <u>a few</u> exercise books for you.

16 어법상 어색한 것은?

① I'll take back my library books.
② Sally took out it from her pocket.
③ Frank wrapped them up himself.
④ Mr. White poured water to put it out.
⑤ The flight attendant turned the "No Smoking" sign on.

17 밑줄 친 ⓐ~ⓓ 중 어법상 어색한 것은?

> There are ⓐ <u>a lot of</u> riddles in the book. ⓑ <u>One of them</u> is very difficult. ⓒ <u>Little</u> people understand ⓓ <u>it</u>.

① ⓐ   ② ⓑ
③ ⓒ   ④ ⓓ
⑤ 어색한 부분 없음

18 밑줄 친 부분을 어법상 바르게 고치지 <u>않은</u> 것은?

① I will introduce you to <u>a little</u> people.
                   → a few
② She has <u>a little</u> dolls on her bed.
        → some
③ Sue ate <u>any</u> ice cream for dessert.
           → some
④ We have <u>few</u> time to prepare for it.
       → any
⑤ We met <u>much</u> foreigners at the hotel.
         → lots of

19 짝지어진 두 문장의 의미가 같은 것은?

① • There are few fish in the pond.
  • There are a few fish in the pond.
② • A lot of Chinese visit Jejudo.
  • Some Chinese visit Jejudo.
③ • He gave some butter to me.
  • He gave a little butter to me.
④ • There isn't any gas station near here.
  • There is a few gas station near here.
⑤ • He put a little salt in his food.
  • He put lots of salt in his food.

20 밑줄 친 부분을 괄호 안의 단어로 바꿔 문장을 다시 쓸 때 빈칸에 알맞은 말을 쓰시오. (주관식)

> Can I try <u>that sweater</u> on? (it)
> → Can I _____ _____ _____?

서술형 평가

01 빈칸에 알맞은 말을 |보기|에서 골라 some, any를 이용하여 올바른 형태로 쓰시오.

| 보기 |
| friend   photo   bread   shampoo |

(1) I'm lonely. I need _____ .

(2) I'll wash my hair. Is there _____ ?

(3) They have no camera, so they can't take _____ .

(4) I'm hungry. Can I eat _____ ?

02 우리말과 뜻이 같도록 괄호 안의 말을 이용하여 문장을 완성하시오.

(1)
학교에서 흥미로운 것을 찾아라.
→ Find _____ _____ in school.
(interesting)

(2)
시각장애인들은 특별한 종류의 시계가 필요하다.
→ _____ _____ _____ special kind of watch. (the)

03 밑줄 친 부분을 우리말로 바르게 해석하시오.

(1) There were few candies in the pot.

→ _____

(2) There were a few candies in the pot.

→ _____

04 밑줄 친 부분을 대명사로 바꿔 문장을 완성하시오.

(1)
A Why didn't you put on your raincoat?
B Oh, I completely forgot! I'll _____ _____ _____ right away.

(2)
A When is Jessy going to throw out her old magazines?
B She's going to _____ _____ _____ tomorrow morning.

독해형 어법

[05~06] 다음 글을 읽고, 물음에 답하시오.

ⓐ Any scientists say the Earth's temperature will be too high by 2030. Then the ice of the North and South Poles will melt, and ⓑ much cities may be under the sea. On the other hand, ⓒ a lot of place may become too dry for farming. We may have very little to eat — very _____ bread and very _____ rice.

05 밑줄 친 ⓐ~ⓒ에서 어법상 어색한 부분을 각각 찾아 고쳐 쓰시오.

ⓐ _____ → _____

ⓑ _____ → _____

ⓒ _____ → _____

06 빈칸에 공통으로 알맞은 말을 쓰시오.

_____

CHAPTER

10

비교 구문

비교란 무엇인가?

비교란 둘 또는 그 이상의 사물이나 사람을 견주어 유사점이나 차이점을 나타내는 것을 말한다.

비교에는 어떤 유형이 있는가?

비교에는 형용사와 부사의 형태를 그대로 사용하는 *원급 비교와, 형태의 변화가 있는 *비교급 비교, 그리고 *최상급 비교가 있다.

원급 비교

- **as+원급+as:** ~만큼 …한(하게)

  Sam spoke **as quietly as** Sujin. Sam은 수진이만큼 조용하게 말했다.

- **as+원급+as+주어+can(could):** 가능한 한 ~하게

  Yuri arrived at the station **as soon as she could**. 유리는 가능한 한 빨리 역에 도착했다.

- **배수사+as+원급+as:** ~보다 몇 배 더 …한(하게)

  This island is **five times as large as** that one. 이 섬이 저 섬보다 5배 더 크다.

비교급 비교

- **비교급+than:** ~보다 더 …한(하게)

  Airplanes are **safer than** cars. 비행기가 자동차보다 더 안전하다.

- **비교급+and+비교급:** 점점 더 ~한

  The weather is getting **colder and colder**. 날씨가 점점 더 추워지고 있다.

- **The+비교급 ~, the+비교급 …:** ~하면 할수록 더 …하다

  The more she thought about it, **the more** she liked it.
  그녀가 그것에 대해 더 많이 생각하면 할수록 그녀는 그것이 더 좋았다.

최상급 비교

- **the+최상급+in(of):** ~ 중에서 가장 …한

  Jerry is **the youngest** player **of** all. Jerry가 모든 선수들 중에서 가장 어린 선수이다.

- **one of the+최상급+복수 명사:** 가장 ~한 것 중 하나

  This is **one of the most expensive watches** in the world.
  이것은 세계에서 가장 비싼 시계들 중 하나이다.

용어 사전

* **원급:** 형용사나 부사의 원래의 상태를 말하는 것으로 두 개의 대상이 차이가 나지 않음을 나타낸다.

* **비교급:** 두 대상을 견주어 둘 중 하나가 다른 쪽보다 우위에 있음을 나타낸다.

* **최상급:** 셋 이상의 비교 대상 중에서 가장 우위에 있음을 나타낸다.

비교급과 최상급의 규칙·불규칙 변화

■ 형용사와 부사의 비교급, 최상급 변화

		비교급 / 최상급	예시
규칙 변화	기본 규칙 변화	+-er / +-est	long-longer-longest, tall-taller-tallest
	-e로 끝나는 경우	+-r / +-st	large-larger-largest, nice-nicer-nicest
	「단모음+단자음」으로 끝나는 경우	자음 반복+-er / -est	big-bigger-biggest, hot-hotter-hottest
	「자음+y」로 끝나는 경우	y → i+-er / -est	pretty-prettier-prettiest, lazy-lazier-laziest
	3음절 이상 또는 -ful, -ous 등으로 끝나는 경우	more / most+원급	beautiful-more beautiful-most beautiful, famous-more famous-most famous
불규칙 변화	good / well-better-best many / much-more-most	bad / ill-worse-worst little-less-least	

A 빈칸에 알맞은 비교급과 최상급을 쓰시오.

1 old - _____ - _____
2 wide - _____ - _____
3 good - _____ - _____
4 hot - _____ - _____
5 strong - _____ - _____
6 bad - _____ - _____
7 dirty - _____ - _____
8 difficult - _____ - _____
9 thin - _____ - _____
10 exciting - _____ - _____

》 정답과 해설 p.21

◆ **far**의 비교급
1. **farther-farthest**: (거리가) 더 먼
   A bird that flies higher can see **farther**.
2. **further-furthest**: (정도가) 심한
   Are there any **further** questions?

B 우리말과 뜻이 같도록 빈칸에 알맞은 말을 |보기|에서 골라 올바른 형태로 쓰시오.

| 보기 |
| fat   easy   much   pretty |

1 나는 영어가 수학보다 더 쉽다고 생각한다.
   → I think that English is _____ than math.
2 Sam은 나의 반에서 가장 뚱뚱한 학생이다.
   → Sam is the _____ student in my class.
3 이것은 이 가게에서 가장 예쁜 드레스이다.
   → This is the _____ dress in this shop.
4 나이 든 농부는 더 많은 땅을 갖기를 원했다.
   → The old farmer wanted to own _____ land.

교과서
문장
응용하기

배운 문법을 이용하여 영어 문장을 써 봅시다.
1 Tom은 Kate보다 현명하다. (wise, than)
   → _____
2 그는 가장 빠른 주자이다. (fast, runner)
   → _____

53 원급 비교

- 원급 비교는 비교하는 대상의 정도가 같음을 나타내며, 형용사나 부사의 원급을 사용한다.

as+원급+as	~만큼 …한(하게)	My brother is **as** tall **as** my father.
not as(so)+원급+as	~만큼 …하지 않은(않게)	Riding a horse is **not as(so)** easy **as** you think.

A 괄호 안에서 알맞은 것을 고르시오.   » 정답과 해설 p.21

1 I am not as tall (as / than) Jimin.

2 This February is as (cold / coldest) as this January.

3 My brother's laptop computer is not (so / more) old as mine.

B 우리말과 뜻이 같도록 빈칸에 알맞은 말을 쓰시오.

1 어떤 풀은 성인 남자의 키만큼 높이 자란다.

→ Some grass grows _____ _____ _____ a man.

2 개는 토끼만큼 빨리 달린다.

→ A dog runs _____ _____ _____ a rabbit.

3 영국은 미국만큼 땅이 크지 않다.

→ England isn't _____ _____ _____ the United States.

C | 보기 |와 같이 비교하는 문장을 쓰시오.

> 보기
> the cooking show = the quiz show (interesting)
> → The cooking show is as interesting as the quiz show.

1 lemonade ≠ lemon juice (sour)

→ _____

2 the chair ≠ the sofa (comfortable)

→ _____

3 the bank = the bookstore (near)

→ _____

4 riding a motorbike = driving a car (dangerous)

→ _____

교과서
문장
응용하기

배운 문법을 이용하여 영어 문장을 써 봅시다.

1 나에게 프랑스는 스페인만큼 아름답다. (to me)   → _____

2 은은 금만큼 가치 있지 않다. (valuable)   → _____

54 비교급·최상급 비교

■ 비교급 비교는 두 사람이나 두 개의 사물을 비교할 때 쓰며, 형용사나 부사의 비교급을 사용한다.

비교급+than	~보다 더 …한(하게)	The Earth is **bigger than** the moon.

cf. '훨씬 더'라는 의미로 비교급을 강조할 때는 부사 much, far, still, even, a lot을 쓰고, very는 쓸 수 없다.
Australia is **much larger than** Korea.

■ 최상급 비교는 세 가지 이상의 대상을 비교할 때 쓰며, 형용사나 부사의 최상급을 사용한다.

the+최상급+in+단수 명사	~에서 가장 …한(하게)	Mercury is **the smallest** planet **in** the solar system.
the+최상급+of+복수 (대)명사	~에서 가장 …한(하게)	The red one is **the cheapest of** the caps.

A 괄호 안의 말을 빈칸에 알맞은 형태로 쓰시오.

1 Ann's hair is _____ than Yuri's. (long)

2 I think hot dogs are _____ than hamburgers. (good)

3 I think Russian is the _____ language in the world. (difficult)

≫ 정답과 해설 p.21

◆ 열등 비교: '~보다 덜 …한'의 뜻을 나타내는 열등 비교는 「less+원급+than」으로 쓴다.
Today is **less hot than** yesterday.
→ Yesterday was hotter than today.

B 밑줄 친 부분을 어법상 바르게 고쳐 쓰시오.

1 The pig is <u>fat</u> than the dog.　　　　　　　_____

2 These buildings are <u>very</u> older than those.　　　_____

3 This backpack is heavier <u>to</u> the other.　　　　_____

4 Eric is the <u>younger</u> athlete of all.　　　　　_____

C 우리말과 뜻이 같도록 괄호 안의 말을 배열하여 문장을 완성하시오.

1 자동차가 TV보다 훨씬 더 비싸다. (is, than, a car, a lot, expensive, a TV, more)
→ _____

2 나는 평소보다 더 일찍 일어났다. (got, usual, I, than, earlier, up)
→ _____

3 고래는 바다에서 가장 큰 동물이다. (animal, a whale, largest, the ocean, the, is, in)
→ _____

교과서 문장 응용하기 배운 문법을 이용하여 영어 문장을 써 봅시다.

1 이 상자는 이 의자보다 더 무겁다. (heavy)　　→ _____

2 에베레스트 산이 가장 높은 산이다. (high)　　→ _____

55 as+원급+as+주어+can / 배수사를 이용한 비교

as+원급+as+주어+can(could) (= as+원급+as possible)	가능한 한 ~하게	We visit Grandma **as** often **as we can**. → We visit Grandma **as** often **as possible**.
배수사+as+원급+as (= 배수사+비교급+than)	~보다 … 배 더 −한(하게) (= … 배 더 −한(하게))	My room is **three times as** large **as** yours. → My room is **three times larger than** yours.

cf. twice는 뒤에 「비교급+than」이 올 수 없다.

A 어법상 <u>어색한</u> 부분을 찾아 고쳐 쓰시오.

» 정답과 해설 p.21

1 I always try to laugh as much to possible.

2 Junho threw the ball as high as he can.

3 He looked into her eyes as longer as possible.

4 The boy shouted, "Help!" more loudly as he could.

5 Pears are as twice expensive as apples these days.

◆ 배수사: '~ 배'를 나타내는 말을 뜻한다. 「기수+times」의 형태로 three times, four times 와 같이 쓰며, '두 배'는 two times 또는 twice로 쓴다.

B 다음 문장을 밑줄 친 부분에 유의하여 바르게 해석하시오.

1 Sue ran to school <u>as fast as she could</u>.

→ _____

2 This watch is <u>four times as expensive as</u> that one.

→ _____

3 The train to Busan is <u>twice as fast as</u> the bus.

→ _____

C 다음 문장과 뜻이 같도록 빈칸에 알맞은 말을 쓰시오.

1 These books are three times as expensive as the used books.

→ These books are _____ _____ _____ _____ _____ the used books.

2 The blue stick is three times longer than the black one.

→ The blue stick is three times _____ _____ _____ the black one.

3 They arrived at the park as early as possible.

→ They arrived at the park as early as _____ _____.

4 Try to read as fast as you can without stopping.

→ Try to read _____ _____ _____ _____ without stopping.

교과서
문장
응용하기

배운 문법을 이용하여 영어 문장을 써 봅시다.

1 Ann은 가능한 한 천천히 수영했다. (slowly)   → _____

2 Tony는 나보다 두 배 더 빠르게 달렸다. (fast)   → _____

비교급+and+비교급 / The+비교급, the+비교급

비교급+and+비교급	점점 더 ~한(하게)	The world is getting **smaller and smaller**.
The+비교급 ~, the+비교급 ...	~하면 할수록 더 …하다	**The sooner** we leave, **the sooner** we arrive.

cf. 「비교급+and+비교급」에서 형용사나 부사가 2음절 이상일 때는 「more and more+원급」으로 쓴다.

He's getting **more and more handsome**.

A 우리말과 뜻이 같도록 괄호 안의 말을 배열하여 문장을 완성하시오. » 정답과 해설 p.21

1 날씨가 더 따뜻해질수록, 나는 기분이 더 좋아진다. (I, better, the, feel)

→ The warmer the weather gets, _____.

2 우리는 돈을 더 많이 벌수록 더 많이 원한다. (more, the, earn, we, money)

→ _____, the more we want.

3 그 오염된 강은 점점 더 깨끗해질 것이다. (get, and, cleaner, will, cleaner)

→ The polluted river _____.

B 우리말과 뜻이 같도록 괄호 안의 말을 이용하여 빈칸에 알맞은 말을 쓰시오.

1 봄에는 날씨가 점점 더 따뜻해진다. (warm)

→ In spring it is getting _____ _____ _____.

2 그 영화배우는 점점 더 유명해졌다. (famous)

→ The movie star has become _____ _____ _____ _____.

3 Mary는 나이가 들수록 더 조용해졌다. (old, quiet)

→ _____ _____ Mary got, _____ _____ she became.

4 네가 영어를 더 열심히 연습할수록 너는 더 빨리 배운다. (hard, fast)

→ _____ _____ you practice English, _____ _____ you learn.

C 다음 문장을 밑줄 친 부분에 유의하여 바르게 해석하시오.

1 The balloon got bigger and bigger.

→ _____

2 The older you get, the wiser you become.

→ _____

교과서 문장 응용하기

배운 문법을 이용하여 영어 문장을 써 봅시다.

1 그 아이는 점점 더 영리해졌다. (smart) → _____

2 우리는 많이 가질수록 더 많이 원한다. (have) → _____

one of the+최상급 / 원급과 비교급을 이용한 최상급

- **one of the+최상급+복수 명사**: '가장 ~한 것 중 하나'라는 뜻으로, 복수 명사가 뒤에 오지만 one이 주어이므로 단수 취급한다.

  One of the best ways is running away.

  The bee is **one of the most diligent** insects.

- **원급과 비교급을 이용한 최상급**: 「No (other) ~ as(so)+원급+as」, 「No (other) ~ 비교급+than」, 「비교급+than any other+단수 명사」를 이용하여 최상의 의미를 나타낼 수 있다.

  Sydney is **the largest** city in Australia.

  → **No (other)** city in Australia is **as(so) large as** Sydney. 「No (other) ~ as(so)+원급+as」

  → **No (other)** city in Australia is **larger than** Sydney. 「No (other) ~ 비교급+than」

  → Sydney is **larger than any other** city in Australia. 「비교급+than any other+단수 명사」

A 우리말과 뜻이 같도록 괄호 안의 말을 이용하여 문장을 완성하시오.   » 정답과 해설 p.21

1 소라는 학교에서 가장 현명한 학생 중 한 명이다. (wise)

  → Sora is _____ in school.

2 이것은 내가 본 것 중 가장 지루한 영화 중 하나이다. (boring)

  → This is _____ I've seen.

3 에디슨은 세계에서 가장 위대한 발명가 중 한 명이었다. (great)

  → Edison was _____ in the world.

4 축구는 세계에서 가장 인기 있는 스포츠 중 하나이다. (popular)

  → Soccer is _____ in the world.

B 다음 문장과 뜻이 같도록 빈칸에 알맞은 말을 쓰시오.

1 This is the cheapest hotel in town.

  → _____ _____ hotel in town is as _____ as this.

  → No other hotel in town is _____ _____ this.

  → This is _____ _____ _____ _____ _____ in town.

2 Pudding is the most popular dessert in this restaurant.

  → No dessert in this restaurant is as _____ _____ pudding.

  → No dessert in this restaurant is _____ _____ _____ pudding.

  → Pudding is _____ _____ than _____ _____ _____ in this restaurant.

교과서 문장 응용하기 | 배운 문법을 이용하여 영어 문장을 써 봅시다.

1 그것은 세계에서 가장 오래된 성 중 하나이다. (castle)   → _____

2 이 책은 다른 어떤 책보다 두껍다. (thick, any)   → _____

➜ 내신적중 실전문제를 풀기 전에 Workbook p.33에 있는 요점정리를 참고하세요.

01 비교급, 최상급의 연결이 바르지 <u>못한</u> 것은?

① short — shorter — shortest

② close — closer — closest

③ lazy — lazyer — lazyest

④ bad — worse — worst

⑤ little — less — least

[02~04] 빈칸에 알맞은 것을 고르시오.

02

> A tiger is _____ a cat.

① big than   ② bigger than

③ biggest than   ④ the bigger than

⑤ the biggest than

03

> Albert Einstein was _____ intelligent person in history.

① as   ② more

③ most   ④ the more

⑤ the most

04

> Maybe she plays tennis as _____ as the famous player.

① good   ② well

③ better   ④ best

⑤ more good

05 빈칸에 알맞은 말이 바르게 짝지어진 것은?

> • Sunrises are as beautiful _____ sunsets.
> • My recipe for cheesecake is better _____ your recipe.

① as — so   ② so — as

③ than — so   ④ so — than

⑤ as — than

06 어법상 어색한 것은?

① A butterfly is much bigger than a fly.

② Sora is twice as fast as her brother.

③ Nights grow short and short in summer.

④ The smaller the box is, the better it is.

⑤ No country is larger than Russia in the world.

07 우리말을 바르게 영작한 것은?

> 이것은 그 서점에서 가장 얇은 책 중의 하나이다.

① This is the thinnest books in the bookstore.

② This is one of thinner books in the bookstore.

③ This is one of the thinner book in the bookstore.

④ This is one of thinnest books in the bookstore.

⑤ This is one of the thinnest books in the bookstore.

08 우리말과 뜻이 같도록 괄호 안의 말을 배열하여 문장을 완성하시오. 주관식

> 가능한 한 빨리 메시지를 남겨 주세요.
> (you, a message, as, leave, can, soon, as)

→ Please _____.

09 다음 문장과 뜻이 같도록 빈칸에 알맞은 것은?

> My wallet and Jiho's smartphone are of almost the same size.
> → My wallet is almost _____ Jiho's smartphone.

① as great as　　② as big as
③ as new as　　④ bigger than
⑤ not so new as

10 두 문장을 한 문장으로 쓸 때 빈칸에 알맞은 것은?

> I have two hats. You have six hats.
> → You have _____ hats as I do.

① twice as fewer　　② twice as more
③ twice as many　　④ three times more
⑤ three times as many

[11~12] 다음 표의 내용과 일치하는 것을 고르시오.

11

Seoul	Busan	Daegu	Jeju
5℃	10℃	12℃	15℃

① Seoul is as cool as Busan.
② Daegu is warmer than Jeju.
③ Jeju is the warmest of the four.
④ Busan is cooler than any other city.
⑤ Daegu is the coolest city of the four.

12

	Age	Height(cm)
Miran	15	155
Sumi	16	152
Jinju	15	150

① Miran is as old as Sumi.
② Sumi is as tall as Jinju.
③ Sumi is not older than Jinju.
④ Miran is the tallest of all.
⑤ Jinju is not as old as Miran.

13 밑줄 친 부분을 어법상 바르게 고쳐 쓰시오. 주관식

> The less you eat, <u>more</u> weight you will lose.

→ _____

14 우리말과 뜻이 같도록 괄호 안의 단어를 이용하여 빈칸에 알맞은 말을 쓰시오. 주관식

> 새 약이 이전 것보다 훨씬 더 효과적이다.

→ The new medicine is _____
_____ than the old one.
(effective)

15 문장의 의미가 나머지 넷과 <u>다른</u> 것은?

① Bob is the best player in our soccer team.

② No other player in our soccer team is as good as Bob.

③ No other player in our soccer team is better than Bob.

④ Bob is better than any other player in our soccer team.

⑤ Bob is one of the best players in our soccer team.

16 밑줄 친 부분이 어법상 <u>어색한</u> 것을 <u>모두</u> 고르면?

① Hojun is <u>very hungrier than</u> me.

② He is <u>more nervous than</u> her.

③ The dog is <u>as cuter as</u> the cat.

④ The sea is <u>deeper than</u> the river.

⑤ She is <u>the most beautiful</u> in her family.

17 |보기|의 문장과 뜻이 같은 것은?

> |보기|
> Coins are heavier than bills.

① Coins are lighter than bills.

② Bills are as heavy as coins.

③ Coins are not as heavy as bills.

④ Bills are as light as coins.

⑤ Bills are not as heavy as coins.

[18~19] 다음 문장과 뜻이 같도록 괄호 안의 단어를 이용하여 빈칸에 알맞은 말을 쓰시오. 주관식

18
> Your score is higher than mine in the math test.
> → My score is ＿＿＿＿＿＿ yours in the math test. (low)

19
> The tower is three times taller than the Eiffel Tower in Paris.
> → The tower is ＿＿＿＿＿＿ as the Eiffel Tower in Paris. (as)

20 우리말을 영작한 것이 <u>어색한</u> 것은?

① 농구는 가장 인기 있는 운동 중 하나이다.

　　→ Basketball is one of the most popular sports.

② 네 가방의 구멍이 점점 더 커지고 있다.

　　→ The hole in your bag is getting bigger and bigger.

③ 민수는 유미보다 사과를 세 배 더 많이 샀다.

　　→ Minsu bought three times more apples than Yumi.

④ 열심히 공부하면 할수록 시험이 더 쉬워질 것이다.

　　→ The hardest you study, the easiest the exam will be.

⑤ 그에게 가능한 한 빨리 전화해 달라고 해 주시겠어요?

　　→ Could you ask him to call me as soon as possible?

서술형 평가

01 |보기|의 내용과 일치하도록 괄호 안의 말을 이용하여 빈칸에 알맞은 말을 쓰시오.

> 보기
> Minsu is a baby, Jina is a child, and I'm a teenager.

(1) Jina is _____ _____ Minsu. (old)

(2) I am _____ _____ Jina. (old)

(3) I am _____ _____ of the three. (old)

(4) Minsu is _____ _____ I am. (young)

(5) Minsu is _____ _____ of the three. (young)

02 괄호 안의 말을 바르게 배열하여 문장을 완성하시오. (단어 하나를 알맞은 형태로 바꿀 것)

(1) I traveled _____ .
   (as, as, I, can, often)

(2) Bee is _____ .
   (of, one, the, insects, busy)

03 우리말과 뜻이 같도록 괄호 안의 지시대로 문장을 완성하시오.

> 앙헬 폭포(Angel Falls)는 세계에서 가장 높은 폭포이다.

(1) Angel Falls is _____ in the world. (최상급 사용)

(2) _____ in the world is _____ Angel Falls. (원급 사용)

(3) _____ in the world is _____ Angel Falls. (비교급 사용)

04 다음 문장과 뜻이 같도록 빈칸에 알맞은 말을 쓰시오.

(1) The chair is not as comfortable as the sofa.
   → The sofa is _____ the chair.

(2) This snake is half as long as that one.
   → That snake is _____ this one.

[05~06] 다음 글을 읽고, 물음에 답하시오.

> Here are the table manners for us to follow: ⓐ <u>가능한 한 음식을 조용히 먹어라.</u> Do not put too much food in your mouth at a time. Do not talk with food in your mouth. However, long ago, it was good manners to make a lot of noise while eating. ⓑ <u>Louder they made noises, the most tasty the meal was.</u> This was a way of letting the cook know how much they liked the food.

05 밑줄 친 ⓐ의 우리말과 뜻이 같도록 괄호 안의 말을 이용하여 빈칸에 알맞은 말을 쓰시오.

(1) Eat your food _____ .
   (possible)

(2) Eat your food _____ .
   (can)

06 밑줄 친 ⓑ에서 어법상 어색한 것을 찾아 바르게 고쳐 문장을 다시 쓰시오.

→ _____

CHAPTER

11

관계사

🍃 **관계사란 무엇인가?**

두 문장을 연결할 때 같은 말의 반복을 피하면서 접속사의 역할을 해 주는 말로, 관계대명사와 관계부사가 있다.

🍃 **관계대명사는 무엇이며, 어떤 것들이 있는가?**

관계대명사는 접속사이자 대명사의 역할을 하며, 선행사에 따라 다음과 같이 달라진다.

	선행사	주격	소유격	목적격
관계대명사	사람	who	whose	who(m)
	사물·동물	which	whose	which
	사람·사물·동물	that	–	that
	없음(선행사 포함)	what	–	what

Mr. Cook is the man **who(that)** lives next to my house. Cook 씨는 나의 옆집에 사는 남자이다.

I met someone **whose** brother is a famous singer. 나는 남자 형제가 유명한 가수인 어떤 사람을 만났다.

Have you found the keys **which(that)** you lost? 너는 잃어버렸던 열쇠들을 찾았니?

Tell me **what** I have to remember. 내가 기억해야 할 것을 말해 줘.

🍃 **관계부사는 무엇이며, 어떤 것들이 있는가?**

관계부사는 접속사이자 부사의 역할을 하며, 선행사에 따라 다음과 같이 달라진다.

	선행사	관계부사의 종류
관계부사	때 (the time, the day 등)	when
	장소 (the place, the house 등)	where
	이유 (the reason 등)	why
	방법 (the way 등)	how

I remember the day **when** I met Erica. 나는 내가 Erica를 만났던 그날을 기억한다.

The hotel **where** we stayed wasn't very clean. 우리가 묵었던 그 호텔은 그다지 깨끗하지 않았다.

The reason **why** I called you was to invite you. 내가 네게 전화했던 이유는 널 초대하기 위해서였다.

I want to know **how** he made many friends. 나는 그가 어떻게 많은 친구를 사귀었는지 알고 싶다.

58 관계대명사 who

관계대명사는 두 문장을 연결하는 접속사와 대명사의 역할을 동시에 하며, 앞에 나온 명사(선행사)를 꾸며 준다.

- 주격 관계대명사 who는 선행사가 사람이면서 주어 역할을 할 때 쓰며, 그 뒤에는 동사가 온다.

  He is the actor. + He played the role of Batman.

  → He is *the actor* **who** played the role of Batman.

  The boy **who** broke the window ran away.

  cf. 의문사 who는 '누구'라는 뜻이며 선행사가 없고, 관계대명사 who는 선행사를 수식하며 해석하지 않는다.

  Do you know **who** the boy is? 〈의문사〉

  Do you know *the boy* **who** is sitting on the bench? 〈관계대명사〉

A 두 문장을 관계대명사 who를 이용하여 한 문장으로 쓰시오. 　》 정답과 해설 p.23

1 I know the lady. + She is standing in front of the theater.

→ _____

2 Emily employed the man. + He looked very diligent.

→ _____

3 A patient is a person. + He receives medical treatment from a doctor.

→ _____

B 밑줄 친 부분을 어법상 바르게 고쳐 쓰시오.

1 I know the boy <u>what</u> came here yesterday.　_____

2 The student who <u>sit</u> next to me is from China.　_____

3 There was an old man <u>who he</u> had a beautiful daughter.　_____

4 The woman <u>when</u> is wearing a hat is a teacher.　_____

C 우리말과 뜻이 같도록 관계대명사를 이용하여 빈칸에 알맞은 말을 쓰시오.

1 나는 나를 도와준 그 경찰관을 절대 잊지 않을 것이다.

→ I'll never forget the policeman _____ _____ _____.

2 그 은행에서 일하는 사람들은 매우 친절하다.

→ The people _____ _____ in the bank are very kind.

3 나의 아빠는 우리에게 날씨에 대해 말해 주는 일기예보관이다.

→ My dad is a weatherman _____ _____ _____ about the weather.

교과서 문장 응용하기 배운 문법을 이용하여 영어 문장을 써 봅시다.

1 Sam은 내게 어제 전화했던 소년이다.　→ _____

2 여기에서 일하는 그 소녀는 내 여동생이다.　→ _____

관계대명사 whose

■ 소유격 관계대명사 whose는 선행사가 사람, 사물, 동물이고 소유격 역할을 할 때 쓰며, 그 뒤에는 명사가 온다.

I know a girl. + The girl's cat is very smart.

→ I know *a girl* **whose** cat is very smart. 〈선행사 – 사람〉

The house is my cousin's. + Its door is green.

→ *The house* **whose** door is green is my cousin's. 〈선행사 – 사물〉

cf. 선행사가 사물 또는 동물일 때 whose는 of which로 바꿔 쓸 수는 있으나, 실제로는 of which를 거의 쓰지 않는다.

A 괄호 안에서 알맞은 것을 고르시오.

» 정답과 해설 p.23

1 Mina is the girl (who / whose) father runs a hotel.

2 I saw a dog (who / whose) tail was very long.

3 We need a pen (what / whose) color is red.

B 두 문장을 관계대명사 whose를 이용하여 한 문장으로 쓰시오.

1 I met a girl. + Her hobby is growing vegetables.

→ _____

2 Mr. White is the writer. + His book won a prize.

→ _____

3 Look at the room. + Its wall is painted blue.

→ _____

4 She is the woman. + Her husband is a football coach.

→ _____

C 우리말과 뜻이 같도록 괄호 안의 말을 배열하여 문장을 완성하시오.

1 우리는 창문이 모두 깨진 차 한 대를 봤다. (all broken, windows, were, whose)

→ We saw a car _____

2 그들은 지붕에 온통 구멍이 난 집에서 살고 있다. (full of, is, roof, whose, holes)

→ They live in the house _____

3 나는 생명의 위험에 빠진 아픈 동물 한 마리를 봤다. (whose, was, in danger, life)

→ I saw a sick animal _____

교과서
문장
응용하기

배운 문법을 이용하여 영어 문장을 써 봅시다.

1 머리카락이 갈색인 그 소녀는 누구니? → _____

2 유미는 이름이 Miya인 검은 고양이 한 마리가 있다. → _____

60 관계대명사 whom

- 목적격 관계대명사 whom(who)은 선행사가 사람이고 목적어 역할을 할 때 쓰며, 그 뒤에는 「주어+동사」가 이어진다.

The woman is Jessica. + You met her this morning.

→ *The woman* **whom(who)** you met this morning is Jessica.

He is *the singer* **whom(who)** I've really wanted to see in person.

A 두 문장을 관계대명사 whom을 이용하여 한 문장으로 쓰시오.   »정답과 해설 p.23

1 There are other people. + We must remember them.

→ _____

2 David has a girlfriend. + He has dated her for a long time.

→ _____

3 What's the name of the boy? + I saw him at the station.

→ _____

B 다음 문장을 두 문장으로 쓸 때 빈칸에 알맞은 말을 쓰시오.

1 Mr. Winslet is the teacher whom I respect very much.

→ Mr. Winslet is the teacher. + _____

2 The people whom we were talking to were very nice.

→ The people were very nice. + _____

3 The woman whom I wanted to see was away on holiday.

→ The woman was away on holiday. + _____

C 우리말과 뜻이 같도록 괄호 안의 말을 배열하여 문장을 완성하시오.

1 너는 Jack이 좋아하는 그 여자를 아니? (whom, likes, Jack)

→ Do you know the woman _____

2 우리가 저녁식사에 초대한 사람들은 오지 않았다. (we, whom, to dinner, invited)

→ The people _____ didn't come.

3 Susie는 내가 믿을 수 있는 사람이다. (I, whom, can, trust)

→ Susie is the person _____

교과서 문장 응용하기 | 배운 문법을 이용하여 영어 문장을 써 봅시다.

1 그는 많은 사람들이 좋아하는 가수이다. (a lot of)   → _____

2 내가 만난 그 남자는 매우 재미있었다. (funny)   → _____

관계대명사 which

- 주격 / 목적격 관계대명사 which는 선행사가 사물 또는 동물일 때 쓰이며, 주어 역할을 할 때는 주격 관계대명사로, 목적어 역할을 할 때는 목적격 관계대명사로 쓰인다.

A dictionary is a book. + It explains words.

→ A dictionary is *a book* **which** explains words. 〈주어 역할〉

This is the desk. + My mother used it thirty years ago.

→ This is *the desk* **which** my mother used thirty years ago. 〈목적어 역할〉

cf. which가 '어느, 어떤'으로 해석이 될 때는 의문사로 쓰인 것이고, 앞의 명사(선행사)를 수식하여 '~한 것'으로 해석될 때는 관계대명사로 쓰인 것이다.

A 두 문장을 관계대명사 which를 이용하여 한 문장으로 쓰시오.

» 정답과 해설 p.23

1 Look at the doll. + It looks like Jenny.

→ _____

2 Can you see the rabbit? + It is hopping in the grass.

→ _____

3 Did you like the meal? + You had it at the restaurant.

→ _____

B 빈칸에 알맞은 말을 | 보기 |에서 골라 관계대명사와 함께 쓰시오.

| 보기 |
| cannot fly   Justin took   you're going to read |

1 Penguins are birds _____.

2 What's the name of the book _____?

3 Have you seen the photos _____?

C 어법상 어색한 부분을 찾아 고쳐 쓰시오.

1 I like the house who has many windows. _____

2 Sam gave Sora a cute dog which were black and white. _____

3 The skirt which Sally bought it yesterday was pretty. _____

교과서 문장 응용하기

배운 문법을 이용하여 영어 문장을 써 봅시다.

1 나는 말을 할 수 있는 새를 갖고 싶다. (have) → _____

2 그는 그가 잃어버린 열쇠를 찾았다. (lose) → _____

62 관계대명사 that

- 관계대명사 that은 선행사가 사람, 사물, 동물인 경우에 주격 관계대명사와 목적격 관계대명사로 쓰일 수 있다. 따라서 who(m)나 which와 바꿔 쓸 수 있다.

Do you know *the girl* **that(who)** is laughing over there?

Let's open *the gifts* **that(which)** I got on my birthday.

- 선행사가 다음과 같을 때는 주로 관계대명사 that을 쓴다.

> - 최상급, 서수, the only, the very, the same, all 등이 선행사를 꾸며 줄 때
> - 선행사가 everything, nothing 등 -thing으로 끝나는 대명사일 때
> - 선행사가 「사람+동물」, 「사람+사물」일 때

That's *the very* question **that** I want to ask you.

She bought *anything* **that** she needed.

A 밑줄 친 부분과 바꿔 쓸 수 있는 말을 쓰시오. ≫ 정답과 해설 p.23

1 The waitress <u>that</u> served us was very polite. _____

2 The woman <u>that</u> you talked about has just appeared. _____

3 The museum <u>that</u> we wanted to visit was shut. _____

4 You can see club posters <u>that</u> are describing their activities. _____

5 Can I talk to the girl <u>that</u> is sitting over there? _____

6 It was his puppy <u>that</u> I wanted to hug. _____

B 두 문장을 관계대명사 that을 이용하여 한 문장으로 쓰시오.

1 This was the only magazine. + Sally wanted to have it.

→ _____

2 Jerry was the first man. + He came to the party.

→ _____

3 Look at the boy and his dog. + They are playing in the park.

→ _____

4 It is the most surprising news. + I've heard it.

→ _____

교과서
문장
응용하기

배운 문법을 이용하여 영어 문장을 써 봅시다.

1 비행기는 하늘을 나는 기계이다. (machine) → _____

2 이것은 내가 여태껏 본 것 중 가장 작은 손목시계이다. (see) → _____

63 관계대명사 what

- 관계대명사 what은 '~(하는) 것'의 뜻으로 선행사를 포함하며 the thing(s) that(which)으로 바꿔 쓸 수 있다.

  The show is the thing. + I waited for the thing.

  → The show is **what(the thing that)** I waited for.

- 명사절을 이끌어 문장에서 주어, 목적어, 보어 역할을 한다.

  What I like is this watch. 〈주어〉

  Do you know **what** he said? 〈목적어〉

  Going fishing is **what** my dad does on weekends. 〈보어〉

  cf. 의문사 what은 '무엇'이라는 의미이다.

  Do you know **what** this is? 〈의문사〉   Do you know **what** they want? 〈관계대명사〉

A 빈칸에 알맞은 말을 |보기|에서 골라 관계대명사와 함께 쓰시오.   » 정답과 해설 p.24

┌─ 보기 ───┐
│   I like to do   he said to me   I bought at that store   │
└──┘

1 I can't believe _____.

2 This dress is _____.

3 _____ in my free time is baking cookies.

B 우리말과 뜻이 같도록 빈칸에 알맞은 말을 쓰시오.

1 Jacob이 한 말은 나를 실망시켰다.

→ _____ Jacob said disappointed me.

→ _____ _____ _____ Jacob said disappointed me.

2 내가 수미에게 들은 것을 너에게 말할게.

→ I'll tell you _____ I heard from Sumi.

→ I'll tell you _____ _____ _____ I heard from Sumi.

C 어법상 어색한 부분을 찾아 고쳐 쓰시오.

1 You'd better do who you want to do.   _____

2 This cell phone is which I really want to have.   _____

3 The thing what Tony said made me happy.   _____

교과서
문장
응용하기

배운 문법을 이용하여 영어 문장을 써 봅시다.

1 Juliet이 말한 것은 사실이다. (true)   → _____

2 이 반지가 내가 오늘 산 것이다. (ring)   → _____

64 관계대명사의 생략

- 목적격으로 사용된 관계대명사 who(m), which, that은 생략할 수 있다.
  Mandy is the girl **(whom)** I play badminton with every day.
  We stayed at a hotel **(which)** Tom recommended to us.
  Do you like the new shoes **(that)** Mom bought you?

- 「주격 관계대명사+be동사」는 생략할 수 있고, 이때 뒤에는 분사구가 남는다.
  The boy **(who is)** jumping in the rain looks excited.
  I bought a necklace **(which is)** made of gold.

A 다음 문장에서 생략할 수 있는 부분을 찾아 밑줄을 그으시오.

1 Sujin is wearing the jacket which I like.
2 The man whom you were speaking with is my husband.
3 Do you know the woman who is jogging in the park?
4 I received a letter which was written in Chinese.

>> 정답과 해설 p.24

◆ 전치사+관계대명사: 관계대명사 앞에 전치사가 쓰인 경우는 관계대명사를 생략할 수 없으며, 관계대명사 that으로 바꿔 쓸 수도 없다.
Daegu is the city (which (that)) I was born in.
→ Daegu is the city in **which** I was born. 〈생략 불가〉
→ Daegu is the city in **that** I was born. (×)

B 다음 문장에서 생략된 부분을 넣어 문장을 다시 쓰시오.

1 Ms. Flower is a kind of person everybody loves.
→ _____

2 Anna bought a dress made in Italy.
→ _____

3 Bob painted a mother looking at her child.
→ _____

C 우리말과 뜻이 같도록 괄호 안의 말을 배열하여 문장을 완성하시오.

1 이것은 나의 아버지가 지으신 집이다. (by, built, the house, my father)
→ This is _____.

2 그것은 그가 그 경매에서 산 그림이다. (he, a painting, the auction, bought, at)
→ That is _____.

교과서 문장 응용하기

배운 문법을 이용하여 영어 문장을 써 봅시다.
1 이것은 내가 어제 본 영화이다. → _____
2 나는 무대 위에서 춤추고 있는 그 소녀를 좋아한다. → _____

65

관계부사 1_ when, where

관계부사는 두 문장을 연결하는 접속사와 부사의 역할을 동시에 한다.

- **관계부사 when**: 선행사가 시간(the day, the time, the year 등)을 나타낼 때 사용한다.

  I remember the day. + My little sister was born on the day.

  → I remember *the day* **when** my little sister was born.

- **관계부사 where**: 선행사가 장소(the place, the city, the house 등)를 나타낼 때 사용한다.

  Jake may know a place. + You can find old books at the place.

  → Jake may know *a place* **where** you can find old books.

A 두 문장을 관계부사를 이용하여 한 문장으로 쓰시오.

1 We arrived at the palace. + The king lived there.

  → _____

2 Fall is the season. + Farmers harvest then.

  → _____

3 This is the village. + A famous poet lives here.

  → _____

4 Do you mean the night? + We played computer games at that time.

  → _____

» 정답과 해설 p.24

◆ 관계대명사 vs. 관계부사:
관계대명사의 뒤에는 불완전한 문장이 오는 반면, 관계부사의 뒤에는 완전한 문장이 온다.
I read the book **which** you told me about.
〈관계대명사〉
I'll be home by the time **when** you'll arrive.
〈관계부사〉

B 우리말과 뜻이 같도록 괄호 안의 말을 배열하여 문장을 완성하시오.

1 나는 너를 만난 날을 잊지 않을 거야. (when, you, met, the day, I)

  → I'll never forget _____.

2 Ian은 최근에 그가 태어난 마을로 돌아갔다. (was born, he, the town, where)

  → Ian recently went back to _____.

3 묘지는 사람들이 묻히는 곳이다. (people, a place, are buried, where)

  → A cemetery is _____.

4 너는 그 쇼가 시작하는 시간을 알고 있니? (when, the show, the time, starts)

  → Do you know _____?

5 그 섬이 내가 휴가를 보냈던 곳이다. (I, my, where, vacation, spent)

  → The island is the place _____.

교과서 문장 응용하기 | 배운 문법을 이용하여 영어 문장을 써 봅시다.

1 우리가 머물렀던 호텔은 매우 작았다.　　　　　　→ _____

2 내일은 우리가 독일어를 공부하는 날이다.　　　　→ _____

66 관계부사 2_ why, how

■ **관계부사 why:** 선행사가 이유(the reason 등)를 나타낼 때 사용한다.

Please tell me the reason. + You don't talk to me for the reason.

→ Please tell me *the reason* **why** you don't talk to me.

■ **관계부사 how:** 선행사가 방법(the way 등)을 나타낼 때 사용한다.

No one knows the way. + The pyramids were built in the way.

→ No one knows **how(the way)** the pyramids were built.

cf. 선행사 the way와 관계부사 how는 동시에 쓸 수 없고, 둘 중 하나만 쓴다.

A 밑줄 친 부분을 어법상 바르게 고쳐 쓰시오.   » 정답과 해설 p.24

1 Tell me the reason <u>how</u> prices go up and down.   _____

2 Everyone wants to know the way <u>how</u> she lost her weight.   _____

3 Please let me know <u>the way</u> how you solved the problem.   _____

4 Do you know the reason <u>which</u> I was interested in the flag? _____

B 두 문장을 관계부사를 이용하여 한 문장으로 쓰시오.

1 I don't know the reason. + Tony got angry for that reason.

→ _____

2 This is the way. + We use chopsticks in that way.

→ _____

3 Tell me the reason. + You were absent for that reason.

→ _____

4 Can you tell me the way? + I can travel with my dog safely in that way.

→ _____

C 우리말과 뜻이 같도록 괄호 안의 말을 이용하여 문장을 완성하시오.

1 네가 그 인형을 만든 방법을 말해 줄래? (made, the doll)

→ Could you tell me _____ _____ _____ _____ _____?

2 소라는 그가 이 소고기 요리를 만든 방법을 안다. (cooked)

→ Sora knows the _____ _____ _____ this beef dish.

교과서
문장
응용하기 | 배운 문법을 이용하여 영어 문장을 써 봅시다.

1 나는 Paul이 우리 동아리에 가입하지 않는 이유를 모른다. → _____

2 네가 그 귀여운 강아지를 얻은 방법을 말해 줄 수 있니? → _____

내신적중 실전문제 1회

[01~02] 빈칸에 알맞은 것을 고르시오.

01

> I met an old woman _____ hair was gray.

① who   ② which
③ that   ④ what
⑤ whose

02

> This is the cafe _____ we can enjoy delicious cakes.

① how   ② what
③ why   ④ when
⑤ where

03 밑줄 친 부분과 바꿔 쓸 수 있는 것은?

> A bus <u>which</u> runs every half hour goes to the airport.

① who   ② whose
③ what   ④ that
⑤ when

04 빈칸에 공통으로 알맞은 말을 쓰시오. 주관식

> • It was the only book _____ he wrote.
> • Everything _____ she said was not true.

05 빈칸에 들어갈 말이 바르게 짝지어진 것은?

> • I miss the time _____ my family had fun in Italy.
> • Jane wants to know the reason _____ he hides the box.

① when — where   ② when — why
③ where — when   ④ where — why
⑤ why — how

06 어법상 <u>어색한</u> 것은?

① This is how I communicate with others.
② I don't know the reason why Paul didn't come to the party.
③ Tell me the way how you finished the project.
④ This is the place where Ms. Brown had a car accident.
⑤ It was the last day of December when she arrived home.

07 밑줄 친 부분에서 생략된 말은?

> <u>The food cooked by the chef</u> tastes good.

① which   ② that
③ which is   ④ what is
⑤ that he is

08 밑줄 친 부분을 한 단어로 바꿔 쓰시오. 주관식

> He bought <u>the things that</u> his son wanted to have.

→ _____

[09~10] 빈칸에 이어질 말로 알맞은 것을 고르시오.

09

> The doctor _____ .

① when I met yesterday was nice
② whose I met yesterday was nice
③ whom I met yesterday was nice
④ which I met yesterday was nice
⑤ what I met yesterday was nice

10

> There is no reason _____ .

① why should apologize to her
② how I should apologize to her
③ why I should apologize to her
④ what I should apologize to her
⑤ who should apologize to her

11 두 문장을 한 문장으로 쓸 때 빈칸에 알맞은 말을 쓰시오. 주관식

> 2025 is the year. They will become adults then.
> → 2025 is _____ _____ _____
> they become adults.

12 밑줄 친 부분의 쓰임이 |보기|와 같은 것은?

> ┌ 보기 ┐
> I don't like people <u>that</u> are never on time.

① It's very nice of you to say <u>that</u>.
② Cheer up! It's not <u>that</u> bad.
③ Who is <u>that</u> person over there?
④ Jim was wearing a hat <u>that</u> was too big for him.
⑤ I think <u>that</u> Korean students have warm hearts.

13 빈칸에 **that**이 들어갈 수 <u>없는</u> 것은?

① I need a robot _____ can do the dishes.
② Yuna is the girl _____ has a beautiful mind.
③ The shirt _____ you are wearing today is very trendy.
④ This is the worst hotel _____ I've ever stayed in.
⑤ I have a friend _____ father works for the post office.

14 우리말을 바르게 영작한 것을 <u>모두</u> 고르면?

> 너는 내가 말한 것을 들었니?

① Did you hear which I said?
② Did you hear that I said?
③ Did you hear what I said?
④ Did you hear the thing what I said?
⑤ Did you hear the thing which I said?

[15~16] 빈칸에 알맞은 말이 나머지 넷과 <u>다른</u> 것을 고르시오.

15 ① _____ he says is not important.

② This is _____ I wanted to know.

③ Tino is a dog _____ helps the blind man.

④ _____ is beautiful is not always good.

⑤ Show me _____ you bought at the shop.

16 ① You're the only friend _____ I have.

② Is there anything _____ I can do?

③ I want the same toy _____ you bought.

④ I want to buy the smartphone _____ color is white.

⑤ Look at the woman and the dog _____ are running.

17 밑줄 친 부분 중 생략할 수 <u>없는</u> 것은?

① Green Music is the music <u>that</u> plants like.

② The man <u>whom</u> I saw last Sunday was an American.

③ The baby <u>who is</u> sleeping on the bed is my sister.

④ Do you see the dogs <u>which</u> are running on the grass?

⑤ The building <u>that was</u> destroyed in the fire has now been rebuilt.

[18~19] 우리말과 뜻이 같도록 빈칸에 알맞은 말을 쓰시오.

18

> 나는 하루에 열 끼를 먹는 여자를 TV에서 보았다.
> → I saw a woman _____ eats ten meals a day on TV.

19

> 이 운동이 그가 빨리 살을 뺀 방법이다.
> → This exercise is _____ he lost his weight fast.

20 어법상 <u>어색한</u> 것끼리 바르게 짝지어진 것은?

> ⓐ I visited the country where I met her.
> ⓑ Tell me the reason why you left me.
> ⓒ Nobody knows the way how the palace was built.
> ⓓ Fall is the season when every creature prepares for winter.
> ⓔ Do you remember the place when we saw Sally?

① ⓐ, ⓑ   ② ⓑ, ⓓ

③ ⓒ, ⓔ   ④ ⓐ, ⓒ, ⓔ

⑤ ⓑ, ⓓ, ⓔ

[01~03] 빈칸에 알맞은 것을 고르시오.

01

_____ happened yesterday was my fault.

① Who　　　　② What
③ How　　　　④ That
⑤ Which

02

Do you want to know the reason _____ she doesn't like you?

① why　　　　② when
③ how　　　　④ what
⑤ where

03

I can give him the only thing _____ I have.

① which　　　　② what
③ that　　　　④ who
⑤ whom

04 밑줄 친 부분과 바꿔 쓸 수 있는 것은?

I will let you know the way I made this chocolate cake.

① why　　　　② which
③ what　　　　④ how
⑤ where

[05~06] 빈칸에 알맞은 관계사를 쓰시오. 주관식

05

The car _____ you want costs thirty million won.

06

July is the month _____ the summer heat actually begins.

07 우리말을 바르게 영작한 것은?

너는 내가 이 양초를 산 가게에 갔었니?

① Did you visit the shop which I bought this candle?
② Did you visit the shop where I bought this candle?
③ Did you visit the shop at where I bought this candle at?
④ Did you visit the shop what I bought this candle at?
⑤ Did you visit the shop how I bought this candle?

[08~09] 밑줄 친 동사의 형태로 알맞은 것을 고르시오.

08

> He was the boy who <u>live</u> next door to me.

① live
② lives
③ lived
④ is living
⑤ were living

09

> We see the kangaroos that <u>be</u> boxing on the street.

① is
② are
③ be
④ was
⑤ being

10 밑줄 친 부분이 어법상 어색한 것은?

① This is all <u>that</u> I ate yesterday.
② She is the woman <u>whose</u> dog barks so loudly.
③ Do you have a tool <u>which</u> I can use now?
④ I can't understand <u>what</u> is written here.
⑤ We saw a man and his monkey <u>which</u> were performing.

11 어법상 어색한 부분을 찾아 고쳐 쓰시오.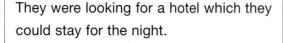

> They were looking for a hotel which they could stay for the night.

_____ → _____

12 빈칸에 공통으로 알맞은 것은?

> • Can you tell me _____ to get downtown from here?
> • She'll explain _____ the coffee machine works.

① that
② what
③ how
④ why
⑤ where

13 밑줄 친 부분 앞에 생략된 말이 나머지 넷과 <u>다른</u> 것은?

① Who's that girl <u>standing</u> in front of the gate?
② The lady <u>crossing</u> the bridge is my neighbor.
③ Do you see the beautiful woman <u>swimming</u> over there?
④ I have a friend <u>interested</u> in classical music very much.
⑤ Look at the elephant <u>drinking</u> beside the river.

14 어법상 올바른 것은?

① Where can we get that we want?
② It is the best film that I have ever seen.
③ We can't buy the pants that price is high.
④ I'm watching the video which you sent it to me.
⑤ The reporter met a man whom was 100 years old.

[15~16] 우리말과 뜻이 같도록 괄호 안의 말을 배열하여 문장을 완성하시오. 주관식

15
> 자신의 고양이가 예쁜 동물 대회에서 우승한 남자가 TV에 나오고 있다. (cat, a man, whose)

→ _____ won the animal beauty contest is on TV.

16
> 내가 테니스를 치곤 했던 코트가 없어졌다.
> (play tennis, I, where, would)

→ The court _____ is gone.

17 괄호 안에 알맞은 말이 바르게 짝지어진 것은?

> ⓐ He was the person (who / which) left the office unlocked.
> ⓑ Do you remember the reason (when / why) we became best friends?
> ⓒ My parents always believe (that / what) I say.

① who — when — that
② who — why — what
③ which — when — that
④ which — when — what
⑤ which — why — what

18 빈칸에 알맞은 말이 바르게 짝지어진 것은?

> • Have you taken the pills _____ the doctor gave you?
> • He is the actor _____ won the award last night.

① who — who
② which — who
③ who — that
④ that — which
⑤ which — which

19 밑줄 친 부분 중 관계대명사 that으로 바꿔 쓸 수 <u>없는</u> 것은?

① I'll save the money <u>which</u> I got from my grandmom.
② I know a lot of people <u>who</u> like hot peppers.
③ This is the book <u>whose</u> cover is designed by me.
④ The people <u>whom</u> I met in Korea were nice.
⑤ He is looking for some books <u>which</u> have many pictures.

20 밑줄 친 부분의 쓰임이 나머지 넷과 <u>다른</u> 것은?

① I saw a man <u>who</u> looks like you.
② I know <u>who</u> the world's richest man is.
③ The people <u>who</u> work for the shop are very kind.
④ The kids <u>who</u> eat lots of sweets will get bad teeth.
⑤ My sister is a college student <u>who</u> is studying history.

서술형 평가

01 | 보기 |에서 알맞은 말을 골라 관계대명사를 이용하여 문장을 완성하시오.

> 보기
> they shine 　　　　 she had a long hair
> the kids ate it 　　his sister is a singer

(1) I know a man _____.
(2) She likes things _____.
(3) I saw a girl _____.
(4) This is the very cake _____.

02 어법상 어색한 것을 찾아 고쳐 쓰시오.

> **A** What do you like to do in your free time?
> **B** That I like to do most in my free time is taking a walk with my puppy.

_____ → _____

03 두 문장을 관계사를 이용하여 한 문장으로 쓰고, 생략할 수 있는 부분에 괄호를 치시오.

(1)
> Mike is looking at the girl.
> She is singing under the tree.

→ Mike is looking at the _____
_____ .

(2)
> Please tell me the story.
> You told Noah that story.

→ Please tell me _____
_____ .

04 | 보기 |에서 알맞은 말을 골라 관계부사를 이용하여 문장을 완성하시오.

> 보기
> Tony got angry 　　　　Rita and I stayed
> she got better at singing

(1) Daniel hit Tony. That was the reason
_____ .

(2) Kate practiced a lot. That is the way
_____ .

(3) That is the hotel _____ .

[05~06] 다음 글을 읽고, 물음에 답하시오.

> When he was young, Clarence Nash made sound of baby chicks, dogs, cats, horses, and many kinds of birds. When he was older, Clarence used to do his animal voices at parties. One time, ⓐWalt Disney heard him talking like a duck. ⓑHe made famous cartoon movies. Disney asked Clarence to speak like a duck in one of his cartoons. Clarence agreed. ⓒThat is the way how Clarence Nash became the voice of the most famous duck of all time — Donald Duck!

05 밑줄 친 ⓐ와 ⓑ의 두 문장을 한 문장으로 쓰시오.

→ _____
_____

06 밑줄 친 ⓒ에서 어법상 어색한 부분을 찾아 고쳐 쓰시오.

_____ → _____

CHAPTER

12

접속사

접속사란 무엇인가?

접속사는 단어와 단어, 구와 구, 절과 절을 연결하는 말이다. 접속사에는 *등위접속사, *종속접속사, *상관접속사가 있다.

종속접속사에는 어떤 것들이 있는가?

명사절을 이끄는 접속사

- **that**: 주어(~하는 것은), 보어(~하는 것이다), 목적어(~하는 것을)

  I think **that** we should try harder. 나는 우리가 더 열심히 노력해야 한다고 생각한다.

부사절을 이끄는 접속사

- **시간**: when, while, as, before, after, until, since

  He gave me a call **when** he arrived. 그는 도착했을 때 내게 전화를 했다.

- **조건**: if, unless

  If you are tired, we can go back home. 네가 피곤하다면, 우리는 집으로 돌아갈 수 있다.

- **이유**: because, since, as

  I got angry **because** Sena was late again. 세나가 또 늦어서 나는 화가 났다.

- **결과**: so, so ~ that ...

  I'm **so** hungry **that** I can eat anything. 나는 너무 배가 고파서 무엇이라도 먹을 수 있다.

- **양보**: though, although, even if, even though

  Though Aiden is young, he is thoughtful. 비록 Aiden은 어리지만, 그는 사려깊다.

상관접속사에는 어떤 것들이 있는가?

both *A* and *B*	A와 B 둘 다	not *A* but *B*	A가 아니라 B
not only *A* but (also) *B* = *B* as well as *A*	A뿐만 아니라 B도	either *A* or *B*	A와 B 둘 중 하나
		neither *A* nor *B*	A와 B 둘 다 아닌

용어 사전

* **등위접속사**: 문법적 역할이 대등한 단어, 구, 절을 연결해 주며, and, but, or, so 등이 있다.
* **종속접속사**: 문법적 역할이 대등하지 않은 종속절을 주절에 연결해 준다.
* **상관접속사**: 두 단어가 짝을 이뤄서 접속사의 역할을 한다.

명령문, and / or ~

- **명령문, and ~**: '…해라, 그러면 ~할 것이다'의 뜻으로, if를 사용하여 바꿔 쓸 수 있다.
Look at this picture, **and** you'll find something interesting.
→ **If** you look at this picture, you'll find something interesting.

- **명령문, or ~**: '…해라, 그렇지 않으면 ~할 것이다'의 뜻으로, if ~ not이나 unless를 사용하여 바꿔 쓸 수 있다.
Keep the salad cold, **or** it will go bad soon.
→ **If** you **don't** keep the salad cold, it will go bad soon.
→ **Unless** you keep the salad cold, it will go bad soon.

A 빈칸에 알맞은 말을 | 보기 |에서 골라 쓰시오. 》 정답과 해설 p.26

보기
you'll be on time   you'll lose weight   you'll be caught

1 Eat less, and _____.
2 Run away right now, or _____ by the bear.
3 Take a taxi, and _____.

B 다음 문장을 밑줄 친 부분에 유의하여 바르게 해석하시오.

1 Be quiet, <u>and</u> you can listen to this music.
→ _____

2 Don't move, <u>or</u> the bees will attack you.
→ _____

3 Wash your hands, <u>or</u> I won't fix you a meal.
→ _____

C 다음 문장과 뜻이 같도록 빈칸에 알맞은 말을 쓰시오.

1 If you read the manual, you will understand what to do.
→ _____, _____ you will understand what to do.
2 If you don't hurry, you won't have time for breakfast.
→ _____, _____ you won't have time for breakfast.

교과서
문장
응용하기

배운 문법을 이용하여 영어 문장을 써 봅시다.

1 일찍 일어나라, 그러면 너는 많은 일을 할 수 있을 것이다.   → _____

2 조심해라, 그렇지 않으면 너는 이 접시를 깨뜨릴 것이다.   → _____

명사절을 이끄는 접속사 that

- 접속사 that이 이끄는 명사절은 문장에서 주어, 보어, 목적어 역할을 한다. 명사절이 주어로 쓰일 때는 가주어 it을 사용하여 바꿔 쓸 수 있으며, 목적절을 이끄는 접속사 that은 생략할 수 있다.

That Kate hates swimming is certain. 〈주어〉

→ **It** is certain **that** Kate hates swimming.

The important thing is **that** you tried your best. 〈보어〉

Sarah knew **(that)** I was lying to her. 〈목적어〉

A 우리말과 뜻이 같도록 빈칸에 알맞은 말을 쓰시오.

》 정답과 해설 p.27

1 우리가 지구를 구해야 한다는 것은 확실하다.

→ _____ is certain _____ we should save the Earth.

2 나는 우리가 세상을 바꿔야 한다고 믿는다.

→ I believe _____ we should change the world.

3 좋은 소식은 John이 그 마라톤 경주에 참가할 거라는 것이다.

→ The good news is _____ John will take part in the marathon race.

B 다음 문장과 뜻이 같도록 빈칸에 알맞은 말을 쓰시오.

1 That koalas sleep for about 19 hours a day is a fun fact.

→ _____

2 That blue whales are the largest sea animals is true.

→ _____

3 That this food has gone bad is certain.

→ _____

C 다음 문장을 괄호 안의 말을 포함시켜 다시 쓰시오.

1 She broke her leg. (It's a pity)

→ _____

2 You will do better next time. (I'm sure)

→ _____

교과서
문장
응용하기

배운 문법을 이용하여 영어 문장을 써 봅시다.

1 수진이의 엄마가 요리사라는 것은 사실이다. (it, true) → _____

2 나는 많은 사람들이 굶주리고 있다는 것을 안다. (starve) → _____

시간의 접속사 1_ when, while, as

when	~할 때	**When** I arrived at the theater, Lissa wasn't there.
while	~하는 동안에	Mom made muffins **while** I was taking a shower.
as	~하면서, ~하고 있을 때	We waved goodbye to Fred **as** he drove away.

cf. 시간의 접속사가 이끄는 절에서 미래를 나타낼 때는 현재시제를 이용한다.

I'll watch a movie **when** the exam *is* over next week.

A 우리말과 뜻이 같도록 빈칸에 알맞은 말을 |보기|에서 골라 쓰시오. » 정답과 해설 p.27

┌ 보기 ┐
　　　　　　　　　while　　as　　when

1 케이크를 만들면서 요리법을 확인해라.

　→ Check out the recipe _____ you make the cake.

2 Tom과 Tony는 언덕 근처에 있는 동안 큰 울음소리를 들었다.

　→ Tom and Tony heard a loud cry _____ they were near the hill.

3 Becky는 쇼핑하러 갈 때 엄마를 위한 선물을 살 것이다.

　→ _____ Becky goes shopping, she will buy a gift for her mom.

B 괄호 안의 말을 바르게 배열하여 문장을 완성하시오.

1 I was reading a book _____.

　(he, called, when, me)

2 _____, I heard a strange voice.

　(as, my, opened, I, eyes)

3 Somebody broke the window _____.

　(they, were, cards, while, playing)

C 다음 문장을 밑줄 친 부분에 유의하여 바르게 해석하시오.

1 <u>While</u> I watched TV, he played online games.

　→ _____

2 I'm shy <u>when</u> I meet new people.

　→ _____

교과서
문장
응용하기

배운 문법을 이용하여 영어 문장을 써 봅시다.

1 내가 Jim에게 전화했을 때, 그는 받지 않았다. (when)　→ _____

2 그는 공부하면서 때때로 음악을 듣는다. (as)　→ _____

시간의 접속사 2_before, after, until, since

before	~하기 전에	Joan worked in a bookstore **before** she became a teacher.
after	~한 후에	You can use this computer **after** I finish this paper.
until	~할 때까지	A baby boy cried **until** his mom came back.
since	~한 이후로 (계속)	Andy has been sick **since** he ate some sushi.

A 괄호 안에서 알맞은 것을 고르시오.

» 정답과 해설 p.27

1 Think deeply (before / after) you make a choice.

2 (Until / Since) my uncle comes back, I will stay here.

3 You should wash your hands (before / while) you eat dinner.

4 Rachel has been interested in stars (as / since) she was ten years old.

5 I'm going to clean the house (until / after) the guests leave.

B 우리말과 뜻이 같도록 알맞은 접속사를 이용하여 괄호 안의 말을 한 문장으로 쓰시오.

1 나는 5살 때부터 영어를 공부하고 있다.

(I have studied English. + I was five.)

→ _____

2 Sam에게 보내기 전에 그 서류를 한 번 더 살펴보아라.

(Look over the paper once more. + You send it to Sam.)

→ _____

3 너는 5킬로그램을 줄일 때까지 계속 운동해야 한다.

(You should keep working out. + You lose five kilograms.)

→ _____

C 괄호 안의 말을 바르게 배열하여 문장을 완성하시오.

1 Sehee waited _____. (the rain, stopped, until)

2 We took a walk _____. (we, had, after, dinner)

3 Take a shower _____. (before, go to bed, you)

4 I have lived here _____. (was, born, since, I)

교과서 문장 응용하기 배운 문법을 이용하여 영어 문장을 써 봅시다.

1 그는 떠나기 전에 그의 가방을 꾸렸다. (pack) → _____

2 Kevin은 버스가 올 때까지 그 책을 읽었다. (come) → _____

조건의 접속사_ if, unless

if	만약 ~라면	If you walk fast, you'll catch the bus.
unless (= if not)	만약 ~하지 않으면	You may get sick **unless** you take some rest. → You may get sick **if** you **don't** take some rest.

cf. 조건의 접속사가 이끄는 절에서 미래를 나타낼 때는 현재시제를 사용한다.

If it *is* cold tomorrow, I'll wear my new coat.

A 빈칸에 알맞은 말을 |보기|에서 골라 쓰시오.

» 정답과 해설 p.27

> |보기|
>
> you lie to me   you were free
>
> you want those pictures   you speak more loudly

1 I'll always be your friend unless _____.

2 I can't hear you unless _____.

3 If _____, you can have them.

4 We could go to the concert together if _____.

B 우리말과 뜻이 같도록 괄호 안의 말을 이용하여 문장을 완성하시오.

1 내가 너를 초대한다면 파티에 오겠니? (invite)

→ Will you come to the party _____ _____ _____?

2 컴퓨터를 사용하지 않을 것이라면 그것을 꺼라. (use)

→ Turn off the computer _____ _____ _____ _____ _____.

3 네가 이 잡지를 원하지 않으면, 나는 그것을 버릴 것이다. (want)

→ _____ _____ _____ _____ _____, I'll throw it away.

C 다음 문장과 뜻이 같도록 빈칸에 알맞은 말을 쓰시오.

1 If you aren't full, we can have lunch together.

→ _____ _____ _____ _____, we can have lunch together.

2 Unless I see you tonight, I'll call you tomorrow.

→ If _____ _____ see you tonight, I'll call you tomorrow.

교과서
문장
응용하기

배운 문법을 이용하여 영어 문장을 써 봅시다.

1 네가 돈이 필요하면 내가 좀 빌려줄 수 있어. (lend)   → _____

2 내가 바쁘지 않으면 너를 도울게. (unless)   → _____

이유의 접속사_ because, since, as

because		Mike got a cold **because** he took a cold bath.
since	~ 때문에	**Since** it was raining, we stayed indoors.
as		I like basketball **as** I can jump higher than my classmates.

A 두 문장을 괄호 안의 말을 이용하여 한 문장으로 쓰시오.

» 정답과 해설 p.27

1 I like science fiction. + It is very interesting. (because)

→ _____

2 I can't eat this anymore. + I have a toothache. (because)

→ _____

3 Sam couldn't arrive on time. + He overslept this morning. (as)

→ _____

4 I laughed at Tony. + He made a funny-looking snowman. (since)

→ _____

◆ 접속사 **as**의 다양한 의미
1. 시간: ~할 때, ~하면서
2. 원인이나 이유: ~ 때문에
3. ~대로, ~처럼
Do in Rome **as** the Romans do. 로마에서는 로마인들이 하는 대로 해라.

B 우리말과 뜻이 같도록 괄호 안의 말을 이용하여 문장을 완성하시오.

1 Sue는 머리가 아파서 병원에 갔다. (because, headache)

→ Sue went to the doctor _____ _____ _____ _____ .

2 나는 무서워서 어젯밤 잠을 잘 수 없었다. (as, scared)

→ _____ _____ _____ _____ , I couldn't sleep last night.

3 우리는 세 시간 동안 걸었기 때문에 피곤했다. (since, walk)

→ _____ _____ _____ _____ _____ _____ , we were tired.

C 괄호 안의 말을 바르게 배열하여 문장을 완성하시오.

1 I can read it _____ . (since, free time, have, I)

2 He drove me there _____ . (I, the bus, as, missed)

3 I'll send him a cap _____ . (it's, since, his birthday)

4 I didn't drink it _____ . (I, because, thirsty, wasn't)

교과서 문장 응용하기 배운 문법을 이용하여 영어 문장을 써 봅시다.

1 나는 열심히 공부했기 때문에 그 시험을 통과했다. (because)   → _____

2 그들은 걷고 싶었기 때문에 공원에 갔다. (as)   → _____

73

결과의 접속사_ so, so ~ that ...

so	그래서	Anna was late for school, **so** Mr. Cruise was angry.
so ~ that ...	매우 ~해서 ...하다	Alex ate **so** much **that** he had to loosen his belt.

cf. 접속사 so가 쓰인 문장은 because를 사용하여 바꿔 쓸 수 있다.

Tom talked about it over and over again, **so** I felt very bored.

→ I felt very bored **because** Tom talked about it over and over again.

A 두 문장을 접속사 so를 이용하여 한 문장으로 쓰시오.

1 It rained heavily. + We put off the game.

→ _____

2 I couldn't sleep at all. + I was very sleepy this morning.

→ _____

3 Rosa was very surprised. + She didn't say anything for minutes.

→ _____

» 정답과 해설 p.27

◆ so that은 '~하기 위해서'의 뜻으로 목적을 나타내는 접속사이다. She swims every day **so that** she can stay healthy. 그녀는 건강을 유지하기 위하여 매일 수영한다.

B 우리말과 뜻이 같도록 빈칸에 알맞은 말을 쓰시오.

1 그 상자는 너무 무거워서 나는 그것을 들지 못했다.

→ The box was _____ _____ _____ I couldn't lift it.

2 Kevin은 너무 늦게 일어나서 경기에 참가하지 못했다.

→ Kevin got up _____ _____ _____ he failed to enter the contest.

3 어떤 애완동물들은 매우 영리해서 그들의 주인을 구한다.

→ Some pets are _____ _____ _____ they save their owners.

C 다음 문장과 뜻이 같도록 빈칸에 알맞은 말을 쓰시오.

1 The clerk is very kind. Every customer likes her.

→ The clerk is very kind, _____ every customer likes her.

→ The clerk is _____ kind _____ every customer likes her.

2 We didn't need a flashlight. The moonlight was very bright.

→ We didn't need a flashlight _____ the moonlight was very bright.

→ The moonlight was _____ _____ _____ we didn't need a flashlight.

교과서
문장
응용하기

배운 문법을 이용하여 영어 문장을 써 봅시다.

1 그들은 서둘렀기에 시간 안에 도착할 수 있었다. → _____

2 수미는 매우 예뻐서 모든 소년들이 그녀를 좋아한다. → _____

양보의 접속사_ though, although, even if, even though

though	비록 ~이지만, 비록 ~일지라도, 비록 ~임에도 불구하고	It was dark, but the man didn't turn on the light. → The man didn't turn on the light **though** it was dark.
although		**Although** he is old, he is very strong and healthy.
even if		**Even if** it was hard, Emma never gave up running.
even though		**Even though** Ian told the truth, nobody believed him.

A 괄호 안의 말을 이용하여 두 문장을 한 문장으로 쓰시오.

» 정답과 해설 p.27

1 He is a good actor. + He is not that popular. (though)

→ _____

2 The package was sent by express. + It would be late. (even if)

→ _____

3 I didn't put much pepper in the soup. + Jack said it was spicy. (although)

→ _____

B 우리말과 뜻이 같도록 빈칸에 알맞은 말을 쓰시오.

1 비록 비가 많이 왔지만, 우리는 우리의 휴가를 즐겼다.

→ _____ _____ _____ a lot, we enjoyed our vacation.

2 수지는 비록 키가 작지만 농구를 잘한다.

→ Suji is good at basketball _____ _____ _____ _____

_____.

3 민지는 캐나다에 5년 동안 살았음에도 불구하고 영어를 잘하지 못한다.

→ _____ _____ _____ _____ Canada for five years, she can't

speak English well.

C 괄호 안의 말을 바르게 배열하여 문장을 완성하시오.

1 _____, they look different.

(they, twins, are, though)

2 _____, I ate them. (I, even if, carrots, hated)

3 _____, they did not believe it.

(the news, even though, true, was)

교과서
문장
응용하기 **배운 문법을 이용하여 영어 문장을 써 봅시다.**

1 그는 비록 앞을 보지 못하지만 소설을 쓴다. (though) → _____

2 그들은 가난할지라도 행복하다. (even though) → _____

상관접속사_ both *A* and *B*, not (only) *A* but (also) *B*, either(neither) *A* or(nor) *B*

■ 상관접속사는 둘 이상의 단어가 짝을 이루어 쓰이는 접속사로 단어와 단어, 구와 구, 절과 절을 대등하게 연결한다.

both *A* and *B*	*A*와 *B* 둘 다	My dad has **both** a bike **and** a motorbike.
not only *A* but (also) *B* (= *B* as well as *A*)	*A*뿐만 아니라 *B*도	Sam is **not only** wise **but (also)** diligent. → Sam is diligent **as well as** wise.
not *A* but *B*	*A*가 아니라 *B*	What I need is **not** a cat **but** a cap.
either *A* or *B*	*A*와 *B* 둘 중 하나	**Either** you **or** I am responsible for the problem.
neither *A* nor *B*	*A*와 *B* 둘 다 아닌	She has **neither** time **nor** money to travel.

cf. 상관접속사의 수 일치: both A and B는 복수 취급하고, 나머지는 B에 일치시킨다.

Both Paul **and** I *were* wearing a blue shirt.

Neither Fiona **nor** I *was* surprised at the news.

A 괄호 안에서 알맞은 것을 고르시오.   » 정답과 해설 p.28

1 My father takes (both / either) milk and sugar in his coffee.

2 I want (neither / either) the shirt or the pants.

3 Matt is intelligent as (well / good) as funny.

4 Not only red (but / and) green looks good on you.

B 빈칸에 알맞은 말을 | 보기 |에서 골라 상관접속사를 이용하여 쓰시오.

> | 보기 |
> warm enough   money   dances perfectly

1 Alex not only sings well _____.

2 This soup is not delicious _____.

3 I don't have either time _____.

C 어법상 어색한 부분을 찾아 고쳐 쓰시오.

1 Neither you or Ann was late for class.   _____

2 Both math and science is good for your future. _____

3 He speaks neither French or English.   _____

교과서 문장 응용하기

배운 문법을 이용하여 영어 문장을 써 봅시다.

1 Mary는 음악과 춤 둘 다를 좋아한다.   → _____

2 Candy는 정직할 뿐만 아니라 친절하다.   → _____

내신적중 실전문제

[01~02] 빈칸에 알맞은 것을 고르시오.

01

> _____ I was sleeping, I had a strange dream.

① So　　　　　② Before
③ After　　　　④ Though
⑤ While

02

> _____ Mr. Robert was very old, he had to keep working.

① That　　　　② If
③ Though　　　④ Even
⑤ Since

[03~04] 밑줄 친 ①~⑤ 중 어법상 어색한 것을 고르시오.

03

> It ① is ② certain ③ what Jacob ④ is enjoying his new ⑤ job.

04

> The Pyramids ① were built ② although the kings of Egypt wanted ③ to live ④ after they ⑤ died.

[05~06] 두 문장의 뜻이 같도록 빈칸에 알맞은 말을 쓰시오.

05

> Turn off the TV, or the baby will wake up.

→ _____ you _____ turn off the TV, the baby will wake up.

06

> Exercising regularly is good for not only your body but also your mind.

→ Exercising regularly is good for your mind _____ _____ _____ for your body.

07 우리말을 바르게 영작한 것은?

> 두통이 너무 심해서 나는 어젯밤 잠을 잘 자지 못했다.

① My headache was very bad that I couldn't sleep well last night.
② My headache was so bad as I couldn't sleep well last night.
③ My headache was so bad that I couldn't sleep well last night.
④ My headache was bad unless I couldn't sleep well last night.
⑤ My headache was bad because I couldn't sleep well last night.

[08~09] 다음 문장과 뜻이 같도록 빈칸에 알맞은 것을 고르시오.

08

> If you don't build a strong house, a storm will blow it down.
> → _____ you build a strong house, a storm will blow it down.

① If   ② As
③ After   ④ While
⑤ Unless

09

> It is not her native language, but Ann speaks English fluently.
> → _____ it is not her native language, Ann speaks English fluently.

① When   ② Because
③ Though   ④ Until
⑤ Since

10 빈칸에 들어갈 말이 나머지 넷과 다른 것은?

① Text me, _____ I'll call you later.
② Push the blue button, _____ the door will open.
③ Tell your parents the truth, _____ they will understand.
④ Go straight forward, _____ you'll get there.
⑤ Wear your coat, _____ you'll catch a cold.

[11~12] 빈칸에 공통으로 알맞은 것을 고르시오.

11

> • They were late _____ there was a traffic jam.
> • Three years have passed _____ he went back to his country.

① as   ② when
③ since   ④ until
⑤ because

12

> • They couldn't watch the musical _____ the tickets were sold out.
> • There was no one _____ I entered the house.

① as   ② that
③ since   ④ even if
⑤ because

[13~14] 우리말과 뜻이 같도록 빈칸에 알맞은 말을 쓰시오.

13

> 나는 일본과 중국 둘 다 가 봤다.
> → I have been to _____ Japan _____ China.

14

> 눈이 너무 심하게 와서 우리는 외출할 수 없었다.
> → It snowed _____ heavily _____ we couldn't go out.

15 우리말을 영작한 것 중 잘못된 것은?

① 더 열심히 공부하지 않는다면 너는 네가 배우는 것을 이해하지 못할 것이다.

→ If you don't study harder, you won't understand what you learn.

② 너는 더 빨리 걷지 않아서 버스를 놓쳤다.

→ Unless you walk faster, you'll miss the bus.

③ 방 안이 매우 더워서 Tony는 재킷을 벗었다.

→ It was very hot in the room, so Tony took off his jacket.

④ 나는 이 도시로 온 이래로 영화를 본 적이 없다.

→ I haven't watched a movie since I came to this city.

⑤ 그는 매우 열심히 일했음에도 불구하고 항상 가난했다.

→ Even though he worked very hard, he was always poor.

16 밑줄 친 부분과 바꿔 쓸 수 있는 것은?

> <u>Although</u> the service was slow, the food was great.

① If   ② Since
③ Unless   ④ While
⑤ Even though

17 우리말과 뜻이 같도록 빈칸에 알맞은 것은?

> 판사들의 결정은 재판이 끝날 때까지 비밀로 지켜져야 했다.
> → The judges' decisions had to be a secret _____ the trial was over.

① as   ② when
③ after   ④ until
⑤ while

18 어법상 어색한 것은?

① We'll leave for Busan when Jack arrives.
② I'll tell you my secret if we will meet again.
③ If I remember correctly, he is a doctor.
④ When she saw me, I was swimming in the pool.
⑤ Your mom will get angry with you if you fail the exam.

19 두 문장을 한 문장으로 쓸 때 빈칸에 알맞은 말이 바르게 짝지어진 것은?

> I don't have any time today. I don't have any plan, either.
> → I have _____ time _____ plan today.

① so — that   ② both — and
③ either — or   ④ neither — nor
⑤ not only — but also

20 밑줄 친 부분의 쓰임이 |보기|와 다른 것은?

> |보기|
> I think <u>that</u> you can be my good friend.

① It is certain <u>that</u> she will keep the promise.
② This is the only present <u>that</u> I got from my mom.
③ He thinks <u>that</u> keeping pets teaches us responsibility.
④ My wish is <u>that</u> I will win first prize in the cooking contest.
⑤ It is true <u>that</u> Border Collies are the smartest dogs.

21 어법상 어색한 것을 찾아 고쳐 쓰시오. 주관식

> Unless I will find my car, I have to walk home.

_____ → _____

22 밑줄 친 ①~⑤ 중 생략할 수 있는 것은?

> People ① believe ② that ③ they can catch ④ a mouse ⑤ with some cheese.

[23~25] 밑줄 친 부분이 어법상 어색한 것을 고르시오.

23 ① He didn't sleep <u>until</u> he finished the work.
② <u>Although</u> she was tired, she kept working.
③ <u>If</u> it's fine tomorrow, I'll go on a picnic.
④ The boy fell asleep under the tree <u>while</u> she was looking for him.
⑤ Put the vacuum cleaner in the corner of the living room <u>though</u> you use it.

24 ① Either you or Emma <u>is</u> a liar.
② Betty as well as I <u>go</u> to see him often.
③ Both loving and being loved <u>are</u> not easy.
④ Neither English nor math <u>is</u> my favorite subject.
⑤ Not only we but also our child <u>wants</u> to go to Disneyland.

25 ① People left the building <u>because</u> the fire.
② I'll show Todd this photo <u>when</u> he comes back.
③ <u>If</u> you read good books, you will become wiser.
④ <u>Though</u> she can't drive, she has bought a new car.
⑤ <u>Unless</u> the animals can find something to eat, they will die.

26 빈칸에 알맞은 말이 바르게 짝지어진 것은?

> **A** Who was with you _____ I called you?
> **B** My TV was broken, so the repairman was with me. But he said _____ he couldn't fix it.

① as — if   ② if — that
③ when — that   ④ that — before
⑤ when — after

27 밑줄 친 **that**의 쓰임이 나머지 넷과 <u>다른</u> 것은?

① I believe <u>that</u> you didn't tell a lie.
② Seaweed is food <u>that</u> comes from the sea.
③ One reason is <u>that</u> people keep polluting water.
④ Henry said <u>that</u> he was doing very well in college.
⑤ It is necessary <u>that</u> he should follow the directions.

서술형 평가

01 빈칸에 알맞은 말을 |보기|에서 골라 쓰시오.

> |보기|
> since   that   when   though

(1) Can you take the garbage out _____ you leave?

(2) _____ the house was destroyed, no one was hurt.

(3) It's necessary _____ we should help the homeless.

(4) I have heard nothing of him _____ I came here.

02 우리말과 뜻이 같도록 괄호 안의 지시대로 문장을 완성하시오.

> 네가 지금 떠나지 않으면 너는 기차를 놓칠 것이다.

(1) _____ now, you'll miss the train. (leave를 포함하여 4 단어)

(2) _____ now, you'll miss the train. (leave를 포함하여 3 단어)

03 다음 문장과 뜻이 같도록 빈칸에 각각 알맞은 말을 쓰시오.

(1)
> You should learn English _____ it is used everywhere.
> → English is used everywhere, _____ you should learn it.

(2)
> I read a book _____ I fall asleep.
> → I fall asleep _____ I read a book.

04 밑줄 친 부분을 괄호 안의 말로 바꿔 문장을 다시 쓸 때 빈칸에 알맞은 말을 쓰시오.

> Not only Anna but also her sister is interested in playing the drums.

(1) _____ interested in playing the drums. (both)

(2) _____ interested in playing the drums. (either)

(3) _____ interested in playing the drums. (neither)

독해형
어법

[05~06] 다음 글을 읽고, 물음에 답하시오.

> ⓐ Everybody knows it. ⓑ Antarctica is a continent. But here's something you do not know. It is also a desert! It rarely rains or snows there, but there is a lot of wind. In fact, Antarctica is the coldest desert in the world! And here's another strange fact: ___ⓒ___ 90% of the world's fresh water is there, you can't drink it ___ⓓ___ it's all ice!

05 밑줄 친 ⓐ와 ⓑ의 두 문장을 한 문장으로 쓰시오.

_____

06 빈칸 ⓒ, ⓓ에 알맞은 말을 각각 쓰시오.

ⓒ _____

ⓓ _____

CHAPTER

13

가정법

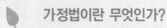

가정법이란 무엇인가?

가정법은 어떤 사실을 반대로 상상하여 말하거나 실현 가능성이 적은 일에 대해 가정하여 말하는 것을 말한다.

If the TV **were not** so loud, I **could** sleep. 〈가정법〉 TV가 그렇게 시끄럽지 않다면, 나는 잠을 잘 수 있을 텐데.

→ I can't sleep because the TV is so loud. 〈*직설법〉 TV가 너무 시끄러워서 나는 잠을 잘 수 없다.

가정법에는 어떤 종류가 있는가?

가정법에는 크게 가정법 과거와 가정법 과거완료가 있다. 가정법 과거는 현재 사실과 반대되는 상황을 가정할 때 쓰고, 해석은 과거가 아닌 현재로 한다. 가정법 과거완료는 과거 사실과 반대되는 상황을 가정할 때 쓰고, 해석은 과거완료가 아닌 과거로 한다.

가정법

가정법 과거

- ~라면, …할(일) 텐데

  If Semin **had** a toothache, he **would go** to the dentist.
  세민이가 치통이 있다면, 치과에 갈 텐데.

가정법 과거완료

- ~했더라면, …했었을(이었을) 텐데

  If I **had remembered** his address, I **would have sent** him a Christmas present.
  내가 그의 주소를 기억했더라면, 그에게 크리스마스 선물을 보냈을 텐데.

I wish 가정법

I wish 가정법 과거

- ~라면(하면) 좋을 텐데

  I wish Wendy **were** here.
  Wendy가 여기 있다면 좋을 텐데.

I wish 가정법 과거 완료

- ~이었다면(했다면) 좋았을 텐데

  I wish you **had listened** to me at that time.
  그때 네가 내 말을 들었다면 좋았을 텐데.

용어 사전

* **직설법**: 사실을 있는 그대로 말하는 것을 직설법이라고 한다. 보통 사용하는 평서문, 의문문, 감탄문은 모두 직설법이다.

76 가정법 과거

- 가정법 과거는 현재의 사실과 반대되는 일이나 실현 가능성이 희박한 일을 가정할 때 쓴다. if절에 be동사를 쓸 때는 주어에 상관없이 were를 쓴다.

형태	If+주어+동사의 과거형(were) ~, 주어+would(could/might)+동사원형 …
의미	~라면, …할(일) 텐데

If I **were** you, I **would ask** my parents for some help.
If your grandfather **saw** your painting, he **would be** proud of you.

- 가정법 과거는 because, as, so 등을 사용하여 직설법으로 나타낸다. 이때 시제는 현재로, 긍정의 내용은 부정, 부정의 내용은 긍정으로 바꿔 쓴다.

If I **had** a map, I **could show** you where you have to go.
→ *Because* I *don't have* a map, I *can't show* you where you have to go.

A 밑줄 친 부분을 어법상 바르게 고쳐 쓰시오.
» 정답과 해설 p.29

1 If it <u>was</u> sunny, we could go on a picnic. _____
2 If I <u>find</u> a wallet in the street, I would take it to the police. _____
3 If Sam grew his own vegetables, he <u>didn't</u> buy them. _____
4 If he <u>is</u> tall, he could be a basketball player. _____

B 우리말과 뜻이 같도록 빈칸에 알맞은 말을 쓰시오.

1 내가 너라면, 그의 말을 믿지 않을 텐데.
→ _____ I _____ you, I _____ _____ his words.
2 소라가 더 열심히 연습하면, 테니스를 더 잘 칠 수 있을 텐데.
→ _____ Sora _____ harder, she _____ _____ better at tennis.

C 다음 문장과 뜻이 같도록 빈칸에 알맞은 말을 쓰시오.

1 If Sally spoke slowly, I could understand her better.
→ Because Sally _____ speak slowly, I _____ _____ her better.
2 Because you don't have more time, you can't stay longer in New York.
→ If you _____ more time, you _____ _____ longer in New York.

교과서
문장
응용하기

배운 문법을 이용하여 영어 문장을 써 봅시다.

1 내가 너라면, 나는 그 콘서트에 갈 텐데. (concert) → _____
2 그가 운동을 한다면, 그는 건강해질 텐데. (healthy) → _____

가정법 과거완료

- 가정법 과거완료는 과거의 사실과 반대되는 일이나 과거에 이루지 못한 것을 가정할 때 쓴다.

형태	If+주어+had+과거분사 ~, 주어+would(could/might)+have+과거분사 …
의미	~했더라면, …했었을(이었을) 텐데

If Matty **had been** stronger, he **could have lifted** the weights.

- 가정법 과거완료를 직설법으로 나타낼 때는 시제는 과거로, 긍정의 내용은 부정, 부정의 내용은 긍정으로 바꿔 쓴다.

If I **had spoken** English well, I **would have talked** with the foreigner.

→ *Because* I *didn't speak* English well, I *didn't talk* with the foreigner.

A 괄호 안에서 알맞은 것을 고르시오.   » 정답과 해설 p.29

1 If you (drunk / had drunk) warm milk, you could have fallen asleep.

2 If you (done / had done) your homework, you would have gotten an A.

3 If there (been / had been) enough snow, the children could have made snowmen.

B 다음 문장과 뜻이 같도록 빈칸에 알맞은 말을 쓰시오.

1 If I had had good seats, I could have enjoyed the play.

→ I _____ _____ good seats, so I _____ _____ the play.

2 If she had been rich, she would have bought the house.

→ _____ she _____ rich, she _____ _____ the house.

3 As it didn't rain, we could go to the pool.

→ If it _____ _____, we _____ _____ _____ to the pool.

C 괄호 안의 말을 빈칸에 알맞은 형태로 쓰시오.

1 If you had called her, _____. (she will be glad)

2 If he'd been online yesterday, _____. (he can read my email)

3 If _____, he could have made the hockey team. (Tim practices hard)

교과서 문장 응용하기 배운 문법을 이용하여 영어 문장을 써 봅시다.

1 내가 배가 고팠다면, 무언가를 먹었을 텐데. → _____

2 날씨가 더 좋았다면, 나는 자전거를 탔을 텐데. → _____

I wish 가정법 과거

- 「I wish+가정법 과거(주어+동사의 과거형(were))」는 '~라면(하면) 좋을 텐데'의 뜻으로 현재 사실과 반대되는 소망을 나타낸다.

  I wish I **had** a good brother.

- 「I wish+가정법 과거」는 「I'm sorry (that)+직설법 현재」로 바꿀 수 있다. 이때 긍정의 내용은 부정, 부정의 내용은 긍정으로 바꿔 쓴다.

  I wish we **could live** in a world without any lies.
  → *I'm sorry (that)* we *can't live* in a world without any lies.

A 우리말과 뜻이 같도록 괄호 안에서 알맞은 것을 고르시오.　　　　　　》 정답과 해설 p.29

1 내가 그를 위해 무언가를 할 수 있다면 좋을 텐데.
→ I wish I (can do / could do) something for him.

2 내가 그 로봇을 살 충분한 돈을 갖고 있으면 좋을 텐데.
→ I wish I (have / had) enough money to buy the robot.

3 그가 영어를 잘하면 좋을 텐데.
→ I wish he (can / could) speak English well.

B 괄호 안의 말을 바르게 배열하여 문장을 완성하시오.

1 I wish _____. (knew, phone number, I, Nancy's)

2 I wish _____. (at, with you, were, I, the park)

3 I wish _____. (barking, the dog, stop, would)

C 다음 문장과 뜻이 같도록 빈칸에 알맞은 말을 쓰시오.

1 I wish I earned a lot of money.
→ I'm sorry _____.

2 I'm sorry I can't read your mind.
→ I wish _____.

3 I'm sorry I can't make a sweater for my father.
→ I wish _____.

교과서
문장
응용하기 | 배운 문법을 이용하여 영어 문장을 써 봅시다.

1 내가 그의 이메일 주소를 알면 좋을 텐데. (address)　　→ _____

2 Miller 씨가 영화배우라면 좋을 텐데. (actor)　　→ _____

I wish 가정법 과거완료

- 「I wish+가정법 과거완료(주어+had+과거분사)」는 '~이었다면(했다면) 좋았을 텐데'의 뜻으로 과거 사실과 반대되는 소망을 나타낸다.
  I wish I **had arrived** earlier here.

- 「I wish+가정법 과거완료」는 「I'm sorry (that)+직설법 과거」로 바꿀 수 있다. 이때 긍정의 내용은 부정, 부정의 내용은 긍정으로 바꿔 쓴다.
  I wish I **had traveled** to Europe last summer.
  → *I'm sorry (that)* I *didn't go* to Europe last summer.

A 우리말과 뜻이 같도록 괄호 안의 말을 이용하여 문장을 완성하시오.   » 정답과 해설 p.30

1 그녀가 바쁘지 않다면 좋았을 텐데. (be)
→ I wish she _____ _____ busy.

2 Jenny가 나에게 초대장을 보냈다면 좋았을 텐데. (send)
→ I wish Jenny _____ _____ me an invitation card.

3 내가 어젯밤에 그렇게 많이 먹지 않았다면 좋았을 텐데. (eat)
→ I wish I _____ _____ so much last night.

B 다음 문장과 뜻이 같도록 빈칸에 알맞은 말을 쓰시오.

1 I wish Mary had taken a bath in the morning.
→ I'm sorry _____.

2 I'm sorry I didn't buy a new guitar.
→ I wish _____.

3 I'm sorry that I didn't understand what the teacher said.
→ I wish _____.

C 다음 문장을 밑줄 친 부분에 유의하여 바르게 해석하시오.

1 I wish I hadn't forgotten my homework.
→ _____

2 I wish I had visited the White House.
→ _____

교과서 문장 응용하기 배운 문법을 이용하여 영어 문장을 써 봅시다.
1 내가 무용 강습을 받았다면 좋았을 텐데. (lesson)   → _____
2 내가 지난 금요일에 쇼핑을 갔다면 좋았을 텐데.   → _____

→ 내신적중 실전문제를 풀기 전에 Workbook p.47에 있는 요점정리를 참고하세요.

[01~04] 빈칸에 알맞은 것을 고르시오.

01

If you _____ there, you could meet him.

① go
② are going
③ went
④ going
⑤ had gone

02

I wish he _____ tell me the truth right now.

① is
② am
③ can
④ could
⑤ may

03

If I had been there, I _____ bungee jumping.

① try
② tried
③ would try
④ had tried
⑤ would have tried

04

A Did you guys have fun?   B Yes, but I wish we _____ more time.

① had
② can have
③ have
④ have have
⑤ had had

05 다음 문장에 이어질 말로 알맞은 것은?

If Alex had enough money, _____.

① he buys a new smartphone
② he will buy a new smartphone
③ he bought a new smartphone
④ he would buy a new smartphone
⑤ he would have bought a new smartphone

06 다음 문장과 뜻이 같도록 빈칸에 알맞은 말을 쓰시오. **주관식**

I wish we could give the charity some help soon.   → I'm sorry that we _____ _____ the charity some help soon.

07 밑줄 친 부분이 어법상 어색한 것은?

① I wish she <u>had gone</u> to the police.
② If the boy practiced enough, he <u>could be</u> a winner.
③ If she <u>had</u> a cellphone, she could have called her parents.
④ I wish I <u>wrote</u> a beautiful poem like the poet.
⑤ If I <u>were</u> him, I would take part in the audition.

08 빈칸에 알맞지 <u>않은</u> 것은?

> I wish _____ last year.

① I had studied harder
② I had learned ballet
③ I had more time to travel
④ I hadn't gone there
⑤ I hadn't wasted my time and money

09 우리말을 바르게 영작한 것은?

> Max가 기차로 갔었더라면 그녀를 봤을 텐데.

① If Max go by train, he would see her.
② If Max went by train, he will see her.
③ If Max went by train, he would see her.
④ If Max went by train, he would have seen her.
⑤ If Max had gone by train, he would have seen her.

10 밑줄 친 부분을 바르게 고친 것은?

> **A** Why isn't William invited to Jody's wedding?
> **B** Well, Jody doesn't like him. If Jody <u>like</u> William, she <u>invites</u> him.

① likes — will invite
② likes — would invite
③ liked — would invite
④ liked — would have invited
⑤ had liked — would have invited

[11~12] 다음 문장과 뜻이 같은 것을 고르시오.

11

> As this movie isn't fun, I am bored.

① If this movie is fun, I wouldn't be bored.
② If this movie were fun, I would be bored.
③ If this movie were fun, I wouldn't be bored.
④ If this movie weren't fun, I would be bored.
⑤ If this movie weren't fun, I wouldn't be bored.

12

> I'm sorry I didn't know the whole story then.

① I wish I know the whole story then.
② I wish I knew the whole story then.
③ I wish I don't know the whole story then.
④ I wish I didn't know the whole story then.
⑤ I wish I had known the whole story then.

13 밑줄 친 ①~⑤ 중 어법상 <u>어색한</u> 것은?

> **A** I wish I ① <u>took</u> a medicine ② <u>when</u> my tooth began ③ <u>to hurt</u>.
> **B** Why do you say ④ <u>that</u>?
> **A** If I had taken medicine, ⑤ <u>I wouldn't have felt</u> miserable all day long.

14 빈칸에 공통으로 알맞은 말을 쓰시오. 주관식

> • If I _____ a bicycle, I could save my time.
> • If the players _____ trained harder, they would have won the game.

[15~16] 밑줄 친 부분을 어법상 바르게 고쳐 쓰시오. 주관식

15

> I wish I <u>arrived</u> at the station on time yesterday.

→ _____

16

> If he had gotten more pocket money, he <u>would go</u> to the amusement park.

→ _____

17 짝지어진 문장의 의미가 <u>다른</u> 것은?

① • If I had enough time, I could have lunch with you.
　• As I don't have enough time, I can't have lunch with you.

② • I wish I had many brothers and sisters.
　• I'm sorry I don't have many brothers and sisters.

③ • I wish I could speak Japanese.
　• I'm sorry I can't speak Japanese.

④ • I wish I were a good daughter.
　• I'm sorry that I am a good daughter.

⑤ • If he had slowed down, he would have lost the race.
　• As he didn't slow down, he didn't lose the race.

[18~19] 빈칸에 알맞은 말이 바르게 짝지어진 것을 고르시오.

18

> • I wish I _____ yoga lessons last year.
> • If he _____ his bike, he would ride it.

① take — repaired
② took — repair
③ took — repaired
④ had taken — repaired
⑤ had taken — had repaired

19

> • If he _____ a liar, he would not tell the truth.
> • If they _____ regularly, they would have been healthy.

① was — exercises
② were — exercised
③ were — had exercised
④ had been — exercised
⑤ had been — had exercised

20 어법상 어색한 것은?

① I wish she kept her promise.
② I wish the police had arrested the thief.
③ If you walked in this rain, you would get very wet.
④ If it started at 8 o'clock, we would come to the party.
⑤ If we had gone to a good restaurant yesterday, we would had a better dinner.

서술형 평가

01 |보기|에서 알맞은 말을 골라 문장을 완성하시오.

> 보기
> go   live   train   read

(1) If I _____ in a palace, I would give parties all the time.

(2) If the sun had shone, we _____ _____ _____ swimming.

(3) If she spent a month on an island, Maria _____ _____ all the books.

(4) If they _____ _____ regularly, the boys would have won the game.

[02~03] 우리말을 괄호 안의 지시대로 영작하시오.

02

> 내가 Ann이라면, 그 선글라스를 살 수 있을 텐데.

(1) _____,
I _____ the sunglasses.
(if를 사용할 것)

(2) _____,
I _____ the sunglasses.
(as를 사용할 것)

03

> 나는 지난밤에 사탕을 많이 먹지 말았어야 했는데.

(1) _____
a lot of candies last night.
(wish를 사용할 것)

(2) _____
a lot of candies last night.
(sorry를 사용할 것)

04 괄호 안의 말을 이용하여 문장을 완성하시오.

> **A** Did you watch the documentary on Channel 7 yesterday?
> **B** No. I wanted to, but I was so busy and never had enough time for it.
> If I _____ some time, I _____ it. (have, watch)

[05~06] 다음 글을 읽고, 물음에 답하시오.

My friend Alan asked me to go to a party the night before the science test. I didn't like science, and I didn't feel like studying. So I went to the party and enjoyed it a lot. The next day, I failed the test, and my parents were disappointed with me. ⓐI'm sorry I went to the party. ⓑ내가 집에서 공부를 했다면 나는 그 시험을 통과했을 텐데.

05 밑줄 친 ⓐ와 뜻이 같도록 빈칸에 알맞은 말을 쓰시오.

I wish _____.

06 밑줄 친 ⓑ의 우리말과 뜻이 같도록 괄호 안의 말을 이용하여 문장을 완성하시오.

If I _____, I _____ the test. (study at home, will pass)

CHAPTER

14

일치와 화법

시제 일치란 무엇인가?

*주절의 시제에 *종속절의 시제를 일치시키는 것을 의미한다. 주절의 시제가 현재일 때는 종속절에 모든 시제를 쓸 수 있으며, 주절의 시제가 과거일 때는 종속절의 시제는 과거나 과거완료로 쓴다.

I **think** that he **missed**(**will miss**) you. 나는 그가 너를 그리워했다고(그리워할 거라고) 생각해.

He **said** that he **studied**(**had studied**) hard. 그는 자기가 공부를 열심히 했다고(했었다고) 말했다.

화법이란 무엇인가?

화법이란 다른 사람의 말을 인용하여 전달하는 방법을 말하며, 화법에는 직접화법과 간접화법이 있다.

화법
- **직접화법:** 인용부호(" ")를 이용하여 그대로 전달

  Andy says, "I am happy." "나는 행복해."라고 Andy가 말한다.

- **간접화법:** 접속사를 이용하여 전달하는 사람의 입장으로 바꿔서 전달

  Andy says that he is happy. Andy는 그가 행복하다고 말한다.

간접의문문은 무엇인가?

간접의문문은 어떤 문장과 의문문을 합쳐 한 문장으로 나타내는 것으로, 두 문장을 하나의 간접의문문으로 바꾸는 과정에서 어순이 변화한다.

〈직접의문문〉 Do you know? + Where does Jason come from?
너는 아니? Jason은 어디 출신이니?

〈간접의문문〉 Do you know **where Jason comes** from? 너는 Jason이 어디 출신인지 아니?
의문사   주어   동사

용어
사전

* **주절:** 문장에서 주어와 동사를 포함하고 있으며 혼자서도 쓰일 수 있는 완전한 문장이다.

* **종속절:** 단독으로 사용될 수 없으며, 주절의 앞이나 뒤에 위치하며 주절의 내용을 도와주는 절이다.

80 시제 일치

- 주절의 시제가 현재인 경우 종속절에는 모든 시제를 쓸 수 있지만, 주절의 시제가 과거인 경우에는 종속절의 시제는 과거 또는 과거완료로 쓴다.

She **says** that Tom **will be**(is/was) a good singer.

I **thought** that I **met**(had met) Mary.

- 종속절의 내용이 일반적인 사실 또는 현재의 습관일 때는 항상 현재시제를, 역사적인 사실일 때는 항상 과거시제를 쓴다.

The scientist **said** that the Earth **is** round. 〈일반적인 사실〉

I **know** that World War II **broke** out in 1939. 〈역사적인 사실〉

A 괄호 안에서 알맞은 것을 고르시오.

» 정답과 해설 p.31

1 Harry says that he (buys / will buy) a new computer tomorrow.

2 Robin was sure that his team (will win / would win) the game.

3 Ann knows that Edison (invents / invented) the light bulb.

4 My teacher taught us that London (is / was) the capital of England.

B 다음 문장의 시제를 바꿔 쓸 때 빈칸에 알맞은 말을 쓰시오.

1 Mina thinks that Sally is at home.

　→ Mina thought that _____.

2 It is strange that he doesn't say hello to me.

　→ It was strange that _____.

3 Yuri didn't know that Shakespeare died in 1616.

　→ Yuri doesn't know that _____.

C 우리말과 뜻이 같도록 괄호 안의 말을 이용하여 문장을 완성하시오.

1 Dona는 해는 동쪽에서 뜬다고 배웠다. (learn, rise)

　→ Dona _____ _____ the sun _____ in the east.

2 그는 매주 일요일에 교회에 간다고 말했다. (say, go to church)

　→ He _____ _____ he _____ _____ _____ every Sunday.

3 그녀는 Ted가 파리에 가 본 적이 있다고 말했다. (say, has been)

　→ She _____ _____ Ted _____ _____ _____ Paris.

교과서 문장 응용하기 배운 문법을 이용하여 영어 문장을 써 봅시다.

1 나는 Bill이 새 직업을 구했다는 소식을 들었다. (get) → _____

2 나는 한국 전쟁이 1950년에 발발한 것을 안다. (break out) → _____

81 평서문의 간접화법

다른 사람의 말을 그대로 전하는 직접화법은 전달자의 입장에서 전달하는 간접화법으로 바꿔 쓸 수 있다.

■ 피전달문이 평서문인 경우 다음과 같이 간접화법으로 만든다.

① 전달 동사를 바꾼다. 〈say → say, say to → tell〉

② 콤마(,)와 인용부호(" ")를 없애고 that을 쓴다. that은 생략 가능하다.

③ 직접화법의 인칭대명사, 부사(구) 등은 전달자의 입장에 맞게 고친다.

④ 전달 동사가 현재일 때는 피전달문의 동사는 시제의 변화가 없지만, 과거일 때는 시제를 알맞게 바꾼다.

〈현재 → 과거, 현재완료나 과거 → 과거완료〉

Jim said to his sister,　　　"I have to work late." 〈직접화법〉

→ Jim **told** his sister **(that)** **he** **had to** work late. 〈간접화법〉

A 다음 문장을 간접화법으로 바꿀 때 괄호 안에서 알맞은 것을 고르시오. 　　》 정답과 해설 p.31

1 Ann said, "Kelly is honest."

→ Ann (said / said to) that Kelly was honest.

2 Paul says to me, "Nobody will know."

→ Paul (tells / told) me that nobody will know.

B 다음 문장을 간접화법으로 바꿀 때 빈칸에 알맞은 말을 쓰시오.

1 Kevin said to me, "I feel great."

→ Kevin _____ me that _____.

2 Colin says to Susan, "I know lots of people."

→ Colin _____ Susan that _____.

3 My brother said, "I saw Ken at a party."

→ My brother _____ that _____.

C 다음 문장을 직접화법으로 바꿀 때 빈칸에 알맞은 말을 쓰시오.

1 Eric says that his mom is a great cook.

→ Eric says, "_____."

2 Josh told us that he was talking on the phone.

→ Josh said to us, "_____."

교과서
문장
응용하기

배운 문법을 이용하여 영어 문장을 써 봅시다.

1 White 부인은 "내 아들은 잘생겼어."라고 말한다. (say)　　→ _____

2 Andy는 가고 싶지 않다고 나에게 말했다. (tell)　　→ _____

82 의문사가 없는 의문문의 간접화법

- 피전달문이 의문사가 없는 의문문인 경우 다음과 같이 간접화법으로 만든다.
  ① 전달 동사를 바꾼다. 〈say to → ask〉
  ② 콤마(,)와 인용부호(" ")를 삭제하고 피전달문을 「if(whether)+주어+동사」의 순으로 바꾼다.
  ③ 직접화법의 인칭대명사는 전달자 입장에 맞추어 바꾸고, 동사의 시제도 주절에 맞게 바꾼다.

  The old man <u>said to</u> me, "<u>Is it</u> raining?"

  → The old man **asked** me **if it was** raining.

A 다음 문장을 간접화법으로 바꿀 때 빈칸에 알맞은 말을 쓰시오.　　　　　　　　》 정답과 해설 p.31

　1 John said to his mother, "Did Ann leave early?"

　　→ John _____.

　2 Nicole said to a woman, "Is there a cafe nearby?"

　　→ Nicole _____.

　3 A man said to me, "Can you take a picture?"

　　→ A man _____.

B 다음 문장을 직접화법으로 바꿀 때 빈칸에 알맞은 말을 쓰시오.

　1 You asked me if I had gotten your letter.

　　→ You said to me, "_____?"

　2 Justin asked his cousin if he could borrow her book.

　　→ Justin said to his cousin, "_____?"

C 우리말과 뜻이 같도록 괄호 안의 말을 배열하여 문장을 완성하시오. (한 단어를 추가할 것)

　1 Ron은 Linda에게 그녀가 노래 부르는 것을 좋아하는지 물었다.

　　(asked, she, singing, liked, Linda)

　　→ Ron _____.

　2 Jason은 내가 그에게 돈을 좀 빌려줄 수 있는지 내게 물었다.

　　(me, I, could lend, him, asked, some money)

　　→ Jason _____.

교과서
문장
응용하기　　**배운 문법을 이용하여 영어 문장을 써 봅시다.**

　1 그녀는 그녀의 남자친구에게 그가 아픈지 물었다.　　→ _____

　2 나는 그 소년들에게 책을 읽는 것을 좋아하는지 물었다.　→ _____

83

의문사가 있는 의문문의 간접화법

- 피전달문이 의문사가 있는 의문문인 경우 다음과 같이 간접화법으로 만든다.
  ① 전달 동사를 바꾼다. ⟨say to → ask⟩
  ② 콤마(,)와 인용부호(" ")를 삭제하고 피전달문을 「의문사+주어+동사」의 어순으로 바꾼다.
  ③ 직접화법의 인칭대명사는 전달자 입장에 맞게 바꾸고, 동사의 시제도 주절의 시제에 맞게 바꾼다.

  The driver <u>said to me</u>, "<u>Where do you want to go?</u>"

  → The driver **asked** me **where I wanted** to go.

A 다음 문장을 | 보기 |와 같이 바꿔 쓰시오.　　　　　　　　　　　　　　　》 정답과 해설 p.31

> **보기**
> Justin: "What are you doing?" → Justin asked me what I was doing.

1 Dean: "Why do you like the book?"
　→ Dean _____.

2 The boss: "What time is the meeting?"
　→ The boss _____.

3 Jason: "Who gave you the laptop?"
　→ Jason _____.

B 다음 문장을 직접화법으로 바꿀 때 빈칸에 알맞은 말을 쓰시오.

1 He asked Fiona who had told her about the job.
　→ He said to Fiona, "_____?"

2 Ronald asked me where Maria parked her car.
　→ Ronald said to me, "_____?"

3 Mr. Erickson asked his daughter how many eggs she wanted.
　→ Mr. Erickson said to his daughter, "_____?"

C 괄호 안의 말을 바르게 배열하여 문장을 완성하시오.

1 Tom asked Ann _____. (went, she, how often, shopping)
2 I asked them _____. (kept, they, where, the money)
3 Linda asked me _____. (the bank, what, closed, time)

> **교과서 문장 응용하기**
>
> 배운 문법을 이용하여 영어 문장을 써 봅시다.
> **1** 나는 그에게 그의 사무실이 어디에 있는지를 물었다. (office) → _____
> **2** 그녀는 나에게 내가 언제 도착했는지를 물었다. (arrive) 　→ _____

84 간접의문문 1

- **의문사가 있는 의문문의 간접의문문:** 「의문사+주어+동사」의 어순으로 쓴다.

  I wonder. + Where did I leave my phone?

  → I wonder **where I left my phone.**

  cf. 간접의문문에서 의문사가 주어로 쓰이면 직접의문문의 어순을 그대로 쓴다.

  Please tell me. + What is causing that noise?

  → Please tell me **what is causing that noise.**

- **의문사가 없는 의문문의 간접의문문:** 「if(whether)+주어+동사」의 어순으로 쓴다.

  I'd like to know. + Does she like the gift?

  → I'd like to know **if(whether) she likes the gift.**

A 두 문장을 간접의문문으로 바꿀 때 빈칸에 알맞은 말을 쓰시오.　　　　　　　　» 정답과 해설 p.32

1 I have no idea. + What's his name?

→ I have no idea ＿＿＿＿＿＿＿＿＿＿＿＿＿＿＿＿＿＿＿ .

2 Can you tell me? + Whose bag is it?

→ Can you tell me ＿＿＿＿＿＿＿＿＿＿＿＿＿＿＿＿＿＿＿ ?

3 I wonder. + Is he a middle school student?

→ I wonder ＿＿＿＿＿＿＿＿＿＿＿＿＿＿＿＿＿ .

B 밑줄 친 부분을 어법상 바르게 고쳐 쓰시오.

1 Could you tell me why is she in such a bad mood?　　　＿＿＿＿＿＿＿＿

2 Do you know what time does the bank open?　　　＿＿＿＿＿＿＿＿

3 I wonder can he speak English.　　　＿＿＿＿＿＿＿＿

4 I'd like to know they took what route.　　　＿＿＿＿＿＿＿＿

C 우리말과 뜻이 같도록 빈칸에 알맞은 말을 쓰시오.

1 너는 Tom이 이탈리아 음식을 좋아하는지 아니?

→ Do you know ＿＿＿＿ ＿＿＿＿ ＿＿＿＿ Italian food?

2 누가 그녀에게 카드를 보냈는지 제게 말해 주세요.

→ Please tell me ＿＿＿＿ ＿＿＿＿ the card to her.

**교과서
문장
응용하기**

배운 문법을 이용하여 영어 문장을 써 봅시다.

1 빵집이 어디에 있는지 말씀해 주실 수 있나요? (bakery)　→ ＿＿＿＿＿＿＿＿＿＿＿＿＿

2 나는 이 꽃병을 누가 깼는지 알고 싶어. (want, vase)　→ ＿＿＿＿＿＿＿＿＿＿＿＿＿

85 간접의문문 2

- 주절의 동사가 생각이나 추측을 나타내는 think, believe, imagine, suppose, guess 등일 때는 간접의문문의 의문사를 문장의 맨 앞에 쓴다.

  Do you think? + When will they come?

  → **When** do you think they will come?

  Do you guess? + Who won the game?

  → **Who** do you guess won the game?

A 두 문장을 간접의문문으로 바꿔 쓰시오.　　　　　　　　　　　　　　　　　　　　　　　》 정답과 해설 p.32

1 Do you imagine? + What will he do?

→ _____

2 Do you think? + How does this robot work?

→ _____

3 Does she guess? + Who borrowed the book?

→ _____

4 Do they suppose? + When will the meeting be held?

→ _____

B 다음 문장을 | 보기 |와 같이 바꿔 쓰시오.

> **보기**
>
> Where do you think she lives?
>
> → Do you think? + Where does she live?

1 Who do you suppose would believe that story?

→ Do you suppose? + _____

2 What do you think you will do next week?

→ Do you think? + _____

3 Where do you imagine she spent her holiday?

→ Do you imagine? + _____

4 How do you believe they will come here?

→ Do you believe? + _____

교과서 문장 응용하기 　배운 문법을 이용하여 영어 문장을 써 봅시다.

1 너는 누가 여기에 산다고 생각하니? (live)　　→ _____

2 너는 그들이 무엇을 만들 것이라고 믿니? (make)　→ _____

　　　　➜ 내신적중 실전문제를 풀기 전에 Workbook p.49에 있는 요점정리를 참고하세요.

» 정답과 해설 p.32

[01~02] 빈칸에 알맞은 것을 고르시오.

01

> My parents believed that I _____.

① am a good son
② cook dinner myself
③ can play football well
④ study math very hard
⑤ would be a great dancer

02

> A Where can I buy some flowers?
> B Sorry, but I have no idea _____.

① whether you buy them
② how can you buy them
③ why should you buy them
④ where you can buy them
⑤ what you should buy them

03 괄호 안에 주어진 동사의 형태로 알맞은 것은?

> I didn't know that she (change) her phone number.

① changes   ② changing
③ will change   ④ has changed
⑤ had changed

04 밑줄 친 ①~⑤ 중 어법상 어색한 것은?

> A What are you ① doing this Saturday?
> B My mother is visiting me, ② so I told her ③ that I ④ will pick her up ⑤ at the airport.

 [05~06] 다음 문장을 간접화법으로 바르게 바꾼 것을 고르시오.

05

> He said to me, "Can I have some bread?"

① He said to me if I can have some bread.
② He said to me whether I could have some bread.
③ He asked me whether he can have some bread.
④ He asked me if he could have some bread.
⑤ He asked me if could he have some bread.

06

> Jenny said to Jim, "I like the bicycle."

① Jenny said to Jim that I like the bicycle.
② Jenny said to Jim that she likes the bicycle.
③ Jenny told Jim that she like the bicycle.
④ Jenny told Jim that she likes the bicycle.
⑤ Jenny told Jim that she liked the bicycle.

[07~08] 다음 문장을 간접화법으로 바꿀 때 빈칸에 알맞은 말이 바르게 짝지어진 것을 고르시오.

07

> Sue said to me, "I didn't do my homework."
> → Sue _____ me that she _____ her homework.

① said — didn't do
② said — hadn't done
③ told — didn't do
④ told — hasn't done
⑤ told — hadn't done

08

> Mia said to me, "Do you like pizza?"
> → Mia _____ me _____ I liked pizza.

① told — if
② told — whether
③ said — whether
④ asked — if
⑤ asked — that

09 우리말을 바르게 영작한 것은?

> 너는 내 키가 얼마나 된다고 생각하니?

① Do you guess how tall am I?
② Do you guess how tall I am?
③ How tall do you guess I am?
④ How tall do you suppose am I?
⑤ How do you suppose I am tall?

[10~11] 빈칸에 알맞지 <u>않은</u> 것을 고르시오.

10

> Who do you _____ will be the winner?

① know   ② think
③ believe   ④ guess
⑤ suppose

11

> Justin said that he _____.

① bought a new bike
② would go shopping
③ travels to Mexico
④ talked to Kevin and Robyn
⑤ gets up at six every day

12 다음 문장을 직접화법으로 바꿀 때 빈칸에 알맞은 말을 쓰시오. 주관식

> Eric asked me what I was doing.
> → Eric said to me, "What _____ _____ _____?

13 어법상 <u>어색한</u> 것은?

① Steve tells me he's ready.
② Yumi told me that she didn't love Jinsu.
③ They asked me if I was scared of him.
④ We asked him whether he could join us.
⑤ Justin asked us when would we go to the park.

14 밑줄 친 부분과 바꿔 쓸 수 있는 것은?

> He asked us <u>if</u> we had heard the strange sound.

① that　　　　　② what
③ when　　　　　④ where
⑤ whether

고난도

15 직접화법을 간접화법으로 바르게 바꾼 것은?

① Pam said to us, "Have you just arrived?"
　→ Pam asked us if we have just arrived.
② James asked, "Can I go?"
　→ James asked that he could go.
③ Julia asked, "Where is my umbrella?"
　→ Julia asked where her umbrella was.
④ Minho asked, "Do I have to do it?"
　→ Minho asked if he has to do it.
⑤ Ann said to her son, "Where have you been?"
　→ Ann asked her son where she had been.

16 우리말과 뜻이 같도록 빈칸에 알맞은 것은?

> 그녀는 나에게 근처에 공원이 있는지 물었다.
> → She asked me ＿＿＿＿＿＿＿＿ a park nearby.

① that there is　　② that there was
③ if is there　　　④ if there is
⑤ if there was

17 다음 문장을 간접화법으로 바꿀 때 빈칸에 알맞은 말을 쓰시오. **주관식**

> She said to me, "Did you see my sister at school?"
> → She asked me if I ＿＿＿＿＿ ＿＿＿＿＿ her sister at school.

18 어법상 어색한 부분을 찾아 고쳐 쓰시오. **주관식**

> Our teacher told us that water boiled at 100°C.

＿＿＿＿＿＿＿＿ → ＿＿＿＿＿＿＿＿

19 우리말과 뜻이 같도록 빈칸에 알맞은 말을 쓰시오. **주관식**

> 너는 누가 그 답을 안다고 생각하니?
> → ＿＿＿＿ ＿＿＿＿ ＿＿＿＿ ＿＿＿＿ knows the answer?

20 어법상 올바른 것은?

① I'd like to know how much is it.
② I wonder where does he come from.
③ Please tell me who stole his wallet.
④ Can you remember where is Bob's house?
⑤ Would you mind telling me you're married?

서술형 평가

01 밑줄 친 부분을 괄호 안에 주어진 말로 바꿔 문장을 다시 쓰시오.

(1)
> Sally <u>thinks</u> online shopping is full of fun. (thought)

→ _____

(2)
> My teacher <u>tells</u> us that the Chinese invented paper. (told)

→ _____

02 두 문장을 한 문장으로 쓸 때 빈칸에 알맞은 말을 쓰시오.

> We learned it. Brazil is the largest country in South America.

→ _____
in South America.

03 우리말과 뜻이 같도록 괄호 안의 말을 배열하여 문장을 완성하시오.

(1)
> 유리가 부모님께 카드를 썼는지 아니?

Do you know _____
to her parents? (if, wrote, Yuri, cards)

(2)
> 우리가 지구를 구하기 위해 뭘 할 수 있다고 생각해?

_____
to save the Earth?
(do, do, we, you, what, can, think)

04 다음 문장을 |보기|와 같이 바꿔 쓸 때 빈칸에 알맞은 말을 쓰시오.

> **보기**
> "I enjoy cooking."
> → Harry said he enjoyed cooking.

(1) "I'll buy you a new bike tomorrow."
→ Ms. Miller told her son that _____
_____.

(2) "How often does Anna go swimming?"
→ David asked me _____
_____.

[05~06] 다음 글을 읽고, 물음에 답하시오.

> Dear Ms. Owl
> ⓐ I don't know. ⓑ Why is this happening to me? ⓒ I got my report card back yesterday. It was terrible! I got 55 points and 60 points. I feel really stupid. What is worse, I have lost my concentration. When I try to study hard, I end up playing computer games. ⓓ I'm getting really far behind. I'm really worried. ⓔ What can I do?   *Alan*

05 밑줄 친 ⓐ와 ⓑ의 두 문장을 한 문장으로 쓰시오.

_____

06 밑줄 친 ⓒ~ⓔ가 간접화법이 되도록 문장을 완성하시오.

ⓒ Alan told Ms. Owl _____
_____.

ⓓ Alan told Ms. Owl _____
_____.

ⓔ Alan asked Ms. Owl _____
_____.

TAPA

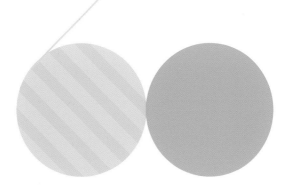

LEVEL 2

| 중학 영어의 특강서 |

핵심문법으로 격파하는

GRAMMAR
TAPA

WORKBOOK

visang

GRAMMAR TAPA
WORKBOOK

LEVEL 2

CONTENTS

» 정답과 해설 p.53

01 1·2형식 문장

■ **1형식:** 「주어+¹_____」로 이루어진 문장이다.
The girl smiles brightly. 그 소녀는 밝게 웃는다.
Dolphins ²_____ in the ocean. 돌고래는 바다에 산다.

■ **2형식:** 「주어+동사+주격보어」로 이루어진 문장이다.
주격보어로는 명사나 형용사가 온다.
She is a musician. 그녀는 음악가이다.
The plan sounds perfect. 그 계획은 완벽하게 들린다.
cf. 감각동사가 쓰인 2형식 문장은 보어로 형용사가 온다.
This bread smells ³_____. 이 빵은 냄새가 좋다.

02 3·4형식 문장

03 4형식 문장의 3형식 전환

■ **3형식:** 「주어+동사+⁴_____」로 이루어진 문장이다.
My sister likes chocolate cake.
내 여동생은 초콜릿 케이크를 좋아한다.

■ **4형식:** 「주어+동사+간접목적어+직접목적어」로 이루어진 문장이다.
My aunt bought ⁵_____ a bike.
나의 이모는 나에게 자전거를 사 주셨다.

■ **4형식:** 「주어+동사+간접목적어+직접목적어」
→ **3형식:** 「주어+동사+직접목적어+⁶_____+간접목적어」

전치사 ⁷_____	give, send, tell, lend, show, teach, write 등
전치사 ⁸_____	make, buy, get, cook 등
전치사 ⁹_____	ask, require 등

04 5형식 문장 1_ 명사, 형용사, to부정사 목적격보어

05 5형식 문장 2_ 동사원형 목적격보어

■ 5형식은 「주어+동사+¹⁰_____+목적격보어」로 이루어진 문장이다. 이때 목적격보어는 동사에 의해 결정된다.

■ **명사 또는 형용사를 목적격보어로 취하는 동사:** call, make, keep, leave 등
My mom calls me "Sleepyhead."
우리 엄마는 나를 '잠꾸러기'라고 부른다.
The news made ¹¹_____ happy.
그 소식은 그녀를 행복하게 했다.
Gloves keep your hands ¹²_____.
장갑은 손을 따뜻하게 유지한다.

■ **to부정사를 목적격보어로 취하는 동사:** want, ask, tell, advise, expect, get 등
Jenna wants me ¹³_____ to her party.
Jenna는 내가 그녀의 파티에 오기를 원한다.

■ ¹⁴_____을 목적격보어로 취하는 동사에는 2가지 종류가 있다.

■ **사역동사:** make, let, have 등 '~가 …하도록 시키다, ~가 …하게 하다'의 뜻을 가진 동사
My brother made us ¹⁵_____.
나의 오빠는 우리를 웃게 했다.
cf. help는 목적격보어로 ¹⁶_____와 동사원형을 모두 쓸 수 있다.
He helped me (to) find my backpack.
그는 내가 나의 배낭을 찾는 것을 도왔다.

■ ¹⁷_____: see, hear, feel 등 '~가 …하는 것을 보다(듣다 / 느끼다)'의 뜻을 가진 동사
I saw you dance on the stage.
나는 네가 무대 위에서 춤을 추는 것을 보았다.

1 다음 문장이 1형식인지, 2형식인지 쓰시오.

(1) Her face became red. _____

(2) The little boy sat on his chair. _____

(3) There are many people there. _____

(4) The man is a university student. _____

2 밑줄 친 부분을 어법상 바르게 고쳐 쓰시오.

(1) The blouse feels very <u>smoothly</u>.

→ _____

(2) The kids are playing <u>happy</u> in the park.

→ _____

(3) The green building looks <u>beautifully</u>.

→ _____

1 다음 문장이 3형식인지, 4형식인지 쓰시오.

(1) Jason bought his son a book. _____

(2) I enjoyed myself at the party. _____

(3) He gave the children gifts. _____

2 우리말과 뜻이 같도록 괄호 안의 말을 배열하여 문장을 완성하시오.

(1) 저에게 접시 좀 건네주시겠어요?

(pass, dish, will, the, me, you)

→ _____

(2) 나는 그 콘서트에 가고 싶다.

(want, the, go, concert, I, to, to)

→ _____

(3) 그는 나에게 멋진 양복을 만들어 줄 것이다.

(will, me, suit, he, make, a, nice)

→ _____

(4) Bob은 교실 청소하는 것을 끝마쳤다.

(finished, classroom, cleaning, the, Bob)

→ _____

1 빈칸에 알맞은 말을 | 보기 |에서 골라 쓰시오.

> | 보기 |
> for   of   to

(1) He gave his toys _____ the poor child.

(2) She bought the new TV _____ us.

(3) The woman showed her secret box _____ them.

(4) The little girl asked many questions _____ me.

2 괄호 안의 말을 바르게 배열하여 문장을 완성하시오.

(1) The old man _____.

(the newspaper, to, his wife, read)

(2) Can I _____?

(ask, of, you, something)

(3) Alan _____.

(his parents, a lie, to, told)

3 다음 문장을 3형식으로 바꿔 쓰시오.

(1) She wrote him several poems.

→ _____

(2) Dad made us coffee.

→ _____

(3) Did you ask him the price?

→ _____

(4) He teaches students history.

→ _____

4 어법상 어색한 부분을 찾아 고쳐 쓰시오.

(1) I'll send a text message for you.

_____ → _____

(2) I got a drink to John.

_____ → _____

1 다음 문장에서 목적격보어를 찾아 밑줄을 그으시오.

(1) He found the movie interesting.

(2) We believe him a king.

(3) They named the ship *Titanic*.

(4) He told them to be quiet.

2 밑줄 친 부분을 어법상 바르게 고쳐 쓰시오.

(1) You should keep the room <u>cleanly</u>.

→ _____

(2) He advised her <u>go</u> see a doctor.

→ _____

(3) The street cat made me <u>sadly</u>.

→ _____

(4) I expect him <u>be</u> a successful writer.

→ _____

3 대화 내용을 한 문장으로 쓸 때 빈칸에 알맞은 말을 쓰시오.

(1) **Harry** Be happy.

　Emma OK, thank you.

　→ Harry told Emma _____ _____ happy.

(2) **Mom** You should stay at home.

　Girl Sure, I will.

　→ Mom advised her _____ _____ at home.

(3) **Man** Will you marry me?

　Woman Of course.

　→ He asked her _____ _____ him.

4 괄호 안의 말을 바르게 배열하여 문장을 완성하시오.

(1) (him, I, think, fat).

→ _____

(2) (elected, president, her, they).

→ _____

(3) (the question, he, found, difficult).

→ _____

(4) (you, play, we, want, the piano, to).

→ _____

1 괄호 안에서 알맞은 것을 <u>모두</u> 고르시오.

(1) The movie made me (laughing / laugh).

(2) I watched the light (go / to go) out.

(3) I helped him (study / to study) math.

(4) Did you hear someone (to sing / sing)?

2 밑줄 친 부분을 어법상 바르게 고쳐 쓰시오.

(1) We will let you <u>knowing</u> about it.

→ _____

(2) I saw Superman <u>to fly</u> in the sky.

→ _____

(3) He had his son <u>watering</u> the grass.

→ _____

(4) I felt something <u>to strike</u> me.

→ _____

3 밑줄 친 부분을 괄호 안의 단어로 바꿔 문장을 다시 쓰시오.

(1) Please <u>allow</u> me to eat chocolate. (let)

→ _____

(2) He <u>asked</u> me to exercise a lot. (had)

→ _____

(3) I <u>got</u> him to carry the heavy box. (made)

→ _____

4 우리말과 뜻이 같도록 괄호 안의 말을 배열하여 문장을 완성하시오.

(1) 나는 그가 그 카페에 들어가는 것을 보았다.

(saw, enter, I, the cafe, him)

→ _____

(2) 우리 엄마는 우리가 눈사람을 만들게 해 주셨다.

(us, a snowman, mom, make, let, our)

→ _____

(3) 그는 내가 에세이 쓰는 것을 도와주었다.

(helped, write, me, he, to, the essay)

→ _____

(4) 나는 그녀가 내 이름을 부르는 소리를 들었다.

(call, I, her, my name, heard)

→ _____

» 정답과 해설 p.53

06 to부정사의 명사적 용법 1_ 주어, 보어

07 to부정사의 명사적 용법 2_ 목적어, 의문사+to부정사

■ **주어 역할:** '~하는 것은, ~하기는'

To get enough sleep is important.

→ ¹_____ is important to get enough sleep.

충분한 잠을 자는 것은 중요하다.

■ **보어 역할:** '~하는 것이다'

My dream is ²_____ _____ around the world.

내 꿈은 전 세계를 여행하는 것이다.

■ **목적어 역할:** '~하는 ³_____, ~하기를'

Brian wants to have a pet at home.

Brian은 집에서 애완동물을 기르고 싶어 한다.

■ **「의문사+to부정사」:** 문장에서 명사처럼 쓰인다. 「의문사+주어+should+동사원형」으로 바꿔 쓸 수 있다.

I don't know ⁴_____ to wear to the party.

나는 그 파티에 무엇을 입고 가야 할 지 모르겠다.

→ I don't know what I should wear to the party.

08 to부정사의 형용사적 용법

■ '⁵_____, ~할'의 뜻으로 (대)명사를 꾸며 준다.

I have something to tell you.

나는 너에게 말할 것이 있다.

■ to부정사가 꾸며 주는 명사가 전치사의 목적어일 경우에는 to부정사 뒤에 전치사를 쓴다.

My sister has many toys to play ⁶_____.

내 여동생은 가지고 놀 장난감이 많이 있다.

09 to부정사의 부사적 용법 1_ 목적, 감정의 원인

10 to부정사의 부사적 용법 2_ 결과, 형용사 수식

■ **목적:** '~하려고, ~하기 위해'라는 뜻이며, 「⁷_____ _____ _____ +동사원형」 또는 「so as to+동사원형」으로 바꿔 쓸 수 있다.

Jennifer went out to walk her dog.

→ Jennifer went out in order to(so as to) walk her dog. Jennifer는 그녀의 개를 산책시키기 위해 외출했다.

■ **감정의 원인:** '~해서, ~하다니'

I was very ⁸_____ to see them again.

나는 그들을 다시 보아서 매우 기뻤다.

■ **결과:** '…해서 (결국) ~하다'

The boy grew up ⁹_____ _____ a great pianist.

그 소년은 자라서 위대한 피아니스트가 되었다.

■ **형용사 수식:** '¹⁰_____

The water in this bottle is safe to drink.

이 병 안의 물은 마시기에 안전하다.

cf. **판단의 근거:** '~하다니, ~하는 것을 보니'

You must be foolish ¹¹_____ _____ such a thing.

그런 것을 믿다니 너는 어리석은 것이 분명하다.

11 too ~ to부정사 / enough to부정사

■ **「too+형용사(부사)+to부정사」:** '너무 ~해서 …할 수 없다'

= 「¹²_____+형용사(부사)+that+주어+can't(couldn't) …」

Sam is too busy to make time for his family.

→ Sam is so busy that he can't make time for his family. Sam은 너무 바빠서 그의 가족을 위한 시간을 내지 못한다.

■ **「형용사(부사)+enough +to부정사」:** '…할 만큼 충분히 ~하다'

= 「so+형용사(부사)+that+주어+¹³_____(could) …」

She is strong enough to lift the box.

→ She is so strong that she can lift the box.

그녀는 그 상자를 들어올릴 수 있을 만큼 충분히 힘이 세다.

12 to부정사의 의미상 주어

■ **「for+목적격」:** 일반적인 형용사 뒤에 쓴다.

This song is difficult ¹⁴_____ _____ to sing.

이 노래는 내가 부르기에는 어렵다.

■ **「¹⁵_____+목적격」:** 사람의 성격이나 태도를 나타내는 형용사 뒤에 쓴다.

It is ¹⁶_____ of you to help the boy.

그 소년을 돕다니 당신은 친절하군요.

1 밑줄 친 부분이 주어인지, 보어인지 쓰시오.

(1) It is easy to ride a horse. _____

(2) My job is to drive a taxi. _____

(3) It is cheap to take the subway. _____

(4) His hope is to become a cook. _____

2 밑줄 친 부분을 어법상 바르게 고쳐 쓰시오.

(1) My dream is to rich.

→ _____

(2) His hobby is collect old cars.

→ _____

(3) Be a professional player is difficult.

→ _____

(4) It is good learn foreign languages.

→ _____

3 다음 문장을 가주어 It을 이용하여 다시 쓰시오.

(1) To drive too fast is dangerous.

→ _____

(2) To read newspapers is a good habit.

→ _____

(3) To see animals at the zoo is fun.

→ _____

(4) To eat too much is bad for your health.

→ _____

4 우리말과 뜻이 같도록 괄호 안의 말을 배열하여 문장을 완성하시오.

(1) 너의 다음 일은 창문을 청소하는 것이다.

(clean, your, is, next job, window, the, to)

→ _____

(2) 그를 만나는 것이 나의 바람이다.

(wish, to, him, is, my, meet)

→ _____

(3) 자기 자신을 아는 것은 매우 어렵다.

(oneself, hard, it, to, know, is, very)

→ _____

1 괄호 안의 말을 빈칸에 알맞은 형태로 쓰시오.

(1) I need _____ to you. (talk)

(2) They wished _____ home. (go)

(3) I plan _____ in the countryside. (live)

(4) She hopes _____ the palace. (visit)

2 괄호 안의 동사와 |보기|의 의문사를 이용하여 빈칸에 알맞은 말을 쓰시오.

보기			
when	where	how	what

(1) He told me _____ _____ _____ for dinner. (eat)

(2) We asked the man _____ _____ _____ to the station. (get)

(3) I don't know _____ _____ _____ for my vacation. (go)

(4) We didn't decide _____ _____ _____, today or tomorrow. (leave)

3 밑줄 친 부분을 어법상 바르게 고쳐 쓰시오.

(1) I want skate on the lake.

→ _____

(2) Please teach me how downloading the file.

→ _____

(3) I didn't expect see you here.

→ _____

4 다음 문장과 뜻이 같도록 빈칸에 알맞은 말을 쓰시오.

(1) We decided where we should meet.

→ We decided _____ _____ _____.

(2) Tell me when to press the button.

→ Tell me _____ _____ _____ press the button.

(3) Do you know what we should do next?

→ Do you know _____ _____ _____ next?

1 괄호 안에서 알맞은 것을 고르시오.

(1) Give me some paper (to write / to write on).

(2) She will buy a new skirt (to wear / wearing).

(3) They don't have any (water to drink / to drink water).

2 밑줄 친 부분을 어법상 바르게 고쳐 쓰시오.

(1) He found a partner to dance.

→ _____

(2) I couldn't find anything to sit.

→ _____

(3) I need a pen to write.

→ _____

(4) We are looking for an apartment to live.

→ _____

3 괄호 안의 말을 바르게 배열하여 문장을 완성하시오.

(1) I have _____.

(toys, play, many, with, to)

(2) She had _____.

(nothing, say, to)

(3) This is the _____.

(in, safe, swim, to, river)

(4) I don't have _____.

(to, time, science, study).

4 우리말과 뜻이 같도록 어법상 어색한 부분을 찾아 고쳐 쓰시오.

(1) 사람들은 함께 이야기할 누군가가 필요하다.

→ People need someone to talk.

_____ → _____

(2) 마실 것 좀 드릴까요?

→ Would you like something drink?

_____ → _____

(3) 나는 책을 살 돈이 없다.

→ I have no money buy books.

_____ → _____

1 빈칸에 알맞은 말을 | 보기 |에서 골라 쓰시오.

> | 보기 |
> to catch the train   to cut the rope
> to win the medal   to find out the truth

(1) Tommy hurried up _____.

(2) She was angry _____.

(3) He used the knife _____.

(4) We were excited _____.

2 밑줄 친 to부정사가 목적을 나타내는지, 원인을 나타내는지 쓰시오.

(1) He was shocked to see the accident. _____

(2) I jog every morning to lose weight. _____

(3) She went to Africa to help sick kids. _____

(4) I am pleased to meet my old friend. _____

3 두 문장을 한 문장으로 쓸 때 빈칸에 알맞은 말을 쓰시오.

(1) They heard the bad news. They were sad.

→ They were sad _____ _____ the bad news.

(2) I got a present. I was very happy.

→ I was very happy _____ _____ a present.

4 다음 문장을 밑줄 친 부분에 유의하여 바르게 해석하시오.

(1) He went there to study the Chinese culture.

→ _____

(2) I was surprised to see Jinny at the cinema.

→ _____

(3) She found her glasses in order to read the magazine.

→ _____

1 밑줄 친 to부정사가 결과를 나타내는지, 형용사를 수식하는지 쓰시오.

(1) This book is difficult to read.   _____

(2) The river is too dirty to swim in.   _____

(3) He woke up to find himself alone.   _____

2 괄호 안의 말을 바르게 배열하여 문장을 완성하시오.

(1) The street is _____.
(cross, dangerous, to)

(2) She _____ herself in the hospital.
(to, find, awoke)

(3) The king _____ 100 years old.
(to, lived, be)

3 우리말과 뜻이 같도록 빈칸에 알맞은 말을 쓰시오.

(1) 그 언어는 읽고 쓰기에 어렵다.
→ The language is difficult _____ _____
_____ _____.

(2) 그녀는 깨어나서 개가 없어진 것을 알았다.
→ She woke up _____ _____ the dog missing.

(3) 이 기계는 사용하기가 쉽다.
→ This machine is _____ _____ _____.

4 다음 문장을 밑줄 친 부분에 유의하여 바르게 해석하시오.

(1) The movie is hard to understand.
→ _____

(2) They entered the room to find it empty.
→ _____

(3) He grew up to become a famous actor.
→ _____

1 밑줄 친 부분을 어법상 바르게 고쳐 쓰시오.

(1) It's so cold to sit outside.
→ _____

(2) I am enough old to travel by myself.
→ _____

(3) My sister was so young that she can't enter the theater. → _____

2 두 문장을 한 문장으로 쓸 때 빈칸에 알맞은 말을 쓰시오.

(1) Bob is tall enough. He can be a basketball player.
→ Bob is _____ _____ _____ be a basketball player.

(2) I am too scared. I can't open my eyes.
→ I am _____ _____ _____ _____ my eyes.

1 괄호 안에서 알맞은 것을 고르시오.

(1) It was foolish (her / of her) to act like that.

(2) It is (necessary / rude) of her to speak so loudly.

(3) It's important (of us / for us) to brush our teeth three times a day.

2 우리말과 뜻이 같도록 빈칸에 알맞은 말을 쓰시오.

(1) 너희들이 이곳에서 노는 것은 위험하다.
→ It's dangerous _____ _____
_____ _____ here.

(2) 그 책을 이곳에 가져오다니 그녀는 영리하다.
→ It is smart _____ _____ _____
_____ the book here.

(3) 가난한 사람들에게 음식을 주다니 그는 친절하다.
→ It is kind _____ _____ _____
_____ food to the poor.

》 정답과 해설 p.54

13	동명사의 쓰임 1_ 주어, 보어
14	동명사의 쓰임 2_ 목적어

■ **주어 역할:** '~하기는, ~하는 것은'

1 _____ about other cultures is interesting.
다른 문화에 대해 배우는 것은 흥미롭다.

■ **보어 역할:** '~하는 것이다'

My goal is 2 _____ high scores on the test.
나의 목표는 시험에서 높은 점수를 받는 것이다.

■ 3 _____ **역할:** '~하는 것을, ~하기를'

Yuna enjoys running along the river.
유나는 강을 따라 달리는 것을 즐긴다.

Thank you for 4 _____ me. 나를 초대해줘서 고마워.

15	동명사나 to부정사만 목적어로 쓰는 동사

5 _____ :	enjoy, finish, stop, mind, give up, practice, imagine, avoid 등
6 _____ :	want, hope, wish, expect, decide, plan, need, agree, promise 등

Jack and I enjoyed 7 _____ kites after school.
Jack과 나는 방과 후에 연날리기를 즐겼다.

I hope 8 _____ _____ from you soon.
나는 곧 네 소식을 듣기를 바란다.

16	동명사와 to부정사 모두 목적어로 쓰는 동사

■ 동명사와 to부정사를 모두 목적어로 쓰는 동사: like, love, hate, begin, start, continue 등

My stomach began hurting(to hurt) suddenly.
갑자기 내 배가 아프기 시작했다.

■ **동명사와 to부정사를 모두 목적어로 쓰며, 의미가 다른 동사**

remember+동명사	(과거에) ~ 했던 것을 기억하다
forget+9 _____	(과거에) ~ 했던 것을 잊다
remember+10 _____	(미래에) ~ 할 것을 기억하다
forget+to부정사	(미래에) 11 _____
try+동명사	시험 삼아 ~해 보다
try+to부정사	12 _____

I 13 _____ _____ you the story.
나는 너에게 그 이야기를 한 것을 기억한다.

I forgot to tell you the story.
나는 너에게 그 이야기를 한다는 것을 잊었다.

I'll 14 _____ _____ the book.
나는 그 책을 한번 읽어 볼 것이다.

The kids try to read the book.
그 아이들은 그 책을 읽으려고 애쓴다.

17	동명사의 관용 표현

15 _____	~하러 가다
spend (on) -ing	(시간·돈을) ~하는 데 쓰다
feel like -ing	~하고 싶다
on(upon) -ing	~하자마자
be used to -ing	~하는 데 익숙하다
be busy -ing	16 _____
How about -ing?	17 _____
look forward to -ing	~하기를 기대하다
cannot help -ing	~하지 않을 수 없다
It's no use -ing	~해도 소용없다

I 18 _____ _____ _____ out for a walk.
나는 산책하러 나가고 싶다.

I spent the weekend watching movies.
나는 영화를 보는 데 주말을 보냈다.

I'll 19 _____ _____ _____ _____ you
soon. 곧 너를 만나길 기대할게.

1 괄호 안의 말을 바르게 배열하여 문장을 완성하시오. (동사는 동명사 형태로 쓸 것)

(1) _____ is very difficult.
(your, understand, children)

(2) His hobby is _____.
(comic, read, books)

(3) _____ is very important.
(leader, the, choose, right)

2 우리말과 뜻이 같도록 빈칸에 알맞은 말을 쓰시오.

(1) 체중을 줄이는 방법은 매일 달리기를 하는 것이다.
→ The way to lose weight is _____ _____ _____.

(2) 자전거를 타는 것은 너의 건강에 좋다.
→ _____ _____ _____ is good for your health.

1 어법상 어색한 부분을 찾아 고쳐 쓰시오.

(1) She didn't give up try to solve the puzzle.
_____ → _____

(2) She is interested in to watch the stars.
_____ → _____

(3) We enjoyed swims in the river.
_____ → _____

2 우리말과 뜻이 같도록 괄호 안의 말을 이용하여 문장을 완성하시오.

(1) 늦어서 죄송합니다.
→ I am _____ _____ _____ late.
(sorry, be)

(2) 그들은 파티를 여는 것에 대해 이야기하고 있다.
→ They are _____ _____ _____ a party. (talk, have)

(3) 시청으로 가는 길을 알려 주셔서 감사합니다.
→ _____ _____ _____ me the way to City Hall. (thanks, show)

1 빈칸에 알맞은 말을 |보기|에서 골라 올바른 형태로 쓰시오.

┌─ 보기 ──────────────────────┐
│   meet   be   open   │
└────────────────────────────┘

(1) I do not wish _____ silent anymore.

(2) I couldn't imagine _____ you here.

(3) Do you plan _____ a new shop?

2 괄호 안의 말을 빈칸에 알맞은 형태로 쓰시오.

(1) She enjoys _____ on weekends. (hike)

(2) He hopes _____ in peace. (live)

(3) I hope you don't mind _____. (wait)

(4) They want _____ studying Korean history. (keep)

3 밑줄 친 부분을 어법상 바르게 고쳐 쓰시오.

(1) I need to give up go on a diet.
→ _____

(2) She promised be on time.
→ _____

(3) He decided take a taxi home.
→ _____

(4) You'd better practice ride your bike.
→ _____

4 우리말과 뜻이 같도록 빈칸에 알맞은 말을 쓰시오.

(1) 그는 그것을 다시 시도하기를 원했다.
→ He _____ _____ _____ it again.

(2) 그녀는 상자 안을 들여다보는 것을 피했다.
→ She _____ _____ into the box.

(3) 그들은 여행에 대해 이야기하기를 멈추었다.
→ They _____ _____ about the trip.

(4) 그녀는 그 빨간 차를 사는 것에 동의했다.
→ She _____ _____ _____ the red car.

1 괄호 안에서 알맞은 것을 <u>모두</u> 고르시오.

(1) I love (playing / to play) with my dogs.

(2) She began (keeping / to keep) a diary in English.

(3) I tried (to meet / meet) him, but he didn't want to meet me.

(4) Remember (to turn / turning) the light off before leaving.

2 괄호 안의 말을 빈칸에 알맞은 형태로 쓰시오.

(1) I remember _____ him at that place last week. (see)

(2) Mia and I started _____ how to play chess. (learn)

(3) You should not forget _____ him tomorrow. (call)

3 어법상 <u>어색한</u> 부분을 찾아 고쳐 쓰시오.

(1) I stopped mailing a letter on the way home.

_____ → _____

(2) We should remember bringing our lunch to the picnic tomorrow.

_____ → _____

(3) I forgot to be in the hospital when I was four.

_____ → _____

4 다음 문장을 밑줄 친 부분에 유의하여 바르게 해석하시오.

(1) He <u>forgot lending</u> her money yesterday.
→ _____

(2) Don't <u>forget to lock</u> the door.
→ _____

(3) <u>Try buying</u> things on the Internet.
→ _____

(4) I <u>tried to keep</u> my eyes open.
→ _____

1 빈칸에 알맞은 말을 |보기|에서 골라 올바른 형태로 쓰시오.

> 보기
> do   write   see

(1) I'm looking forward to _____ you.

(2) He is busy _____ the invitation cards.

(3) I don't want to spend my time _____ nothing.

2 어법상 <u>어색한</u> 부분을 찾아 고쳐 쓰시오.

(1) Will you go shop with me tomorrow?

_____ → _____

(2) It's no use ask your mom.

_____ → _____

(3) How about eat out tonight?

_____ → _____

3 다음 문장을 밑줄 친 부분에 유의하여 바르게 해석하시오.

(1) They <u>couldn't help laughing</u> at his funny face.
→ _____

(2) I'm <u>looking forward to visiting</u> Turkey.
→ _____

(3) He <u>is used to speaking</u> in front of many people.
→ _____

4 우리말과 뜻이 같도록 빈칸에 알맞은 말을 쓰시오.

(1) 아빠와 나는 오늘 밤 낚시하러 갈 것이다.
→ My dad and I will _____ _____ tonight.

(2) 나는 뜨거운 것을 마시고 싶다.
→ I _____ _____ _____ something hot.

» 정답과 해설 p.54

18 현재완료의 쓰임과 형태

- 현재완료는 「have(has)+¹_____」로 나타내며, 과거에 일어난 일이 현재까지 영향을 미칠 때 쓴다. 특정한 ²_____ 시점을 나타내는 부사(구)나 ³_____이 이끄는 부사절과는 같이 쓸 수 없다.

I have been to London before. 〈현재완료〉
나는 전에 런던에 다녀온 적이 있다.

I went to London last year. 〈과거〉
나는 작년에 런던에 갔다.

19 현재완료의 부정문과 의문문

부정문	주어+have(has) not+과거분사 ~.
의문문	⁴_____+주어+과거분사 ~?

They have not(haven't) seen a rainbow.
그들은 무지개를 본 적이 없다.

She ⁵_____ _____ played soccer before.
그녀는 전에 축구를 해 본 적이 없다.

Have you finished your homework? 네 숙제를 다 끝냈니?

- Yes, I ⁶_____. / No, I haven't.
응, 끝냈어. / 아니, 끝내지 못했어.

20 현재완료의 의미 1_ 완료

- '(벌써, 지금 막) ~했다'는 뜻으로, 주로 already(이미, 벌써), yet(아직), ⁷_____(지금 막) 등의 부사와 쓰여 과거에 일어난 일이 현재에 막 완료된 경우를 나타낸다.

Today's guest has just ⁸_____.
오늘의 손님이 지금 막 도착했다.

We have ⁹_____ had dinner. 우리는 이미 저녁을 먹었다.

The students haven't finished reading the book ¹⁰_____. 학생들은 아직 그 책을 읽는 것을 끝마치지 못했다.

21 현재완료의 의미 2_ 결과

- '~해 버렸다 (그래서 현재 …하다)'는 뜻으로, 과거에 일어난 일이 현재의 결과에 대한 원인일 때 쓴다.

I've ¹¹_____ my arm. I cannot play basketball now.
나는 팔이 부러졌다. 나는 지금 농구를 할 수 없다.

He ¹²_____ _____ his smartphone since yesterday.
그는 어제 그의 스마트폰을 잃어버렸다.

22 현재완료의 의미 3_ 경험

- '¹³_____'는 뜻으로, 주로 ever, never, once, twice, ~ times, before 등의 부사와 쓰여 과거부터 현재까지의 경험을 나타낸다.

I ¹⁴_____ _____ to France three times.
나는 프랑스에 세 번 가 본 적이 있다.

They have eaten pasta many times ¹⁵_____.
그들은 이전에 파스타를 여러 번 먹어 본 적이 있다.

23 현재완료의 의미 4_ 계속

- '~해 오고 있다'는 뜻으로, 주로 ¹⁶_____(~ 동안), since (~ 이후로) 등의 말과 쓰여 과거에 시작된 동작이 현재까지 계속되는 경우를 나타낸다.

She ¹⁷_____ _____ in this town for 10 years.
그녀는 10년 동안 이 마을에서 살고 있다.

I have learned Japanese ¹⁸_____ last year.
나는 작년부터 일본어를 배워왔다.

1 괄호 안의 말을 빈칸에 알맞은 형태로 쓰시오.

(1) He has just _____ out. (go)

(2) I have _____ my wallet at home. (leave)

(3) I have _____ my passport. (lose)

(4) Tom has _____ all of his money. (spend)

2 괄호 안에서 알맞은 것을 고르시오.

(1) Pat (rides / has ridden) a camel twice.

(2) We (have been / went) to India two years ago.

(3) When (did you buy / have you bought) your notebook computer?

(4) We (have swum / swam) in this lake before.

3 밑줄 친 부분을 어법상 바르게 고쳐 쓰시오.

(1) We has just opened the textbook.

→ _____

(2) He has arrived one hour ago.

→ _____

(3) She has live in this town for 10 years.

→ _____

(4) I visit Korean Folk Village last week.

→ _____

4 괄호 안의 말을 이용하여 우리말을 영작하시오. (동사는 현재완료 시제로 쓸 것)

(1) 나는 이미 내 숙제를 끝냈다.

(already, do my homework)

→ _____

(2) David는 일주일 동안 계속 병원에 있다.

(be in hospital, for)

→ _____

(3) 나는 태국 음식을 한 번 먹어 본 적이 있다.

(eat Thai food, once)

→ _____

1 괄호 안에서 알맞은 것을 고르시오.

(1) I (have not crossed / have crossed not) the road at a red light.

(2) I (never have seen / have never seen) such a large park before.

(3) (Have they known / Have known they) each other for 10 years?

2 다음 문장에 not을 넣어 부정문으로 바꿔 쓰시오.

(1) I have touched your bag.

→ _____

(2) Scientists have found a new planet.

→ _____

(3) I have done my English homework.

→ _____

3 다음 문장을 의문문으로 바꿔 쓰시오.

(1) She has visited Los Angeles before.

→ _____

(2) You have returned the book to the library.

→ _____

(3) You have thought about the future of Korea.

→ _____

4 괄호 안의 말을 빈칸에 알맞은 형태로 쓰시오.

(1) I _____ _____ _____ my own car. (never, have)

(2) _____ you _____ _____ such a beautiful garden? (ever, see)

(3) They _____ _____ _____ their work yet. (finish, not)

1 빈칸에 알맞은 말을 |보기|에서 골라 올바른 형태로 쓰시오.

> |보기|
> hear   finish   come   go

(1) They _____ not _____ painting the wall yet.

(2) My parents _____ already _____ to bed.

(3) My mom _____ just _____ back from the office.

(4) The students _____ already _____ about the festival.

2 밑줄 친 부분을 어법상 바르게 고쳐 쓰시오.

(1) Ron and Jina just have got married.

→ _____

(2) I have written already a letter to her.

→ _____

3 괄호 안의 말을 바르게 배열하여 문장을 완성하시오.

(1) He _____.
(my store, has, walked into, just)

(2) Ashley _____.
(already, fixed, has, the door)

(3) I _____.
(just, watched, an animation, have)

4 우리말과 뜻이 같도록 빈칸에 알맞은 말을 쓰시오.

(1) Joanne은 이미 10개의 메시지를 보냈다.
→ Joanne _____ 10 messages.

(2) Smith 씨는 막 말에서 떨어졌다.
→ Mr. Smith _____ off the horse.

(3) 그는 아직 이곳에 도착하지 않았다.
→ He _____ here _____.

1 빈칸에 알맞은 말을 |보기|에서 골라 올바른 형태로 쓰시오.

> |보기|
> lose   repair   stop

(1) It _____ _____ snowing. It is fine now.

(2) I _____ _____ my car key. I can't open my car now.

(3) She _____ _____ the broken phone. She can use it now.

2 괄호 안의 말을 바르게 배열하여 문장을 완성하시오.

(1) He _____ on the subway.
(left, his, has, sunglasses)

(2) The thief _____.
(my, has, stolen, expensive bag)

3 두 문장을 한 문장으로 쓸 때 괄호 안의 말을 이용하여 빈칸에 알맞은 말을 쓰시오.

(1) He washed his shoes. So, his shoes are clean now. (wash)
→ He _____ _____ his shoes.

(2) My sister broke my camera. So, I don't have a camera now. (break)
→ My sister _____ _____ my camera.

4 우리말과 뜻이 같도록 빈칸에 알맞은 말을 쓰시오.

(1) 나는 그녀의 전화번호를 잊어버렸다. (그녀에게 전화할 수 없다.)
→ I _____ _____ her phone number.

(2) 그 남자는 자기 나라로 가버렸다. (지금 여기에 없다.)
→ The man _____ _____ _____ his country.

1 빈칸에 알맞은 말을 |보기|에서 골라 올바른 형태로 쓰시오.

> | 보기 |
> study　　travel　　see

(1) I _____ _____ Japanese before.

(2) Sarah _____ _____ a ghost before.

(3) Henry _____ _____ by airplane many times.

2 괄호 안의 말을 빈칸에 알맞은 형태로 쓰시오.

(1) I _____ _____ to the Great Wall three times. (be)

(2) She _____ _____ the lottery once. (win)

(3) He _____ _____ in Ulsan before. (work)

3 우리말과 뜻이 같도록 빈칸에 알맞은 말을 쓰시오.

(1) 나는 전에 예랑이를 만난 적이 있다.
　　→ I _____ _____ Yerang before.

(2) 우리는 런던에 여러 번 가 보았다.
　　→ We _____ _____ to London several times.

(3) 그녀는 그 작가의 소설을 읽은 적이 있다.
　　→ She _____ _____ the writer's novel.

4 다음 문장을 밑줄 친 부분에 유의하여 바르게 해석하시오.

(1) I have eaten frogs once.
　　→ _____

(2) I have watched a sunrise twice.
　　→ _____

(3) My family have had a pet before.
　　→ _____

---

1 괄호 안에서 알맞은 것을 고르시오.

(1) We have known him (for / since) 10 years.

(2) I have had the camera (for / since) 2004.

(3) Angelina has collected coins from other countries (for / since) many years.

2 괄호 안의 말을 빈칸에 알맞은 형태로 쓰시오.

(1) It _____ _____ heavily for 2 days. (snow)

(2) He _____ _____ in Korea since 1999. (be)

(3) She _____ _____ him since she first met him. (love)

3 우리말과 뜻이 같도록 빈칸에 알맞은 말을 쓰시오.

(1) 그들은 3년 동안 여기에서 일하고 있다.
　　→ They _____ _____ here _____ 3 years.

(2) Jack은 지난 달부터 요리를 배우고 있다.
　　→ Jack _____ _____ to cook _____ last month.

(3) James는 20년 동안 학생들에게 수학을 가르치고 있다.
　　→ James _____ _____ students math _____ 20 years.

4 다음 문장을 밑줄 친 부분에 유의하여 바르게 해석하시오.

(1) She has practiced dancing for 2 years.
　　→ _____

(2) We have been best friends since childhood.
　　→ _____

» 정답과 해설 p.55

24 can, could

■ **can**: 능력, 허락, 요청 등의 의미를 나타내며, 부정형은
「1_____(can't)+동사원형」으로 쓴다.

2_____	Anna can(is able to) solve the problem. Anna는 그 문제를 풀 수 있다.
3_____	You can(may) watch TV after finishing your homework. 너는 숙제를 마친 후에 TV를 봐도 좋다.
요청	Can you hand me the pencil case? 나한테 그 필통 좀 건네줄래?

■ **could**: 의문문에 쓰여 정중한 요청을 나타낸다.

25 will

■ will은 미래에 대한 예정, 의지 또는 요청의 의미를 나타내며, 부정형은 「will not(4_____)+동사원형」으로 쓴다.

5_____	My sister will be ten years old next year. 내 여동생은 내년이면 열 살이 될 것이다.
6_____	I will try my best. 나는 최선을 다해 노력할 것이다.
요청	Will you open the door? 문을 열어주시겠어요?

26 may, might

■ **may**: 허락 또는 불확실한 추측의 의미를 나타내며, 부정형은 「may not+동사원형」으로 쓴다.

7_____	You may take my umbrella with you. 너는 내 우산을 가져가도 좋다.
8_____	Mike may know how to play this game. Mike는 이 게임을 하는 방법을 알지도 모른다.

■ **might**: 주로 불확실한 추측을 나타낸다.

27 must, have to

■ **must**: 강한 추측 또는 의무를 나타내며, 부정형 「must not+동사원형」은 금지의 의미를 나타낸다.

■ **have to**: 의무를 나타내며, 부정형 「don't have to+동사원형」은 불필요의 의미를 나타낸다.

9_____	He is tall with red hair. He must be Jerry. 그는 붉은 머리에 키가 크다. 그는 Jerry임이 틀림없다.
10_____	I must take this book back to the library. 나는 이 책을 도서관에 반납해야 한다.
금지	You 11_____ _____ _____ to your friends. 너는 친구들에게 거짓말하면 안 된다.
의무	You 12_____ _____ (must) finish your report today. 너는 네 보고서를 오늘 끝내야 한다.
불필요	We don't have to go to school on Saturday. 우리는 토요일에 학교에 갈 필요가 없다.

28 should, had better

■ **should**: 도덕적 의무 또는 충고를 나타내며 의무를 나타낼 때 ought to와 바꿔 쓸 수 있다. 「should not(shouldn't)+동사원형」은 금지를 나타낸다.

13_____	You should(ought to) be quiet in the library. 도서관에서는 조용히 해야 한다.
14_____	You should(ought to) take some rest. 너는 휴식을 좀 취하는 것이 좋겠다.

■ **had better**: 충고의 의미를 나타내며, 부정형은 「had better not+동사원형」으로 쓴다.
You 15_____ _____ _____ waste your money. 너는 네 돈을 낭비하지 않는 것이 좋겠다.

29 used to, would

■ **used to**: 과거의 습관이나 과거의 상태를 나타낸다.
I 16_____ _____ _____ swimming on weekends.
나는 주말마다 수영하러 가곤 했었다.

■ **would**: 과거에 반복되었던 행동을 나타낼 때 쓰며, 과거의 상태를 나타낼 때는 쓸 수 없다.
I 17_____ _____ my grandparents every Christmas.
나는 크리스마스마다 조부모님을 방문하곤 했다.

1 밑줄 친 부분의 의미를 |보기|에서 골라 쓰시오.

> ┌─ 보기 ┌─
> 　　　허락　　　능력　　　요청
> └────────────────────┘

(1) Can you pass me the salt, please?　_____

(2) He can play the cello very well.　_____

(3) You can stay in my house tonight.　_____

2 괄호 안에서 알맞은 것을 고르시오.

(1) Hyemi (was / could) able to get home before six.

(2) He couldn't speak Chinese last year, but he (can / is able) speak it now.

(3) I have a bad cold, so I (could / couldn't) go to work.

3 다음 문장과 뜻이 같도록 빈칸에 알맞은 말을 쓰시오.

(1) Can I sit here?

→ _____ I sit here?

(2) Can you drive a truck?

→ Are you _____ _____ drive a truck?

(3) I wasn't able to walk when I was two.

→ I _____ walk when I was two.

4 다음 문장을 밑줄 친 부분에 유의하여 바르게 해석하시오.

(1) You can ride my bike.

→ _____

(2) Could you tell me the time, please?

→ _____

(3) Jane wasn't able to catch the first train.

→ _____

(4) My grandparents can use a computer.

→ _____

---

1 다음 문장을 will을 이용하여 미래를 나타내는 문장으로 바꿀 때 빈칸에 알맞은 말을 쓰시오.

(1) It isn't cold this morning.

→ It _____ cold this afternoon.

(2) We are fifteen years old this year.

→ We _____ sixteen years old next year.

(3) He cuts down trees every weekend.

→ He _____ down trees next Saturday.

2 괄호 안의 말을 바르게 배열하여 문장을 완성하시오.

(1) When _____ the plant? (water, will, you)

(2) I _____ again. (not, do, will, that)

(3) _____ the way to the bus stop? (will, you, me, show)

(4) _____ for Sena's birthday? (buy, you, what, will)

3 어법상 어색한 부분을 찾아 고쳐 쓰시오.

(1) Will does he take a trip?

_____ → _____

(2) He not will call you.

_____ → _____

(3) My sister will is a musician in the future.

_____ → _____

4 우리말과 뜻이 같도록 빈칸에 알맞은 말을 쓰시오.

(1) 그는 샌드위치를 먹을 것이다.

→ He _____ sandwiches.

(2) 나는 이 편지들을 보내지 않을 것이다.

→ I _____ these letters.

1 밑줄 친 부분이 허락의 의미인지, 추측의 의미인지 쓰시오.

(1) You <u>may</u> be surprised to hear it. _____

(2) You <u>may</u> eat my cookies. _____

(3) <u>May</u> I speak to Mr. Jo, please? _____

(4) He <u>may</u> not meet his friends today. _____

2 괄호 안에서 알맞은 것을 <u>모두</u> 고르시오.

(1) (May / Can) I get some water?

(2) You (can / might) like the shirt.

(3) I (may / might) go over to Jane's house later.

(4) She is Andy's classmate. She (may / can) know his number.

3 괄호 안의 말을 이용하여 우리말을 영작하시오.

(1) 내가 너의 스마트폰을 써도 되니?
(may, smartphone)

→ _____

(2) 너는 방과 후에 영화를 보러 가도 된다.
(may, go to the movies)

→ _____

(3) 그녀는 수지의 어머니가 아닐지도 모른다.
(might, Suji's mother)

→ _____

4 다음 문장을 밑줄 친 부분에 유의하여 바르게 해석하시오.

(1) <u>May</u> I borrow your white dress?

→ _____

(2) I <u>might</u> be in the office this evening.

→ _____

(3) He <u>may not</u> be a doctor.

→ _____

1 밑줄 친 부분이 의무의 의미인지, 추측의 의미인지 쓰시오.

(1) You <u>must</u> not sleep in the class. _____

(2) He sings well. He <u>must</u> be a singer. _____

(3) You <u>must</u> be quiet in the museum. _____

2 괄호 안에서 알맞은 것을 고르시오.

(1) My leg hurts. It (must / has to) be broken.

(2) You are not late. You (must not / don't have to) hurry.

(3) You (must not / don't have to) touch the horse. It will kick you.

3 다음 문장과 뜻이 같도록 빈칸에 알맞은 말을 쓰시오.

(1) You must wear a uniform to school.

→ You _____ _____ wear a uniform to school.

(2) She must go to the market to buy some sugar.

→ She _____ _____ go to the market to buy some sugar.

4 우리말과 뜻이 같도록 빈칸에 알맞은 말을 쓰시오.

(1) 너는 또 지각해서는 안 된다.

→ You _____ _____ _____ late again.

(2) 그들은 두 시간 동안 걸어야 했다.

→ They _____ _____ _____ for two hours.

(3) 너는 내 미래에 대해 걱정할 필요 없다.

→ You _____ _____ _____ _____ about my future.

1 빈칸에 알맞은 말을 |보기|에서 골라 should 또는 should not을 이용하여 문장을 완성하시오.

|보기|
play   get   take

(1) You _____ care of your old parents.

(2) He _____ some exercise for his health.

(3) You caught a cold. You _____ in the rain.

2 괄호 안에서 알맞은 것을 고르시오.

(1) She (has better / had better) get some rest.

(2) You (don't should / should not) watch TV all night.

(3) You (had better not / had not better) give so much money to young children.

3 괄호 안의 말을 바르게 배열하여 문장을 완성하시오.

(1) _____ any noise here.
(had, not, you, make, better)

(2) _____ more sleep.
(get, to, Eric, ought)

(3) _____ those colorful clothes.
(not, should, you, wear)

4 우리말과 뜻이 같도록 빈칸에 알맞은 말을 쓰시오.

(1) 너는 다른 사람들에게 친절해야 한다.
→ You _____ _____ _____ to other people.

(2) 너는 패스트푸드를 먹어서는 안 된다.
→ You _____ _____ _____ _____ fast food.

1 빈칸에 알맞은 말을 |보기|에서 골라 쓰시오.

|보기|
be a lake   climb that tree
cook for my parents

(1) Paul would _____ when young.

(2) I would _____ when I lived with them.

(3) There used to _____ around here.

2 괄호 안에서 알맞은 것을 고르시오.

(1) She (would / used to) be a teacher before.

(2) Susan would (often help / often helps) me with my homework.

(3) Tom (would play / used play) basketball with us.

3 다음 문장과 뜻이 같도록 빈칸에 알맞은 말을 쓰시오.

(1) Jenny worked in a bank before, but she doesn't work there now.
→ Jenny _____ _____ _____ in a bank.

(2) There was an apple tree in the backyard before, but now there isn't.
→ _____ _____ _____ _____ an apple tree in the backyard.

4 어법상 어색한 부분을 찾아 고쳐 쓰시오.

(1) My father used to reading books to me.
_____ → _____

(2) There use to be a church over there.
_____ → _____

(3) I would often to go fishing with him.
_____ → _____

» 정답과 해설 p.55

30	수동태의 쓰임과 형태
31	수동태의 부정문과 의문문

■ **수동태:** 「주어+be동사+과거분사+¹_____+목적격(행위자)」

She is ² _____ by everyone.
그녀는 모든 사람들에게 사랑받는다.

■ **부정문:** 「주어+be동사+³_____+과거분사+by+목적격(행위자)」

The bridge was not(wasn't) built in the 1895.
그 다리는 1895년에 건설되지 않았다.

■ **의문문:** 「(의문사)+be동사+주어+⁴_____+by+목적격(행위자)?」

⁵_____ this chair made by your father?
이 의자는 네 아버지에 의해 만들어졌니?

⁶_____ was the wine glass broken?
그 와인 잔은 언제 깨졌니?

32	수동태의 시제 / 조동사가 있는 수동태

■ **수동태과거:** 「was(were)+과거분사」

Chinese food ⁷_____ cooked by Cheng.
중국 음식이 Cheng에 의해 요리되었다.

■ **수동태미래:** 「will be+과거분사」

The fence will be ⁸_____ by Tom.
그 울타리는 Tom에 의해 칠해질 것이다.

■ **조동사를 포함하는 문장의 수동태:** 「조동사+be+과거분사」

Animals should ⁹_____ protected (by people).
동물들은 (사람들에게) 보호받아야 한다.

33	4형식 문장의 수동태

■ 4형식 문장은 두 가지의 수동태를 만들 수 있다.

Mom gave me some apple juice.
엄마가 나에게 약간의 사과 주스를 주셨다.

→ ¹⁰_____ was given some apple juice by Mom.
〈간접목적어가 주어〉: 「간접목적어+be동사+과거분사+직접목적어」

→ Some apple juice was given ¹¹_____ by Mom. 〈직접목적어가 주어〉: 「직접목적어+be동사+과거분사+전치사+간접목적어」

■ **직접목적어를 주어로 수동태를 만들 때 쓰는 전치사**

¹²_____	give, teach, tell, send 등
¹³_____	make, buy, get, cook 등
of	ask, inquire 등

34	5형식 문장의 수동태 1_ 명사, 형용사, to부정사 목적격보어
35	5형식 문장의 수동태 2_ 동사원형 목적격보어

■ 목적격보어가 명사나 형용사, to부정사인 경우, 수동태를 만들 때 목적격보어는 원래의 형태대로 주격보어가 된다.

She ¹⁴_____ Aunt Jenny by us.
그녀는 우리에 의해 Jenny 아줌마라고 불렸다.

You ¹⁵_____ _____ to explain this by them.
너는 그들에게 이것을 설명하도록 요청받았다.

■ 목적격보어가 동사원형인 경우, 수동태를 만들 때 목적격보어를 ¹⁶_____로 바꿔 쓴다.

I was made to clean my room by my father.
내가 내 방을 청소하도록 아버지가 시키셨다.

cf. 목적격보어가 현재분사인 경우, 「be동사+과거분사+현재분사」로 쓴다.
Justin was heard ¹⁷_____ by a lot of people.
Justin이 울고 있는 것이 많은 사람들에게 들렸다.

36	**by 이외의 전치사를 쓰는 수동태**

be interested in	~에 관심이 있다
be worried about	~에 대해 걱정하다
be surprised ¹⁸_____	~에 놀라다
be satisfied with	~에 대해 만족하다
be disappointed at	~에 대해 실망하다
be pleased with	~에 기뻐하다
be made of(from)	~로 만들어지다
be known to	~에게 알려져 있다
be known ¹⁹_____	~로 유명하다
be filled ²⁰_____	~로 가득하다
be covered with	~로 덮여 있다
be crowded with	~로 붐비다

1 다음 문장을 수동태로 바꿔 쓰시오.

(1) Many people buy the book.

→ _____

(2) Chinese people drink tea.

→ _____

(3) Ms. Bin raises two children.

→ _____

(4) The police caught the thief.

→ _____

FOCUS 31 수동태의 부정문과 의문문

1 괄호 안에서 알맞은 것을 고르시오.

(1) (Did / Was) your watch repaired?

(2) The glass wasn't (broke / broken) by Mary.

(3) When was television (inventing / invented)?

(4) That play (didn't / wasn't) written by Shakespeare.

2 다음 문장을 수동태의 부정문으로 바꿔 쓰시오.

(1) They raise cats and dogs in the house.

→ _____

(2) Mr. Kang directed this movie.

→ _____

(3) My children eat a lot of fruits and vegetables.

→ _____

3 다음 문장을 수동태의 의문문으로 바꿔 쓰시오.

(1) You clean this room every day.

→ _____

(2) My brother fixed the bike.

→ _____

(3) Aesop wrote *The Fox and the Grapes*.

→ _____

4 괄호 안의 말을 바르게 배열하여 문장을 완성하시오. (필요한 경우, 단어의 형태를 바꿀 것)

(1) When _____ ?
(break, the window, was)

(2) _____ by him?
(this song, is, sing)

(3) _____ on food.
(spend, not, was, that money)

FOCUS 32 수동태의 시제 / 조동사가 있는 수동태

1 괄호 안에서 알맞은 것을 고르시오.

(1) Some cakes will (bake / be baked) for her.

(2) You should (put / be put) your glasses here.

(3) This parcel must (send / be sent) right now.

2 빈칸에 알맞은 말을 | 보기 |에서 골라 올바른 형태로 쓰시오.

┌─ 보기 ┐
take   change   clean

(1) The plan may _____ _____ by him.

(2) The beautiful photo _____ _____ by me last year.

(3) My room will _____ _____ in thirty minutes.

3 다음 문장을 수동태로 바꿀 때 빈칸에 알맞은 말을 쓰시오.

(1) You should dry your pants.
→ Your pants _____.

(2) He can train the elephants.
→ The elephants _____ by him.

(3) My brother carried the big boxes.
→ The big boxes _____ by my brother.

1 괄호 안에서 알맞은 것을 고르시오.

(1) History was taught (to / for) them by Mr. Kim.

(2) Spaghetti will be cooked (to / for) us by Mom.

(3) The bag was bought (to / for) me by my best friend.

(4) A funny story was told (to / for) us by the old woman.

2 괄호 안의 말을 바르게 배열하여 문장을 완성하시오. (필요한 경우, 단어의 형태를 바꿀 것)

(1) A small box _____.
(to, was, me, send)

(2) A house _____.
(my dog, for, is, make)

(3) I _____ that man.
(how to drive, was, teach, by)

3 밑줄 친 부분을 주어로 바꿔 문장을 다시 쓰시오.

(1) He showed me wonderful magic.
→ _____

(2) Tony gave her an interesting book.
→ _____

(3) She bought me dinner last night.
→ _____

4 대화의 빈칸에 알맞은 말을 쓰시오.

(1) A Did the girl's grandma make her the doll?
B No. The doll _____ the girl by her mom.

(2) A Did Mr. Lee give you the package?
B No. The package _____ me by Mr. Jin.

1 다음 문장을 수동태로 바꿔 쓰시오.

(1) Doing yoga makes us healthy.
→ _____

(2) They call an elevator a lift in England.
→ _____

(3) He told me to stay longer.
→ _____

2 다음 문장을 능동태로 바꿔 쓰시오.

(1) He was elected class president by us.
→ _____

(2) The bottle was found empty by me.
→ _____

(3) He was asked to close the door by her.
→ _____

3 어법상 어색한 부분을 찾아 고쳐 쓰시오.

(1) The boy is thought to be very diligently.
_____ → _____

(2) I was told turn off the computer by him.
_____ → _____

(3) I am expected being a lawyer by her.
_____ → _____

4 우리말과 뜻이 같도록 괄호 안의 말을 이용하여 문장을 완성하시오.

(1) 나는 아빠에게서 세차해 달라는 부탁을 받았다.
(ask, wash)
→ I _____ the car by Dad.

(2) Daniel은 그의 선생님으로부터 열심히 공부하라는 말을 들었다. (tell, study)
→ Daniel _____ hard by his teacher.

(3) 그는 아내에게서 조심히 운전하라는 충고를 들었다.
(advise, drive)
→ He _____ carefully by his wife.

1 빈칸에 알맞은 말을 |보기|에서 골라 올바른 형태로 쓰시오.

┌ 보기 ┐
sing   enter   carry

(1) Kelly was seen _____ her room.

(2) The bell boy was made _____ the suitcase by the man.

(3) The bird was heard _____ a beautiful song by me.

2 다음 문장을 수동태로 바꿔 쓰시오.

(1) The crocodile watched the deer drink water.

→ _____

(2) Mom made Tom brush the baby's hair.

→ _____

(3) He felt the ground shake.

→ _____

3 괄호 안의 말을 바르게 배열하여 문장을 완성하시오.

(1) He _____ out of the building.
(walk, watched, was, to)

(2) She _____ to the library by him.
(made, was, go, to)

(3) The boy _____ the drums by us.
(heard, was, to, play)

4 어법상 어색한 부분을 찾아 고쳐 쓰시오.

(1) The sun was watched rise.

_____ → _____

(2) I was made stop smoking by the doctor.

_____ → _____

(3) He was seen help the workers by his boss.

_____ → _____

1 괄호 안에서 알맞은 것을 고르시오.

(1) My parents were not satisfied (with / at) the result.

(2) I am interested (in / to) playing hockey.

(3) Jane was pleased (with / in) the show.

(4) Cheese is made (to / from) milk.

2 빈칸에 알맞은 말을 쓰시오.

(1) He was surprised _____ her words.

(2) The mountain is covered _____ trees.

(3) Her eyes were filled _____ tears.

3 다음 문장을 밑줄 친 부분에 유의하여 바르게 해석하시오.

(1) The water park was crowded with people.

→ _____

(2) This box is made of gold.

→ _____

(3) His name is known to all the people.

→ _____

(4) The restaurant is known for fresh food.

→ _____

4 우리말과 뜻이 같도록 빈칸에 알맞은 말을 쓰시오.

(1) 우리 부모님은 나를 걱정하신다.
→ My parents _____ _____ me.

(2) 너는 어떤 종류의 취미에 관심이 있니?
→ What kind of hobby _____ you _____ _____?

(3) 그는 그녀의 선물에 실망했다.
→ He _____ _____ _____ her present.

» 정답과 해설 p.56

| 37 | 현재분사의 쓰임과 형태 |
| 38 | 과거분사의 쓰임과 형태 |

| 현재분사 | 「동사원형+[1]_____」 | 능동과 진행 |
| 과거분사 | 「동사원형+-ed」 | [2]_____과 완료 |

The woman [3]_____ over there is my music teacher. 저쪽에서 뛰고 있는 그 여자는 내 음악 선생님이다.

Don't touch that [4]_____ window.
저 깨진 창문을 만지지 마라.

| 39 | [5]_____을 나타내는 분사 |

| 현재분사 | ~한 기분이 들게 하는 | surprising, boring, tiring, exciting, disappointing, satisfying, confusing, shocking 등 |
| 과거분사 | ~한 기분이 드는 | surprised, bored, tired, excited, disappointed, satisfied, confused, shocked 등 |

The news was very [6]_____. 그 소식은 매우 놀라웠다.

People were very [7]_____ at the news.
사람들은 그 소식에 매우 놀랐다.

| 40 | 현재분사와 동명사 |

| 8 | _____ | ~하고 있는 | running girls 달리는 소녀들 |
| 9 | _____ | ~하기 위한 | running shoes 운동화 |

My father is folding paper. 〈현재분사〉
나의 아버지는 종이를 접고 계신다.

My hobby is folding paper frogs. 〈동명사〉
내 취미는 종이 개구리를 접는 것이다.

| 41 | 분사구문 |

- 부사절을 분사구문으로 만들 때는 부사절의 접속사와 [10]_____를 생략하고 동사를 「[11]_____+-ing」로 바꾼다. 분사구문은 이유, 때, 양보, 조건, 동시동작 등 다양한 의미를 나타낸다.

When he arrived at the station, he met his old friend.

→ [12]_____ at the station, he met his old friend.
그 역에 도착했을 때, 그는 그의 오랜 친구를 만났다.

FOCUS 37 현재분사의 쓰임과 형태

1 괄호 안의 말을 빈칸에 알맞은 형태로 쓰시오.

(1) The _____ horse must be Tony's. (run)

(2) Look at the farmers _____ in the field. (work)

(3) A strange man is _____ at me. (look)

2 밑줄 친 부분을 수식하는 부분을 찾아 밑줄을 그으시오.

(1) Who is the girl sitting on the bench?

(2) The man reading a book is a famous actor.

(3) The cell phone ringing in the kitchen is yours.

3 괄호 안의 말을 바르게 배열하여 문장을 완성하시오.

(1) I love the _____.
(towards, girl, walking, us)

(2) The _____ is my aunt.
(wearing, lady, a, dress, white)

4 우리말과 뜻이 같도록 괄호 안의 말을 배열하여 문장을 완성하시오. (필요한 경우, 단어의 형태를 바꿀 것)

(1) 그 웃고 있는 아기는 그들을 행복하게 했다.
(smile, made, the, baby)
→ _____ them happy.

(2) 그 호수에서 수영하고 있는 아이는 진주이다.
(swim, the, in, child, lake)
→ The _____ is Jinju.

1 괄호 안에서 알맞은 것을 고르시오.

(1) Every dog (has / have) its day.

(2) I have six kittens. (Every / Each) of the kittens has a name.

(3) Every (girl / girls) has a dream in her heart.

2 어법상 <u>어색한</u> 부분을 찾아 고쳐 쓰시오.

(1) Every building in Seoul are very modern.

_____ → _____

(2) Each of the book is cheap.

_____ → _____

(3) Each day and each hour bring us something new.

_____ → _____

(4) Every students in my class didn't do the homework.

_____ → _____

3 우리말과 뜻이 같도록 빈칸에 알맞은 말을 쓰시오.

(1) 이 거리의 모든 집이 똑같다.

→ _____ house on this street _____ the same.

(2) 너희들 각각이 표 한 장당 60달러를 지불해야 한다.

→ _____ of you _____ to pay $60 per ticket.

(3) 그 극장의 모든 좌석이 자리가 찼다.

→ _____ _____ in the theater is taken.

4 다음 문장을 밑줄 친 부분에 유의하여 바르게 해석하시오.

(1) What is in <u>each</u> box?

→ _____

(2) <u>Every</u> member in the club has his / her own talent.

→ _____

1 괄호 안에서 알맞은 것을 고르시오.

(1) All his money (was / were) stolen.

(2) (Both / All) of my parents work.

(3) (All / Both) teenagers like the songs of the group.

(4) Both of his (brother / brothers) are famous musicians.

2 다음 문장에서 어법상 <u>어색한</u> 부분을 찾아 고쳐 쓰시오.

(1) I will buy all three shirt.

_____ → _____

(2) Both of the bus go to the subway station.

_____ → _____

(3) All of the food have gone.

_____ → _____

(4) Both of the man love the lady.

_____ → _____

3 다음 문장과 뜻이 같도록 빈칸에 알맞은 말을 쓰시오.

(1) Every window is open.

→ All the _____ _____ open.

(2) Every room in this building has a heating system.

→ All the _____ in this building _____ a heating system.

(3) Every worker has to wear a uniform during working hours.

→ All _____ _____ to wear a uniform during working hours.

4 우리말과 뜻이 같도록 빈칸에 알맞은 말을 쓰시오.

(1) 그녀의 모든 음악은 대부분의 사람들을 감동시킨다.

→ _____ of her _____ moves most people.

(2) Jimmy는 장갑을 양쪽 다 잃어버렸다.

→ Jimmy has lost _____ of his _____.

1 괄호 안에서 알맞은 것을 고르시오.

(1) The teacher always gives (ourselves / us) a lot of homework.

(2) I bought (myself / me) a new pair of shoes.

(3) **A** Who fixed the computer?

B Mr. Lee fixed it (itself / himself).

2 밑줄 친 부분을 어법상 바르게 고쳐 쓰시오.

(1) He hurt <u>him</u> while he was running.

→ _____

(2) Mary made the dress for <u>himself</u>.

→ _____

(3) Don't worry about us. We can take care of <u>ourself</u>.

→ _____

3 빈칸에 알맞은 말을 | 보기 |에서 골라 재귀대명사와 함께 쓰시오. (필요한 경우 단어의 형태를 바꿀 것)

| 보기 |
think about   burn   cover

(1) I picked up a hot plate. So I _____.

(2) It's cold. _____ with a blanket, Jim.

(3) They never think about other people. They only _____.

4 다음 문장을 밑줄 친 부분에 유의하여 바르게 해석하시오.

(1) I wrote this poem <u>myself</u>.

→ _____

(2) She said to <u>herself</u>, "I am the prettiest in the world."

→ _____

(3) Mary got up late and didn't have time to wash <u>herself</u>.

→ _____

---

1 다음 문장과 뜻이 같도록 빈칸에 알맞은 말을 쓰시오.

(1) I often go on a trip by myself.

→ I often go on a trip _____.

(2) The car operated automatically.

→ The car operated _____ _____.

(3) My 10-year-old sister baked this cake without any help.

→ My 10-year-old sister baked this cake _____ _____.

2 대화의 빈칸에 알맞은 말을 재귀대명사를 이용하여 쓰시오.

(1) **A** Can I have these cookies?

B _____ _____ to all of them.

(2) **A** How was her vacation?

B Great. She _____ _____.

(3) **A** Did he go to the festival with his girlfriend?

B No. He went there _____ _____.

3 어법상 어색한 부분을 찾아 고쳐 쓰시오.

(1) Tim and Jane, help yourself to anything you like.

_____ → _____

(2) My tooth has come out for itself.

_____ → _____

(3) Between ourself, I didn't do my best.

_____ → _____

4 다음 문장을 밑줄 친 부분에 유의하여 바르게 해석하시오.

(1) Children must not be home <u>by themselves</u> at night.

→ _____

(2) <u>Help yourself</u> to these cookies on the table.

→ _____

» 정답과 해설 p.57

48 -thing+형용사 / the+형용사

■ -thing, -body, -one으로 끝나는 대명사: 형용사가 ¹_____에서 수식한다.

I feel cold. Give me something hot. 추워. 뜨거운 것 좀 줘.

■ the+형용사: '~한 사람들' = 「형용사+복수 보통명사」

The young have to respect the ²_____.
젊은 사람들은 나이 든 사람들을 존경해야 한다.

49 수량형용사

■ (대)명사 앞에 쓰여 명사의 수와 양을 나타내는 형용사이다.

	몇 개의 / 약간의	⁴_____	많은	
셀 수 있는 명사 앞	a few	few	many	a lot of / lots of
셀 수 없는 명사 앞	³_____	little	⁵_____	

There is ⁶_____sugar in the bowl.
그릇에 설탕이 거의 없다.

50 some, any

■ some은 '어떤 ~, 몇몇의'라는 뜻으로 긍정문과 권유문에, any는 '어떤 ~도, 아무 ~도'라는 뜻으로 ⁷_____과 의문문에 쓰인다.

⁸_____ boy asked me how to get to the library.
어떤 소년이 나에게 도서관에 어떻게 가는지 물었다.

Are there ⁹_____ forks on the table?
식탁 위에 포크가 있니?

51 이어동사

■ 이어동사는 「타동사+부사」이며, 목적어에 따라 어순이 다르다.

목적어가 명사인 경우	「동사+명사+부사」/「동사+부사+명사」
목적어가 ¹⁰_____인 경우	「동사+대명사+부사」

It's time to turn off the radio.
= It's time to turn the radio ¹¹_____.
이제 라디오를 끌 시간이다.

My aunt tried ¹²_____ on at the clothing shop.
나의 숙모는 그 옷가게에서 그것들을 입어 보셨다.

FOCUS 48 -thing+형용사 / the+형용사

1 괄호 안에서 알맞은 것을 고르시오.

(1) (A / The) beautiful are not always happy.

(2) The young (like / likes) adventures.

(3) (Something nice / Nice something) will happen.

2 우리말과 뜻이 같도록 괄호 안의 말을 배열하여 문장을 완성하시오.

(1) 나는 비행기에서 읽을 것이 없었다.

→ _____ on the plane.
(have, I, to, didn't, read, anything)

(2) 나는 먹을 달콤한 것을 원한다.

→ I want _____.
(sweet, eat, something, to)

FOCUS 49 수량형용사

1 괄호 안에서 알맞은 것을 고르시오.

(1) There (is / are) a little water in the pool.

(2) I ate too (many / much) ice cream last night.

(3) Few (people / person) came to the party because of the heavy rain.

2 다음 문장을 밑줄 친 부분에 유의하여 바르게 해석하시오.

(1) There are <u>few</u> clouds in the sky.

→ _____

(2) I have <u>a little</u> time to have lunch.

→ _____

(3) Tom has <u>few</u> friends at school.

→ _____

3 어법상 어색한 부분을 찾아 고쳐 쓰시오.

(1) I didn't have many homework yesterday.

_____ → _____

(2) The weather will be nice in a little days.

_____ → _____

(3) A lot of beer are in the glass.

_____ → _____

4 우리말과 뜻이 같도록 괄호 안의 말을 배열하여 문장을 완성하시오.

(1) 겨울 내내 눈이 거의 오지 않았다.

(winter, had, snow, little, all, we)

→ _____

(2) 병 안에 몇 개의 캔디가 있다.

(are, there, in, few, jar, a, candies, the)

→ _____

(3) 나는 커피를 많이 마시지 않는다.

(much, don't, drink, coffee, I)

→ _____

FOCUS 50 some, any

1 어법상 어색한 부분을 찾아 고쳐 쓰시오.

(1) There aren't some cars in the parking lot.

_____ → _____

(2) I need any sugar to make pancakes.

_____ → _____

(3) Are there some questions about this chapter?

_____ → _____

2 우리말과 뜻이 같도록 빈칸에 알맞은 말을 쓰시오.

(1) 나는 일본에 친구가 몇 명 있다.

→ I have _____ _____ in Japan.

(2) 냉장고에 아무 음식이라도 있니?

→ Is there _____ _____ in the fridge?

(3) 차 좀 더 드시겠어요?

→ Would you like _____ _____ _____ ?

---

1 괄호 안에서 알맞은 것을 모두 고르시오.

(1) I'll (pick her up / pick Jane up) at 5.

(2) We (turned it on / turned on it) to keep cool.

(3) Please (hand in your essay / hand in it) by tomorrow.

(4) I (took off my wet boots / took my wet boots off) when I got back.

2 밑줄 친 부분을 괄호 안의 단어로 바꿔 문장을 다시 쓰시오.

(1) Why don't you call up Mr. Jo? (him)

→ _____

(2) The doctor put on his white gown. (it)

→ _____

(3) I'll wake up the tourists when we get there. (them)

→ _____

3 괄호 안의 말을 바르게 배열하여 문장을 완성하시오.

(1) Fire engines arrived to _____.

(out, a fire, put)

(2) Did you _____?

(turn, the light, off)

(3) The woman _____ on the table.

(it, put, down)

4 우리말과 뜻이 같도록 괄호 안의 말을 이용하여 문장을 완성하시오.

(1) 그 신발을 신어 봐도 될까요? (try on)

→ Can I _____?

(2) 장난감들을 같은 곳으로 치워라. (put away)

→ _____ in the same place.

(3) 너의 주머니에서 그것을 꺼내라. (take out)

→ _____ of your pocket.

» 정답과 해설 p.58

52 비교급과 최상급의 규칙 · 불규칙 변화

■ 규칙 변화

	비교급 / 최상급
기본 규칙 변화	+ 1 _____ / + -est
-e로 끝나는 경우	+ -r / + -st
「단모음+단자음」으로 끝나는 경우	자음 반복 + -er /-est
「자음+y」로 끝나는 경우	y → i + -er /-est
3음절 이상 또는 -ful, -ous 등으로 끝나는 경우	more / 2 _____ + 원급

■ 불규칙 변화

good / well - 3 _____ - best
bad / ill - worse - 4 _____
many / much - more - most
little - less - least

53 원급 비교
54 비교급 · 최상급 비교

원급 비교	「5 _____ +원급+as」	~만큼 …한(하게)
	「not as(so)+원급+as」	~만큼 …하지 않은(않게)
비교급 비교	「비교급+6 _____」	~보다 더 …한(하게)
최상급 비교	「7 _____ +최상급 (+in/of+명사)」	~에서 가장 …한(하게)

My brother is as tall 8 _____ my father.
내 오빠는 아버지만큼 키가 크다.
The Earth is 9 _____ than the moon.
지구는 달보다 더 크다.
Mercury is the 10 _____ planet in the solar
system. 수성은 태양계에서 가장 작은 행성이다.
cf. 비교급을 강조할 때 쓰는 부사: 11 _____, far, still, even, a lot

55 as+원급+as+주어+can / 배수사를 이용한 비교
56 비교급+and+비교급 / The+비교급, the+비교급
57 one of the+최상급 / 원급과 비교급을 이용한 최상급

「as+원급+as+주어+can(could)」 (= as+원급+as 12 _____)	가능한 한 ~하게
「배수사+as+원급+as」 (= 배수사+비교급+than)	~보다 … 배 더 -한(하게)
「비교급+and+비교급」	점점 더 ~한(하게)
「The+비교급 ~, the+비교급 …」	~하면 할수록 더 …하다
「one of the+최상급+복수 명사」	가장 ~한 것 중 하나

We visit Grandma as often as we can.
→ We visit Grandma as often as possible.
우리는 가능한 한 자주 할머니를 찾아 뵙는다.
My room is twice as large as yours.
→ My room is twice 13 _____ _____ yours.
내 방은 너의 방보다 두 배 더 크다.
The world is getting smaller 14 _____ smaller.
세계가 점점 더 작아지고 있다.
The sooner we leave, 15 _____ · _____ we arrive.
우리는 더 빨리 출발할수록 더 빨리 도착한다.
The bee is one of the most diligent 16 _____.
벌은 가장 부지런한 곤충 중 하나이다.

■ 원급과 비교급을 이용한 최상급

원급	「17 _____ (other) ~ as(so)+원급+as」
비교급	「No (other) ~ 비교급+than」
	「비교급+than any other+18 _____」

Sydney is the largest city in Australia.
시드니가 호주에서 가장 큰 도시이다.
→ No (other) city in Australia is as(so) large as Sydney. 호주의 그 어떤 도시도 시드니만큼 크지 않다.
→ No (other) city in Australia is larger than Sydney.
호주의 그 어떤 도시도 시드니보다 크지 않다.
→ Sydney is 19 _____ _____ any other city in Australia. 시드니는 호주의 그 어떤 도시보다 더 크다.

1 빈칸에 알맞은 비교급과 최상급을 쓰시오.

(1) nice — _____ — _____

(2) fat — _____ — _____

(3) pretty — _____ — _____

(4) many — _____ — _____

(5) ill — _____ — _____

(6) well — _____ — _____

2 괄호 안의 말을 빈칸에 알맞은 형태로 쓰시오.

(1) I like bread _____ than rice. (well)

(2) His grade is _____ than mine. (bad)

3 괄호 안에서 알맞은 것을 고르시오.

(1) My sister is (wisest / wiser) than me.

(2) This is the (most tall / tallest) tree in our yard.

(3) Summer is the (hotest / hottest) time of the year.

(4) I think the Russian grammar is (difficulter / more difficult) than the English grammar.

4 우리말과 뜻이 같도록 빈칸에 알맞은 말을 쓰시오.

(1) 그녀는 예전보다 일을 적게 한다.

→ She works _____ than she used to.

(2) 그는 나의 가장 나쁜 적이다.

→ He is my _____ enemy.

(3) 그녀는 그보다 더 많은 돈을 번다.

→ She earns _____ money than he does.

(4) 이것은 이 가게에서 가장 좋은 재킷이다.

→ This is the _____ jacket in this shop.

1 두 문장을 한 문장으로 쓸 때 as ~ as와 괄호 안의 말을 이용하여 문장을 완성하시오.

(1) I get up at six. My sister gets up at six, too.

→ I get up _____ _____ _____ my sister. (early)

(2) This necklace costs $1,000. That ring costs $1,000, too.

→ This necklace is _____ _____ _____ that ring. (expensive)

2 어법상 어색한 부분을 찾아 고쳐 쓰시오.

(1) Your hands are as colder as ice.

_____ → _____

(2) Yujin spoke so quietly as Yuna.

_____ → _____

(3) My grade isn't as high as Mary.

_____ → _____

3 괄호 안의 말을 바르게 배열하여 문장을 완성하시오.

(1) The scene is _____.
(beautiful, as, as, a picture)

(2) I don't know _____ you do.
(people, as, so, many)

(3) Mice are _____.
(as, not, big, cats, as)

4 우리말과 뜻이 같도록 빈칸에 알맞은 말을 쓰시오.

(1) 호수는 바다만큼 깊지 않다.

→ A lake isn't _____ _____ _____ an ocean.

(2) Frank는 그 피아니스트만큼 피아노를 잘 친다.

→ Frank plays the piano _____ _____ _____ the pianist.

(3) 버스는 KTX만큼 빠르지 않다.

→ A bus can't go _____ _____ _____ KTX train.

1 괄호 안에서 알맞은 것을 고르시오.

(1) Roses are (much / very) prettier than sunflowers.

(2) Baseball is the most exciting of all the (sport / sports).

(3) History books are less (funny / funnier) than comic books.

2 괄호 안의 말을 빈칸에 알맞은 형태로 쓰시오.

(1) Your candy tastes _____ than mine. (sweet)

(2) August is usually _____ than June. (hot)

(3) My family is _____ of all. (important)

(4) This is _____ bridge in this country. (wide)

3 두 문장의 내용과 일치하도록 빈칸에 알맞은 말을 쓰시오.

(1) Ann is younger than Judy. Judy is younger than Tony.
→ Ann is _____ _____ of all.

(2) Mina is wiser than Yumi. Yumi is wiser than Bomi.
→ Mina is _____ _____ of the three.

4 다음 문장과 뜻이 같도록 빈칸에 알맞은 말을 쓰시오.

(1) Bob is more handsome than Andy.
→ Andy is _____ _____ _____ Bob.

(2) Music isn't as interesting as art to me.
→ Art is _____ _____ _____ music to me.

(3) An airplane is faster than a train.
→ A train is _____ _____ an airplane.

1 다음 문장과 뜻이 같도록 빈칸에 알맞은 말을 쓰시오.

(1) I want you to speak as clearly as possible.
→ I want you to speak as clearly as _____ _____.

(2) She spoke as slowly as possible.
→ She spoke as slowly as _____ _____.

(3) Jean eats twice as fast as Seri.
→ Jean eats twice _____ _____ Seri.

(4) I have one-third more books than he has.
→ I have one-third _____ _____ _____ _____ he has.

2 괄호 안의 말을 바르게 배열하여 문장을 완성하시오.

(1) He read books _____.
(possible, as, as, much)

(2) I'll wait for you _____.
(as, I, long, can, as)

(3) Russia is _____.
(as, twice, Brazil, big, as)

(4) He received _____.
(than, three times, me, more presents)

3 다음 문장을 밑줄 친 부분에 유의하여 바르게 해석하시오.

(1) I'll finish it as quickly as I can.
→ _____

(2) She kicked the ball as far as possible.
→ _____

(3) She ate three times as much as I did.
→ _____

(4) This rope is five times thicker than that one.
→ _____

1 빈칸에 알맞은 말을 |보기|에서 골라 「비교급+and+비교급」 형태로 쓰시오.

> |보기|
> important   fast   loud

(1) He drove _____ until she told him to slow down.

(2) The noise outside became _____ _____.

(3) The Internet is becoming _____ _____ in our lives.

2 어법상 어색한 부분을 찾아 고쳐 쓰시오.

(1) The higher we climb, thinner the air is.

_____ → _____

(2) You are getting tall and tall every year.

_____ → _____

3 우리말과 뜻이 같도록 빈칸에 알맞은 말을 쓰시오.

(1) 그는 점점 더 가난해졌다.

→ He got _____ _____ _____.

(2) 네가 빨리 운전할수록, 우리는 그곳에 더 일찍 도착할 것이다.

→ _____ _____ you drive, _____ _____ we will get there.

(3) 호텔이 싸면 쌀수록 서비스는 더 나쁘다.

→ _____ _____ the hotel is, _____ _____ the service is.

4 다음 문장을 밑줄 친 부분에 유의하여 바르게 해석하시오.

(1) Your English is getting better and better.

→ _____

(2) The older the girl grew, the more beautiful she became.

→ _____

1 괄호 안에서 알맞은 것을 고르시오.

(1) I think Vincent van Gogh is one of the greatest (artist / artists) ever.

(2) (No / Any) show is so funny as this.

(3) This is deeper than any other (lake / lakes) in this area.

2 |보기|와 같이 최상급 표현을 이용하여 문장을 완성하시오.

> |보기|
> He is a very good actor.
> → He is one of the best actors in Korea.

(1) The ant is a very busy insect.

→ The ant is _____ in the world.

(2) Today is a very cold day.

→ Today is _____ this winter.

3 어법상 어색한 부분을 찾아 고쳐 쓰시오.

(1) Some of the students like music better than no other subject.

_____ → _____

(2) No other students is politer than Eric in his class.

_____ → _____

4 우리말과 뜻이 같도록 괄호 안의 단어를 이용하여 문장을 완성하시오.

> '대부'는 가장 흥미로운 영화이다. (interesting)

(1) The Godfather is the _____ _____ movie.

(2) The Godfather is _____ _____ _____ any other movie.

(3) _____ movie is _____ _____ than The Godfather.

(4) _____ movie is _____ _____ as The Godfather.

» 정답과 해설 p.58

58	관계대명사 who	59	관계대명사 whose
60	관계대명사 whom	61	관계대명사 which
62	관계대명사 that		

■ **관계대명사**: 접속사와 대명사의 역할을 동시에 하며, 앞에 나온 명사(¹_____)를 꾸며 준다.

선행사	주격	소유격	목적격
사람	who	whose	who(m)
사물·동물	which	whose	which
사람·사물·동물	that	–	that
없음(선행사포함)	what	–	what

The boy ²_____ broke the window ran away.
〈주격 관계대명사〉 창문을 깬 그 소년은 도망가 버렸다.

The house ³_____ door is green is my cousin's.
〈소유격 관계대명사〉 문이 녹색인 저 집은 내 사촌의 집이다.

The woman ⁴_____ you met this morning is Jessica. 〈목적격 관계대명사〉 네가 오늘 아침에 만난 여자는 Jessica이다.

A dictionary is a book ⁵_____ explains words.
〈주격 관계대명사〉 사전은 어휘를 설명하는 책이다.

■ 관계대명사 that은 who(m)나 which와 바꿔 쓸 수 있으며, 선행사가 다음과 같을 때 주로 쓴다.

> • 최상급, 서수, the only, the very, the same, all 등이 선행사를 꾸며 줄 때
> • 선행사가 -thing으로 끝나는 대명사일 때
> • 선행사가 「사람+동물」, 「사람+사물」일 때

Do you know the girl that(who) is laughing over there? 저기에서 웃고 있는 소녀를 아니?

Let's open the gifts that(which) I got on my birthday.
내가 내 생일에 받은 선물들을 열어 보자.

That's the very question ⁶_____ I want to ask you. 그것이 바로 내가 너에게 묻고 싶은 질문이다.

She bought anything ⁷_____ she needed.
그녀는 그녀가 필요한 (것은) 무엇이든지 샀다.

| 63 | 관계대명사 what |

■ ⁸_____를 포함하는 관계대명사로, ⁹_____의 뜻이다. the thing(s) that(which)으로 바꿔 쓸 수 있다.

The show is what(the thing that) I waited for.
그 쇼는 내가 기다렸던 것이다.

¹⁰_____ I like is this watch.
내가 마음에 들어하는 것은 이 시계다.

Do you know what he said?
너는 그가 말한 것이 무엇인지 아니?

| 64 | 관계대명사의 생략 |

■ ¹¹_____으로 쓰인 관계대명사 who(m), which, that은 생략할 수 있다.

Do you like the new shoes (which(that)) Mom bought you? 엄마가 네게 사 준 새 신발이 마음에 드니?

■ 「주격 관계대명사+¹²_____」는 생략할 수 있다.

The boy (¹³_____ _____) jumping in the rain looks excited. 빗속에서 점프하고 있는 그 소년은 신나 보인다.

| 65 | 관계부사 1_ when, where |
| 66 | 관계부사 2_ why, how |

■ 관계부사는 접속사와 부사의 역할을 동시에 한다.

선행사	시간	장소	이유	방법
관계부사	¹⁴_____	where	¹⁵_____	how

cf. the way와 how는 동시에 쓸 수 없고 둘 중 하나만 쓴다.

I remember the day when my little sister was born. 나는 내 여동생이 태어난 날을 기억한다.

Jake may know a place ¹⁶_____ you can find old books. Jake는 네가 고서를 찾을 수 있는 장소를 알지도 모른다.

Please tell me the reason why you don't talk to me. 나와 말하지 않는 이유를 제발 말해줘.

No one knows ¹⁷_____ the pyramids were built. 아무도 피라미드가 어떻게 지어졌는지(지어진 방법을) 알지 못한다.

1 두 문장을 관계대명사 who를 이용하여 한 문장으로 쓰시오.

(1) Once there was a king. He had a beautiful wife.

→ _____

(2) Eric is the man. He gave her flowers and chocolates.

→ _____

(3) I called the student. He was absent yesterday.

→ _____

2 선행사를 수식하는 관계대명사절을 찾아 밑줄을 그으시오.

(1) The man who stole my purse was caught by a brave young man.

(2) The child who is lying on the bed is my little brother.

3 괄호 안의 말을 바르게 배열하여 문장을 완성하시오.

(1) There are _____.
(baseball, playing, some boys, are, who)

(2) _____ is my friend.
(who, the man, them, to, is, talking)

(3) _____ are very strong.
(live, the people, on the island, who)

4 다음 문장을 밑줄 친 부분에 유의하여 바르게 해석하시오.

(1) There are many people <u>who</u> want to meet you.

→ _____

(2) People <u>who</u> play sports need lots of water.

→ _____

1 두 문장을 관계대명사 whose를 이용하여 한 문장으로 쓰시오.

(1) He had a date with a girl. Her name is Amy.

→ _____

(2) He is a singer. His voice sounds very sweet.

→ _____

(3) I saw a cat. Its eyes were blue.

→ _____

2 빈칸에 알맞은 말을 |보기|에서 골라 올바른 관계대명사와 함께 쓰시오.

> **보기**
> dog is sick   seat is blue
> title is *The Little Prince*

(1) I'm looking for a book _____.
(2) Dave _____ looks so sad.
(3) I have a bicycle _____.

3 괄호 안의 말을 바르게 배열하여 문장을 완성하시오.

(1) I know the girl _____.
(famous, whose, is, a, sister, painter)

(2) I want the room _____.
(are, walls, pink, whose)

(3) Is there a student _____?
(Peter, name, whose, is)

4 다음 문장을 밑줄 친 부분에 유의하여 바르게 해석하시오.

(1) He wants a car <u>whose</u> roof can be opened.

→ _____

(2) Bring me the bag <u>whose</u> color is gold.

→ _____

(3) She has a cat <u>whose</u> fur is white.

→ _____

1 두 문장을 관계대명사 who(m)를 이용하여 한 문장으로 쓰시오.

(1) I won't forget the people. I met them during my trip.

→ _____

(2) The woman left for France. You wanted to meet her.

→ _____

(3) He is the man. She wants to marry him.

→ _____

2 다음 문장을 두 문장으로 쓸 때 빈칸에 알맞은 말을 쓰시오.

(1) This is the lady whom I went there with.
→ This is the lady.

_____

(2) He is the doctor whom I told you about.
→ He is the doctor.

_____

3 괄호 안의 말을 바르게 배열하여 문장을 완성하시오.

(1) Tim is the boy _____.
(fought, I, whom, with)

(2) The girl _____ became an English teacher.
(whom, English, taught, you)

4 다음 문장을 밑줄 친 부분에 유의하여 바르게 해석하시오.

(1) I want to dance with the one <u>whom</u> I really love.

→ _____

(2) He is the man <u>whom</u> I have been looking for.

1 두 문장을 관계대명사 which를 이용하여 한 문장으로 쓰시오.

(1) She has some shirts. They are too small for her.

→ _____

(2) These are candies. Jiyun gave me them yesterday.

→ _____

2 괄호 안에서 알맞은 것을 고르시오.

(1) Have you read this magazine (which / who) I have brought?

(2) This is an animal which (has / have) a long neck.

(3) The movie which they saw yesterday (was / were) moving.

3 다음 문장을 두 문장으로 쓸 때 빈칸에 알맞은 말을 쓰시오.

(1) He has two horses which run very fast.
→ He has two horses.

_____

(2) This is the doll house which I made last month.
→ This is the doll house.

_____

4 다음 문장을 밑줄 친 부분에 유의하여 바르게 해석하시오.

(1) I ate some food <u>which</u> tasted salty.

→ _____

(2) I borrowed books <u>which</u> are about animals.

→ _____

(3) Have you seen the money <u>which</u> I left on the table?

→ _____

FOCUS 62 관계대명사 that

1 괄호 안에서 알맞은 것을 모두 고르시오.

(1) It is the best film (which / that) I have ever seen.

(2) On the street I met an old lady (who / that) was selling vegetables.

(3) Have you listened to the song (that / which) I told you about?

2 밑줄 친 부분과 바꿔 쓸 수 있는 말을 쓰시오.

(1) My friend that I used to play with moved to Gangwondo.

→ _____

(2) Roses are the flowers that my grandparents like best.

→ _____

(3) The boy that broke the classroom mirror ran away.

→ _____

FOCUS 63 관계대명사 what

1 괄호 안에서 알맞은 것을 모두 고르시오.

(1) What (make / makes) me happy is her smile.

(2) We must do (the thing that / what) is right.

(3) What we want to do now (is / are) to get some sleep.

2 빈칸에 알맞은 말을 |보기|에서 골라 쓰시오. (관계대명사를 추가할 것)

> 보기
> I really need   they believe
> you have

(1) _____ is my parents' love.

(2) Be satisfied with _____.

(3) They'll fight for _____.

3 우리말과 뜻이 같도록 빈칸에 알맞은 말을 쓰시오.

(1) You must be interested in _____ _____ _____. (그들이 말하는 것)

(2) He gave the girl _____ _____ _____. (그가 가지고 있던 것)

(3) _____ _____ _____ _____ was his rudeness. (우리를 화나게 한 것)

4 다음 문장을 밑줄 친 부분에 유의하여 바르게 해석하시오.

(1) My parents always buy what is very cheap.

→ _____

(2) I don't believe what you are talking about.

→ _____

(3) What people say is often different from what they think.

→ _____

FOCUS 64 관계대명사의 생략

1 생략할 수 있는 부분을 찾아 밑줄을 그으시오.

(1) Look at the man who is playing the guitar.

(2) This is the newspaper story which was written by my cousin.

(3) This is the boy who they found in the woods.

(4) Do you like the blouse that Nancy is wearing?

2 빈칸에 생략된 말을 쓰시오.

(1) The bag _____ I lent you is my favorite.

(2) That is the guy _____ I saw downtown last night.

(3) The children _____ _____ laughing happily are my friend's children.

1 괄호 안에서 알맞은 것을 고르시오.

(1) I arrived in Paris (when / where) I always wanted to live.

(2) I'm going to Japan in December (when / where) it snows a lot.

(3) That is the factory (when / where) they make lots of cars.

2 두 문장을 관계부사를 이용하여 한 문장으로 쓰시오.

(1) My office is not far from the place. I live there.

→ _____

(2) 2014 was the year. Brazil hosted the World Cup then.

→ _____

3 괄호 안의 말을 바르게 배열하여 문장을 완성하시오. (관계부사를 추가할 것)

(1) Is there _____?

(can, a place, I, ride a skateboard)

(2) Winter is _____.

(go skiing, we, the season, can)

(3) This is _____.

(is buried, the great poet, the place)

4 |보기|와 같이 문장을 바꿀 때 빈칸에 알맞은 말을 쓰시오.

┌ 보기 ┐
My dad was born in Busan.
→ Busan is the place where my dad was born.
└─────┘

(1) We spent our vacation in that city.

→ That city is _____.

(2) I arrived at her house at seven o'clock.

→ Seven o'clock is _____
_____.

1 괄호 안에서 알맞은 것을 고르시오.

(1) She likes (the way / the way how) her boyfriend dresses.

(2) I know the reason (why / how) Peter is so sad.

(3) Parents don't like the (reason / way) their teenage children speak to others.

2 두 문장을 관계부사를 이용하여 한 문장으로 쓰시오.

(1) Tell me the reason. She called me for that reason.

→ _____

(2) Bob told me the way. He finished the work in that way.

→ _____

3 괄호 안의 말을 바르게 배열하여 문장을 완성하시오.

(1) _____ is clear now.

(he, why, upset, the reason, was)

(2) Please tell me _____.

(passed, the way, the test, you)

4 |보기|와 같이 문장을 바꿀 때 빈칸에 알맞은 말을 쓰시오.

┌ 보기 ┐
I solved the difficult problem in that way.
→ That is the way I solved the difficult problem.
└─────┘

(1) Lots of fish died in the river because of this.

→ This is _____.

(2) I got the old book through this way.

→ This is _____.

» 정답과 해설 p.59

67 명령문, and / or ~

명령문, ¹ _____ ~	…해라, 그러면 ~할 것이다
명령문, or ~	…해라, 그렇지 않으면 ~할 것이다

Look at this picture, and you'll find something interesting. 이 그림을 봐라, 그러면 너는 재미있는 무언가를 발견할 것이다.

Keep the salad cold, ² _____ it will go bad soon. 샐러드를 차갑게 보관해라, 그렇지 않으면 곧 상할 것이다.

68 명사절을 이끄는 접속사 that

■ that이 이끄는 명사절이 주어로 쓰일 때는 가주어 it을 사용하여 바꿔 쓸 수 있고, 목적절을 이끄는 접속사 that은 생략할 수 있다.

That Kate hates swimming is certain.

→ ³ _____ is certain that Kate hates swimming.
Kate가 수영을 싫어하는 것은 확실하다.

Sarah knew (⁴ _____) I was lying to her.
Sarah는 내가 그녀에게 거짓말을 하고 있었다는 걸 알고 있었다.

69 시간의 접속사 1 **70** 시간의 접속사 2

⁵ _____	~할 때
while	~하는 동안에
as	~하면서, ~하고 있을 때
before	~하기 전에
⁶ _____	~한 후에
until	~할 때까지
since	~한 이후로 (계속)

Mom made muffins ⁷ _____ I was taking a shower. 내가 샤워를 하고 있는 동안에 엄마가 머핀을 만드셨다.

A baby boy cried ⁸ _____ his mom came back.
한 남자 아기가 엄마가 돌아올 때까지 울었다.

Andy has been sick ⁹ _____ he ate some sushi.
Andy는 초밥을 좀 먹은 이후 계속 아프다.

71 조건의 접속사 **72** 이유의 접속사
73 결과의 접속사 **74** 양보의 접속사

조건	if	만약 ~라면
	unless (= if not)	만약 ~하지 않으면
이유	because, since, as	¹⁰ _____
결과	so	그래서
	so ~ that ...	매우 ~해서 …하다
양보	though, although, even if, even though	비록 ~이지만, 비록 ~일지라도, 비록 ~임에도 불구하고

¹¹ _____ you walk fast, you'll catch the bus.
네가 빨리 걸으면 너는 그 버스를 탈 것이다.

You may get sick ¹² _____ you take some rest.
좀 쉬지 않으면 너는 아프게 될지도 모른다.

¹³ _____ it was raining, we stayed indoors.
비가 오고 있었기 때문에 우리는 실내에 머물렀다.

Alex ate ¹⁴ _____ much that he had to loosen his belt. Alex는 너무 많이 먹어서 허리띠를 풀어야 했다.

¹⁵ _____ he is old, he is very strong and healthy.
그는 비록 나이 들었지만 힘이 아주 세고 건강하다.

75 상관접속사

both A ¹⁶ _____ B	A와 B 둘 다
not (only) A but (also) B (= B as well as A)	A뿐만 아니라 B도
not A but B	¹⁷ _____
either A or B	A와 B 둘 중 하나
neither A nor B	A와 B 둘 다 아닌

My dad has ¹⁸ _____ a bike and a motorbike.
나의 아빠는 자전거와 오토바이 둘 다 가지고 있다.

Either you ¹⁹ _____ I am responsible for the problem. 너와 나 둘 중 한 사람이 그 문제에 책임이 있다.

1 다음 문장과 뜻이 같도록 빈칸에 알맞은 말을 쓰시오.

(1) Unless you wake up now, you will miss the plane.

→ _____, _____ you will miss the plane.

(2) If you tell him the truth, he will forgive you.

→ _____, _____ he will forgive you.

2 다음 문장을 밑줄 친 부분에 유의하여 바르게 해석하시오.

(1) Try to eat more vegetables, <u>and</u> you will be healthy.

→ _____

(2) Clean the bathroom, <u>or</u> your roommate will get angry.

→ _____

1 |보기|와 같이 괄호 안의 말을 이용하여 대답을 완성하시오.

┌ 보기 ┐
A Will it snow tomorrow? (think)
B Yes, I think that it will snow tomorrow.

(1) **A** Did you turn off the light? (remember)
B Yes, _____.

(2) **A** Will she do well on the test? (think)
B Yes, _____.

2 두 문장을 접속사 **that**을 이용하여 한 문장으로 쓰시오.

(1) It's true. The Earth is round.

→ _____

(2) The store was closed. Did you know?

→ _____

1 빈칸에 알맞은 말을 |보기|에서 골라 쓰시오.

┌ 보기 ┐
she lived in Hong Kong
she looked out the window

(1) It was raining when _____.

(2) As _____, she learned English.

2 두 문장을 괄호 안의 접속사를 이용하여 한 문장으로 쓰시오. (접속사로 시작할 것)

(1) I have some free time. I usually see a movie. (when)

→ _____

(2) He was playing soccer. He got hurt. (as)

→ _____

3 우리말과 뜻이 같도록 빈칸에 알맞은 말을 쓰시오.

(1) 그는 어렸을 때 그림을 잘 그렸다.
→ He was good at painting _____ _____ _____ _____.

(2) 내가 일하고 있는 동안 그들이 내 케이크를 먹었다.
→ _____ _____ _____ _____, they ate my cake.

4 문장을 밑줄 친 부분에 유의하여 바르게 해석하시오.

(1) <u>As</u> he is having a meal, he reads the newspaper.

→ _____

(2) <u>When</u> I was ten, I moved into this city.

→ _____

1 두 문장을 괄호 안의 접속사를 이용하여 한 문장으로 쓰시오.

(1) I kept waiting. He showed up. (until)
→ I kept _____.

(2) She can't go swimming. She has a cold. (since)
→ She can't _____.

(3) I took a shower. I came back home. (after)
→ I took _____.

2 우리말과 뜻이 같도록 빈칸에 알맞은 말을 쓰시오.

(1) 네가 성공할 때까지 포기하지 마라.
→ Don't give up _____ _____ _____.

(2) 질문에 답하기 전에 손을 들어라.
→ Raise your hand _____ _____ _____ the question.

(3) 아침을 먹은 후에, 우리는 산책을 했다.
→ _____ _____ _____ _____, we took a walk.

3 괄호 안의 말을 바르게 배열하여 문장을 완성하시오.

(1) We had better go _____.
(the weather, worse, before, gets)

(2) Go straight _____.
(the park, until, get to, you)

(3) _____, we enter a room.
(we, our shoes, after, take off)

4 다음 문장을 밑줄 친 부분에 유의하여 바르게 해석하시오.

(1) I knew nothing about that <u>until</u> you told me.
→ _____

(2) She has not seen him <u>since</u> she moved.
→ _____

1 괄호 안에서 알맞은 것을 고르시오.

(1) If you (have / don't have) any questions, raise your hand.

(2) Your parents will be proud of you (if / unless) you pass the test.

(3) Unless you (want / don't want) to try something new, you don't have to.

2 빈칸에 알맞은 말을 |보기|에서 골라 문장을 완성하시오.

┌ 보기 ┐
you take this aspirin
the weather is good
you stop shouting
└────────────────────────┘

(1) If _____, you'll feel better.

(2) We will call the police unless _____ _____.

(3) We will eat outdoors if _____ _____.

3 다음 문장과 뜻이 같도록 빈칸에 알맞은 말을 쓰시오.

(1) If you don't eat this now, you'll feel hungry soon.
→ _____, you'll feel hungry soon.

(2) Unless you take the textbook to your home, you can't do your homework.
→ _____, you can't do your homework.

4 괄호 안의 말을 바르게 배열하여 문장을 완성하시오.

(1) _____, stop eating fast food.
(gain weight, unless, want, you, to)

(2) _____, you won't catch a cold.
(put on, you, if, your coat)

FOCUS 72 이유의 접속사_ because, since, as

1 두 문장을 괄호 안의 접속사를 이용하여 한 문장으로 쓰시오.

(1) My parents got angry. I got a bad grade.
(because)
→ My _____ .

(2) The sun is very bright. I can't open my eyes.
(as)
→ As _____ .

2 빈칸에 알맞은 말을 |보기|에서 골라 because를 이용하여 문장을 완성하시오.

> | 보기 |
> he works there
> its food is good
> we didn't have enough time

(1) The restaurant is crowded _____
_____ .

(2) We couldn't have lunch _____
_____ .

(3) Henry lives in Jejudo _____
_____ .

3 괄호 안의 말을 바르게 배열하여 문장을 완성하시오.

(1) I stayed home _____ .
(was, cold, because, very, it)

(2) _____, I couldn't pick you up. (busy, as, was, I)

4 다음 문장의 밑줄 친 부분을 바르게 해석하시오.

(1) Mary can't buy the shoes <u>since they are too expensive</u>.
→ _____

(2) We can't climb the mountain <u>as it is snowing hard</u>.
→ _____

FOCUS 73 결과의 접속사_ so, so ~ that ...

1 두 문장을 접속사 so를 이용하여 한 문장으로 쓰시오.

(1) The teacher understands us. We like him.
→ _____

(2) I missed the train. I couldn't arrive at the meeting on time.
→ _____
_____

2 우리말과 뜻이 같도록 빈칸에 알맞은 말을 쓰시오.

(1) 나는 치통이 있어서 치과에 갔다.
→ I had a toothache, _____ _____
_____ to the dentist.

(2) 내 고향은 너무 작아서 소문이 정말 빨리 퍼진다.
→ My hometown is _____ _____
_____ news travels so fast.

3 괄호 안의 말을 바르게 배열하여 문장을 완성하시오.

(1) You speak _____ .
(that, can't, quietly, hear you, so, we)

(2) It snowed _____ .
(go out, so, I, that, heavily, couldn't)

(3) Harry studied _____ .
(so, the test, he, passed, hard, that)

4 다음 문장을 밑줄 친 부분에 유의하여 바르게 해석하시오.

(1) I was <u>so</u> surprised <u>that</u> I didn't know what to say.
→ _____

(2) The waiter was <u>so</u> rude <u>that</u> we were angry.
→ _____

1 다음 문장과 뜻이 같도록 빈칸에 알맞은 말을 쓰시오.

(1) He was smiling, but he was worried about it.

→ _____ he was smiling, he was worried about it.

(2) I was feeling sick, but I went to work early.

→ I went to work early _____ _____

_____ _____ _____.

(3) It was very hot, but we didn't turn on the air conditioner.

→ _____ _____ it was very hot, we didn't turn on the air conditioner.

2 두 문장을 괄호 안의 접속사를 이용하여 한 문장으로 쓰시오. (접속사로 시작할 것)

(1) She was tired. She worked hard. (though)

→ _____

(2) It was very cold. The girl wasn't wearing gloves. (even though)

→ _____

3 괄호 안의 말을 바르게 배열하여 문장을 완성하시오.

(1) Tim can do a lot of things by himself _____.

(can't, even though, walk, he)

(2) _____, you have to visit her often. (lives, though, far away, she)

4 다음 문장을 밑줄 친 부분에 유의하여 바르게 해석하시오.

(1) Even though I see her every day, I never speak to her.

→ _____

(2) I am still hungry, though I had a big lunch.

→ _____

1 괄호 안에서 알맞은 것을 고르시오.

(1) Either you or Mike (have / has) to come to pick me up.

(2) Not only my sister but also I (want / wants) the computer.

(3) Her kids as well as she (like / likes) fried chicken.

2 빈칸에 알맞은 말을 쓰시오.

(1) Fashion is not only a business _____ _____ an art.

(2) You can choose either coffee _____ tea.

(3) Neither the students _____ the teacher knew the song.

3 괄호 안의 말을 이용하여 우리말을 영작하시오.

(1) 그는 우리에게 좋은 충고뿐만 아니라 많은 돈도 주었다. (not only, good advice, a lot of money)

→ _____

(2) 채소와 고기 둘 다 우리의 건강을 위해 필수적이다. (both, vegetables, meat, necessary)

→ _____

(3) 나는 공포 영화뿐만 아니라 로맨틱 영화도 좋아한다. (as well as, horror movies, romantic movies)

→ _____

4 다음 문장을 밑줄 친 부분에 유의하여 바르게 해석하시오.

(1) Either my husband or I have to take our children to the museum.

→ _____

(2) The boss as well as I was satisfied with the result.

→ _____

» 정답과 해설 p.60

76 가정법 과거

■ ¹_____의 사실과 반대되는 일이나 실현 가능성이 희박한 일을 가정할 때 쓴다.

형태	If+주어+동사의 ²_____(were) ~, 주어+would(could/might)+동사원형 ...
의미	~라면, ···할(일) 텐데

If I ³_____ you, I would ask my parents for some help. 내가 너라면, 부모님에게 도움을 요청할 텐데.

If your grandfather ⁴_____ your painting, he would be proud of you.
만약 네 할아버지가 네 그림을 보신다면, 너를 자랑스러워하실 텐데.

77 가정법 과거완료

■ ⁵_____의 사실과 반대되는 일이나 과거에 이루지 못한 것을 가정할 때 쓴다.

형태	If+주어+⁶_____+과거분사 ~, 주어+would (could/might)+have+과거분사 ...
의미	~했더라면, ···했을(이었을) 텐데

If Matty had been stronger, he could have ⁷_____ the weights.
Matty가 좀 더 힘이 셌다면, 그 역기를 들어 올릴 수 있었을 텐데.

78 I wish 가정법 과거
79 I wish 가정법 과거완료

■ 「I wish+가정법 ⁸_____(주어+동사의 과거형(were))」는 현재 사실과 반대되는 소망을, 「I wish+가정법 ⁹_____(주어+had+과거분사)」는 과거 사실과 반대되는 소망을 나타낸다.

I wish+가정법 과거	~라면(하면) ¹⁰_____ 텐데
I wish+가정법 과거완료	~이었다면(했다면) ¹¹_____ 텐데

I wish I ¹²_____ a good brother.
내게 좋은 형제가 있으면 좋을 텐데.

I wish I ¹³_____ _____ earlier here.
내가 여기에 더 일찍 도착했다면 좋았을 텐데.

■ 「I wish+가정법 과거」는 「I'm sorry (that)+직설법 ¹⁴_____」로, 「I wish+가정법 과거완료」는 「I'm sorry (that)+직설법 과거」로 바꿔 쓸 수 있다.

FOCUS 76 가정법 과거

1 괄호 안의 말을 빈칸에 알맞은 형태로 쓰시오.

(1) If you drove carefully, I _____ you my car. (can lend)

(2) If I _____ you, I would buy the digital camera. (be)

(3) If she knew his address, she _____ a letter to him. (will write)

2 밑줄 친 부분을 어법상 바르게 고쳐 쓰시오.

(1) If he didn't have a test, he can go on a date with Julia.
→ _____

(2) If you saw a UFO, what will you do?
→ _____

3 다음 문장과 뜻이 같도록 빈칸에 알맞은 말을 쓰시오.

(1) As I don't live in the country, I'm not happy.
→ If I _____ in the country, I _____ _____ happy.

(2) If they were able to speak Chinese, they could get the job.
→ As they _____ able to speak Chinese, they _____ _____ the job.

4 괄호 안의 말을 이용하여 우리말을 영작하시오.

(1) 내가 영화배우가 아니라면 요리사가 될 텐데.
(a movie star, will be a cook)
→ _____

(2) 나에게 충분한 사과가 있다면 애플파이를 만들 수 있을 텐데. (have, apples, can bake, an apple pie)
→ _____

1 괄호 안의 말을 빈칸에 알맞은 형태로 쓰시오.

(1) If I had been diligent when young, I
_____ in life.
(can succeed)

(2) If he _____ the accident, he
would have been very shocked.
(see)

(3) If Bob had been more careful, he
_____ the glass.
(won't break)

2 다음 문장과 뜻이 같도록 빈칸에 알맞은 말을 쓰시오.

(1) If I had married her, I could have lived a
happy life.
→ As I _____ her, I _____ a
happy life.

(2) As we didn't have a key, we couldn't get
into that house.
→ If we _____ a key, we _____
into that house.

3 괄호 안의 말을 이용하여 문장을 완성하시오.

(1) If _____, he would have
stayed longer with us. (he, feel good)

(2) If _____, they wouldn't
have gotten lost. (they, listen to the guide)

4 다음 문장을 밑줄 친 부분에 유의하여 바르게 해석하시오.

(1) If you hadn't gone camping, <u>you couldn't
have met</u> many nice people.
→ _____

(2) If he had studied music, <u>he would have
been</u> a great musician.
→ _____

1 다음 문장과 뜻이 같도록 빈칸에 알맞은 말을 쓰시오.

(1) I'm sorry Karen doesn't agree with me.
→ I wish _____ with me.

(2) I wish she were my girlfriend.
→ I'm sorry _____.

(3) We're sorry it is true.
→ We wish _____.

2 우리말과 뜻이 같도록 어법상 어색한 부분을 찾아 고쳐 쓰
시오.

(1) 나에게 진정한 친구가 있다면 좋을 텐데.
→ I wish I have a true friend.
_____ → _____

(2) 네가 여기에 우리와 함께 있다면 좋을 텐데.
→ I wish you are here with us.
_____ → _____

1 다음 문장을 |보기|와 같이 바꿔 쓰시오.

> 보기
> I painted the wall white.
> → I wish I hadn't painted the wall white.

(1) He wasn't honest with his friends.
→ I wish _____.

(2) Grace didn't do it earlier.
→ I wish _____.

2 다음 문장을 밑줄 친 부분에 유의하여 바르게 해석하시오.

(1) I wish he <u>had seen</u> the movie with me.
→ _____

(2) I wish it <u>had been</u> sunny last Sunday.
→ _____

80 시제 일치

주절의 시제	종속절의 시제
1 _____	모든 시제 가능
2 _____	과거 / 과거완료

I thought that I met(had met) Mary.
나는 내가 Mary를 만났다고(만났었다고) 생각했다.

종속절의 시제	
항상 3 _____	종속절의 내용이 일반적인 사실 또는 현재의 습관일 때
항상 4 _____	종속절의 내용이 역사적 사실일 때

The scientist said that the Earth 5 _____ round.
그 과학자는 지구가 둥글다고 말했다.

I know that World War II 6 _____ out in 1939.
나는 제2차 세계대전이 1939년에 일어난 것을 알고 있다.

81 평서문의 간접화법

① 전달 동사를 바꾼다. 〈say → say, say to → tell〉
② 콤마(,)와 인용부호(" ")를 없애고 that을 쓴다. (that 생략 가능)
③ 직접화법의 인칭대명사, 부사(구) 등은 전달자의 입장에 맞게 고친다.
④ 전달 동사가 현재일 때는 피전달문의 동사는 시제의 변화가 없지만, 과거일 때는 〈현재 → 7 _____, 현재완료나 과거 → 과거완료〉로 바꾼다.

Jim said to his sister, "I have to work late."
Jim은 그의 여동생에게 "나 야근해야 해."라고 말했다.

→ Jim 8 _____ his sister (that) he had to work late. Jim은 그의 여동생에게 그가 야근해야 한다고 말했다.

82 의문사가 없는 의문문의 간접화법

① 전달 동사를 바꾼다. 〈say to → 9 _____〉
② 콤마(,)와 인용부호(" ")를 삭제하고 피전달문을 「if(whether)+주어+동사」의 순으로 바꾼다.

③ 직접화법의 인칭대명사는 전달자 입장에 맞추어 바꾸고, 동사의 시제도 주절에 맞게 바꾼다.

The old man said to me, "Is it raining?"
그 노인은 나에게 "비가 오고 있습니까?"라고 말했다.

→ The old man asked me 10 _____ it 11 _____ raining. 그 노인은 나에게 비가 오고 있는지를 물었다.

83 의문사가 있는 의문문의 간접화법

① 전달 동사를 바꾼다. 〈say to → ask〉
② 콤마(,)와 인용부호(" ")를 삭제하고 피전달문을 「12 _____ +주어+동사」의 어순으로 바꾼다.
③ 직접화법의 인칭대명사는 전달자 입장에 맞게 바꾸고, 동사의 시제도 주절의 시제에 맞게 바꾼다.

The driver said to me, "Where do you want to go?" 운전사는 나에게 "어디로 가기를 원합니까?"라고 말했다.

→ The driver asked me 13 _____ I 14 _____ to go. 운전사는 나에게 어디로 가기를 원하는지 물었다.

84 간접의문문 1 **85** 간접의문문 2

의문사가 있을 때	「의문사+주어+동사」
의문사가 없을 때	「if(15 _____)+주어+동사」

I wonder. + Where did I leave my phone?
나는 궁금하다.   내가 내 전화기를 어디에 뒀지?

→ I wonder 16 _____ I 17 _____ my phone.
나는 내가 어디에 내 전화기를 두었는지 궁금하다.

I'd like to know. + Does she like the gift?
나는 알고 싶다.   그녀가 그 선물을 마음에 들어하나?

→ I'd like to know 18 _____ she 19 _____ the gift. 그녀가 그 선물을 마음에 들어하는지 알고 싶다.

■ 주절의 동사가 생각이나 추측을 나타내는 think, believe, imagine, suppose, guess 등일 때는 간접의문문의 의문사를 문장의 맨 앞에 쓴다.

Do you think? + When will they come?
넌 생각하니?   그들은 언제 올까?

→ 20 _____ do you think they will come?
그들이 언제 올 것이라고 생각하니?

1 괄호 안에서 알맞은 것을 <u>모두</u> 고르시오.

(1) Sally says that Mr. Kim (is / was) very funny.

(2) They think that there (are / were) dragons in the past.

(3) My history teacher told us that the French Revolution (had broken / broke) out in 1789.

2 다음 문장의 시제를 바꿔 쓸 때 빈칸에 알맞은 말을 쓰시오.

(1) He says that his father goes hiking every Sunday.
→ He said that _____ every Sunday.

(2) I hear that he left for his hometown.
→ I heard that _____.

(3) They think that Andrew will be home tonight.
→ They thought that _____ tonight.

3 어법상 <u>어색한</u> 부분을 찾아 고쳐 쓰시오.

(1) She didn't say that she buys the jacket on sale.
_____ → _____

(2) He explained that Marilyn Monroe had died in 1962.
_____ → _____

4 우리말과 뜻이 같도록 괄호 안의 말을 이용하여 문장을 완성하시오.

(1) 우리는 여름보다 겨울에 해가 늦게 뜬다는 것을 배웠다.
→ We learned that the sun _____ later in winter than in summer. (rise)

(2) 그녀는 그녀의 아들이 성공할 것이라고 믿는다.
→ She believes that her son _____. (succeed)

1 다음 문장을 간접화법으로 바꿀 때 괄호 안에서 알맞은 것을 고르시오.

(1) She says to me, "I am your teacher."
→ She (says to / tells) me that she is my teacher.

(2) He said to us, "I want to take your picture now."
→ He told us that he wanted to take our picture (now / then).

2 괄호 안의 말을 바르게 배열하여 문장을 완성하시오.

(1) You said _____.
(had walked, that, you, that morning, to school)

(2) Sally says _____.
(there, found, that, a strange box, she)

(3) The girl said _____.
(that, would, she, the next day, go swimming)

3 다음 문장을 간접화법으로 바꿀 때 빈칸에 알맞은 말을 쓰시오.

(1) Amy said to him, "I don't know your phone number."
→ Amy told him that _____.

(2) He said to me, "I saw your friend yesterday."
→ He told me that _____.

4 다음 문장을 직접화법으로 바꿀 때 빈칸에 알맞은 말을 쓰시오.

(1) Kate says that she likes the white blouse.
→ Kate says, "_____."

(2) Julia told me that she had seen the movie two days before.
→ Julia said to me, "_____."

1 다음 문장을 | 보기 |와 같이 바꿔 쓰시오.

> | 보기 |
> **Alex** Do you believe what Jury said?
> → Alex asked me if I believed what Jury had said.

(1) **Policeman** Is this your car?
  → The policeman asked me _____
  _____.

(2) **Mom** Do you feel better now?
  → Mom asked me _____
  _____.

2 다음 문장을 간접화법으로 바꿀 때 어법상 어색한 부분을 찾아 고쳐 쓰시오.

(1) Lily said to me, "Do I know you?"
  → Lily asked me whether she knew you.
  _____ → _____

(2) He said to Sue, "Will you marry me?"
  → He asked Sue that she would marry him.
  _____ → _____

3 다음 문장을 직접화법으로 바꿀 때 빈칸에 알맞은 말을 쓰시오.

(1) Alice asked him if he loved her.
  → Alice said to him, "_____
  _____?"

(2) My math teacher asked me whether I could solve that problem.
  → My math teacher said to me, "_____
  _____?"

4 괄호 안의 말을 바르게 배열하여 문장을 완성하시오.

(1) Clara asked the man _____.
  (a cat, had, if, he, seen)

(2) The waiter asked us _____.
  (were, whether, ready to order, we)

1 다음 문장을 간접화법으로 바꿀 때 빈칸에 알맞은 말을 쓰시오.

(1) He said to me, "What makes you think so?"
  → He asked me _____.

(2) Harry said to Jane, "How old is your dog?"
  → Harry asked Jane _____.

2 다음 문장을 직접화법으로 바꿀 때 빈칸에 알맞은 말을 쓰시오.

(1) I asked her what her father had said about it.
  → I said to her, "_____?"

(2) He asked me where I came from.
  → He said to me, "_____?"

(3) Tony asked us what time we would arrive.
  → Tony said to us, "_____?"

3 괄호 안의 말을 바르게 배열하여 문장을 완성하시오.

(1) She _____.
  (who, asked, had broken, them, the window)

(2) He _____.
  (felt, his son, that day, how, asked, he)

4 밑줄 친 부분을 어법상 바르게 고쳐 쓰시오.

(1) They asked me when I <u>am</u> going to leave there.
  → _____

(2) Eric asked us how long we <u>have</u> lived there.
  → _____

(3) The boy asked him what the weather was like <u>today</u>.
  → _____

1 두 문장을 한 문장으로 쓰시오.

(1) Can you tell me? What should I do?

→ _____

(2) I'm not sure. Is the man diligent?

→ _____

(3) I wonder. Where are my old friends?

→ _____

2 밑줄 친 부분을 어법상 바르게 고쳐 쓰시오.

(1) Have you wondered when <u>was the bike invented</u>?

→ _____

(2) He wanted to know how much <u>was my new bag</u>.

→ _____

(3) I wonder whether <u>do you love</u> me.

→ _____

3 괄호 안의 말을 바르게 배열하여 문장을 완성하시오.

(1) We can't remember _____ the bus stop. (go, we, how, to)

(2) Please tell me _____ to Korea. (your, if, is, first visit, this)

(3) Do you know _____ yesterday? (felt, why, Judy, angry)

4 우리말과 뜻이 같도록 빈칸에 알맞은 말을 쓰시오.

(1) 우리는 내일 무슨 일이 일어날지 궁금하다.

→ We wonder _____ _____ _____ tomorrow.

(2) 내가 그를 전에 본 적이 있는지 모르겠다.

→ I don't know _____ _____ _____ _____ before.

---

1 두 문장을 한 문장으로 쓰시오.

(1) Do they guess? How long is this bridge?

→ _____

(2) Does the teacher think? Who is wrong?

→ _____

(3) Do you suppose? What time will they leave?

→ _____

2 밑줄 친 부분을 어법상 바르게 고쳐 쓰시오.

(1) Who do you think <u>am I</u>?

→ _____

(2) <u>Do you believe which foods</u> are good for us?

→ _____

(3) What do you imagine <u>will Dad buy</u> for you?

→ _____

3 괄호 안의 말을 바르게 배열하여 문장을 완성하시오.

(1) What do you imagine _____? (doing, the kids, are, now)

(2) _____ his promise? (think, why, he, you, do, broke)

(3) _____ from here? (you, how far, suppose, is, do, it)

4 우리말과 뜻이 같도록 빈칸에 알맞은 말을 쓰시오.

(1) 이 단어가 무슨 뜻이라고 생각하니?

→ _____ do you think _____ _____ _____?

(2) 누가 다음 대통령이 될 것이라고 추측하니?

→ _____ do you guess _____ _____ the next president?

Answer

CHAPTER 01 문장의 형식

요점정리 노트 p.2

1 동사 **2** live **3** good **4** 목적어 **5** me **6** 전치사 **7** to
8 for **9** of **10** 목적어 **11** her **12** warm **13** to come
14 동사원형 **15** laugh **16** to부정사 **17** 지각동사

FOCUS 01   p.3

1 (1) 2형식 (2) 1형식 (3) 1형식 (4) 2형식 **2** (1) smooth
(2) happily (3) beautiful

FOCUS 02   p.3

1 (1) 4형식 (2) 3형식 (3) 4형식 **2** (1) Will you pass me the
dish? (2) I want to go to the concert. (3) He will make me
a nice suit. (4) Bob finished cleaning the classroom.

FOCUS 03   p.3

1 (1) to (2) for (3) to (4) of **2** (1) read the newspaper
to his wife (2) ask something of you (3) told a lie to his
parents **3** (1) She wrote several poems to him. (2) Dad
made coffee for us. (3) Did you ask the price of him?
(4) He teaches history to students. **4** (1) for → to
(2) to → for

FOCUS 04   p.4

1 (1) interesting (2) a king (3) *Titanic* (4) to be quiet **2** (1)
clean (2) to go (3) sad (4) to be **3** (1) to be (2) to stay
(3) to marry **4** (1) I think him fat. (2) They elected her
president. (3) He found the question difficult. (4) We want
you to play the piano.

FOCUS 05   p.4

1 (1) laugh (2) go (3) study, to study (4) sing **2** (1) know
(2) fly(flying) (3) water (4) strike(striking) **3** (1) Please let
me eat chocolate. (2) He had me exercise a lot. (3) I made
him carry the heavy box. **4** (1) I saw him enter the cafe.
(2) Our mom let us make a snowman. (3) He helped me to
write the essay. (4) I heard her call my name.

CHAPTER 02 to부정사

요점정리 노트 p.5

1 It **2** to travel **3** 것을 **4** what **5** ~하는 **6** with **7** in order to
8 happy **9** to be **10** ~하기(에) **11** to believe **12** so **13** can
14 for me **15** of **16** nice

FOCUS 06   p.6

1 (1) 주어 (2) 보어 (3) 주어 (4) 보어 **2** (1) to be rich (2) to
collect(collecting) (3) To be(Being) (4) to learn **3** (1) It is
dangerous to drive too fast. (2) It is a good habit to read
newspapers. (3) It is fun to see animals at the zoo. (4) It is
bad for your health to eat too much. **4** (1) Your next job
is to clean the window. (2) To meet him is my wish. / My
wish is to meet him. (3) It is very hard to know oneself.

FOCUS 07   p.6

1 (1) to talk (2) to go (3) to live (4) to visit **2** (1) what to
eat (2) how to get (3) where to go (4) when to leave **3** (1)
to skate (2) to download (3) to see **4** (1) where to meet
(2) when I should (3) what to do

FOCUS 08   p.7

1 (1) to write on (2) to wear (3) water to drink **2** (1)
to dance with (2) to sit on (3) to write with (4) to live in
3 (1) many toys to play with (2) nothing to say (3) safe
river to swim in (4) time to study science **4** (1) talk →
talk with (2) drink → to drink (3) buy → to buy

FOCUS 09   p.7

1 (1) to catch the train (2) to find out the truth (3) to cut
the rope (4) to win the medal **2** (1) 원인 (2) 목적 (3) 목적 (4)
원인 **3** (1) to hear (2) to get **4** (1) 그는 중국 문화를 공부하기
위해 그곳에 갔다. (2) 나는 영화관에서 Jinny를 보고 놀랐다. (3) 그녀는
잡지를 읽기 위해 안경을 찾았다.

FOCUS 10   p.8

1 (1) 형용사 수식 (2) 형용사 수식 (3) 결과 **2** (1) dangerous to cross (2) awoke to find (3) lived to be **3** (1) to read and write (2) to find (3) easy to use **4** (1) 그 영화는 이해하기에 어렵다. (2) 그들은 그 방에 들어가서 방이 비어 있다는 것을 알았다. (3) 그는 자라서 유명한 배우가 되었다.

FOCUS **11** p.8

1 (1) too (2) old enough (3) couldn't **2** (1) tall enough to (2) too scared to open

FOCUS **12** p.8

1 (1) of her (2) rude (3) for us **2** (1) for you to play (2) of her to bring (3) of him to give

CHAPTER **03** 동명사

요점정리 노트 p.9

1 Learning **2** getting **3** 목적어 **4** inviting **5** 동명사 **6** to부정사 **7** flying **8** to hear **9** 동명사 **10** to부정사 **11** ~할 것을 잊다 **12** ~하려고 노력하다 **13** remember telling **14** try reading **15** go -ing **16** ~하느라 바쁘다 **17** ~하는 게 어때? **18** feel like going **19** look forward to seeing

FOCUS **13** p.10

1 (1) Understanding your children (2) reading comic books (3) Choosing the right leader **2** (1) running every day (2) Riding a bike

FOCUS **14** p.10

1 (1) try → trying (2) to watch → watching (3) swims → swimming **2** (1) sorry for being (2) talking about having (3) Thanks for showing

FOCUS **15** p.10

1 (1) to be (2) meeting (3) to open **2** (1) hiking (2) to live (3) waiting (4) to keep **3** (1) going (2) to be (3) to take (4) riding **4** (1) wanted to try (2) avoided looking (3) stopped talking (4) agreed to buy

FOCUS **16** p.11

1 (1) playing, to play (2) keeping, to keep (3) to meet (4) to turn **2** (1) seeing (2) learning(to learn) (3) to call **3** (1) mailing → to mail (2) bringing → to bring (3) to be → being **4** (1) 그는 어제 그녀에게 돈을 빌려준 것을 잊어버렸다. (2) 문을 잠그는 것을 잊지 마라. (3) 인터넷에서 물건을 한번 사 보아라. (4) 나는 눈을 뜨고 있으려고 노력했다.

FOCUS **17** p.11

1 (1) seeing (2) writing (3) doing **2** (1) shop → shopping (2) ask → asking (3) eat → eating **3** (1) 그들은 그의 재미있는 얼굴을 보고 웃지 않을 수 없었다. (2) 나는 터키를 방문하기를 기대하고 있다. (3) 그는 많은 사람들 앞에서 말하는 데 익숙하다. **4** (1) go fishing (2) feel like drinking

CHAPTER **04** 시제

요점정리 노트 p.12

1 과거분사 **2** 과거 **3** when **4** Have(Has) **5** has not **6** have **7** just **8** arrived **9** already **10** yet **11** broken **12** has lost **13** ~한 적이 있다 **14** have been **15** before **16** for **17** has lived **18** since

FOCUS **18** p.13

1 (1) gone (2) left (3) lost (4) spent **2** (1) has ridden (2) went (3) did you buy (4) have swum **3** (1) have just opened (2) arrived (3) has lived (4) visited **4** (1) I have already done my homework. (2) David has been in hospital for a week. (3) I have eaten Thai food once.

FOCUS **19** p.13

1 (1) have not crossed (2) have never seen (3) Have they known **2** (1) I have not(haven't) touched your bag. (2) Scientists have not(haven't) found a new planet. (3) I have not(haven't) done my English homework. **3** (1) Has she visited Los Angeles before? (2) Have you returned the book to the library? (3) Have you thought about the future of Korea? **4** (1) have never had (2) Have, ever seen (3) have not finished

1 (1) have, finished (2) have, gone (3) has, come (4) have, heard   **2** (1) have just got (2) have already written   **3** (1) has just walked into my store (2) has already fixed the door (3) have just watched an animation   **4** (1) has already sent (2) has just fallen (3) has not(hasn't) arrived, yet

1 (1) has stopped (2) have lost (3) has repaired   **2** (1) has left his sunglasses (2) has stolen my expensive bag   **3** (1) has washed (2) has broken   **4** (1) have forgotten (2) has gone to

1 (1) have studied (2) has seen (3) has traveled   **2** (1) have been (2) has won (3) has worked   **3** (1) have met (2) have been (3) has read   **4** (1) 나는 개구리를 한 번 먹어 본 적이 있다. (2) 나는 일출을 두 번 본 적이 있다. (3) 나의 가족은 애완동물을 전에 키운 적이 있다.

1 (1) for (2) since (3) for   **2** (1) has snowed (2) has been (3) has loved   **3** (1) have worked, for (2) has learned, since (3) has taught, for   **4** (1) 그녀는 2년 동안 춤을 연습해왔다. (2) 우리는 어린 시절부터 단짝 친구이다.

CHAPTER **05** 조동사

요점정리 노트 ·· p.16

1 cannot   2 능력   3 허락   4 won't   5 예정   6 의지   7 허락   8 추측
9 강한 추측   10 의무   11 must not lie   12 have to   13 도덕적 의무   14 충고   15 had better not   16 used to go
17 would visit

1 (1) 요청 (2) 능력 (3) 허락   **2** (1) was (2) can (3) couldn't
3 (1) May (2) able to (3) couldn't   **4** (1) 너는 내 자전거를 타도

된다. (2) 시간 좀 말해 주시겠어요? (3) Jane은 첫 기차를 탈 수 없었다. (4) 나의 조부모님은 컴퓨터를 사용하실 수 있다.

1 (1) will not(won't) be (2) will be (3) will cut   **2** (1) will you water (2) will not do that (3) Will you show me (4) What will you buy   **3** (1) Will does → Will (2) not will → will not (won't) (3) will is → will be   **4** (1) will eat (2) will not(won't) send

1 (1) 추측 (2) 허락 (3) 허락 (4) 추측   **2** (1) Can (2) might (3) may, might (4) may   **3** (1) May I use your smartphone? (2) You may go to the movies after school. (3) She might not be Suji's mother.   **4** (1) 너의 하얀색 드레스를 빌려도 되니? (2) 나는 오늘 저녁에 사무실에 있을지도 모른다. (3) 그는 의사가 아닐지도 모른다.

1 (1) 의무 (2) 추측 (3) 의무   **2** (1) must (2) don't have to (3) must not   **3** (1) have to (2) has to   **4** (1) must not be (2) had to walk (3) don't have(need) to worry

1 (1) should take (2) should get (3) should not play   **2** (1) had better (2) should not (3) had better not   **3** (1) You had better not make (2) Eric ought to get (3) You should not wear   **4** (1) should be kind (2) ought not to eat

1 (1) climb that tree (2) cook for my parents (3) be a lake   **2** (1) used to (2) often help (3) would play   **3** (1) used to work (2) There used to be   **4** (1) reading → read (2) use → used (3) to go → go

CHAPTER **06** 수동태

요점정리 노트 ·· p.20

1 by 2 loved 3 not 4 과거분사 5 Was 6 When 7 was 8 painted 9 be 10 I 11 to me 12 to 13 for 14 was called 15 were asked 16 to부정사 17 crying 18 at 19 for 20 with

FOCUS 30   p.21

1 (1) The book is bought by many people. (2) Tea is drunk by Chinese people. (3) Two children are raised by Ms. Bin. (4) The thief was caught by the police.

FOCUS 31   p.21

1 (1) Was (2) broken (3) invented (4) wasn't 2 (1) Cats and dogs are not(aren't) raised in the house by them. (2) This movie was not(wasn't) directed by Mr. Kang. (3) A lot of fruits and vegetables are not(aren't) eaten by my children. 3 (1) Is this room cleaned by you every day? (2) Was the bike fixed by my brother? (3) Was *The Fox and the Grapes* written by Aesop? 4 (1) was the window broken (2) Is this song sung (3) That money was not spent

FOCUS 32   p.21

1 (1) be baked (2) put (3) be sent 2 (1) be changed (2) was taken (3) be cleaned 3 (1) should be dried (2) can be trained (3) were carried

FOCUS 33   p.22

1 (1) to (2) for (3) for (4) to 2 (1) was sent to me (2) is made for my dog (3) was taught how to drive by 3 (1) I was shown wonderful magic by him. (2) She was given an interesting book by Tony. (3) Dinner was bought for me last night by her. 4 (1) was made for (2) was given to

FOCUS 34   p.22

1 (1) We are made healthy by doing yoga. (2) An elevator is called a lift in England (by them). (3) I was told to stay longer by him. 2 (1) We elected him class president. (2) I found the bottle empty. (3) She asked him to close the door. 3 (1) diligently → diligent (2) turn → to turn (3) being → to be 4 (1) was asked to wash (2) was told to study (3) was advised to drive

FOCUS 35   p.23

1 (1) to enter (2) to carry (3) to sing 2 (1) The deer was watched to drink water by the crocodile. (2) Tom was made to brush the baby's hair by Mom. (3) The ground was felt to shake by him. 3 (1) was watched to walk (2) was made to go (3) was heard to play 4 (1) rise → to rise (2) stop → to stop (3) help → to help

FOCUS 36   p.23

1 (1) with (2) in (3) with (4) from 2 (1) at (2) with (3) with 3 (1) 그 워터파크는 사람들로 붐볐다. (2) 이 상자는 금으로 만들어져 있다. (3) 그의 이름은 모든 사람들에게 알려져 있다. (4) 그 식당은 신선한 음식으로 유명하다. 4 (1) are worried about (2) are interested in (3) was disappointed at

CHAPTER 07 분사

요점정리 노트 ·· p.24

1 -ing 2 수동 3 running 4 broken 5 감정 6 surprising 7 surprised 8 현재분사 9 동명사 10 주어 11 동사원형 12 Arriving

FOCUS 37   p.24

1 (1) running (2) working (3) looking 2 (1) sitting on the bench (2) reading a book (3) ringing in the kitchen 3 (1) girl walking towards us (2) lady wearing a white dress 4 (1) The smiling baby made (2) child swimming in the lake

FOCUS 38   p.25

1 (1) lost (2) written (3) broken 2 (1) called Captain Q (2) painted by my mom (3) cooked in the Korean way 3 (1) the roof painted red (2) buy a used car (3) My car was examined 4 (1) His given name is (2) found the stolen wallet (3) was filled with balls

FOCUS 39   p.25

1 (1) shocking (2) bored (3) satisfied (4) tiring 2 (1)

pleased (2) boring (3) exciting (4) interested   3 (1) frightening (2) confused (3) shocked   4 (1) interested in taking pictures (2) The tired student (3) heard the surprising news

FOCUS 40   p.26

1 (1) 동명사 (2) 현재분사 (3) 동명사 (4) 현재분사   2 (1) shopping bag (2) girls singing   3 (1) sleeping room (2) drinking water (3) burning building   4 (1) 수영장에서는 수영복을 입어라. (2) 그 남자들은 부엌에서 요리를 하고 있다.

FOCUS 41   p.26

1 (1) 양보 (2) 조건 (3) 이유   2 (1) Leaving now (2) Having much to do (3) Reading the letter   3 (1) As he ran into the room (2) If you take off right now   4 (1) 상자를 열었을 때 나는 강아지 한 마리를 발견했다. (2) 그녀의 집 근처에 사는데도 나는 그녀를 전혀 본 적이 없다.

CHAPTER 08 대명사

요점정리 노트 ···································· p.27

1 the, other 2 another 3 others 4 the others 5 each 6 단수 7 all 8 복수 9 is 10 is 11 복수 12 has 13 friends 14 yourself 15 themselves 16 by oneself 17 저절로 18 for themselves 19 Help yourself to

FOCUS 42   p.28

1 (1) The other (2) another   2 (1) another (2) the other (3) one   3 (1) it → one (2) the other → another (3) another → the other   4 (1) 나는 이 모자가 마음에 안 들어요. 다른 것을 보여주세요. (2) 나는 선물을 세 개 샀다. 하나는 아빠 것이고, 다른 하나는 엄마 것이고, 나머지 하나는 내 강아지의 것이다. (3) 여기에 공이 두 개 있다. 하나는 야구공이고 다른 하나는 테니스 공이다.

FOCUS 43   p.28

1 (1) Some, others (2) Some, the others   2 (1) the others → others (2) others → the others   3 (1) Some, others (2) Some, the others   4 (1) 그들 중 몇몇은 아파트에 살고, 나머지는 (아파트에) 살지 않는다. (2) 카페에 많은 사람들이 있다. 어떤 사람들은 커피를 마시고 어떤 사람들은 주스를 마신다.

FOCUS 44   p.29

1 (1) has (2) Each (3) girl   2 (1) are → is (2) book → books (3) bring → brings (4) students → student   3 (1) Every, is (2) Each, has (3) Every seat   4 (1) 각각의 상자 안에는 무엇이 있니? (2) 그 동아리의 모든 회원은 자신만의 재능을 가지고 있다.

FOCUS 45   p.29

1 (1) was (2) Both (3) All (4) brothers   2 (1) shirt → shirts (2) bus → buses (3) have → has (4) man → men   3 (1) windows are (2) rooms, have (3) workers have   4 (1) All, music (2) both, gloves

FOCUS 46   p.30

1 (1) us (2) myself (3) himself   2 (1) himself (2) herself (3) ourselves   3 (1) burned myself (2) Cover yourself (3) think about themselves   4 (1) 내가 직접 이 시를 썼다. (2) 그녀는 "내가 세상에서 제일 예뻐."라고 혼잣말을 했다. (3) Mary는 늦게 일어나서 (자신을) 씻을 시간이 없었다.

FOCUS 47   p.30

1 (1) alone (2) of, itself (3) for, herself   2 (1) Help yourself (2) enjoyed herself (3) by himself   3 (1) yourself → yourselves (2) for → of (3) ourself → ourselves   4 (1) 아이들은 밤에 그들끼리만 집에 있으면 안 된다. (2) 탁자 위에 있는 이 쿠키들을 마음껏 드세요.

CHAPTER 09 형용사와 부사

요점정리 노트 ···································· p.31

1 뒤 2 old 3 a little 4 거의 없는 5 much 6 little 7 부정문 8 Some 9 any 10 대명사 11 off 12 them

FOCUS 48   p.31

1 (1) The (2) like (3) Something nice   2 (1) I didn't have anything to read (2) something sweet to eat

FOCUS 49 p.31

1 (1) is (2) much (3) people　2 (1) 하늘에 구름이 거의 없다.
(2) 나는 점심 먹을 시간이 약간 있다. (3) Tom은 학교에서 친구가 거의 없
다.　3 (1) many → much (2) little → few (3) are → is　4 (1)
We had little snow all winter. (2) There are a few candies
in the jar. (3) I don't drink much coffee.

FOCUS 50 p.32

1 (1) some(aren't) → any(are) (2) any → some (3) some →
any　2 (1) some friends (2) any food (3) some more tea

FOCUS 51 p.32

1 (1) pick her up (2) turned it on (3) hand in your essay
(4) took off my wet boots, took my wet boots off　2 (1)
Why don't you call him up? (2) The doctor put it on. (3) I'll
wake them up when we get there.　3 (1) put out a fire
(put a fire out) (2) turn off the light(turn the light off) (3) put
it down　4 (1) try on the shoes(try the shoes on) (2) Put
away the toys(Put the toys away) (3) Take it out

CHAPTER 10 비교 구문

요점정리 노트 p.33

1 -er 2 most 3 better 4 worst 5 as 6 than 7 the 8 as
9 bigger 10 smallest 11 much 12 possible 13 larger
than 14 and 15 the sooner 16 insects 17 No 18 단수 명
사 19 larger, than

FOCUS 52 p.34

1 (1) nicer, nicest (2) fatter, fattest (3) prettier, prettiest
(4) more, most (5) worse, worst (6) better, best　2 (1)
better (2) worse　3 (1) wiser (2) tallest (3) hottest (4) more
difficult　4 (1) less (2) worst (3) more (4) best

FOCUS 53 p.34

1 (1) as early as (2) as expensive as　2 (1) colder → cold
(2) so → as (3) Mary → Mary's (grade)　3 (1) as beautiful
as a picture (2) so many people as (3) not as big as cats

4 (1) as(so) deep as (2) as well as (3) as(so) fast as

FOCUS 54 p.35

1 (1) much (2) sports (3) funny　2 (1) sweeter (2) hotter
(3) the most important (4) the widest　3 (1) the youngest
(2) the wisest　4 (1) less handsome than (2) more
interesting than (3) slower than

FOCUS 55 p.35

1 (1) you can (2) she could (3) faster than (4) as many
books as　2 (1) as much as possible (2) as long as I can
(3) twice as big as Brazil (4) three times more presents
than me　3 (1) 나는 가능한 한 빨리 그것을 끝낼 것이다. (2) 그녀는
가능한 한 멀리 그 공을 찼다. (3) 그녀는 나보다 세 배 더 많이 먹었다.
(4) 이 밧줄은 저것(저 밧줄)보다 다섯 배 더 두껍다.

FOCUS 56 p.36

1 (1) faster and faster (2) louder and louder (3) more and
more important　2 (1) thinner → the thinner (2) tall and
tall → taller and taller　3 (1) poorer and poorer (2) The
faster, the earlier (3) The cheaper, the worse　4 (1) 너의 영
어 실력이 점점 더 좋아지고 있다. (2) 그 소녀는 나이가 들수록 더 아름다
워졌다.

FOCUS 57 p.36

1 (1) artists (2) No (3) lake　2 (1) one of the busiest
insects (2) one of the coldest days　3 (1) no → any
(2) students → student　4 (1) most interesting (2) more
interesting than (3) No, more interesting (4) No, as(so)
interesting

CHAPTER 11 관계사

요점정리 노트 p.37

1 선행사 2 who 3 whose 4 whom(who) 5 which 6 that
7 that 8 선행사 9 ~(하는) 것 10 What 11 목적격 12 be동사
13 who is 14 when 15 why 16 where 17 how(the way)

1 (1) Once there was a king who had a beautiful wife.
(2) Eric is the man who gave her flowers and chocolates.
(3) I called the student who was absent yesterday.
2 (1) who stole my purse (2) who is lying on the bed
3 (1) some boys who are playing baseball (2) The man who is talking to them (3) The people who live on the island **4** (1) 너를 만나고 싶어 하는 많은 사람들이 있다. (2) 스포츠를 하는 사람들은 많은 물이 필요하다.

1 (1) He had a date with a girl whose name is Amy. (2) He is a singer whose voice sounds very sweet. (3) I saw a cat whose eyes were blue. **2** (1) whose title is *The Little Prince* (2) whose dog is sick (3) whose seat is blue **3** (1) whose sister is a famous painter (2) whose walls are pink (3) whose name is Peter **4** (1) 그는 지붕이 열릴 수 있는 자동차를 원한다. (2) 나에게 색깔이 금색인 가방을 가져와라. (3) 그녀는 털이 하얀 고양이를 가지고 있다.

1 (1) I won't forget the people who(m) I met during my trip. (2) The woman who(m) you wanted to meet left for France. (3) He is the man who(m) she wants to marry.
2 (1) I went there with her. (2) I told you about him. **3** (1) whom I fought with (2) whom you taught English **4** (1) 나는 내가 정말로 사랑하는 사람과 춤을 추고 싶다. (2) 그는 내가 찾고 있던 남자이다.

1 (1) She has some shirts which are too small for her.
(2) These are candies which Jiyun gave me yesterday.
2 (1) which (2) has (3) was **3** (1) They run very fast.
(2) I made it last month. **4** (1) 나는 짠맛이 나는 음식을 조금 먹었다. (2) 나는 동물에 관한 책을 빌렸다. (3) 너는 내가 탁자 위에 둔 돈을 본 적이 있니?

1 (1) that (2) who, that (3) that, which **2** (1) who(m)
(2) which (3) who

1 (1) makes (2) the thing that, what (3) is **2** (1) What I really need (2) what you have (3) what they believe
3 (1) what they say (2) what he had (3) What made us angry **4** (1) 나의 부모님은 항상 매우 싼 것을 사신다. (2) 나는 네가 말하고 있는 것을 믿지 않는다. (3) 사람들이 말하는 것은 종종 그들이 생각하는 것과 다르다.

1 (1) who is (2) which was (3) who (4) that **2** (1) which (that) (2) who(m)(that) (3) who(that), are

1 (1) where (2) when (3) where **2** (1) My office is not far from the place where I live. (2) 2014 was the year when Brazil hosted the World Cup. **3** (1) a place where I can ride a skateboard (2) the season when we can go skiing (3) the place where the great poet is buried **4** (1) the place where we spent our vacation (2) the time when I arrived at her house

1 (1) the way (2) why (3) way **2** (1) Tell me the reason why she called me. (2) Bob told me how he finished the work. **3** (1) The reason why he was upset (2) the way you passed the test **4** (1) the reason why lots of fish died in the river (2) the way I got the old book

CHAPTER 12 접속사

요점정리 노트 ·· p.42

1 and 2 or 3 It 4 that 5 when 6 after 7 while 8 until
9 since 10 ~ 때문에 11 If 12 unless 13 Since(Because / as)
14 so 15 Although 16 and 17 A가 아니라 B 18 both
19 or

1 (1) Wake up now, or (2) Tell him the truth, and **2** (1) 더

많은 채소를 먹으려고 노력해, 그러면 건강해질 거야.　(2) 욕실을 청소해, 그렇지 않으면 너의 룸메이트가 화를 낼 거야.

FOCUS **68**　　　　　　　　　　　　　　　　p.43

1 (1) I remember that I turned off the light　(2) I think that she will do well on the test　**2** (1) It's true that the Earth is round.　(2) Did you know that the store was closed?

FOCUS **69**　　　　　　　　　　　　　　　　p.43

1 (1) she looked out the window　(2) she lived in Hong Kong　**2** (1) When I have some free time, I usually see a movie.　(2) As he was playing soccer, he got hurt.　**3** (1) when he was young　(2) While I was working　**4** (1) 그는 식사를 하면서 신문을 읽는다.　(2) 내가 10살이었을 때 나는 이 도시로 이사를 왔다.

FOCUS **70**　　　　　　　　　　　　　　　　p.44

1 (1) waiting until he showed up　(2) go swimming since she has a cold　(3) a shower after I came back home　**2** (1) until you succeed　(2) before you answer　(3) After we had breakfast　**3** (1) before the weather gets worse　(2) until you get to the park　(3) After we take off our shoes　**4** (1) 네가 나에게 말할 때까지 나는 그것에 대해 아무것도 몰랐다.　(2) 그녀는 이사한 이후로 그를 보지 못했다.

FOCUS **71**　　　　　　　　　　　　　　　　p.44

1 (1) have　(2) if　(3) want　**2** (1) you take this aspirin　(2) you stop shouting　(3) the weather is good　**3** (1) Unless you eat this now　(2) If you don't take the textbook to your home　**4** (1) Unless you want to gain weight　(2) If you put on your coat

---

FOCUS **72**　　　　　　　　　　　　　　　　p.45

1 (1) parents got angry because I got a bad grade　(2) the sun is very bright, I can't open my eyes　**2** (1) because its food is good　(2) because we didn't have enough time　(3) because he works there　**3** (1) because it was very cold　(2) As I was busy　**4** (1) 그것들이 너무 비싸기 때문에　(2) 눈이 심하게 오고 있기 때문에

FOCUS **73**　　　　　　　　　　　　　　　　p.45

---

1 (1) The teacher understands us, so we like him.　(2) I missed the train, so I couldn't arrive at the meeting on time.　**2** (1) so I went　(2) so small that　**3** (1) so quietly that we can't hear you　(2) so heavily that I couldn't go out　(3) so hard that he passed the test　**4** (1) 나는 너무 놀라서 무슨 말을 해야 할지 몰랐다.　(2) 웨이터가 너무 무례해서 우리는 화가 났다.

FOCUS **74**　　　　　　　　　　　　　　　　p.46

1 (1) Though(Although)　(2) though(although) I was feeling sick　(3) Even if(though)　**2** (1) Though she was tired, she worked hard.　(2) Even though it was very cold, the girl wasn't wearing gloves.　**3** (1) even though he can't walk　(2) Though she lives far away　**4** (1) 나는 그녀를 매일 봄에도 불구하고 그녀와 절대 말을 하지 않는다.　(2) 나는 점심을 많이 먹었지만 여전히 배고프다.

FOCUS **75**　　　　　　　　　　　　　　　　p.46

1 (1) has　(2) want　(3) like　**2** (1) but also　(2) or　(3) nor　**3** (1) He gave us not only good advice but (also) a lot of money.　(2) Both vegetables and meat are necessary for our health.　(3) I like romantic movies as well as horror movies.　**4** (1) 나의 남편 또는 내가 우리의 아이들을 박물관에 데리고 가야 한다.　(2) 나뿐만 아니라 사장도 그 결과에 만족했다.

CHAPTER **13**　가정법

요점정리 노트 ·· p.47

1 현재　**2** 과거형　**3** were　**4** saw　**5** 과거　**6** had　**7** lifted　**8** 과거 **9** 과거완료　**10** 좋을　**11** 좋았을　**12** had　**13** had arrived　**14** 현재

FOCUS **76**　　　　　　　　　　　　　　　　p.47

1 (1) could lend　(2) were　(3) would write　**2** (1) could go　(2) would　**3** (1) lived, would be　(2) aren't, can't get　**4** (1) If I weren't a movie star, I would be a cook.　(2) If I had enough apples, I could bake an apple pie.

FOCUS **77**　　　　　　　　　　　　　　　　p.48

1 (1) could have succeeded　(2) had seen　(3) wouldn't have broken　**2** (1) didn't marry, couldn't live　(2) had had,

---

could have gotten　　**3** (1) he had felt good　(2) they had listened to the guide　　**4** (1) 네가 캠핑을 가지 않았다면, 많은 좋은 사람들을 만나지 못했을 것이다.　(2) 그가 음악을 공부했다면, 훌륭한 음악가가 되었을 것이다.

FOCUS 78　　　　　　　　p.48

1 (1) Karen agreed　(2) (that) she is not(isn't) my girlfriend　(3) it were not(weren't) true　　**2** (1) have → had　(2) are → were

FOCUS 79　　　　　　　　p.48

1 (1) he had been honest with his friends　(2) Grace had done it earlier　　**2** (1) 그가 나와 함께 그 영화를 봤다면 좋았을 텐데.　(2) 지난 일요일에 날이 맑았다면 좋았을 텐데.

CHAPTER 14 일치와 화법

요점정리 노트 ··· p.49

1 현재　2 과거　3 현재　4 과거　5 is　6 broke　7 과거　8 told 9 ask　10 if　11 was　12 의문사　13 where　14 wanted 15 whether　16 where　17 left　18 if(whether)　19 likes 20 When

FOCUS 80　　　　　　　　p.50

1 (1) is, was　(2) were　(3) broke　　**2** (1) his father goes hiking　(2) he had left for his hometown　(3) Andrew would be home　　**3** (1) buys → bought(had bought)　(2) had died → died　　**4** (1) rises　(2) will succeed

FOCUS 81　　　　　　　　p.50

1 (1) tells　(2) then　　**2** (1) that you had walked to school that morning　(2) that she found a strange box there (3) that she would go swimming the next day　　**3** (1) she didn't know his phone number　(2) he had seen my friend the day before　　**4** (1) I like the white blouse　(2) I saw the movie two days ago

FOCUS 82　　　　　　　　p.51

1 (1) if that was my car　(2) if I felt better then　　**2** (1) you → me　(2) that → if(whether)　　**3** (1) Do you love me　(2) Can you solve this problem　　**4** (1) if he had seen a cat (2) whether we were ready to order

FOCUS 83　　　　　　　　p.51

1 (1) what made me think so　(2) how old her dog was **2** (1) What did your father say about it　(2) Where do you come from　(3) What time will you arrive　　**3** (1) asked them who had broken the window　(2) asked his son how he felt that day　　**4** (1) was　(2) had　(3) that day

FOCUS 84　　　　　　　　p.52

1 (1) Can you tell me what I should do?　(2) I'm not sure if (whether) the man is diligent.　(3) I wonder where my old friends are.　　**2** (1) the bike was invented　(2) my new bag was　(3) you love　　**3** (1) how we go to　(2) if this is your first visit　(3) why Judy felt angry　　**4** (1) what, will, happen (2) if(whether), I, have, seen, him

FOCUS 85　　　　　　　　p.52

1 (1) How long do they guess this bridge is?　(2) Who does the teacher think is wrong?　(3) What time do you suppose they will leave?　　**2** (1) I am　(2) Which foods do you believe　(3) Dad will buy　　**3** (1) the kids are doing now (2) Why do you think he broke　(3) How far do you suppose it is　　**4** (1) What, this, word, means　(2) Who, will, be

Memo

T·A·P·A 영역별 집중 학습으로 영어 고민을 한 방에 타파 합니다.

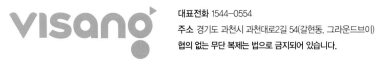

대표전화 1544-0554
주소 경기도 과천시 과천대로2길 54(갈현동, 그라운드브이)
협의 없는 무단 복제는 법으로 금지되어 있습니다.

G2

LEVEL 2

핵심문법으로 격파하는

GRAMMAR
TAPA

정답과 해설

visang

GRAMMAR TAPA

정답과 해설

LEVEL 2

FOCUS 01   p.9

A 1 1형식 2 2형식 3 1형식 4 2형식 **B** 1 주어, 동사, 부사구 2 주어, 동사, 보어 3 주어, 동사, 부사구 4 주어, 동사, 보어 **C** 1 looks busy 2 tastes sweet 3 felt tired

교과서 문장 응용하기 1 His bag is under the chair. 2 She looks happy.

FOCUS 02   p.10

A 1 3형식 2 4형식 3 3형식 4 4형식 5 3형식 **B** 1 you 2 him 3 us 4 me **C** 1 sent him fan letters 2 asked me many questions 3 made his sister cookies 4 showed us her new bag

교과서 문장 응용하기 1 We grow three apple trees. 2 He gave her a diamond ring.

FOCUS 03   p.11

A 1 for 2 of 3 to **B** 1 to them 2 for Mira 3 of me **C** 1 Josh's sister bought a red hat for him. 2 Kate lent her earphones to me. 3 Minsu made a paper airplane for his brother. 4 He sometimes asks funny questions of his classmates.

교과서 문장 응용하기 1 Kevin showed his pictures to me. 2 She bought some snacks for us.

FOCUS 04   p.12

A 1 Kitty 2 to study 3 sad **B** 1 to win 2 angry 3 to sing **C** 1 him a kind neighbor 2 made us excited 3 told them to start 4 call me a liar

교과서 문장 응용하기 1 He keeps his body healthy. 2 Our teacher told us to be quiet.

FOCUS 05   p.13

A 1 wash 2 jump 3 save 4 to solve 5 falling

B 1 go(going) 2 keep 3 touch(touching) 4 know **C** 1 heard someone ask 2 see my brother ride 3 makes us water 4 let the child go 5 help the boy carry

교과서 문장 응용하기 1 I had him fix my chair. 2 Her mother saw her wash(washing) the dishes.

내신적중 실전문제   pp.14~18

01 ④	02 ①	03 send the homework to our teacher
04 ⑤	05 ③	06 ②, ④ 07 ②, ④, ⑤
08 ③	09 ②	10 ④ 11 feels soft 12 ③
13 ④	14 ②	15 to dress 16 shake(shaking)
17 ②	18 ①	19 ① 20 ①, ④ 21 ② 22 ③
23 ④	24 ②	25 to knock → knock(knocking)
26 ③	27 ⑤	

서술형 평가

01 ⑴ She bought me a new pair of shoes.
   ⑵ She bought a new pair of shoes for me.

02 ⑴ told me to bake muffins
   ⑵ saw Jessica shop

03 ⑴ ~을 만들었다, 3형식 ⑵ ~에게 …을 만들어 주었다, 4형식 ⑶ ~에게 …을 만들어 주었다, 3형식 ⑷ ~가 …하게 시켰다, 5형식

04 ⑴ coldly → cold ⑵ warmly → warm

05 ⑴ ⓒ ⑵ ⓔ ⑶ ⓓ ⑷ ⓐ ⑸ ⓑ

06 We usually give nicknames to our friends.

---

01 smell은 감각동사이므로 보어로 형용사가 와야 한다. ①, ②, ③, ⑤는 부사이고 ④는 형용사이다.

02 빈칸 뒤에 목적어와 목적격보어가 나오고, 목적격보어가 동사원형인 것으로 보아 빈칸에는 지각동사 watched가 알맞다.

03 목적어가 두 개이지만 주어진 단어에 전치사 to가 있으므로, 「주어 + 동사 + 직접목적어 + 전치사 + 간접목적어」인 3형식 문장이 알맞다.

04 첫 번째 빈칸에는 '~에게'의 뜻으로 쓰인 전치사 to, 두 번째 빈칸에는 동사 ask의 목적격보어를 이끄는 to부정사의 to가 필요하다.

05 want는 목적격보어로 to부정사를 쓰고, 사역동사 have는

목적격보어로 동사원형을 쓴다.

06 ②「동사(cook) + 간접목적어 + 직접목적어」의 어순인 4형식 문장이다. ④「동사(cook) + 직접목적어 + 전치사(for) + 간접목적어」의 어순인 3형식 문장이다.

07 |보기|는「주어 + 동사 + 명사 보어」의 2형식 문장이다.
① 1형식 ②, ④, ⑤ 2형식 ③ 3형식

08 목적격보어로 동사원형이 쓰인 5형식 문장이므로 빈칸에는 사역동사(have, let)와 지각동사(see, help)가 알맞다. ③의 tell은 목적격보어로 to부정사를 쓰는 동사이므로 알맞지 않다.

09 make가 5형식 문장의 동사일 때는 목적격보어 자리에 명사, 형용사, 동사원형을 쓸 수 있다. ②는 to부정사이므로 알맞지 않다.

10 목적격보어 자리에 to부정사가 있으므로 동사원형을 목적격보어로 쓰는 watched는 알맞지 않다.

11 '~한 느낌이다'라는 뜻의 동사 feel은 주격보어로 형용사를 쓴다.

12 ③은 4형식 문장의 직접목적어이고, ①, ②, ④, ⑤는 5형식 문장의 목적격보어이다.

13 4형식 문장을 3형식으로 전환할 때 동사 get은 간접목적어 앞에 전치사 for를 쓴다.

14 ②「주어 + 동사 + 목적어 + 목적격보어」인 5형식 문장이다.
① 5형식, 3형식 ③ 4형식, 3형식 ④ 2형식, 1형식 ⑤ 5형식, 4형식 문장이다.

15 advise는 목적격보어로 to부정사를 쓰는 동사이다.

16 지각동사 feel은 목적격보어로 동사원형이나 현재분사를 쓰는 동사이다.

17 ①, ③, ④, ⑤는「주어 + 동사 + 목적어 + 목적격보어」인 5형식 문장이지만 ②는「주어 + 동사 + 간접목적어 + 직접목적어」인 4형식 문장이다.

18 감각동사 look이 2형식 문장에 쓰이면 보어로 형용사를 쓰므로 ①은 sadly가 아닌 sad가 알맞다.

19 |보기|와 ①은 5형식 문장의 목적격보어로 쓰였다. ② 2형식 문장의 주격보어, ③, ④ 3형식 문장의 목적어, ⑤ 4형식 문장의 직접목적어로 쓰였다.

20 help의 목적격보어로는 동사원형과 to부정사를 모두 쓸 수 있다.

21 '~가 …하는 것을 보다'는「지각동사 see + 목적어 + 목적격보어(동사원형)」의 형태로 쓴다.

22 |보기|와 ③은「동사 + 간접목적어 + 직접목적어」의 형태인 4형식 문장이다. ①, ④, ⑤ 3형식 ② 5형식

23 ④ make가 5형식 문장에 쓰이면 목적격보어로 부사가 아니라 형용사를 쓰므로 happily는 happy로 고쳐야 한다.
①, ② 2형식 문장의 형용사 보어 ③ 1형식 문장의 부사 ⑤ 5형식 문장의 형용사 보어

24 ① let은 사역동사이므로 목적격보어로 동사원형을 쓴다. (to show → show)
③ find의 목적격보어는 형용사가 알맞다. (interest → interesting)
④ advise는 목적격보어로 to부정사를 쓴다. (jogging → to jog)
⑤ get은 사역의 의미를 가지는 동사이지만, 목적격보어로 to부정사를 쓴다. (wait → to wait)

25 hear는 지각동사이므로 목적격보어 자리에 동사원형이나 현재분사가 온다.

26 ①, ②, ④, ⑤의 make는 5형식 동사이고 ③의 make는 4형식 동사이다.

27 ⑤ 4형식을 3형식으로 전환할 때 buy는 간접목적어 앞에 전치사 for를 쓰는 동사이므로 to me는 for me로 바꾸는 것이 알맞다.

서술형 평가

01 4형식 문장은「주어 + 동사 + 간접목적어 + 직접목적어」의 어순으로 쓰고, 3형식 문장은「주어 + 동사 + 직접목적어 + 전치사 + 간접목적어」의 어순으로 쓴다. 이때 동사가 buy이므로 전치사는 for를 쓴다.

02「주어 + 동사 + 목적어 + 목적격보어」형태의 5형식 문장으로 나타낸다. (1)은 to 부정사가, (2)는 동사원형이 목적격보어 자리에 온다.

03 (1) this beef dish가 목적어인 3형식 문장 (2) me가 간접목적어, this beef dish가 직접목적어인 4형식 문장 (3) this beef dish가 목적어인 3형식 문장 (4) me가 목적어, cook이 목적격보어인 5형식 문장

04 (1) 2형식 문장의 주격보어와 (2) 5형식 문장의 목적격보어는 모두 형용사로 쓴다.

[05~06]

우리는 우리의 친구들에게 보통 별명을 붙인다. 내 친구들은 나를 '마이클 잭슨'이라고 부른다. 난 곱슬머리를 갖고 있다. 또, 노래를 잘 하고 춤도 잘 춘다. 장소에 붙는 별명들도 있다. 뉴욕은 '빅 애플(큰 사과)'이고 파리는 '빛의 도시', 아리조나는 '발렌타인 주'이다. 이런 별명들

에는 흥미로운 유래가 있다. 예를 들면 아리조나는 2월 14일에 주가 되었다. 파리의 밤 불빛은 밝다.

05 (1) 「주어＋동사」의 1형식 문장
    (2) 「주어＋동사＋보어」의 2형식 문장
    (3) 「주어＋동사＋목적어」의 3형식 문장
    (4) 「주어＋동사＋간접목적어＋직접목적어」의 4형식 문장
    (5) 「주어＋동사＋목적어＋목적격보어」의 5형식 문장

06 ⓐ는 4형식 문장이므로 전치사를 이용하려면 3형식 문장인 「주어＋동사＋직접목적어＋전치사＋간접목적어」의 어순으로 쓴다. 동사가 give이므로 전치사는 to가 알맞다.

CHAPTER 02 to부정사

FOCUS 06　　　　p.21

A 1 It, to read 2 It, to write 3 It, to play 4 It, to eat B 1 is to see 2 is to become 3 His dream is to invent C 1 to wash tennis shoes 2 to finish the puzzle in an hour 3 to have a check-up with the dentist

교과서 문장 응용하기 1 It is a good exercise to ride a bike(bicycle). 2 My wish is to pass the test(exam).

FOCUS 07　　　　p.22

A 1 to play 2 to take 3 to go 4 to marry
B 1 what to cook 2 how to read 3 when to call
4 where to visit C 1 when, should start 2 how to make 3 where to go

교과서 문장 응용하기 1 Mary hopes to meet him again.
2 I don't know what to buy.

FOCUS 08　　　　p.23

A 1 to talk 2 to show 3 to sit on 4 to eat with
B 1 someone to help me 2 many places to visit
3 something warm to wear 4 many ways to solve the problem C 1 book to read 2 key to open

3 friend to depend(rely) on 4 time to go shopping

교과서 문장 응용하기 1 We don't have time to go there.
2 Michael needed a chair to sit on.

FOCUS 09　　　　p.24

A 1 to ask 2 to get 3 to save 4 to see B 1 to have(eat) lunch 2 to hear the news 3 to miss the ball C 1 order to study 2 in(so) order(as) to buy

교과서 문장 응용하기 1 They sat on the sofa to take a rest. 2 I was glad to see Paul at(in) the park.

FOCUS 10　　　　p.25

A 1 to learn 2 to be 3 to move 4 to find
B 1 to be 2 easy to carry 3 to use C 1 나의 할머니는 80세까지 사셨다. 2 그 질문에 대답하는 것을 보니 그는 똑똑한 것이 분명하다. 3 Fred는 새 전화기를 샀지만, 결국 그것을 또 잃어버렸다.

교과서 문장 응용하기 1 The poet lived to be 87 years old.
2 Sunglasses are proper to wear in summer.

FOCUS 11　　　　p.26

A 1 too 2 enough 3 enough 4 too B 1 too young to get 2 long enough to reach 3 too old to walk C 1 so, that, can't think 2 so, that, can sleep

교과서 문장 응용하기 1 She is too young to understand the book. 2 He was kind enough to carry my bag.

FOCUS 12　　　　p.27

A 1 for, to 2 of, to 3 for, to 4 of, to B 1 natural for Penny to get 2 careless of him to open
3 difficult for her to say 4 foolish of you to miss
C 1 for me to 2 of him to save 3 of them to take
4 for us to understand

교과서 문장 응용하기 1 It is important for him to exercise regularly. 2 It is kind of you to lend me your pen.

▲▲▲▲▲▲▲▲▲▲▲▲▲▲▲▲▲▲

01 ④　02 ①　03 ①　04 ⑤　05 enough to
have　06 ④　07 ②　08 ②　09 ⑤　10 ①
11 to eat → to eat with　12 what →
when　13 ⑤　14 ①　15 ①　16 ④　17 ①
18 ②　19 in(so) order(as) to　20 too, to
swim　21 ①, ⑤　22 ⑤　23 ④　24 ②　25 ④
26 ③　27 ②

서술형 평가

01 (1) ⓐ, ⓒ　(2) ⓓ　(3) ⓑ, ⓔ, ⓕ
02 (1) how to get　(2) how I should get
03 to(so as to / in order to) take pictures of
04 (1) so early that she could have
　　(2) early enough to have
05 several ways to give advice
06 It's important for you to know when to give strong advice and when to make a suggestion.

01 '그 아이에게 카드를 보내기로 결정했다'는 의미가 되도록 decide의 목적어 역할을 하는 to부정사 형태가 알맞다.

02 to work out regularly가 진주어이므로 빈칸에는 가주어 It이 알맞다.

03 ①은 '~해서 (결국) …하다'는 뜻의 결과를 나타내며, | 보기 |와 ②, ③, ④, ⑤는 '~하기 위해'의 뜻으로 목적의 의미를 나타내는 부사적 용법의 to부정사이다.

04 to부정사가 꾸며 주는 명사가 전치사의 목적어이므로 전치사가 필요하다.
play with: '~와 함께 놀다' / live in: '~에 살다'

05 '…할 만큼 충분히 ~하다'는 「형용사(부사) + enough + to부정사」로 표현한다.

06 to부정사의 의미상 주어는 「for(of) + 목적격」이며, ④는 사람의 성격을 나타내는 형용사 nice가 있으므로 for가 아닌 of를 써야 한다.

07 | 보기 |와 ②는 명사적 용법 중 주어로 쓰인 to부정사이다.
① 명사적 용법 중 보어 ③ 명사적 용법 중 목적어 ④ 부사적 용법 중 감정의 원인 ⑤ 형용사적 용법

08 형용사 뒤에 빈칸이 있고 to부정사가 이어지고 있으므로 '…할 만큼 충분히 ~하다'라는 의미인 「형용사 + enough + to부

정사」를 써야 한다.

09 ⑤ 「too ~ to부정사」는 부정어 not이 없어도 부정의 의미이므로 can 대신 cannot이 알맞다.

10 ①은 날씨를 나타내는 비인칭 주어이다. ②, ③, ④, ⑤는 뒤에 오는 to부정사를 대신하는 가주어이다.

11 to부정사가 수식하는 명사는 a spoon and chopsticks이며, 명사가 전치사의 목적어이므로 전치사 with를 써야 한다.

12 저녁에 약을 먹었다는 말로 보아 의사가 말해 준 것은 약을 먹는 시간일 것이다. 따라서 '언제 ~할지'의 뜻을 가진 「when + to부정사」를 써야 한다.

13 ① 명사 time을 꾸며 주는 to부정사 (→ to leave)
② 「too + 형용사 + to부정사」 (→ to say)
③ 부사적 용법 중 결과를 나타내는 to부정사 (→ to find)
④ 「형용사 + enough + to부정사」 (→ good enough)
⑤ '무엇을 ~할지'의 뜻을 가진 「what + to부정사」

14 -thing으로 끝나는 대명사는 형용사가 뒤에서 수식하므로 「대명사 + 형용사 + to부정사」의 어순으로 쓴다.

15 to부정사 앞에 의미상 주어가 필요하며, impossible은 사람의 성격을 나타내는 형용사가 아니므로, 「for + 목적격」 형태로 쓴다.

16 ①은 목적어, ②, ⑤는 보어, ③은 진주어로 쓰여 모두 명사 역할을 하는 to부정사이다. ④는 형용사 역할을 하며 명사 time을 꾸미는 to부정사이다.

17 ①, ③, ④, ⑤는 목적을 나타내는 부사 역할을 하는 to부정사인 반면, ②는 보어로 쓰인 명사 역할의 to부정사이다.

18 ②는 형용사를 꾸미는 부사 역할을 하는 to부정사이다. ①은 「의문사 + to부정사」로, 목적어로 쓰인 명사 역할, ③은 주어로 쓰인 명사 역할, ④, ⑤는 보어로 쓰인 명사 역할이다.

19 목적을 나타내는 to부정사는 in order to 또는 so as to로 바꿔 쓸 수 있다.

20 「so + 형용사(부사) + that + 주어 + can't(couldn't) + 동사원형 ~」은 「too + 형용사(부사) + to부정사」로 바꿔 쓸 수 있다.

21 '너무 ~해서 …할 수 없다'라는 뜻은 「too + 형용사 + to부정사」 또는 「so + 형용사 + that + 주어 + can't …」로 쓸 수 있다.

22 nice, kind, stupid, careful은 사람의 성격이나 태도를 나타내는 형용사이므로 to부정사의 의미상 주어를 「of + 목적격」의 형태로 쓴다. ⑤의 necessary는 전치사 for가 필요하므로 알맞지 않다.

23 「의문사 + to부정사」는 「의문사 + 주어 + should + 동사원형」으

로 바꿔 쓸 수 있다.

24 「형용사(부사)+enough+to부정사」의 형태가 알맞다. ②는 빈칸 앞이 be동사이므로 알맞지 않다.

25 ⓐ 명사적 용법 (목적어 역할), ⓑ 형용사적 용법, ⓒ 명사적 용법 (보어 역할), ⓓ 명사적 용법 (주어 역할), ⓔ 형용사적 용법의 to부정사이다.

26 ③ '점심으로 무엇을 먹을지'라는 뜻이 되어야 하므로 why를 what으로 고쳐야 한다.

27 ① 가주어는 it으로 쓴다. (That → It)
③ to부정사가 수식하는 명사가 전치사의 목적어이면 to부정사 뒤에 전치사를 쓴다. (to write → to write on)
④ brave는 사람의 성격을 나타내는 형용사이므로 「of+목적격」으로 의미상 주어를 쓴다. (for you → of you)
⑤ difficult는 사람의 성격을 나타내는 형용사가 아니므로 「for+목적격」으로 의미상 주어를 쓴다. (of me → for me)

서술형 평가

01 (1) 명사적 용법: ⓐ 목적어 역할 ⓒ 주어 역할
(2) 형용사적 용법: ⓓ 명사 수식
(3) 부사적 용법: ⓑ 결과 ⓔ 감정의 원인 ⓕ 목적

02 '어떻게 ~할지'라는 의미로 목적어 역할을 할 때는 「how+to 부정사」 또는 「how+주어+should+동사원형」으로 나타낸다.

03 '~하기 위해'라는 목적의 의미는 「to(so as to/in order to)+동사원형」의 부사적 용법으로 나타낸다.

04 '…할 만큼 충분히 ~하다'의 뜻은 「so+형용사(부사)+that+주어+can ...」이나 「형용사+enough+to부정사」로 바꿔 쓸 수 있다.

[05~06]

> 영어로 충고를 하는 방법이 몇 가지 있다. 어떤 방법들은 아주 강력하다. 다른 방법들은 그만큼 강력하지 않다. 언제 강한 충고를 하고 언제 제안을 해야 할지를 아는 것이 중요하다. 예를 들면 미국과 캐나다에서는 친한 친구나 가족 구성원에게 강한 충고를 할 수 있다. 상사나 친구에게는 강한 충고를 해서는 안 된다. 대신, 제안을 해야 한다.

05 to부정사의 형용사적 용법으로 명사 뒤에서 수식하는 「명사+to부정사」의 어순으로 쓰는 것이 알맞다.

06 to부정사가 주어인 경우, 가주어는 it을 쓰며, 형용사가 important이므로 의미상 주어는 「for+목적격」으로 나타낸다. when giving과 when to making은 '언제 ~해야 할지'의

의미로 know의 목적어 역할을 하는 「의문사+to부정사」의 형태가 되어야 한다.
(That → It / of you → for you / giving → to give / to making → to make)

CHAPTER 03 동명사

FOCUS 13　　　　p.35

A 1 Getting **2** having **3** taking **4** flying
B 1 Is riding a motorcycle hard? **2** My homework is writing an email in English. **3** Going out at night is dangerous. **C 1** It, to cheat **2** to meet

교과서 문장 응용하기 **1** Playing tennis is fun. / It is fun to play tennis. **2** His job is taking(to take) pictures.

FOCUS 14　　　　p.36

A 1 playing **2** watching **3** winning **4** painting **5** helping **B 1** without finishing his lunch **2** Thank you for not forgetting **3** enjoy talking about sports **4** mind taking the medicine **5** gave up smoking
C 1 mind eating **2** avoided talking **3** worried about washing **4** afraid of swimming

교과서 문장 응용하기 **1** Did you finish cleaning your room? **2** We talked about changing the plan.

FOCUS 15　　　　p.37

A 1 shutting **2** drawing **3** to go **4** cooking **5** to have **B 1** setting **2** passing **3** to bring **4** to buy
C 1 gave up fixing **2** want to get **3** finish writing

교과서 문장 응용하기 **1** Anne enjoys watching TV in her free time. **2** I hope to see you soon.

FOCUS 16　　　　p.38

A 1 breathing(to breathe) **2** working(to work) **3** to

hand **4** to tell **B 1** seeing **2** to pack **3** giving
C 1 나는 작년에 그 책을 읽었던 것을 잊어버렸다. **2** 그는 내 이름을 기억해 내려고 애썼다.

교과서 문장 응용하기 1 I remember seeing her before.
2 Yuri forgot to bring the coupons.

FOCUS 17　　　　　　　　　　　p.39

A 1 living **2** seeing **3** buying **4** worrying
B 1 ski → skiing **2** read → reading **3** to run → running **4** join → joining **C 1** no use regretting
2 cannot help asking **3** On(Upon) hearing **4** is used to sleeping

교과서 문장 응용하기 1 I feel like going home now.
2 I look forward to working with you.

내신적중 실전문제
pp.40~44

01 ④　**02** ④　**03** ④　**04** ②　**05** On(Upon)
arriving　**06** ⑤　**07** ⑤　**08** ②　**09** ⑤　**10** ①
11 to sleep　**12** making　**13** ③　**14** ③　**15** ⑤
16 ①　**17** ④　**18** learning to cook　**19** ②
20 ①, ②　**21** ①　**22** ①　**23** ①　**24** ④　**25** ③
26 answer → answering　**27** ⑤

서술형 평가
01 (1) Swimming(To swim) in deep water is
　　(2) Learning(To learn) a foreign language is
02 (1) remember sending　(2) remember to send
03 (1) to do → doing　(2) to doing → to do
04 (1) 울지 않을 수 없다　(2) 쇼핑하러 가고 싶다
　　(3) 준비하느라 바쁘다
05 ⓐ going　ⓑ to go　ⓒ leaving
　　ⓓ Spending(To spend)
06 나는 네게 몇 권의 책을 돌려줄 것을 잊었어.

01 동사를 주어로 사용하기 위해서는 동명사 또는 to부정사의 형태로 써야 한다.
02 without은 전치사이므로 동명사를 목적어로 쓴다.
03 agree는 to부정사를 목적어로 쓰는 동사이다.

04 practice는 동명사를 목적어로 쓰는 동사이다.
05 '~하자마자'라는 의미의 동명사의 관용 표현인 「on(upon) -ing」를 쓴다.
06 첫 번째 빈칸에는 '(미래에) ~할 것을 잊다'의 의미를 나타낼 「forget + to부정사」의 to부정사가 알맞고, need는 to부정사를 목적어로 쓰는 동사이다.
07 첫 번째 빈칸에는 전치사의 목적어인 동명사가 와야 하고, 두 번째 빈칸에는 '(과거에) ~했던 것을 잊다'의 의미인 「forget + 동명사」가 필요하다.
08 ② hope는 to부정사만을 목적어로 쓰는 동사이다.
09 ⑤ plan은 to부정사만을 목적어로 쓰는 동사이다.
10 |보기|와 ②, ③, ④, ⑤는 보어로 쓰인 동명사이고 ①은 현재진행형을 만드는 현재분사이다.
11 동사 try가 '~하려고 노력하다'의 의미로 쓰일 때는 목적어로 to부정사를 쓴다.
12 finish는 동명사를 목적어로 쓰는 동사이다.
13 ③ 「look forward to -ing」는 '~하기를 기대하다'라는 의미이므로 join은 joining으로 고쳐야 한다.
14 '(과거에) ~했던 것을 기억하다'는 의미는 「remember + 동명사」로 쓴다.
15 ① 전치사 뒤에는 동명사가 온다. (solve → solving)
② imagine은 동명사를 목적어로 쓴다. (to be → being)
③ 「spend + 시간(돈) + -ing」 형태로 쓴다. (collect → collecting)
④ next week가 있으므로 「remember + to부정사」를 써서 '(미래에) ~할 것을 기억하다'의 의미가 되어야 한다.
(inviting → to invite)
16 stop은 동명사를, hope는 to부정사를 목적어로 쓰는 동사이다.
17 ④ '~을 기대하다'는 「look forward to -ing」로 나타내므로 to working으로 고쳐야 한다.
18 enjoy는 동명사를 목적어로 쓰는 동사이므로 learn을 동명사 형태로 바꾼다.
19 '시험 삼아 ~해 보다'라는 뜻일 때는 「try + 동명사」로, '~하려고 노력하다'라는 뜻일 때는 「try + to부정사」로 쓴다.
20 ① 「be busy -ing」는 '~하느라 바쁘다'는 뜻이므로 to clean은 cleaning이 되어야 한다. ② 「cannot help -ing」는 '~하지 않을 수 없다'는 뜻이므로 to love는 loving이 되어야 한다.
21 ① promise는 to부정사만 목적어로 쓰므로 to take로 고쳐

22 ① decide는 to부정사만 목적어로 쓰는 동사이므로 to be로 고쳐야 한다.

23 ① want는 to부정사만 목적어로 쓰는 동사이므로 동명사로 바꿔 쓸 수 없다.

24 '~해도 소용없다'는 「It is no use -ing」로 나타내고, '~에게 …하라고 충고하다'는 「advise + 목적어 + to부정사」로 쓴다.

25 ③ 동사 love는 to부정사와 동명사 중 어떤 것을 목적어로 쓰더라도 뜻이 달라지지 않는다.

26 「How about ~?」은 목적어로 동명사를 쓴다.

27 ① expect, ③ plan은 목적어로 to부정사만 쓰고 ② enjoy, ④ mind는 목적어로 동명사만 쓴다.
(① → to see ② → playing ③ → to study ④ → working)

서술형 평가

01 동사가 주어로 올 때는 동명사나 to부정사의 형태이며, 이때는 단수 취급한다. (1) 깊은 물에서 수영하는 것은 위험하며, (2) 외국어를 배우는 것은 도움이 된다는 내용이 되어야 한다.

02 (1) 「remember + 동명사」: '~했던 것을 기억하다' (과거의 일)
(2) 「remember + to부정사」: '~할 것을 기억하다' (미래의 일)

03 (1) '~하는 게 어때?'는 「How about -ing?」로 나타낸다.
(2) need는 to부정사만을 목적어로 쓴다.

04 (1) 「cannot help -ing」: '~하지 않을 수 없다'
(2) 「feel like -ing」: '~하고 싶다' / 「go -ing」: '~하러 가다'
(3) 「be busy -ing」: '~하느라 바쁘다'

[05~06]

> 안녕, Alan.
> 이번 주말에 등산 가자는 것에 대한 네 이메일을 받았어, 좋아, 난 가고 싶어. 며칠간 도시를 떠나는 것을 정말 기대하고 있어. 시골에서 시간을 보내는 것은 날 행복하게 할 거야. 토요일 아침에 우리가 몇 시에 출발하는 거지? 아, 그건 그렇고, 네게 책 몇 권을 돌려줄 것을 잊었어. 내일 아침 네 집에 들를게.
> Jessy가.

05 ⓐ 전치사는 동명사를 목적어로 쓴다. ⓑ want는 to부정사를 목적어로 쓴다. ⓒ 「look forward to -ing」: '~하기를 기

대하다' ⓓ 동사가 주어로 올 때는 동명사 또는 to부정사의 형태이다.

06 「forget + to부정사」: '~할 것을 잊다' (미래의 일)

CHAPTER 04 시제

FOCUS 18　　　　　p.47

A **1** went **2** have been **3** has seen **4** got **5** started **B** **1** has kept **2** have known **3** have been **4** have met **5** has, walked **C** **1** have been **2** lost **3** has learned **4** was

교과서 문장 응용하기 **1** I have met Matt before. **2** Jim has already eaten(had) lunch.

FOCUS 19　　　　　p.48

A **1** Have **2** have not(haven't) **3** found **4** heard **B** **1** I have not(haven't) traveled in Thailand. **2** Have they sold all the tickets? **3** My sister has not(hasn't) spoken to Andrew. **4** Has Yuri bought him a present? **C** **1** Has your cousin returned to Mexico? **2** We have not seen the new room yet. **3** Have you read the comic book?

교과서 문장 응용하기 **1** has not(hasn't) read his letter yet **2** you (ever) been to New York

FOCUS 20　　　　　p.49

A **1** has already called **2** has just made **3** has already done **4** have just finished **B** **1** have already sent **2** have just had(eaten) **3** studied, yet **C** **1** 그녀는 벌써 떠났다. **2** 나는 지금 막 설거지하는 것을 마쳤다. **3** 그는 아직 공항에 도착하지 않았다.

교과서 문장 응용하기 **1** Kenny has just arrived in Seoul. **2** I have already bought the book.

A 1 have broken **2** have sold **3** has taken my umbrella **4** has told me   **B 1** has gone to **2** has left her wallet **3** have washed the shirt   **C 1** 그 선수들은 경기장을 떠나 버렸다. **2** 내 여동생이 그 케이크를 먹어 버렸다.

교과서 문장 응용하기 **1** I have lost my cap(hat). **2** The woman has gone out.

A 1 have met **2** has climbed **3** has eaten **4** has played   **B 1** has ever been to Mars **2** has made a pizza many times **3** have flown a kite before   **C 1** 우리는 그의 콘서트를 한 번 본 적이 있다. **2** 그들은 워터파크에 가 본 적이 전혀 없다. **3** Bob은 전에 말을 타 본 적이 있다.

교과서 문장 응용하기 **1** I have been to China twice. **2** Peter has heard the news before.

A 1 has worked **2** has been **3** since **4** for **B 1** since **2** for **3** has been   **C 1** have lived here since last year **2** has had a cold for two days **3** has enjoyed baseball for three years **4** has broken down since last Monday **5** has worn glasses since she was six

교과서 문장 응용하기 **1** It has rained since last Saturday. **2** I have used the computer for 3(three) years.

내신적중 실전문제   pp.53~56

01 ③   **02** ②   **03** ②   **04** watch → watched
05 No, I haven't   **06** Have you heard
07 ④   **08** ④   **09** ④   **10** ②   **11** ③   **12** ②
13 ③   **14** ⑤   **15** ①   **16** ③   **17** ①   **18** have, lived   **19** has, lost   **20** ⑤

서술형 평가

01 (1) Jack has not(hasn't) touched a spider before.
   (2) Has Jack touched a spider before?
02 ⓐ, ⓓ / ⓑ, ⓕ / ⓒ, ⓔ
03 (1) has made since   (2) has made, for
04 (1) Yes, I have, I haven't played
   (2) No, he hasn't, has eaten
05 ⓐ has left → left   ⓓ since → for
06 We have had a new teacher, Mr. Cheng, since March.

01 '영국에 가서 지금 서울에 없다'는 뜻이므로 결과의 의미를 나타내는 현재완료가 알맞다. ④의 have been to는 '~에 가 본 적이 있다'의 의미로 경험을 나타낸다.

02 '전에 들어 본 적이 없어서 지금 알지 못한다'는 뜻이므로 현재완료가 알맞다. 현재완료의 부정문은 「have(has) not + 과거분사」로 나타낸다.

03 현재완료는 과거의 특정 시간을 나타내는 부사(구)인 ①, ③, ④, ⑤와는 함께 쓸 수 없다.

04 현재완료는 「have(has) + 과거분사」로 나타낸다.

05 Have you ever been to ~?는 '~에 가 본 적 있니?'라는 경험을 묻는 현재완료 의문문이고, 대답은 Yes, I have. 또는 No, I haven't.로 한다. 언젠가 가 보고 싶다고 했으므로 아직 가 본 적이 없다는 응답이 알맞다.

06 경험을 묻는 표현이므로 현재완료 의문문인 「Have(Has) + 주어 + 과거분사 ~?」를 이용한다.

07 과거부터 지금까지 계속 배우고 있으므로 계속의 의미를 나타내는 현재완료로 표현하며, '~ 동안'은 for로 나타낸다.

08 ⓐ 계속, ⓑ 결과, ⓒ 경험, ⓓ 완료, ⓔ 경험의 용법으로 쓰인 현재완료이다.

09 한 시간 전부터 지금까지 계속 찾고 있으므로 계속의 의미를 나타내는 현재완료가 알맞다. 주어가 3인칭 단수이므로 「has + 과거분사」로 쓴다.

10 3시간 전부터 페인트칠을 시작하여 이제 문이 파란색으로 칠해졌으므로 완료의 의미를 나타내는 현재완료가 알맞다.

11 일정 기간 앞에는 for를 쓰고, 과거의 특정 시점 앞에는 since를 쓴다.

12 현재완료시제는 when이 이끄는 부사절이나 ago 등 구체적인 과거를 나타내는 부사적 표현과 함께 쓸 수 없다.

13 A는 경험을 묻는 현재완료 의문문이므로 「Have + 주어 + 과거분사 ~?」로 쓴다. an hour ago라는 과거의 구체적 시점을 밝혔으므로 B의 빈칸에는 과거시제가 알맞다.

14 |보기|와 ⑤는 계속의 의미를 나타내는 현재완료이다.
①, ③ 경험 ② 완료 ④ 결과

15 |보기|와 ①은 경험의 의미를 나타내는 현재완료이다.
②, ⑤ 계속 ③, ④ 완료

16 |보기|와 ③은 완료의 의미를 나타내는 현재완료이다.
①, ⑤ 계속 ② 경험 ④ 결과

17 ① 현재완료는 과거의 특정 시점을 나타내는 부사구(last spring)와 함께 쓰지 않는다.

18 과거부터 현재까지 계속 살고 있으므로 계속을 나타내는 현재완료로 표현한다.

19 휴대전화 배터리를 잃어버려서 지금도 가지고 있지 않다는 의미이므로 결과를 나타내는 현재완료로 표현한다.

20 ⑤ two months ago는 과거의 특정 시점을 나타내는 말이므로 현재완료와 함께 쓸 수 없다.

서술형 평가

01 (1) 3인칭 단수 현재완료의 부정문은 「has not(hasn't) + 과거분사 ~.」로 쓴다.
(2) 3인칭 단수 현재완료의 의문문은 「Has + 주어 + 과거분사 ~?」로 쓴다.

02 ⓐ, ⓓ 완료, ⓑ, ⓕ 결과, ⓒ, ⓔ 경험을 나타내는 현재완료이다.

03 치즈케이크를 3시에 만들기 시작해서 아직도 계속 만들고 있으므로 현재완료 형태가 알맞다. 시작 시점을 나타내는 three o'clock 앞에는 since를, 기간을 나타내는 two hours 앞에는 for를 쓴다.

04 (1) Nick은 드럼을 쳐 본 적이 있으므로 긍정으로 대답하고, 하프는 연주해 본 적이 없으므로 경험을 나타내는 현재완료의 부정형을 쓴다. (2) Dave는 멕시코 음식은 먹어 본 적이 없으므로 부정으로 대답하고, 스페인 음식은 먹어 본 적이 있으므로 경험을 나타내는 현재완료의 긍정형을 쓴다.

[05~06]

> 난 학교에서 정말 열심히 공부하고 있다. 우리가 1년 전 이 마을로 이사 왔기 때문에 나는 이 학교에 겨우 9월부터 다니기 시작했다. 우리 중국어 선생님은 12월에 학교를 떠났다. 지난 3월, 새 선생님인 Cheng 선생님이 오셨다. 여전히 그 선생님이 계신다. 그는 아주 친절하고 우리에게 시험을 자주 내지 않으신다. 사실, 우리는 석 달 동안 중국어 시험을 보지 않았다. 하지만 내일 시험을 볼 것이기 때문에, 나는 공부를 더 해야 한다.

05 ⓐ 과거의 일을 나타내므로 현재완료가 아니라 과거시제를 쓴다. ⓓ '3개월 동안'이라는 계속의 의미여야 하므로 기간을 나타내는 전치사 for를 쓴다.

06 3월부터 지금까지 계속 Cheng 씨가 선생님이므로 현재완료로 쓰고, '3월 이후부터 계속 ~'이라는 의미가 되도록 since를 써서 기간의 시작점을 나타낸다.

CHAPTER 05 조동사

FOCUS 24   p.59

A 1 능력 2 허락 3 요청 4 능력 5 요청 **B** 1 can 2 is able to 3 wasn't able to **C** 1 You can spend 2 I couldn't sleep 3 Could you turn off

교과서 문장 응용하기 1 Minho can(is able to) speak Chinese. 2 Can(Could) you lend me your notebook?

FOCUS 25   p.60

A 1 go 2 will not(won't) 3 Will 4 invite **B** 1 will eat 2 will take 3 will not(won't) wear **C** 1 I'll make you some sandwiches. 2 I won't tell a lie again. 3 He will not do your homework for you. 4 Will you show us her album?

교과서 문장 응용하기 1 Sue will give you the gift later. / Sue will give the gift to you later. 2 I will go fishing with my father.

A 1 (b) 2 (c) 3 (a)　**B** 1 may be absent from school　2 might rain later　3 May I open　4 may not be true　**C** 1 너는 그 쿠키들을 먹어도 좋다.　2 지금 TV를 봐도 되나요?　3 Andy는 지금 공원에 있을지도 모른다.
4 세나는 축구를 좋아하지 않을지도 모른다.

교과서 문장 응용하기　1 May I come in?　2 You may(might) be wrong.

A 1 must not　2 have to　3 don't have to　4 have to
B 1 Sam must be angry.　2 You must not call me at work.　3 Tom doesn't have to wash the dishes.
4 They have to decide the winner.　**C** 1 우리는 그 호텔을 찾아야 한다.　2 그 동물들에게 먹이를 주어서는 안 된다.
3 그녀는 Tony에게 사과할 필요가 없다.

교과서 문장 응용하기　1 We must(have to) leave now.
2 John must be sick.

A 1 keep　2 should not go　3 had better　4 had better not　**B** 1 ought to　2 should not(shouldn't)
C 1 should wash your hands　2 had better tell
3 should not talk loud　4 had better not leave

교과서 문장 응용하기　1 You should not(shouldn't) forget your password.　2 You had better not drink coffee.

A 1 would　2 to eat　3 used to　4 would　**B** 1 우리는 작은 마을에 살았었다.　2 그는 머리가 길었었다.　3 Andy는 화가 날 때 방 밖으로 나가곤 했다.　**C** 1 I used to get up late　2 the house would shake　3 used to be here
4 he would sing a song

교과서 문장 응용하기　1 I used to(would) take a walk after dinner.　2 Nicole used to have brown hair.

내신적중 실전문제　　　pp.65~68

01 ②　　02 ②　　03 ④　　04 ①　　05 ⑤　　06 will not(won't) be able to solve the problem
07 don't have to　　08 ①　　09 ④　　10 used to
11 ⑤　　12 ③　　13 had not better → had better not　14 ③　　15 ④　　16 ①　　17 ③　　18 ③
19 ④　　20 ④

서술형 평가

01 (1) 그녀는 좀 쉬는 게 좋겠다.
　　(2) Ron은 나의 가장 친한 친구였다.
02 (1) Can　(2) has to　(3) ought to
03 (1) ⓐ → come　(2) ⓑ → have
　　(3) ⓔ → must not
04 (1) should(had better) drink warm milk before bedtime
　　(2) should not(shouldn't / had better not) watch TV for too long
05 Go in that direction, and you will(may / can) find the museum.
06 (1) can understand　(2) are able to understand

01 과거에 반복되었던 행동은 '~하곤 했다'라는 의미의 used to 또는 would로 나타낸다.

02 '~해도 좋다'는 허락의 의미는 may로 나타낸다.

03 건강에 대한 조언을 구하는 말에 대한 대답으로는 '패스트 푸드를 먹지 말라'는 내용의 ④가 알맞다. 금지는 「should not+동사원형」으로 나타낼 수 있다.

04 '~할 수 있다'라는 뜻으로 능력을 나타내는 be able to는 조동사 can과 바꿔 쓸 수 있다.

05 '~하는 게 좋겠다'라는 뜻으로 충고를 나타내는 should는 had better로 바꿔 쓸 수 있다.

06 능력을 나타내는 can의 미래형은 will be able to로 쓰며, 부정형은 will not(won't)으로 쓴다.

07 'No'라고 했으므로 그럴 필요가 없다는 내용이 되도록 불필요를 나타내는 don't have to가 알맞다.

08 A의 빈칸에는 현재의 능력을 묻는 can이 알맞다. B의 말은 '어렸을 때는 못했지만, 지금은 할 수 있다'라는 내용이 되어야 하므로, B의 빈칸에는 couldn't가 알맞다.

09 첫 번째 문장은 우산을 가져가는 게 좋겠다는 내용이어야 하므로 충고를 나타내는 had better를 쓴다. 두 번째 문장은 과거 시점이므로 의무를 나타내는 have to의 과거형인 had to를 쓴다.

10 '과거에는 있었지만 지금은 없다'는 뜻이므로 과거의 상태를 나타내는 used to가 알맞다.

11 |보기|와 ⑤는 '~임에 틀림없다'는 강한 추측의 의미이다. ①, ②는 '~해야 한다'는 의무이고 ③, ④는 '~해서는 안 된다'는 금지의 의미이다.

12 |보기|와 ③은 '~해도 좋다'는 허락을, ①, ②, ④, ⑤는 '~할 수 있다'는 능력을 나타낸다.

13 had better의 부정형은 had better not이다.

14 ③ must not은 '~해서는 안 된다'는 뜻으로 금지를 나타내고, don't have to는 '~할 필요가 없다'는 뜻으로 불필요를 나타낸다.

15 ④ should not은 '~해서는 안 된다'라는 뜻으로 금지를 나타내며, must는 '~해야 한다'라는 뜻으로 의무를 나타낸다.

16 ①은 '~일지도 모른다'는 추측을 나타내고, ②, ③, ④, ⑤는 '~해도 좋다'는 허락을 나타낸다.

17 will, can, would, could는 요청의 의미를 가진 조동사지만, ③ may는 요청의 의미를 나타낼 수 없다.

18 내용상 예정, 의지를 나타내는 ①, 추측을 나타내는 ②, 충고를 나타내는 ④, ⑤가 모두 알맞다. ③은 과거의 습관을 나타내므로 알맞지 않다.

19 영어 성적을 향상시키고 싶다는 내용이므로 ④ '이제는 영어를 공부할 필요가 없다'는 불필요의 의미는 어색하다.

20 과속하지 말고 주의해서 운전해야 한다는 '의무'의 내용이다. ④ may는 허락이나 추측을 나타내는 조동사이므로 어색하다.

서술형 평가

01 (1) had better는 '~하는 게 좋겠다'는 충고의 의미를 나타낸다. (2) used to는 '(과거에) ~였다'는 과거의 상태를 나타낸다.

02 (1) 허가를 나타내는 may는 can으로, (2) '~해야 한다'는 의미의 must는 have(has) to로, (3) 도덕적 의무를 나타내는 should는 ought to로 각각 바꿔 쓸 수 있다.

03 (1) must 다음에는 동사원형이 온다. (2) ⓑ의 문장의 주어는 You이므로 have to를 써야 한다. (3) 금지를 나타내는 must의 부정형은 must not이다.

04 (1) '~하라'는 충고는 You should ~.나 You had better ~.로, (2) '~하지 마라'는 충고는 You should not ~.이나 You had better not ~.으로 쓴다.

[05~06]

> 몸짓 언어는 일본, 미국, 그리스, 멕시코 혹은 그 어떤 곳에서든, 모든 곳에서 여러분을 도와줄 것이다. 사람의 말은 이해할 수 없을지 모르지만, <u>사람의 몸짓 언어는 이해할 수 있다</u>. 어떻게 박물관에 가는지 알고 싶다고 치자. 그저 거리의 사람에게 물어보아라. 그는 대개 몸을 돌린 후 가리킬 것이다. <u>그 방향으로 가라, 그러면 박물관을 찾을 것이다(찾을지도 모른다 / 찾을 수 있다)</u>.

05 '그 방향으로 가라, 그러면 박물관을 찾아야 한다'는 말은 문맥상 어색하므로 '그 방향으로 가라, 그러면 박물관을 찾을 것이다(찾을지도 모른다 / 찾을 수 있다)'라는 의미가 되도록 have to를 will(may / can)으로 바꾸어야 한다.

06 '~할 수 있다'는 의미는 can 또는 be able to로 나타내며, 조동사 다음에는 동사원형을 쓴다.

CHAPTER 06 수동태

FOCUS 30　　p.71

A 1 him **2** misunderstood **3** was parked **B 1** is driven by **2** are grown by **3** is respected by
C 1 This room is used by my daughter. **2** A mouse is run after by a cat. **3** This movie was made in 2017 by the director. **4** Stamps are sold in the post office (by them).

교과서 문장 응용하기 1 were planted by Mary **2** is spoken in Montreal (by people)

FOCUS 31　　p.72

A 1 is not grown **2** was not built **3** is not run **4** is not made **5** were not washed **B 1** Was, invented, was **2** Was, painted, wasn't, was **3** When was, introduced **C 1** 부정문: This sad poem wasn't(was not) written by Mike. 의문: Was this sad poem written by Mike? **2** 부정문: This art gallery isn't(is not) closed at 5 o'clock by them. 의문문: Is this art gallery closed at 5 o'clock by them?

 **1** These shoes weren't(were not) made by him. **2** When was the email sent?

FOCUS 32   p.73

A 1 was built **2** will be washed **3** should be thrown **4** can be done **B 1** was repaired **2** will be used **3** may be carried **C 1** The bathroom was cleaned by Brian yesterday. **2** The pictures will be copied by the secretary. **3** The problem must be solved by Sam.

교과서 문장 응용하기 **1** was played by a band **2** may be sold soon

---

FOCUS 33   p.74

A 1 to **2** for **3** to **B 1** Some sandwiches were made for us by Dad. **2** A new computer was gotten for me by Mom. **C 1** were told a scary story by Andy, was told (to) them by Andy **2** was asked a hard question by Mr. Tullock, was asked of me by Mr. Tullock

교과서 문장 응용하기 **1** are taught Chinese by Ming **2** was made for me by my brother

---

FOCUS 34   p.75

A 1 I was made happy easily by him. **2** Bob was told to exercise by us. **3** A petrol station is called a gas station in America (by them). **4** We were asked to bring some food to the party by Emma. **5** The rabbit was named Sally by me. **B 1** was told to stop surfing the Internet **2** was kept warm by his dog **3** was found easy to use by many people **4** are advised to drink lots of water for their health

교과서 문장 응용하기 **1** was elected leader of the tennis club **2** was advised to exercise by the doctor

---

FOCUS 35   p.76

A 1 was seen to jog **2** was watched to run across **3** are helped to do **B 1** talk → to talk **2** look after → to look after **3** touch → to touch **C 1** was heard to sing **2** were made to feel **3** were seen to eat

교과서 문장 응용하기 **1** was seen to cross the road by us **2** was made to bring the map by Bob

---

FOCUS 36   p.77

A 1 to **2** in **3** with **4** with **B 1** to → with **2** of → with **3** of → at **C 1** am worried about **2** was surprised at **3** is made of(from)

교과서 문장 응용하기 **1** The mountain is covered with snow. **2** She is known for her beauty.

● ● ● ● 내신적중 실전문제   pp.78~82

01 ④	02 ③	03 ③	04 ⑤	05 ④	06 ③
07 with	08 ③	09 ⑤	10 ②	11 ⑤	
12 be touched		13 made	14 ③		15 ③
16 ③	17 ⑤	18 ⑤	19 ③	20 come → to come(coming)	
21 for → to		22 ④	23 ③		
24 ③	25 ④	26 ④	27 ②		

서술형 평가

01 (1) are wrapped by (2) are not wrapped by
   (3) Are, wrapped by

02 wasn't, was invented by

03 (1) are covered with (2) was surprised at

04 (1) must not be pushed
   (2) A baby dog is called a puppy
   (3) A good dinner was given to us

05 ⓐ two women were heard to talk by me
   ⓑ I am made very happy by him

06 will be bought for him by me

---

01 겨울 기간 동안 문이 '잠긴다'는 수동의 표현이 알맞으므로 「be동사＋과거분사」의 수동태를 쓴다.

02 「by + 행위자」가 있는 것으로 보아 수동태가 필요하며, 과거 시제이고 문장의 주어가 복수이므로 be동사는 were를 쓴다.

03 조동사가 있는 문장의 수동태는 「조동사 + be + 과거분사」의 형태로 쓴다.

04 미래를 나타내는 부사구 next Friday가 있는 것으로 보아 생일 파티가 '열릴 것이다'라는 의미가 되도록 미래시제의 수동 태 「will be + 과거분사」로 쓴다.

05 의문사가 없는 의문문의 수동태는 「Be동사 + 주어 + 과거분 사 + by + 목적격(행위자)?」의 형태이다. 시제가 과거이고 주 어가 단수이므로 be동사는 was를 쓴다.

06 동사 buy를 쓴 4형식 문장을 수동태로 바꾸면 직접목적어 만을 주어로 쓸 수 있으며, 간접목적어 앞에는 for를 쓴다.

07 '~로 가득하다'는 be filled with로 표현한다.

08 ③ 수동태에서 행위자가 대명사이면 「by + 목적격」으로 나타 낸다. (they → them)

09 ⑤ '~에 관심이 있다'는 be interested in으로 쓴다. (at → in)

10 ② 목적어가 없는 2형식 문장은 수동태로 바꿀 수 없다.

11 ①, ②, ③, ④에는 수동태의 행위자의 앞에 쓰는 by가 알맞 고, ⑤에는 with가 알맞다.
be satisfied with: '~에 만족하다'

12 「조동사 + not + be + 과거분사」의 조동사 수동태의 부정형을 써야 한다.

13 의문사가 있는 수동태의 의문문은 「의문사 + be동사 + 주어 + 과거분사 ~?」의 형태이다.

14 「지각동사 + 목적어 + 동사원형」의 수동태 구문은 목적어를 주 어로 하고, 나머지는 「be동사 + 과거분사 + to부정사」로 쓴다.

15 5형식 문장을 수동태로 바꾸면 목적어를 주어로 하고, 동사 는 「be동사 + 과거분사」로 바꾼 뒤 to부정사는 그대로 쓴다.

16 첫 번째 문장에는 '~에게 알려지다'라는 뜻의 be known to 가 필요하다. 두 번째 문장은 직접목적어를 주어로 하는 4형식 문장의 수동태로, 동사가 teach이므로 전치사는 to를 쓴다.

17 ⑤ 사역동사가 있는 5형식 문장의 수동태는 목적격보어인 동 사원형을 to부정사로 바꾼다. (say → to say)

18 '누가 '모나리자'를 그렸는가?'에 대한 대답으로, B의 답은 사 물 It이 주어이고 「by + 행위자」가 있으므로 수동태로 쓴다. 과거시제로 묻고 있으므로 과거시제로 답한다.

19 ③ 수동태의 의문문은 「Be동사 + 주어 + 과거분사 + by + 목적 격(행위자)?」의 형태이므로 바르게 바꾸면 Were his glasses found in his room by him?이 알맞다.

20 지각동사가 있는 5형식 능동태 문장의 목적격보어가 동사원 형이면 수동태에서는 to부정사로 바꿔 쓴다.

21 동사 send가 있는 4형식 문장을 직접목적어가 있는 수동태로 바꿀 때는 간접목적어 앞에 전치사 to를 쓴다.

22 첫 번째 문장에는 '~로 붐비다'라는 뜻의 be crowded with 가, 두 번째 문장에는 '~에 기뻐하다'라는 뜻의 be pleased with가 쓰이는 것이 자연스럽다.

23 ③ 창문을 깬 것은 Jennifer가 아니므로 수동태의 부정문 인 「be동사 + not + 과거분사」로 써야 한다. (→ wasn't[was not] broken)

24 사역동사가 쓰인 5형식 문장의 수동태인 「be동사 + made + to부정사」를 능동태로 바꾸면 「made + 목적어 + 동사원형」이 되어야 한다.

25 능동태로는 The doctor told him to avoid sweet foods. 로 쓸 수 있으며, 이때 목적격보어로 쓰인 to부정사는 수동태 에도 그대로 쓴다.

26 미래시제의 수동태는 「will be + 과거분사」로 쓴다.

27 의문사가 있는 의문문의 수동태는 「의문사 + be동사 + 주어 + 과거분사 + by + 목적격(행위자)?」의 형태가 알맞다.

서술형 평가

01 (1) 수동태 긍정문은 「주어 + be동사 + 과거분사 + by + 목적격 (행위자).」의 형태이다.
(2) 수동태 부정문은 「주어 + be동사 + not + 과거분사 + by + 목적격(행위자).」의 형태이다.
(3) 수동태 의문문은 「be동사 + 주어 + 과거분사 + by + 목적격 (행위자)?」의 형태이다.

02 수동태 질문에 대한 대답은 be동사를 사용하며, 이어지는 내 용도 'Alexander Graham Bell에 의해 발명되었다'는 수동 의 의미여야 하므로 「was + 과거분사 + by」가 알맞다.

03 (1) be covered with: '~로 덮여 있다'
(2) be surprised at: '~에 놀라다'

04 (1) 조동사가 있는 문장의 수동태 부정형은 「조동사 + not + be + 과거분사」의 순서이다.
(2) 5형식 문장의 수동태는 목적어(a baby dog)가 주어로 오 고 「be동사 + 과거분사 + 목적격보어(a puppy)」의 순서이다.
(3) 직접목적어가 주어로 온 4형식 문장의 수동태는 「be동

사＋과거분사＋to＋간접목적어」의 순서이다.

[05~06]

> 　한 가게에서 나는 두 여성이 옆 코너에서 이야기하는 것을 들었다. "Jimmy와 나는 이제 10년째 함께하는 중이고 그는 나를 정말 행복하게 해."라고 한 사람이 말하길, "그래서 나는 아무리 몹시 비싸더라도 <u>그가 가장 좋아하는 음식을 사 줄 거야.</u>"라고 했다. "음, 난 Benny에 대해서는 선택권이 없어."라고 그녀의 친구가 대답했다. 나는 코너를 돌았다. 두 여성 모두 비싼 고양이 음식을 사고 있었다.

05 ⓐ 지각동사(hear)가 있는 문장의 수동태는 「주어＋be동사＋과거분사＋to부정사」의 형태이다. ⓑ 목적격보어가 형용사인 문장의 수동태는 「주어＋be동사＋과거분사＋형용사＋by＋목적격(행위자)」의 형태이다.

06 동사가 buy인 경우에는 간접목적어만을 주어로 수동태를 만들 수 있으며, will buy의 수동형은 will be bought이다.

CHAPTER 07 분사

FOCUS 37　　　　p.85

A 1 taking **2** reading **3** sleeping **4** rising **5** drinking　**B 1** these barking dogs **2** man playing the piano **3** my legs are shaking **4** saved the drowning boy　**C 1** swim → swimming **2** waited → waiting **3** stood → standing **4** wear → wearing

 **1** I am watching a TV show. **2** The smiling boy is my boyfriend.

FOCUS 38　　　　p.86

A 1 called **2** covered **3** learned **4** written **B 1** taken **2** stolen **3** sent **4** left　**C 1** is a picture painted **2** is a used chair **3** have an earphone made

 **1** The classroom was cleaned by

Jane.　**2** I like baked potatoes.

FOCUS 39　　　　p.87

A 1 tiring **2** boring **3** interested **4** confused **5** shocking　**B 1** was satisfied with his grade **2** looked disappointed with your address **C 1** (a) interesting (b) interested　**2** (a) exciting (b) excited

 **1** The service was satisfying.　**2** We were satisfied with the service.

FOCUS 40　　　　p.88

A 1 현재분사 **2** 동명사 **3** 현재분사 **4** 동명사　**B 1** That sleeping bag **2** the burning building　**C 1** (a) 그들은 대기실에 있다. (b) 줄 서서 기다리고 있는 많은 사람들이 있었다. **2** (a) 나의 꿈은 내 전용 수영장을 갖는 것이다. (b) 헤엄치고 있는 돌고래들을 봐.

 **1** The exciting game made us happy.　**2** Their goal is winning the race.

FOCUS 41　　　　p.89

A 1 Being busy **2** Turning left **3** Living next door to him　**B 1** When she came back home **2** Because he had a headache　**3** While I was reading a novel **4** If you turn right

 **1** Feeling tired, I didn't go to her party.　**2** Having dinner, Somi got a phone call.

내신적중 실전문제　　　　pp.90~94

01 ②	02 ③	03 ③	04 flying	05 ④
06 ②	07 ④	08 ①	09 ①	10 ④　11 ①
12 ①	13 ④	14 Be → Being	15 ④	16 ⑤
17 ⑤	18 ②	19 ⑤	20 ④	21 Lifting

a heavy flower pot　**22** ⓑ covering → covered　**23** ④　**24** ①　**25** Taking **26** cooked　**27** ③

01 the cake decorated with fruit
02 (1) interested → interesting (2) boring → bored
03 ⓐ, ⓒ, ⓕ / ⓑ, ⓓ, ⓔ
04 (1) Turning right (2) Sleeping in class
   (3) Cleaning the house
05 ⓐ Being ⓑ excited
06 I turning to correct him

01 '50년 전에 지어진'이라는 수동의 의미로 명사(apartment)를 꾸며야 하므로 과거분사가 알맞다.

02 '머리핀을 하고 있는'이라는 능동의 의미로 명사(girl)를 꾸며야 하므로 현재분사가 알맞다.

03 감정을 느끼는 주체가 사람이므로 과거분사가 알맞다.

04 빈칸은 목적어의 상태를 설명하는 목적격보어 자리이며, 'Teddy가 드론을 날리는 것'이라는 능동의 의미이므로 현재분사 flying이 알맞다.

05 '깨진'은 수동의 의미를 포함하므로 명사(windows)를 꾸미는 과거분사로 쓰는 것이 알맞다.

06 '노래를 부르면서'라는 진행의 의미이므로 현재분사를 보어로 쓰는 것이 알맞다.

07 '~하면'이라는 조건을 나타내는 문장은 If you use the Internet으로 쓸 수 있고, 이 문장에서 접속사와 주어인 If you를 생략하고 use를 「동사원형＋-ing」 형태로 바꾸어 분사구문으로 쓴다.

08 ㅣ보기ㅣ와 ②, ③, ④, ⑤는 현재분사이고 ①은 용도를 나타내는 동명사로 쓰였다.

09 surprise는 감정을 나타내는 분사로 쓰이면 감정을 느끼는 사람(you)이 주어일 때 과거분사로, 감정을 불러일으키는 것 (news)이 주어일 때 현재분사로 나타낸다.

10 문맥상 이유를 나타내는 접속사 As, Since, Because와 때를 나타내는 접속사 When은 자연스럽지만, 양보를 나타내는 Though는 어색하다.

11 분사구문 뒤에 이어지는 내용으로 보아 '두꺼운 코트를 입었음에도 불구하고'라는 양보의 의미여야 하므로 접속사는 Though가 쓰여야 한다.

12 분사구문 뒤에 이어지는 내용으로 보아 '할 일이 많기 때문에'라는 이유의 의미여야 하므로 접속사는 Because가 쓰여야 한다.

13 명사(book)를 뒤에서 꾸며 주는 수동의 의미를 지닌 과거분사가 알맞다.

14 Though she was only six years old, she went to elementary school.을 분사구문으로 바꾼 문장이므로 be동사는 「동사원형＋-ing」의 형태로 써야 한다.

15 ④ 분사구문으로 바꿀 때는 접속사와 주어를 생략하고 문장의 동사를 현재분사로 바꿔야 하므로 ④의 두 번째 문장은 Being cheap, the jeans are nice.가 알맞다.

16 ⑤는 동사의 목적어 역할을 하는 동명사이고, ①, ②, ③, ④는 형용사 역할을 하는 현재분사이다.

17 ⑤는 주어 역할을 하는 동명사이고 ①, ②, ③, ④는 분사구문이다.

18 ② 동사 excite는 사람이 주어로 그 감정을 느끼는 주체일 때는 과거분사 형태로 써야 하므로, ②의 exciting은 excited로 고쳐야 한다.

19 첫 번째 문장은 명사 the dog이 '달려오고 있는' 능동을 나타내야 하므로 빈칸에는 현재분사가 알맞고, 두 번째 문장은 명사 music이 '내려받은'의 수동의 의미로 수식을 받아야 하므로 빈칸에는 과거분사가 알맞다.

20 첫 번째 문장의 주어는 감정을 느끼는 '사람'이므로 빈칸에는 과거분사가, 두 번째 문장의 주어는 감정을 유발하는 사물 our field trip이므로 빈칸에는 현재분사가 알맞다.

21 접속사 As와 주어 I를 생략하고 동사 lifted를 「동사원형＋-ing」로 바꾼다.

22 ⓑ '눈으로 덮인'이라는 수동의 의미로 쓰여 the top of the mountain을 수식해야 하므로 과거분사 covered로 고쳐야 한다.

23 ④ 주어인 사람이 느끼는 감정을 나타내므로 과거분사 형태인 shocked로 고쳐야 한다.

24 ① '숨겨진 진실'이라는 수동의 의미여야 하므로 과거분사 형태인 hidden으로 고쳐야 한다.

25 조건을 나타내는 분사구문이어야 하므로 take의 현재분사형이 알맞다.

26 '요리된'이라는 수동의 의미로 명사(food)를 뒤에서 수식해야 하므로 과거분사형이 알맞다.

27 ①, ②, ④, ⑤는 시간을 나타내는 분사구문이고 ③은 이유를 나타내는 분사구문이다.

01 '장식된'이라는 수동의 의미이므로 decorate는 과거분사

decorated로 쓰고, 그 이하가 뒤에서 명사 the cake를 수식한다.

02 감정을 나타내는 동사 interest와 bore가 분사로 쓰이면 감정을 유발하는 능동의 의미일 때는 현재분사로, 감정을 느끼는 수동의 의미일 때는 과거분사로 쓴다.

03 ⓐ, ⓒ, ⓕ 명사의 동작이나 상태를 설명하는 형용사 역할을 하는 현재분사
ⓑ 목적어, ⓓ 보어, ⓔ 주어 역할을 하는 동명사

04 (1) 조건, (2) 이유, (3) 때를 나타내는 분사구문이며, 접속사와 주어 없이 「동사원형＋-ing」의 형태로 쓴다.

[05~06]

> 나는 10대 소년이었을 때 어머니와 함께 우리 친척들을 방문하기 위해 장시간의 버스 여행을 했다. 당시 어머니는 40세였지만, 더 젊어 보였다. 돌아오는 여행길에 잘생긴 운전사가 우리가 탑승하는 것을 돕기 위해 버스 밖에 서 있었다. "네 누나의 가방을 들어주렴."이라고 그가 제안했다. 내가 그의 말을 정정하려고 돌아설 때, 어머니는 팔꿈치로 나를 건드리셨다. 그녀는 신이 나 보였고 "신경 쓰지 마, 동생아. 이 분이 하시는 말 들었지."라고 말했다.

05 ⓐ 접속사와 주어가 생략되어 있으므로 분사구문임을 알 수 있다. 분사구문은 「동사원형＋-ing」의 형태이므로 Being이 알맞다.
ⓒ 감정을 나타내는 동사는 문장의 주어인 사람이 감정을 느낄 때는 과거분사형으로 쓴다.

06 분사구문은 접속사와 주어를 생략하고 동사에 -ing를 붙여서 만든다. 부사절의 주어와 주절의 주어가 다르므로 부사절의 주어는 그대로 쓴다.

CHAPTER **08** 대명사

FOCUS 42   p.97

A 1 One, the other 2 One, another, the others
3 One, another, the other 4 another **B** 1 One, the other 2 One, the others

교과서 문장 응용하기 **1** One is a comic book and the other is a cookbook. **2** One lives in Paris, another lives in New York, and the other lives in London.

FOCUS 43   p.98

A 1 Some 2 others 3 the others 4 the others
B 1 the others → others 2 the other → the others
3 the other → others **C** 1 Some, others 2 Some, others 3 Some, the others

교과서 문장 응용하기 **1** Some are rich, but others are poor. **2** Some of them are Jane's (books) and the others are Tom's (books).

FOCUS 44   p.99

A 1 Each 2 water park 3 has 4 Each 5 each
B 1 member 2 every 3 has **C** 1 each child
2 Every country 3 Every student 4 each of

교과서 문장 응용하기 **1** Each group makes different cakes. **2** Every visitor wants to see this show.

FOCUS 45   p.100

A 1 are 2 is 3 want 4 days 5 were **B** 1 (a) 모든 사람이 참석했다. (b) 파티를 위한 모든 것이 준비되었다.
2 (a) 그 자매들은 둘 다 부지런하다. (b) 나는 이 두 권의 책을 모두 읽었다. **C** 1 all day 2 Both of them

교과서 문장 응용하기 **1** All of us have to study hard.
2 I like both of those pictures.

FOCUS 46   p.101

A 1 himself 2 myself 3 ourselves 4 itself
5 yourself **B** 1 Y 2 N 3 Y 4 N **C** 1 myself
2 herself 3 himself 4 themselves

교과서 문장 응용하기 **1** Sally sometimes talks to herself in the mirror. **2** My father himself made this chair. / My father made this chair himself.

FOCUS 47   p.102

A 1 enjoyed themselves 2 by herself 3 help yourselves **B** 1 나는 혼자서 그 일을 할 수 있다.
2 Bob은 혼자 힘으로 수프를 만들었다. 3 이 돌은 그 자체로

충분히 희귀하다.　**C 1** of itself　**2** for herself　**3** by themselves

교과서 문장 응용하기　**1** My friends enjoyed themselves at the concert.　**2** The old man lives in that house by himself.

내신적중 실전문제

pp.103~106

01 ④　02 ⑤　03 ⑤　04 ④　05 Some, others　06 One, the other　07 ②　08 ③
09 ②　10 ⑤　11 ④　12 boys → boy　13 ④
14 ⑤　15 ④　16 yourself　17 another　18 ①
19 ④　20 ②

서술형 평가

01 One, the others
02 One, another, the other
03 (1) him → himself　(2) Some → One
　　(3) the others → the other
04 ⓐ, ⓓ, ⓔ / ⓑ, ⓒ
05 get → gets
06 ⓑ Some　ⓒ Others

01 '어떤 사람들은 ~하고, 또 어떤 사람들은 …하다'는 의미는 「some ~ others …」로 쓴다.

02 문맥상 '우리끼리 이야기지만'이라는 뜻의 between ourselves가 알맞다.

03 주어와 목적어가 같은 사람들을 지칭하므로 재귀대명사 themselves가 알맞다.

04 by oneself는 '혼자서'를 의미하는 재귀대명사의 관용 표현이다.

05 '어떤 사람들은 ~하고, 또 어떤 사람들은 …한다'는 「some ~, others …」로 나타낸다.

06 두 개의 사물 중 하나는 one, 다른 하나는 the other로 표현한다.

07 '모든 사람들'이라는 뜻으로는 all을 쓰며, 이때는 복수 취급한다. ④ every는 형용사로 쓰이므로 명사 없이는 쓸 수 없고, ⑤ each는 단수 취급해야 한다.

08 all이 복수 명사와 함께 쓰이면 복수 취급하며, 「every + 단수 명사」는 항상 단수 취급한다.

09 대상이 셋일 때는 하나는 one, 다른 하나는 another, 나머지 하나는 the other로 표현한다.

10 ①, ②, ③, ④는 목적어 역할을 하는 재귀 용법이며, ⑤는 주어 you를 강조하는 강조 용법의 재귀대명사이다.

11 ④ 앞에 나온 명사와 같은 종류의 불특정한 것을 가리킬 때 그것이 단수형이면 one을 쓴다. ①, ②, ③, ⑤의 빈칸에는 '또 다른 (것)'의 의미인 another를 쓸 수 있다.

12 each 뒤에는 단수 명사와 단수 동사가 온다.

13 ④ help oneself는 '마음껏 먹다'의 의미인 관용어구이므로, 재귀대명사를 생략할 수 없다. ①, ②, ③, ⑤는 모두 재귀대명사가 강조 용법으로 쓰였으므로 생략할 수 있다.

14 ⑤ 수영 선수가 자신에게 실망한 것이므로 himself 또는 herself가 알맞다.

15 ④는 동사의 목적어 역할을 하는 재귀 용법으로 쓰였고, 나머지는 모두 강조 용법으로 쓰인 재귀대명사이다.
|보기|, ①, ③, ⑤ 주어 강조 ② 목적어 강조

16 첫 번째 문장에는 '~을 마음껏 먹다'라는 뜻의 help yourself to가 알맞으며, 두 번째 문장의 빈칸에는 생략된 주어 you를 강조하는 재귀대명사 yourself가 알맞다.

17 첫 번째 문장에는 '(여러 개 중 막연한) 또 다른 하나'를 나타내는 another가 알맞으며, 두 번째 문장에는 '(셋 중) 하나는 ~, 또 하나는 …, 나머지 하나는 -'의 「one ~, another … the other -」가 알맞다.

18 ① both 다음에는 복수 명사가 오고, both는 복수 취급한다. (is → are)

19 ④ 정해진 수에서 나머지 전부를 가리킬 때는 the others를 쓴다. (others → the others)

20 ② for oneself는 '혼자 힘으로'라는 뜻이다.

서술형 평가

01 특정한 수의 사물 중에서 하나를 가리킬 때는 one, 나머지 모두를 가리킬 때는 the others로 표현한다.

02 '(셋 중의) 하나는 ~, 또 하나는…, 나머지 하나는 -'을 나타낼 때는 「one ~, another … the other -」를 쓴다.

03 주어와 일치하는 대상이 목적어로 올 때는 재귀대명사를 쓰며, 둘 중 하나는 one, 다른 하나는 the other로 지칭한다.

04 ⓐ, ⓓ, ⓔ는 목적어 역할을 하는 재귀적 용법으로 쓰인 재귀대명사이고 ⓑ, ⓒ는 강조 용법으로 쓰인 재귀대명사이며 생략이 가능하다.

기분이 가라앉는가? 우울한가? 당신은 혼자가 아니다. 모든 사람은 서글퍼진다. 어떤 사람들은 그저 어쩌다가 한 번 슬픈 기분을 느낀다. 또 어떤 이들은 자주 슬픈 기분을 느낀다. 10대들 중 절반이 넘는 수가 적어도 한 달에 한 번은 슬픈 기간을 거친다. 슬픈 기분일 때는 그것이 영원히 지속될 것처럼 느낄지도 모른다. 하지만 대개 슬픔의 감정은 아주 오래 가지는 않고, 몇 시간, 혹은 하루나 이틀 지속된다.

05 「every＋명사」가 주어로 오면 단수 취급한다.

06 '어떤 이들은 ~하고, 또 어떤 이들은 …하다'의 뜻은 「some ~, others …」로 나타낸다.

CHAPTER **09** 형용사와 부사

FOCUS **48** p.109

A 1 nothing important **2** the poor **3** something interesting **4** the handicapped **B 1** I know somebody smart. **2** There is someone strange at the door. **3** Do you have anything special in mind? **4** I'm looking for something interesting. **C 1** 우리는 노인들을 위한 특별한 집을 짓는다. **2** 젊은이들은 그들의 손에 미래를 쥐고 있다. **3** 그는 집 없는 사람들을 위해 텐트를 설치했다.

교과서 문장 응용하기 **1** Bob told me something funny. **2** We should help the poor.

FOCUS **49** p.110

A 1 much **2** few **3** many, a few **4** Many, A lot of **5** a little **B 1** a few → a little **2** much → many **3** few → little **4** little → few **5** few → a few **6** many → much **C 1** (a) 나는 몇 가지 질문이 있다. (b) 나는 질문이 거의 없다. **2** (a) Sue는 책 읽을 시간이 약간 있다. (b) Sue는 책 읽을 시간이 거의 없다.

교과서 문장 응용하기 **1** There are few carrots in the basket. **2** Give the roses a little water every day.

FOCUS **50** p.111

A 1 some **2** any **3** any **4** some **B 1** some → any **2** some → any **3** some → any **4** any → some **C 1** some water **2** any special plans **3** any time **4** some pictures

교과서 문장 응용하기 **1** We ate(had) some sandwiches for lunch. **2** Do you have any questions?

FOCUS **51** p.112

A 1 Take off your hat / Take your hat off **2** Turn down the volume / Turn the volume down **3** Wake me up **4** take it back **B 1** Turn it on to boil the rice. **2** He put it out with his clothes. **3** Mom took them out from the fridge. **4** Mr. Cook handed them out to the students. **C 1** 이 코트를 입어라, 오늘은 무척 춥다. **2** 지나는 신문 읽는 것을 멈추고 그것을 내려놓았다.

교과서 문장 응용하기 **1** Turn on the fan. / Turn the fan on. **2** You should give it up.

• • • •
내신적중 실전문제 pp.113~116

| 01 ① | 02 ④ | 03 the, young | 04 ② | 05 ⑤ |
| 06 ① | 07 ② | 08 ② | 09 ① | 10 ②, ③ |

11 much → many(a lot of / lots of) **12** ⑤
13 ③, ⑤ **14** a little **15** ① **16** ② **17** ③
18 ④ **19** ③ **20** try it on

서술형 평가

01 (1) some friends (2) any shampoo
(3) any photos (4) some bread

02 (1) something interesting (2) The blind need

03 (1) 사탕이 거의 없는 (2) 사탕이 조금 있는

04 (1) put it on (2) throw them out

05 ⓐ Any → Some ⓑ much → many(a lot of / lots of) ⓒ place → places

06 little

01 내용상 '실수를 거의 하지 않는다'는 뜻이 자연스럽고, 명사 mistake가 셀 수 있는 명사이므로 few가 알맞다.

02 내용상 '할 일이 많지 않다'는 뜻이 자연스럽고, 명사 work가 셀 수 없는 명사이므로 much가 알맞다.

03 「형용사+복수 보통명사(~ people)」는 '~한 사람들'이라는 의미로, 「the+형용사」로 바꿔 쓸 수 있다.

04 긍정문에는 '몇몇의, 약간의'라는 뜻의 some을, 부정문에는 '어떤 ~도, 아무 ~도'라는 뜻의 any를 쓴다.

05 첫 번째 빈칸에는 '몇몇의, 약간의'라는 뜻으로 권유문에 쓰이는 some이 알맞다. 두 번째 문장은 '그의 책들 중 몇 권만 읽었다'는 의미여야 하므로 빈칸에는 셀 수 있는 명사 앞에 쓰는 a few가 알맞다.

06 sugar는 셀 수 없는 명사이므로 수량형용사 many로 수식할 수 없다.

07 「타동사+부사」에서 목적어가 명사이면 「타동사+목적어+부사 / 타동사+부사+목적어」의 어순이고, 대명사이면 「타동사+목적어+부사」의 어순이므로 ②는 적절하지 않다.

08 -thing으로 끝나는 대명사는 형용사가 뒤에서 수식하므로 괄호 안의 말을 배열하면 The students saw something wrong with the plants.이다.

09 이어동사의 목적어가 대명사이므로 「동사+대명사+부사」의 순서로 쓰며, 괄호 안의 말을 배열하면 You should hand it in by tomorrow morning.이다.

10 -thing 또는 -one으로 끝나는 대명사는 형용사가 뒤에서 수식한다. (① sweet something → something sweet ④ interesting something → something interesting ⑤ professional someone → someone professional)

11 셀 수 있는 명사(things) 앞에 much는 쓸 수 없으므로 many, a lot of, lots of로 고쳐야 한다.

12 ①, ②, ③ -thing, -one으로 끝나는 대명사는 형용사가 대명사의 뒤에서 수식한다. ④ 「the+형용사」는 '~한 사람들'이라는 의미로 복수 취급한다. (① cold something → something cold ② strange someone → someone strange ③ exciting anything → anything exciting ④ is → are)

13 긍정문에서 '몇몇의, 약간의'라는 의미로 셀 수 없는 명사(water) 앞에 쓸 수 있는 것은 some과 a little이다.

14 syrup은 셀 수 없는 명사이므로 '약간의'라는 뜻의 수량형용사로는 a little을 쓴다.

15 ③ example은 셀 수 있는 명사이므로 수량형용사는 a little이 아닌 a few나 some이 적절하다.

16 ② 목적어가 대명사이면 「타동사+목적어+부사」의 어순으로만 쓴다. (took out it → took it out)

17 ⓒ people은 셀 수 있는 명사이므로 '거의 없는'이라는 뜻의 수량형용사를 쓰려면 Few로 고쳐야 한다.

18 ④ few는 '거의 없는'의 뜻으로 셀 수 있는 명사를 수식한다. time은 셀 수 없는 명사이므로, '거의 없는'의 뜻으로 셀 수 없는 명사를 수식하는 little로 고쳐야 한다. any는 부정문과 의문문에 쓰이므로 알맞지 않다.

19 ③ butter는 셀 수 없는 명사이므로 '약간의, 몇몇의'라는 의미의 some은 a little로 바꿔 쓸 수 있다.

20 이어동사의 목적어가 대명사일 경우는 「동사+목적어+부사」의 어순이므로 try it on으로 써야 한다.

서술형 평가

01 (1) 외로운 것과 관계있는 것은 친구를 가지는 것이다.
(2) 머리를 감는 것과 관계있는 것은 샴푸이다.
(3) 카메라가 없으니 사진을 못 찍을 것이다.
(4) 배가 고픈 것과 관계있는 것은 빵이다.
(1) 긍정문과 (4) 권유문에는 some을, (2) 의문문과 (3) 부정문에는 any를 사용하며, 셀 수 있는 명사인 경우에는 복수형을 쓴다.

02 (1) -thing으로 끝나는 명사는 형용사가 뒤에서 수식한다.
(2) '~하는 사람들'은 「the+형용사」로 나타내며, 복수 취급한다.

03 셀 수 있는 명사 앞에 쓰이는 수량형용사 few는 '거의 없는'이라는 뜻이고 a few는 '약간의'라는 뜻이다.

04 「타동사+부사」로 이루어진 이어동사의 목적어가 대명사이면 타동사와 부사 사이에 위치한다. (1) raincoat는 단수명사이므로 대명사는 it이 알맞다. (2) magazines는 복수명사이므로 대명사는 them이 알맞다.

[05~06]

> 어떤 과학자들은 지구의 기온이 2030년까지 과도하게 높아질 것이라고 말한다. 그런 다음 북극과 남극의 얼음이 녹을 것이고, 많은 도시들이 바다 밑에 있게 될지도 모른다. 반면에, 많은 장소들은 농경을 하기에는 너무 건조해질지 모른다. 우리는 먹을 것이 거의 없을 것이다. 빵도, 쌀도 거의 없을 것이다.

05 ⓐ 긍정문에서 '조금, 약간'의 의미를 갖는 수량형용사로는

some을 쓴다. ⓑ 셀 수 있는 명사의 복수형 앞에 오는 수량 형용사로는 many, a lot of, lots of를 쓴다. ⓒ a lot of 다음에 셀 수 있는 명사가 올 때는 복수 명사로 쓴다.

06 '빵도 쌀도 거의 없다'는 의미여야 하고, bread와 rice는 둘 다 셀 수 없는 명사이므로, 수량형용사 little이 알맞다.

CHAPTER 10 비교 구문

FOCUS 52　　　　p.119

A 1 older, oldest **2** wider, widest **3** better, best **4** hotter, hottest **5** stronger, strongest **6** worse, worst **7** dirtier, dirtiest **8** more difficult, most difficult **9** thinner, thinnest **10** more exciting, most exciting **B 1** easier **2** fattest **3** prettiest **4** more

교과서 문장 응용하기 **1** Tom is wiser than Kate. **2** He is the fastest runner.

FOCUS 53　　　　p.120

A 1 as **2** cold **3** so **B 1** as tall as **2** as fast as **3** as(so) big as **C 1** Lemonade is not(isn't) as(so) sour as lemon juice. **2** The chair is not(isn't) as(so) comfortable as the sofa. **3** The bank is as near as the bookstore. **4** Riding a motorbike is as dangerous as driving a car.

교과서 문장 응용하기 **1** France is as beautiful as Spain to me. **2** Silver isn't as(so) valuable as gold.

FOCUS 54　　　　p.121

A 1 longer **2** better **3** most difficult **B 1** fatter **2** much(far / still / even / a lot) **3** than **4** youngest **C 1** A car is a lot more expensive than a TV. **2** I got up earlier than usual. **3** A whale is the largest animal in the ocean.

교과서 문장 응용하기 **1** This box is heavier than this chair. **2** Mt. Everest is the highest mountain.

FOCUS 55　　　　p.122

A 1 to → as **2** can → could **3** longer → long **4** more → as **5** as twice → twice as **B 1** Sue는 가능한 한 빨리 학교로 뛰어갔다. **2** 이 시계는 저것보다 네 배 더 비싸다. **3** 부산으로 가는 기차는 버스보다 두 배 더 빠르다. **C 1** three times more expensive than **2** as long as **3** they could **4** as fast as possible

교과서 문장 응용하기 **1** Ann swam as slowly as possible(she could). **2** Tony ran twice as fast as I.

FOCUS 56　　　　p.123

A 1 the better I feel **2** The more money we earn **3** will get cleaner and cleaner **B 1** warmer and warmer **2** more and more famous **3** The older, the quieter **4** The harder, the faster **C 1** 그 풍선은 점점 더 커졌다. **2** 나이가 들면 들수록 더 현명해진다.

교과서 문장 응용하기 **1** The child got smarter and smarter. **2** The more we have, the more we want.

FOCUS 57　　　　p.124

A 1 one of the wisest students **2** one of the most boring movies **3** one of the greatest inventors **4** one of the most popular sports **B 1** No other, cheap / cheaper than / cheaper than any other hotel **2** popular as / more popular than / more popular, any other dessert

교과서 문장 응용하기 **1** It is one of the oldest castles in the world. **2** This book is thicker than any other book.

내신적중 실전문제
pp.125~128

01 ③　**02** ②　**03** ⑤　**04** ②　**05** ⑤　**06** ③
07 ⑤　**08** leave a message as soon as you can　**09** ②　**10** ⑤　**11** ③　**12** ④　**13** the more　**14** much(far / even / still / a lot) more

effective   15 ⑤   16 ①, ③   17 ⑤   18 lower than   19 three times as tall   20 ④

서술형 평가

01 (1) older than   (2) older than   (3) the oldest
(4) younger than   (5) the youngest

02 (1) as often as I could
(2) one of the busiest insects

03 (1) the highest fall   (2) No (other) fall, as(so) high as   (3) No (other) fall, higher than

04 (1) more comfortable than
(2) twice as long as

05 (1) as quietly as possible
(2) as quietly as you can

06 The louder they made noises, the more tasty the meal was.

---

01 ③ lazy는 「자음 + y」로 끝나는 형용사이므로 y를 i로 바꾸고 -er, -est를 붙인다. (lazy - lazier - laziest)

02 '~보다 더 …한'의 의미는 「비교급 + than」으로 나타낸다.

03 '가장 ~한'의 의미는 「the + 최상급」으로 나타내며, intelligent는 앞에 most를 붙여 최상급을 만든다.

04 '~만큼 …한'을 뜻하는 「as + 원급 + as」의 동등 비교 표현이어야 하며, 동사 plays를 원급이 수식해야 하므로 부사 well이 알맞다.

05 '~만큼 …한'은 「as + 원급 + as」 형태로 나타내며, '~보다 더 …한'은 「비교급 + than」으로 나타낸다.

06 ③ '점점 더 ~한'은 「비교급 + and + 비교급」으로 나타낸다. (short and short → shorter and shorter)

07 '가장 ~한 것 중 하나'라는 뜻은 「one of the + 최상급 + 복수 명사」로 나타낸다.

08 '가능한 한 ~하게'는 「as + 원급 + as + 주어 + can(could)」로 나타낸다.

09 거의 같은 크기이므로 「as + 원급 + as」의 원급 비교가 알맞으며, '크기'를 나타내는 형용사 big을 이용한다.

10 '~보다 몇 배 더 …한'이라는 뜻의 「배수사 + as + 원급 + as」 구문이 알맞다. 배수사가 세 배 이상일 때는 ~ times로 쓴다.

11 ① 서울은 부산보다 시원하다.
② 대구는 제주도보다 시원하다.
④ 부산은 서울보다 따뜻하다.

⑤ 대구는 넷 중 가장 시원한 도시이다.

12 ① 미란이는 수미보다 더 어리다.
② 수미는 진주보다 키가 더 크다.
③ 수미는 진주보다 나이가 더 많다.
⑤ 진주는 미란이와 나이가 같다.

13 '~하면 할수록 더 …할 것이다'라는 의미여야 하므로 「The + 비교급 ~, the + 비교급 …」의 형태가 알맞다.

14 '~보다 훨씬 더 …한'은 비교급 강조 부사 much, far, even, still, a lot 등을 비교급 앞에 써서 나타낸다. effective는 3음절 이상의 단어이므로 more를 붙여 비교급을 만든다.

15 ①, ②, ③, ④는 'Bob이 우리 축구팀에서 가장 훌륭한 선수이다'라는 의미이고 ⑤는 'Bob은 우리 축구팀에서 가장 훌륭한 선수 중 한 명이다'라는 의미이다.

16 ① very는 비교급을 강조할 수 없다. (very → much(far / even / still / a lot)) ③ 「as + 원급 + as」의 원급 비교여야 한다. (cuter → cute)

17 |보기|의 문장은 '동전이 지폐보다 무겁다'는 뜻이므로 ⑤의 '지폐는 동전만큼 무겁지 않다'는 뜻과 일치한다.

18 '너의 수학시험 점수가 내 점수보다 높다.'는 '내 수학시험 점수가 너의 점수보다 낮다.'와 같은 뜻이며, 2개를 비교하고 있으므로 「비교급 + than」으로 쓴다.

19 배수사를 이용한 비교 표현은 「배수사 + 비교급 + than」 또는 「배수사 + as + 원급 + as」로 쓴다.

20 ④ '~하면 할수록 더 …하다'는 「The + 비교급 ~, the + 비교급…」으로 나타낸다. (The hardest → The harder, the easiest → the easier)

서술형 평가

01 a teenager > a child > a baby의 순서로 나이가 많으므로 (1), (2), (4)에는 비교급이 알맞다. 셋 중에서 a teenager가 나이가 가장 많으므로 (3)에는 최상급이 알맞다. 셋 중에 민수는 a baby로 가장 어리므로 (5)에는 최상급이 알맞다.

02 (1) 「as + 원급 + as + 주어 + can」의 순서로 쓰되, travel이 과거시제로 쓰였으므로 can을 could로 바꿔 쓴다.
(2) 「one of the + 최상급 + 복수 명사」: '가장 ~한 것 중 하나'

03 (1) 「the + 최상급」, (2) 「No (other) ~ + as(so) + 원급 + as」, (3) 「No (other) ~ + 비교급 + than」으로 최상급을 표현한다.

04 (1) 소파가 의자보다 더 편안하다는 뜻이므로 「비교급 + than」이 알맞다.
(2) 이 뱀이 저 뱀의 절반 길이라는 것은 저 뱀이 이 뱀의 두

배 길이라는 뜻이므로 「twice + as + 원급 + as」가 알맞다.

[05~06]

> 여기, 우리가 따라야 할 식탁예절이 있다. <u>가능한 한 음식을 조용히 먹어라.</u> 입에 한 번에 많은 음식을 넣지 마라. 입에 음식을 넣은 채 말하지 마라. 하지만, 예전에는 먹으면서 많은 소리를 내는 것이 좋은 예절이었다. 소리가 크면 클수록 식사가 더 맛있는 것이었다. 이 방법은 요리사에게 그들이 그 음식을 얼마나 마음에 들어 하는지를 알려주는 방법이었다.

05 '가능한 한 ~하게'는 「as + 원급 + as + possible」 또는 「as + 원급 + as + 주어 + can」으로 나타낸다.

06 '~하면 할수록 더욱 더 …하다'는 「The + 비교급, the + 비교급 …」으로 나타낸다.

CHAPTER 11 관계사

FOCUS 58   p.131

A **1** I know the lady who is standing in front of the theater. **2** Emily employed the man who looked very diligent. **3** A patient is a person who receives medical treatment from a doctor. **B** **1** who **2** sits **3** who **4** who **C** **1** who helped me **2** who work **3** who tells us

교과서 문장 응용하기 **1** Sam is the boy who called me yesterday. **2** The girl who works here is my (little) sister.

FOCUS 59   p.132

A **1** whose **2** whose **3** whose **B** **1** I met a girl whose hobby is growing vegetables. **2** Mr. White is the writer whose book won a prize. **3** Look at the room whose wall is painted blue. **4** She is the woman whose husband is a football coach. **C** **1** whose windows were all broken. **2** whose roof is full of holes. **3** whose life was in danger.

교과서 문장 응용하기 **1** Who is the girl whose hair is brown? **2** Yumi has a black cat whose name is Miya.

FOCUS 60   p.133

A **1** There are other people whom we must remember. **2** David has a girlfriend whom he has dated for a long time. **3** What's the name of the boy whom I saw at the station? **B** **1** I respect him very much. **2** We were talking to them. **3** I wanted to see her. **C** **1** whom Jack likes? **2** whom we invited to dinner **3** whom I can trust.

교과서 문장 응용하기 **1** He is a singer whom(who) a lot of people like. **2** The man whom(who) I met was very funny.

FOCUS 61   p.134

A **1** Look at the doll which looks like Jenny. **2** Can you see the rabbit which is hopping in the grass? **3** Did you like the meal which you had at the restaurant? **B** **1** which cannot fly **2** which you're going to read **3** which Justin took **C** **1** who → which **2** were → was **3** it 삭제

교과서 문장 응용하기 **1** I want to have a bird which can talk. **2** He found the key which he lost.

FOCUS 62   p.135

A **1** who **2** whom(who) **3** which **4** which **5** who **6** which **B** **1** This was the only magazine that Sally wanted to have. **2** Jerry was the first man that came to the party. **3** Look at the boy and his dog that are playing in the park. **4** It is the most surprising news that I've heard.

교과서 문장 응용하기 **1** An airplane is a machine that(which) flies in the sky. **2** This is the smallest watch that I've ever seen.

A 1 what he said to me **2** what I bought at that store. **3** What I like to do **B 1** What / The thing that(which) **2** what / the thing that(which)
C 1 who → what **2** which → what **3** The thing what → The thing which(that) 또는 What

교과서 문장 응용하기 **1** What Juliet said is true. **2** This ring is what I bought today.

A 1 which **2** whom **3** who is **4** which was
B 1 Ms. Flower is a kind of person who(m)(that) everybody loves. **2** Anna bought a dress which(that) was made in Italy. **3** Bob painted a mother who(that) is looking at her child. **C 1** the house built by my father **2** a painting he bought at the auction

교과서 문장 응용하기 **1** This is the movie (which(that)) I saw(watched) yesterday. **2** I like the girl (who is) dancing on the stage.

A 1 We arrived at the palace where the king lived. **2** Fall is the season when farmers harvest. **3** This is the village where a famous poet lives. **4** Do you mean the night when we played computer games?
B 1 the day when I met you **2** the town where he was born **3** a place where people are buried
4 the time when the show starts **5** where I spent my vacation

교과서 문장 응용하기 **1** The hotel where we stayed was very small. **2** Tomorrow is the day when we study German.

A 1 why **2** how 삭제 **3** the way 삭제 **4** why
B 1 I don't know the reason why Tony got angry.
2 This is how we use chopsticks. **3** Tell me the reason why you were absent. **4** Can you tell me how I can travel with my dog safely? **C 1** how you made the doll **2** way he cooked

교과서 문장 응용하기 **1** I don't know the reason why Paul doesn't join our club. **2** Can you tell me how(the way) you got the cute puppy?

내신적중 실전문제 1회　　　　pp.140~142

01 ⑤	02 ⑤	03 ④	04 that	05 ②	06 ③
07 ③	08 what	09 ③	10 ③	11 the year when	
12 ④	13 ⑤	14 ③, ⑤	15 ③		
16 ④	17 ④	18 who	19 how	20 ③	

01 사람(an old woman)이 선행사이고 빈칸 뒤에 명사(hair)가 이어지므로 소유격 관계대명사 whose가 알맞다.

02 장소를 나타내는 the cafe가 선행사이므로 관계부사 where 가 알맞다.

03 사물(a bus)을 선행사로 하는 주격 관계대명사 which는 that으로 바꿔 쓸 수 있다.

04 the only가 선행사를 수식하거나, 선행사가 -thing으로 끝나는 대명사일 때는 관계대명사 that을 쓴다.

05 첫 번째 문장은 선행사가 때를 나타내는 the time이므로 빈 칸에는 관계부사 when이 알맞다. 두 번째 문장은 선행사가 이유를 나타내는 the reason이므로 빈칸에는 관계부사 why 가 알맞다.

06 ③ 선행사가 the way 등의 방법을 나타낼 때는 관계부사 how를 사용하며, 이때 the way와 how 둘 중 하나만 쓸 수 있다. 따라서 the way 혹은 how 중 하나를 삭제해야 한다.

07 '그 주방장에 의해 요리되는 음식'이므로 선행사 food 뒤에 「주격 관계대명사+be동사」인 which is 또는 that is가 생략된 것이다.

08 the things that은 선행사를 포함하는 관계대명사 what으로 바꿔 쓸 수 있다.

09 선행사가 사람(the doctor)이고 관계대명사 뒤에 「주어+동사」의 어순이 되어야 하므로 목적격 관계대명사 whom을 사용한 ③이 알맞다.

10 선행사가 이유를 나타내는 reason이므로 관계부사 why가

적절하며, why 뒤에는 완전한 문장이 와야 하므로 주어와 동사가 있는 ②가 알맞다.

11 the year는 때를 나타내는 선행사이므로 관계부사 when으로 연결한다.

12 |보기|와 ④는 앞의 선행사를 수식하는 주격 관계대명사이다. ① 지시대명사 ② 부사 ③ 지시형용사 ⑤ 명사절을 이끄는 접속사

13 ⑤ 선행사가 사람(a friend)이고, 빈칸 다음에 명사가 온 것으로 보아 소유격 관계대명사 whose를 쓰며, 소유격은 that으로 바꿔 쓸 수 없다.

14 '~하는 것'의 뜻으로 목적어 역할을 하는 what 또는 the thing which(that)를 사용한다.

15 ①, ②, ④, ⑤ 빈칸 앞에 선행사가 없으므로 선행사를 포함하는 관계대명사 what(What)이 알맞다.
③ 선행사가 동물인 a dog이므로 주격 관계대명사 which 혹은 that이 알맞다.

16 ① the only, ③ the same 등이 선행사를 수식하거나 ② -thing으로 끝나는 대명사, ⑤ 「사람 + 동물」이 선행사인 경우에는 관계대명사 that을 쓴다. ④ 선행사가 사물(the smartphone)이고 빈칸 뒤에 명사가 오므로 빈칸에는 소유격 관계대명사 whose가 알맞다.

17 ④ 「주격 관계대명사 + be동사」인 which are를 생략할 수 있지만, 주격 관계대명사만 단독으로 생략할 수는 없다.

18 선행사가 사람(a woman)이고 주어 역할을 하므로 주격 관계대명사 who가 알맞다.

19 '~한 방법'을 의미하는 관계부사는 how이다.

20 ⓒ 선행사가 the way 등의 방법을 나타낼 때는 관계부사 how를 사용하지만, 이때 the way와 how 둘 중 하나만 쓴다. (the way 삭제 혹은 how 삭제)
ⓔ 선행사가 장소를 나타내는 the place이므로 관계부사 where를 써야 한다. (when → where)

내신적중 실전문제 2회
pp.143~146

01 ②	02 ①	03 ③	04 ④	05 which(that)
06 when	07 ②	08 ③	09 ②	10 ⑤

11 which → where   12 ③   13 ⑤   14 ②
15 A man whose cat   16 where I would play tennis   17 ②   18 ②   19 ③   20 ②

서술형 평가

01 (1) whose sister is a singer   (2) which(that) shine   (3) who(that) had a long hair   (4) that the kids ate

02 That → What

03 (1) girl (who(that) is) singing under the tree   (2) the story (which(that)) you told Noah

04 (1) why Tony got angry   (2) she got better at singing   (3) where Rita and I stayed

05 Walt Disney, who(that) made famous cartoon movies heard him talking like a duck.

06 the way how → the way 또는 how

01 선행사를 포함하여 '~하는 것'의 의미로 쓰이는 관계대명사는 what이다.

02 선행사가 이유를 나타내는 the reason이므로 관계부사 why가 알맞다.

03 선행사가 the only의 수식을 받으므로 관계대명사 that이 알맞다.

04 방법을 나타내는 선행사 the way 대신 관계부사 how를 쓸 수 있다.

05 선행사가 사물(the car)이므로 관계사는 which 또는 that이 알맞다.

06 선행사가 때를 나타내는 the month이므로 관계부사 when이 알맞다.

07 선행사가 장소(the shop)이므로 관계부사 where를 써야 한다.

08 주격 관계대명사절의 동사는 선행사의 인칭과 수, 시제에 일치시켜야 한다. 선행사(the boy)가 3인칭 단수이고 시제가 과거이므로 lived가 알맞다.

09 주격 관계대명사 that의 선행사(kangaroos)가 복수이므로 복수동사 are가 알맞다.

10 선행사(a man and his monkey)가 「사람 + 동물」이므로 관계대명사는 that을 써야 한다.

11 관계사 뒤가 완전한 문장이므로 관계대명사 which를 장소를 나타내는 관계부사 where로 고쳐야 한다.

12 첫 번째 문장의 빈칸에는 「의문사 + to부정사」의 형태로 '~하는 방법'을 나타내는 how가 알맞다. 두 번째 문장의 빈칸에는 방법을 나타내는 관계부사 how가 알맞다.

13 모두 「주격 관계대명사 + be동사」가 생략된 문장이다.

⑤는 선행사가 3인칭 단수의 '동물'이므로 which is가, ①, ②, ③, ④는 선행사가 3인칭 단수의 '사람'이므로 who is가 생략되었다.

14 ① '우리가 원하는 것'이라는 의미여야 하므로 that을 관계대명사 what으로 고친다. ③ 선행사 the pants의 가격에 대한 이야기이므로 that을 소유격 관계대명사 whose로 고친다. ④ 관계대명사 which가 뒤에 이어지는 절의 목적어를 대신하므로 it을 삭제한다.
⑤ 목적격 관계대명사 whom을 주격 관계대명사 who로 고친다.

15 문장의 cat은 a man이 소유한 고양이이고 문장의 주어는 a man이므로 선행사 a man 뒤에 소유격 관계대명사 whose를 쓴다.

16 장소를 나타내는 선행사 the court 뒤에 관계부사 where를 쓰고 주어와 조동사, 동사의 순서대로 쓴다.

17 ⓐ 주어인 선행사가 사람이므로 주격 관계대명사 who가 알맞다. ⓑ 선행사가 이유를 나타내는 the reason이므로 관계부사 why가 알맞다. ⓒ '내가 말하는 것'이라는 의미여야 하므로 선행사를 포함하는 관계대명사 what이 알맞다.

18 첫 번째 문장은 목적어인 사물이 선행사이므로 목적격 관계대명사 which 혹은 that이 알맞다. 두 번째 문장은 주어인 사람이 선행사이므로 주격 관계대명사 who 혹은 that이 알맞다.

19 ③ 소유격 관계대명사는 that으로 바꿔 쓸 수 없다.

20 ①, ③, ④, ⑤는 앞에 선행사가 있는 것으로 보아 관계대명사이고 ②는 간접의문문에 쓰인 의문사이다.

서술형 평가

01 (1) 선행사 a man을 가리키는 대명사에 알맞은 his sister is a singer를 쓰되, his가 소유격이므로 소유격 관계대명사 whose로 바꾼다.
(2) 선행사 things를 가리키는 대명사는 they이므로 they shine을 주격 관계대명사 which(that)로 바꾼다.
(3) 선행사 a girl을 가리키는 대명사는 she이므로 she had a long hair를 주격 관계대명사 who(that)로 바꾼다.
(4) 선행사 cake를 가리키는 대명사는 it이므로 the kids ate it을 쓰되, the very가 선행사를 꾸며 주고 있으므로 목적격 관계대명사 that을 쓰고 it을 삭제한다.

02 '~하는 것'의 뜻으로 선행사를 포함하여 주어 역할을 하는 관계대명사는 what이다.

03 (1) 선행사가 사람(the girl)이므로 who 또는 that으로 연결

하며, 「주격 관계대명사+be동사」는 생략할 수 있다.
(2) 선행사가 사물(the story)이므로 which나 that으로 연결하며, 목적격 관계대명사는 생략할 수 있다.

04 빈칸 앞에 나온 선행사 (1) the reason, (2) the way, (3) the hotel에 알맞은 관계부사를 사용하고 빈칸에 어울리는 내용을 |보기|에서 찾아 쓴다. 단, (2)의 the way와 how는 둘 중 하나만 써야 하므로 관계부사 없이 내용을 연결한다.

[05~06]

Clarence Nash는 어렸을 때 병아리, 개, 고양이, 말, 그리고 많은 종류의 새 소리를 냈다. 그가 더 나이가 들었을 때, Clarence는 파티에서 그의 동물 목소리를 내곤 했다. 한 번은, Walt Disney가 그가 오리처럼 이야기하는 것을 들었다. 그는 유명한 만화영화들을 만들었다. Disney는 Clarence에게 그의 영화 중 한 편에서 오리처럼 말해달라고 부탁했다. 그것이 Clarence Nash가 역대 가장 유명한 목소리가 된 방법이다. 바로 도널드 덕 말이다!

05 선행사인 주어가 사람(Walt Disney)이므로 주격 관계대명사 who 또는 that으로 연결한다.

06 방법을 나타내는 선행사인 thy way와 관계부사 how는 둘 중 하나만 쓴다.

CHAPTER **12** 접속사

FOCUS 67   p.149

A **1** you'll lose weight **2** you'll be caught **3** you'll be on time **B** **1** 조용히 해라, 그러면 너는 이 음악을 들을 수 있을 것이다. **2** 움직이지 마라, 그렇지 않으면 벌들이 널 공격할 것이다. **3** 손을 씻어라, 그렇지 않으면 나는 네게 식사를 차려 주지 않을 것이다. **C** **1** Read the manual, and **2** Hurry, or

교과서 문장 응용하기 **1** Get up early, and you can do many things. **2** Be careful, or you will break this plate.

A 1 It, that **2** that **3** that　**B 1** It is a fun fact that koalas sleep for about 19 hours a day. **2** It is true that blue whales are the largest sea animals. **3** It is certain that this food has gone bad.　**C 1** It's a pity that she broke her leg. **2** I'm sure (that) you will do better next time.

교과서 문장 응용하기　**1** It is true that Sujin's mom is a cook. **2** I know (that) many(a lot of) people are starving.

A 1 as **2** while **3** When　**B 1** when he called me **2** As I opened my eyes **3** while they were playing cards　**C 1** 내가 TV를 보는 동안에 그는 온라인 게임을 했다. **2** 나는 새로운 사람들을 만날 때 수줍어한다.

교과서 문장 응용하기　**1** When I called Jim, he didn't answer. **2** As he studies, he sometimes listens to music.

A 1 before **2** Until **3** before **4** since **5** after
B 1 I have studied English since I was five. **2** Look over the paper once more before you send it to Sam. **3** You should keep working out until you lose five kilograms.　**C 1** until the rain stopped **2** after we had dinner **3** before you go to bed **4** since I was born

교과서 문장 응용하기　**1** He packed his bag before he left. **2** Kevin read the book until the bus came.

A 1 you lie to me **2** you speak more loudly **3** you want those pictures **4** you were free　**B 1** if I invite you **2** unless you use it **3** Unless you want this magazine　**C 1** Unless you are full **2** I don't

교과서 문장 응용하기　**1** If you need money, I can lend you some. **2** I'll help you unless I'm busy. / Unless I'm busy, I'll help you.

A 1 I like science fiction because it is very interesting. **2** I can't eat this anymore because I have a toothache. **3** Sam couldn't arrive on time as he overslept this morning. **4** I laughed at Tony since he made a funny-looking snowman.

B 1 because she had a headache **2** As I was scared **3** Since we walked for 3(three) hours
C 1 since I have free time **2** as I missed the bus **3** since it's his birthday **4** because I wasn't thirsty

교과서 문장 응용하기　**1** I passed the exam because I studied hard. **2** They went to the park as they wanted to walk.

A 1 It rained heavily, so we put off the game. **2** I couldn't sleep at all, so I was very sleepy this morning. **3** Rosa was very surprised, so she didn't say anything for minutes.　**B 1** so heavy that **2** so late that **3** so smart that　**C 1** so / so, that **2** because / so bright that

교과서 문장 응용하기　**1** They hurried, so they could arrive in time. **2** Sumi is so pretty that every boy likes her.

A 1 Though he is a good actor, he is not that popular. **2** Even if the package was sent by express, it would be late. **3** Although I didn't put much pepper in the soup, Jack said it was spicy.
B 1 Though(Although) it rained **2** even though(if) she is short **3** Though(Although) Minji lived in
C 1 Though they are twins **2** Even if I hated carrots **3** Even though the news was true

교과서 문장 응용하기　**1** Though he is blind, he writes a

novel. **2** Even though they are poor, they are happy.

FOCUS 75　　　　　　　p.157

A **1** both **2** either **3** well **4** but **B** **1** but also
dances perfectly **2** but warm enough **3** or money
C **1** or(Neither) → nor(Either) **2** is → are **3** or(neither)
→ nor(either)

교과서 문장 응용하기 **1** Mary likes both music and dance.
2 Candy is not only honest but also kind(kind as
well as honest).

내신적중 실전문제
pp.158~162

01 ⑤	02 ③	03 ③	04 ②	05 If, don't
06 as well as	07 ③	08 ⑤	09 ③	10 ⑤
11 ③	12 ①	13 both, and	14 so, that	
15 ②	16 ⑤	17 ④	18 ②	19 ④	20 ②
21 will find → find	22 ②	23 ⑤	24 ②	
25 ①	26 ③	27 ②		

서술형 평가
01 (1) when (2) Though (3) that (4) since
02 (1) If you don't leave (2) Unless you leave
03 (1) because, so (2) before, after
04 (1) Both Anna and her sister are
　 (2) Either Anna or her sister is
　 (3) Neither Anna nor her sister is
05 Everybody knows (that) Antarctica is a
　 continent.
06 ⓒ though(even though / even if / although)
　 ⓓ because(as / since)

01 '잠을 자고 있는 동안에'라는 의미여야 하므로 시간의 접속사
　 while이 알맞다.

02 '비록 매우 나이가 들었지만'이라는 의미여야 하므로 양보의
　 접속사 though가 알맞다.

03 ③ 가주어 It이 가리키는 진주어는 that이 이끄는 절이 되어
　 야 한다. (→ that)

04 ② the kings of Egypt ~ died.가 앞 문장에 대한 이유

를 나타내므로 이유의 접속사를 써야 한다. (→ because
(as / since))

05 「명령문, or ~」는 if ~ not 또는 unless를 이용하여 바꿔 쓸
　 수 있다.

06 「not only A but also B」는 「B as well as A」로 바꿔 쓸 수
　 있다.

07 '너무 ~해서 …하다'는 의미의 결과를 나타낼 때는 「so ~ that
　 …」을 이용한다.

08 if ~ not은 unless를 이용하여 바꿔 쓸 수 있다.

09 '모국어는 아니지만 유창하게 말한다'는 뜻이므로 양보의 접
　 속사 though가 알맞다.

10 ⑤ 「명령문, or ~」로 '…해라, 그렇지 않으면 ~할 것이다'라는
　 뜻을 나타내야 한다.
　 ①, ②, ③, ④ 「명령문, and~」로 '…해라, 그러면 ~할 것이다'
　 라는 뜻을 나타내야 한다.

11 첫 번째 문장의 빈칸에는 '~ 때문에'라는 이유를 나타내는 접
　 속사가, 두 번째 문장의 빈칸에는 '~한 이후로'라는 시간을 나
　 타내는 접속사가 필요하므로 since가 알맞다.

12 첫 번째 문장의 빈칸에는 '~ 때문에'라는 이유를 나타내는 접
　 속사가, 두 번째 문장의 빈칸에는 '~할 때'라는 시간을 나타내
　 는 접속사가 필요하므로 as가 알맞다.

13 'A와 B 둘 다'는 「both A and B」로 표현한다.

14 '너무 ~해서 …하다'는 「so ~ that …」으로 표현한다.

15 ② You missed the bus because you didn't walk faster.
　 로 영작하는 것이 올바르다. 주어진 문장은 '만약 네가 더 빨
　 리 걷지 않는다면, 너는 버스를 놓칠 것이다.'라는 의미이다.

16 although는 '비록 ~이지만'이라는 의미로 though, even
　 though, even if와 바꿔 쓸 수 있다.

17 '~할 때까지'의 뜻으로 계속의 의미를 나타내는 시간의 접속
　 사는 until이다.

18 ② 시간이나 조건을 나타내는 접속사가 이끄는 절에서는 미
　 래시제 대신 현재시제를 쓴다. (will meet → meet)

19 '오늘은 시간도 계획도 없다'는 뜻이 되도록 'A도 B도 아닌'이
　 라는 의미의 상관접속사 「neither A nor B」가 알맞다.

20 ②는 목적격 관계대명사로, ①, ③, ④, ⑤는 명사절을 이끄는
　 접속사로 쓰였다.

21 조건의 접속사가 이끄는 절에서는 미래를 나타낼 때 현재시
　 제를 쓴다.

22 목적어 역할을 하는 명사절을 이끄는 접속사 that은 생략할 수 있다.

23 ⑤ '청소기를 사용한 후에 거실 구석에 두어라'는 뜻이어야 하므로 '~한 후에'라는 뜻의 접속사 after가 알맞다.

24 「*B* as well as *A*」가 주어일 때는 동사의 수를 B에 일치시키므로 goes가 알맞다.

25 ① because는 절을 이끄는 접속사이므로 뒤에 주어와 동사가 와야 한다. 명사를 쓰려면 because를 전치사 because of로 바꿔야 한다.

26 첫 번째 문장의 빈칸에는 '내가 너에게 전화했을 때'의 의미가 되도록 as 또는 when이 알맞고, 두 번째 문장의 빈칸에는 명사절을 이끄는 접속사 that이 알맞다.

27 ②는 앞의 선행사 food를 수식하는 관계대명사이다. ①, ③, ④, ⑤는 명사절을 이끄는 접속사로 쓰였다.

01 (1) '~할 때'라는 의미의 접속사 when, (2) '비록 ~이지만'이라는 의미의 접속사 though, (3) 진주어 역할을 하는 명사절을 이끄는 접속사 that, (4) '~이후로'라는 의미의 접속사 since가 알맞다.

02 '~하지 않으면'이라는 부정의 조건은 if ~ not이나 unless로 나타낸다.

03 (1) because와 so를 이용하여 「결과＋because＋이유」, 「이유＋so＋결과」와 같이 쓴다. (2) 내용상 I read a book이 먼저 한 일, I fall asleep이 나중에 한 일이어야 자연스러우므로 before와 after를 쓴다.

04 (1) 「both *A* and *B*」: 'A와 B 둘 다' (복수 취급)
(2) 「either *A* or *B*」: 'A와 B 둘 중 하나' (B에 수 일치)
(3) 「neither *A* or *B*」: 'A와 B 둘 다 아닌' (B에 수 일치)

[05~06]

> 모두가 안다. 남극대륙은 대륙이다. 하지만 여기 여러분이 모르는 어떤 것이 있다. 그것은 사막이기도 하다! 그곳에는 비나 눈이 거의 내리지 않지만, 바람이 많이 분다. 사실, 남극대륙은 세계에서 가장 추운 사막이다! 그리고 여기 또 다른 낯선 사실이 있다. 비록 세계의 신선한 물의 90%가 거기에 있지만, 모두 얼음이기 때문에 마실 수 없다!

05 know의 목적어로 명사절이 왔으므로 접속사 that을 사용하

여 연결하며, 이때의 that은 생략할 수 있다.

06 ⓒ '그곳에 있지만'이라는 뜻이 되도록 양보의 의미를 나타내야 한다.
ⓓ '얼음이기 때문에'라는 뜻이 되도록 이유의 의미를 나타내야 한다.

CHAPTER **13** 가정법

FOCUS **76** p.165

A **1** were **2** found **3** wouldn't **4** were **B** **1** If, were, wouldn't believe **2** If, practiced, could be **C** **1** doesn't, can't understand **2** had, could stay

교과서 문장 응용하기 **1** If I were you, I would go to the concert. **2** If he worked out, he would become healthy.

FOCUS **77** p.166

A **1** had drunk **2** had done **3** had been
B **1** didn't have, couldn't enjoy **2** As(Because), wasn't, didn't buy **3** had rained, couldn't have gone **C** **1** she would have been glad **2** he could have read my email **3** Tim had practiced hard

교과서 문장 응용하기 **1** If I had been hungry, I would have eaten(had) something. **2** If the weather had been better, I would have ridden a bike.

FOCUS **78** p.167

A **1** could do **2** had **3** could **B** **1** I knew Nancy's phone number **2** I were at the park with you **3** the dog would stop barking **C** **1** (that) I don't earn a lot of money **2** I could read your mind **3** I could make a sweater for my father

교과서 문장 응용하기 **1** I wish I knew his email address. **2** I wish Mr. Miller were an actor.

A 1 hadn't been **2** had sent **3** hadn't eaten
B 1 (that) Mary didn't take a bath in the morning
2 I had bought a new guitar **3** I had understood what the teacher said **C 1** 내가 나의 숙제를 잊지 않았다면 좋았을 텐데. **2** 내가 백악관을 방문했다면 좋았을 텐데.

교과서 문장 응용하기 1 I wish I had taken dance lessons.
2 I wish I had gone shopping last Friday.

내신적중 실전문제   pp.169~172

01 ③ 02 ④ 03 ⑤ 04 ⑤ 05 ④ 06 can't give
07 ③ 08 ③ 09 ⑤ 10 ③ 11 ③ 12 ⑤
13 ① 14 had 15 had arrived 16 would have gone 17 ④ 18 ④ 19 ③ 20 ⑤

서술형 평가

01 (1) lived (2) would have gone
　　(3) would read (4) had trained
02 (1) If I were Ann, could buy
　　(2) As I'm not Ann, can't buy
03 (1) I wish I hadn't eaten
　　(2) I'm sorry (that) I ate
04 had had, would have watched
05 I hadn't gone to the party
06 had studied at home, would have passed

01 주절이 조동사의 과거형인 가정법 과거 문장이므로 빈칸에는 if절의 동사의 과거형이 알맞다.

02 부사구 right now로 보아 현재 사실과 반대되는 소망을 나타내는 「I wish + 가정법」이 되도록 빈칸에는 동사의 과거형이 알맞다.

03 if절의 동사(had been)로 보아 가정법 과거완료 문장이므로, 주절의 빈칸에는 「would + have + 과거분사」 형태가 알맞다.

04 과거 사실과 반대되는 소망을 나타내는 「I wish + 가정법 과거완료」가 되도록 빈칸에는 「had + 과거분사」 형태가 알맞다.

05 if절의 동사(had)로 보아 가정법 과거 문장이므로 「would + 동사원형」의 형태가 알맞다.

06 가정법이 과거시제 긍정문이므로 직설법은 현재시제 부정문

으로 써야 한다.

07 ③ 주절의 동사로 보아 가정법 과거완료 문장이므로 if절은 「had + 과거분사」 형태가 되어야 한다. (→ had had)

08 부사 last year로 보아 과거 사실과 반대되는 소망을 나타내는 문장이어야 하므로 「I wish + 가정법 과거완료(had + 과거분사)」가 되어야 한다. ③의 had는 have의 단순과거시제이다.

09 '~했더라면 …했었을 텐데'의 뜻은 과거 사실과 반대되는 가정을 나타내므로 가정법 과거완료 「If + 주어 + had + 과거분사 ~, 주어 + would have + 과거분사 …」의 형태로 쓴다.

10 Jody가 William을 좋아하지 않는다는 현재 사실에 대한 반대를 가정하므로 가정법 과거인 「If + 주어 + 동사의 과거형 ~, 주어 + would + 동사원형 …」이 되어야 한다.

11 직설법이 현재시제 부정문이면 가정법은 과거시제 긍정문으로 쓴다.

12 직설법이 과거시제 부정문이므로 I wish 가정법 과거완료의 긍정문으로 바꿔 쓸 수 있다.

13 ① began으로 보아 과거의 일을 나타내므로 과거 사실과 반대되는 소망을 표현하는 가정법 과거완료 문장이어야 한다. (→ had taken)

14 첫 번째 문장은 '자전거가 있으면'이라는 의미여야 하므로 빈칸에 동사 have를 쓰되, 주절의 동사로 보아 가정법 과거 문장이므로 과거형 had가 알맞다. 두 번째 문장은 주절의 동사로 보아 가정법 과거완료 문장이므로 if절은 「had + 과거분사」 형태가 되어야 한다.

15 yesterday로 보아 과거 사실과 반대되는 소망을 나타내므로 「I wish + 가정법 과거완료(had + 과거분사)」의 형태가 되어야 한다.

16 If절의 동사(had gotten)로 보아 가정법 과거완료 문장이므로 주절의 동사는 「would + have + 과거분사」의 형태가 되어야 한다.

17 ④ 「I wish + 가정법 과거」는 현재 사실과 반대되는 소망을 나타내며 「I'm sorry (that) + 직설법 현재」로 바꿔 나타내고, 긍정은 부정으로 바꾼다. 따라서 두 번째 문장의 동사로는 am이 아닌 am not을 써야 한다.

18 첫 번째 문장은 last year로 보아 과거 사실과 반대되는 소망을 나타내므로 「had + 과거분사」 형태를 쓴다. 두 번째 문장은 주절의 동사가 「would + 동사원형」인 것으로 보아 가정법 과거 문장이므로 if절에는 과거형 동사를 쓴다.

19 첫 번째 문장은 주절의 시제로 보아 가정법 과거인 「If + 주어 + 동사의 과거형 ~」이며, be동사는 인칭과 수에 상관없이

were로 쓴다. 두 번째 문장은 주절의 시제로 보아 가정법 과거완료인 「If + 주어 + had + 과거분사 ~」의 형태를 쓴다.

20 ⑤ '어제 좋은 식당에 갔었더라면'의 뜻을 가진 가정법 과거완료 문장이므로 would had는 would have had가 되어야 한다.

서술형 평가

01 내용상 관계있는 동사를 쓰되 올바른 형태로 바꾼다.
(1) 주절의 would give로 보아 가정법 과거이므로 빈칸에는 동사의 과거형을 쓴다.
(2) if절의 had shone으로 보아 가정법 과거완료이므로 「조동사 과거형 + have + 과거분사」의 형태로 쓴다.
(3) if절의 spent로 보아 가정법 과거이므로 「조동사 과거형 + 동사원형」의 형태로 쓴다.
(4) 주절의 would have won으로 보아 가정법 과거완료이므로 「had + 과거분사」의 형태로 쓴다.

02 현재 사실에 대한 가정은 가정법 과거로 나타내며, 직설법은 현재시제로 쓴다. 가정법의 긍정(부정)은 직설법에서 부정(긍정)의 내용으로 바꿔 쓴다.

03 과거 일에 대한 유감이나 아쉬움은 「I wish + 가정법 과거완료」로 나타내며, I'm sorry (that) ~을 사용해서 직설법 과거로 바꿔 쓸 수 있다.

04 과거의 사실과 반대되는 가정을 나타내므로 「If + 주어 + had + 과거분사~, 주어 + 조동사의 과거형 + have + 과거분사 …」의 가정법 과거완료가 알맞다.

[05~06]

> 내 친구 Alan이 과학 시험 전날 밤 내게 파티에 가자고 물어봤다. 나는 과학을 싫어해서, 공부하고 싶지 않았다. 그래서 난 파티에 갔고 아주 즐겁게 보냈다. 그 다음 날 나는 그 시험에 낙제했고 부모님은 내게 실망하셨다. 내가 그 파티에 갔던 것이 유감이다. <u>내가 집에서 공부를 했다면 나는 그 시험을 통과했을 텐데.</u>

05 과거 일에 반대되는 가정을 나타내므로 「I wish + 가정법 과거완료」로 쓴다.

06 '~했다면, …했을 텐데'라는 의미로 과거의 사실과 반대되는 일을 가정할 때는 가정법 과거완료로 나타낸다.

CHAPTER **14** 일치와 화법

FOCUS 80   p.175

A 1 will buy **2** would win **3** invented **4** is
B 1 Sally was at home **2** he didn't say hello to me **3** Shakespeare died in 1616 **C 1** learned that, rises **2** said that, goes to church **3** said that, had been to

교과서 문장 응용하기 **1** I heard (that) Bill got a new job. **2** I know (that) the Korean War broke out in 1950.

FOCUS 81   p.176

A 1 said **2** tells **B 1** told, he felt great **2** tells, he knows lots of people **3** said, he had seen Ken at a party **C 1** My mom is a great cook **2** I am talking on the phone

교과서 문장 응용하기 **1** Ms. White says, "My son is handsome." **2** Andy told me (that) he didn't want to go.

FOCUS 82   p.177

A 1 asked his mother if(whether) Ann had left early **2** asked a woman if(whether) there was a cafe nearby **3** asked me if(whether) I could take a picture **B 1** Did you get my letter **2** Can I borrow your book **C 1** asked Linda if(whether) she liked singing **2** asked me if(whether) I could lend him some money

교과서 문장 응용하기 **1** She asked her boyfriend if(whether) he was sick. **2** I asked the boys if(whether) they liked to read(reading) books.

FOCUS 83   p.178

A 1 asked me why I liked the book **2** asked me what time the meeting was **3** asked me who had given me the laptop **B 1** Who told you about the job **2** Where does Maria park her car **3** How many eggs do you want **C 1** how often she went shopping **2** where they kept the money **3** what time the bank closed

교과서 문장 응용하기 **1** I asked him where his office was. **2** She asked me when I arrived.

FOCUS 84　　p.179

A 1 what his name is **2** whose bag it is
3 if(whether) he is a middle school student
B 1 she is **2** the bank opens **3** if(whether) he can speak **4** what route they took **C 1** if(whether) Tom likes **2** who sent

교과서 문장 응용하기 **1** Could you tell me where the bakery is? **2** I want to know who broke this vase.

FOCUS 85　　p.180

A 1 What do you imagine he will do? **2** How do you think this robot works? **3** Who does she guess borrowed the book? **4** When do they suppose the meeting will be held? **B 1** Who would believe that story? **2** What will you do next week? **3** Where did she spend her holiday? **4** How will they come here?

교과서 문장 응용하기 **1** Who do you think lives here? **2** What do you believe they will make?

내신적중 실전문제
pp.181~184

01 ⑤　**02** ④　**03** ⑤　**04** ④　**05** ④　**06** ⑤
07 ⑤　**08** ④　**09** ③　**10** ①　**11** ③　**12** are you doing　**13** ⑤　**14** ⑤　**15** ③　**16** ⑤　**17** had seen　**18** boiled → boils　**19** Who do you think　**20** ③

서술형 평가

01 (1) Sally thought online shopping was full of fun.　(2) My teacher told us that the Chinese invented paper.

02 We learned (that) Brazil is the largest country
03 (1) if Yuri wrote cards
(2) What do you think we can do
04 (1) she would buy him a new bike the next day
(2) how often Anna went swimming
05 I don't know why this is happening to me.
06 ⓒ (that) he had gotten his report card back the day before　ⓓ that he was getting really far behind　ⓔ what he could do

01 주절의 동사인 believed와 시제를 일치시켜야 하므로 과거시제인 ⑤만 올 수 있다.

02 간접의문문은 「의문사＋주어＋동사」의 어순으로 쓴다.

03 주절의 시제가 과거이므로 종속절의 시제는 과거 또는 과거완료(had＋과거분사)가 알맞다.

04 ④ 전달 동사 tell이 과거시제로 쓰였으므로 will이 아닌 would로 고쳐 시제를 일치시켜야 한다.

05 의문사가 없는 의문문의 간접화법은 전달 동사 said to를 asked로 바꾸고, if나 whether로 연결한다. 피전달문의 I는 he가 되고, 전달 동사가 과거이므로 can은 과거형으로 쓴다.

06 평서문의 간접화법은 전달 동사 said to를 told로, 피전달문의 I는 말하는 사람인 Jenny의 대명사 she로, 시제는 전달 동사가 과거이므로 liked로 바꾼다.

07 평서문의 간접화법이므로 said to는 told로, 전달 동사가 과거이므로 피전달문의 didn't do는 과거완료 hadn't done으로 바꾼다.

08 의문사가 없는 의문문의 간접화법이므로 said to는 asked로 바꾸고, 피전달문은 if 혹은 whether로 연결한다.

09 추측을 나타내는 동사 guess가 주절의 동사로 쓰인 간접의문문의 의문사는 문장의 맨 앞에 위치한다.

10 간접의문문의 의문사가 문장의 맨 앞에 위치해 있으므로 빈칸에는 생각이나 추측을 나타내는 동사만 쓸 수 있다.

11 주절의 동사인 said가 과거시제이므로 시제를 일치시켜야 한다. 따라서 현재시제인 ③은 쓸 수 없다. ⑤는 현재의 습관을 나타내므로 시제 일치에서 예외가 된다.

12 간접화법의 주절도 과거시제, 전달문도 과거시제이므로, 직접화법에서 인용부호 안의 시제는 현재시제로 쓴다.

13 ⑤ 의문사가 있는 의문문의 간접화법에서 피전달문은 「의문

사＋주어＋동사」의 어순으로 쓴다. (when would we go →
when we would go)

14 의문사가 없는 의문문을 간접화법으로 바꿀 때는 「주어＋동
사」 앞에 if 또는 whether를 쓴다.

15 ① 전달동사가 과거이면 피전달문의 현재완료는 과거완료가
되어야 한다. (have → had)
② 의문사가 없는 의문문의 간접화법은 if나 whether로 연결
한다. (that → if(whether))
④ 전달 동사가 asked이므로 피전달문의 동사는 과거시제가
되어야 한다. (has → had)
⑤ 인용문의 you는 말을 듣는 상대방인 her son이므로 인칭
대명사는 he가 되어야 한다. (she → he)

16 직접화법인 의문문 Is there a park nearby?를 간접화법으
로 바꾼 것이므로 「if＋주어＋동사」의 어순으로 쓰고, 주절의
시제가 과거이므로 과거시제로 쓴다.

17 직접화법에서 인용부호 안의 시제가 과거이므로 간접화법의
종속절의 시제는 과거완료로 쓴다.

18 물이 100℃에서 끓는 것은 일반적인 사실이므로 주절의 시제
와 상관없이 항상 현재시제로 써야 한다.

19 생각을 나타내는 동사 think를 주절의 동사로 쓴 간접의문문
이어야 하므로 의문사 who가 문장 맨 앞에 와야 한다.

20 ①, ②, ③, ④ 의문사가 있는 의문문의 간접 화법
⑤ 의문사가 없는 의문문의 간접화법
(① is it → it is ② where does he come → where he
comes ④ where is Bob's house → where Bob's house is
⑤ you're married → if(whether) you're married)

서술형 평가

01 (1) 주절의 동사가 현재에서 과거로 바뀌었으므로 종속절의
시제도 과거로 쓴다.
(2) 역사적인 사실은 주절의 동사와 상관없이 과거시제로 쓴다.

02 주절의 동사가 과거이지만 종속절은 일반적인 사실을 나타내
므로 종속절의 시제는 현재형으로 쓴다.

03 (1) know의 목적어 역할을 하면서 의문사가 없는 간접의문
문은 「if＋주어＋동사」의 어순으로 쓴다.
(2) 동사 think가 쓰였으므로 의문사를 문장 앞에 두어 「의문
사＋do you think＋주어＋동사」의 어순으로 쓴다.

04 (1) 피전달문이 평서문이므로 that으로 연결하며, 동사 will
은 would로, you는 her son이므로 him으로, tomorrow는
the next day로 바꿔 쓴다.

② 피전달문이 의문사가 있는 의문문이므로 「의문사＋주
어＋동사」의 순서로 쓴다. 이때 how often은 분리하지 않으
며, go는 과거형 went로 바꿔 쓴다.

[05~06]

> Owl 선생님께.
> 　전 모르겠어요. 왜 제게 이런 일이 일어나는 거죠? 저
> 는 제 성적표를 어제 돌려받았어요. 끔찍했어요! 저는 55
> 점과 60점을 받았어요. 전 정말 멍청하다고 느껴요. 더
> 나쁜 것은, 전 제 집중력을 잃었다는 것이에요. 제가 열
> 심히 공부하려고 노력할 때면, 저는 결국 컴퓨터 게임을
> 하게 됩니다. 저는 점점 아주 뒤처지고 있어요. 정말 걱
> 정이 되어요. 제가 무엇을 할 수 있을까요?
> 　　　　　　　　　　　　　　　　　　　Alan 드림

05 의문사가 있는 절이 know의 목적어 역할을 하는 간접의문
문이 되도록 「의문사＋주어＋동사」의 순서로 쓴다.

06 ⓒ 피전달문이 평서문이므로 that으로 연결하고, I는 Alan
을 가리키므로 he로, 피전달문의 과거형은 과거완료로,
yesterday는 the day before로 바꿔 쓴다.
ⓓ 피전달문이 평서문이므로 that으로 연결하며, 피전달문의
현재진행형은 과거진행형으로 바꿔 쓴다.
ⓔ 의문사가 있는 피전달문이므로 「의문사＋주어＋동사」의
어순이며 피전달문의 can은 could로 바꿔 쓴다.

Memo

Memo

Memo

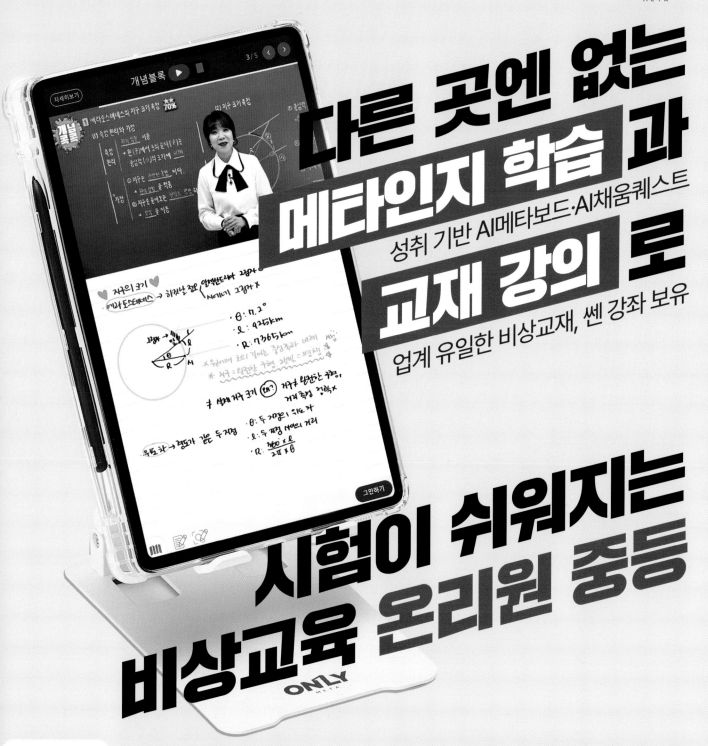

T·A·P·A   영역별 집중 학습으로 영어 고민을 한 방에 타파 합니다.

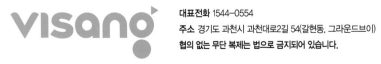

대표전화 1544-0554
주소 경기도 과천시 과천대로2길 54(갈현동, 그라운드브이)